PAY TO THE ORDER OF
PUERTO RICO

Alexander Odishelidze
and Arthur Laffer

Allegiance Press
The Right Answers for America

Copyright © 2004 by Alexander Odishelidze

Pay to the Order of Puerto Rico
by Alexander Odishelidze

Printed in the United States of America

ISBN 1-594672-89-X

All rights reserved. No part of this publication may be reproduced or transmitted in any form or by any means without written permission of the author.

Allegiance Press
10640 Main Street
Suite 204
Fairfax, VA 22030
www.allegiancepress.com

(703) 934-4411

Table of Contents

	Acknowledgements vii
Foreword	*Lawrence Kudlow* 9
Introduction 1	*Alexander Odishelidze* 13
Introduction 2	*Arthur Laffer* 19
Section I	**Economy** 25
Chapter 1	My Odyssey to Freedom 27
Chapter 2.	The Last Colony 39
Chapter 3	America Delivers 51
Chapter 4	The Price of Dependence 59
Chapter 5	Pitorro and Panas (Moonshine and Breadfruit) 95
Chapter 6	The American Taxpayer's Commonwealth Burden 103
Chapter 7	Making Lemons into Lemonade 159
Chapter 8	Biography of a Tax Gimmick 173

Section II	**Status**	**213**
Chapter 9	The Young Bill: The Roar of the Coqui	215
Chapter 10.	Eulogies for the Young Bill	257
Chapter 11	The Cries of Patriots	291
Chapter 12	The Eternal Territory	303
Section III	**Character**	**319**
Vignette 1	Moncho's Other Family Business	321
Chapter 13	Mainlining Our Kids	329
Vignette 2	A New Friend of Commonwealth	351
Chapter 14	Welcome to the *Laundromat a la Boriqua*	355
Section IV	**Identity**	**379**
Chapter 15	"Mejorando La Raza" (Improving the Race)	381
Chapter 16	The Last, Full Measure	399
Chapter 17	More Than a Hero, Less Than a Citizen	437
Afterword	*Alexander Odishelidze*	439

Acknowledgements

I wish I had the space to thank all those who have helped me develop this book over the years. However, the people that deserve particular mention are: Chuck Donovan who has been my relentless Editor/Researcher who added the depth to this work that I could not have achieved on my own, Professor Gonzalo Cordova, Ph.D. who has given me the cultural and racial insights into Puerto Rico and Manuel Rodriguez Orellana who originally opened my eyes to the Puerto Rico political status dilemma.

Foreword

The United States was founded on economic and political freedom. A "City on the Hill," to use Ronald Reagan's phrase, metaphorically describes American exceptionalism. This freedom enables all our citizens to successfully pursue unlimited opportunities to use their God-given talents to work, produce, take risks, invest, and grow wealthy while keeping the prosperous fruits of their enterprise.

All too often in the 20th century, opportunities to do just this were being taken for granted. But not by a young Alex Odishelidze, who risked life and limb to escape communist oppression and make a new start in America.

Mr. Odishelidze's passion to succeed in business should be taught in American business schools. As World War II raged across the European continent, a young Alexander Odishelidze witnessed carnage by Communists and murder of his own family members in his mother country. He vividly recalls indoctrination through loudspeakers placed in the public squares, and before his escape to freedom, first in Canada and then New York, was honored by Marshall Tito for his devotion to the Party.

He charged head-first into the insurance business and was quickly spotted as a go-getter. And no one was going faster than Alex Odishelidze. With every deal, every sale, every promotion, he knew that more opportunities were around the corner.

Through his work in the insurance industry, Mr. Odishelidze has uncovered a gaping hole in Puerto Rico's economic system. U.S. companies can now not only manufacture their products in Puerto Rico tax free, but also assign the licenses to manufacture those products to its Puerto Rican subsidiaries and keep the tax-free profits, even if the actual work was done in China or elsewhere. This takes even more jobs from American workers. Americans are subsidizing Puerto Rico to the tune of $22 billion per year!

My dear friend Arthur Laffer, who nearly single-handedly revolutionized American economic thought, brings a great deal of insight to this book. By developing the Laffer Curve, he captured the incentive effects on work and investment from changing tax-rates.

Dr. Laffer shows how higher after-tax economic rewards from lower tax-rates will expand the economic pie as human behavior responds to growth incentives by supplying added work, investment, and risk-taking. In short, when it pays more, after-tax, to work and produce, then people respond immediately. As a result, rising national income and production from lower tax-rates actually throw off higher tax revenues within a relatively short time.

For years, Art Laffer has advised top Puerto Rican officials and is in a unique position to analyze this situation. In 1979, Art Laffer drafted a report for the incoming governor of Puerto Rico on how to mend the island's economic ills. He notes that the purpose of this book is to shine more light on the myriad opportunities for economic prosperity.

Laffer points out that in 1987, Puerto Rico cut the top marginal rate on personal income taxes. A respected study showed that Puerto Rican taxpayers declared 50 percent more income than the previous year. The total number of taxpayers increased by one third and total tax revenues increased by 28 percent.

These extremely able and insightful men have combined their efforts to show the American people that the current support system for Puerto Rico is unfair to American taxpayers and unjust for the residents of Puerto Rico. However, unlike the days when empires ruled colonies around the world, rules and regulations could be changed by executive decision.

Such is not the case with Puerto Rico. Only the Congress can alter Puerto Rico's status. Numerous Members of Congress from diverse parts of the country agree with Odishelidze and Laffer's position to allow Puerto Rican self-determination. However, many Americans are unfamiliar with Puerto Rico's unique status and its impact on the American economy. Odishelidze and Laffer provide an eye-opening look at how Puerto Rico's status siphons tax dollars from hard-working Americans, while impeding its own economic progress.

The authors give a detailed chronology of Section 931 of the Internal Revenue Code. From its inception in 1921, which exempted from federal income taxes all income of individuals and corporations that originates in U.S. possessions, including Puerto Rico, subject to certain key limitations.

Mr. Odishelidze and Dr. Laffer reveal key facts about Puerto Rico under this system such as the fact that unemployment has risen significantly and has outpaced that of the mainland United States. They also show the intense lobbying efforts by pharmaceutical companies and other U.S. concerns to preserve the status quo in Puerto Rico's tax system.

This tax structure, while well-meaning in the early 20th century, no longer has any purpose in the Puerto Rican economy, and in fact, is counterproductive. During the more than eighty years it has been in effect it has only helped to create jobs in a fifteen to twenty year period.

Odishelidze and Laffer show that every working middle and upper-middle class American contributes $400 annually to the upkeep of Puerto Rico.

Yet, what are the results of this misguided tax and political status policy when we compare Puerto Rico to the other fifty states?

Puerto Rico is second in out-of-wedlock births, fourth in high energy costs, and dead last in per capita income. The United States has also spent billions on improving Puerto Rico from 1981-2001. Some of those expenditures include: Food Stamps, $19.25 billion; Educationally Deprived Children Program, $3.59 billion; nearly $1 billion on public housing and a half billion dollars on a school lunch program.

Even more alarming, grants given to Puerto Rico from the United States account for significant portions of local departmental budgets. For example, the Public Housing Administration in Puerto

Rico received a grant of $200 million from the federal government. This accounted for 92.9% of its budget. The Puerto Rican Education Department received $875.9 million, which accounts for 35% of its budget.

The poverty level in Puerto Rico is extremely high, despite a close relationship with the United States.

The authors also demonstrate how Washington works with the 1996 effort to change Puerto Rico's status. Mr. Odishelidze shows the strong power of the pharmaceutical lobbies, which benefit handsomely from Section 936. He takes the reader inside breakfast meetings with then-Vice President Al Gore and stands his ground against the Vice President's skepticism.

The authors go on to document that the United States is not getting a return on its investment. They make the case that the federal government should move away from the current system of tax subsidies for corporations. They show that Puerto Rico has splendid opportunities ahead of it, but needs a new fiscal system to realize its long-term potential. The work of Alexander Odishelidze and Arthur Laffer will surely open that discussion.

Lawrence Kudlow

Introduction 1

If anyone had told me 43 years ago, when I first came to America, that the years of my youth in Nazi-occupied Belgrade and later in Communist Yugoslavia would drive me to develop a passion for Puerto Rico's self-determination, I would have advised them to seek professional help.

Back then ideology wasn't even on my radar screen. I was 19 years old and I had just arrived in the land of my fantasies, America, the land of opportunity that made millionaires out of anyone who dared dream the dream. I was here, in the country of gleaming alabaster cities and amber waves of grain, where you could open a business, make a profit and not have to go to jail for it. Your only price for this great privilege was just to pay a few dollars in taxes, and only if you made the money. How much better could life get?

To most native-born Americans, raised in the protective cocoon of this nation's freedoms, the above words may seem silly, even to the point of being ridiculously obvious. Perhaps it is precisely because those freedoms are so obvious that they are ignored by those who were born here, where the main focus in life becomes a good job, a house in the suburbs, and a gold watch when the company puts you out to pasture. If you were raised, however, where those "obvious" freedoms did not exist, coming to America allows you to see them clearly, to touch them, to feel them, and to mold them into a life of unimaginable possibility.

In the beginning, I thought that the freedom to accumulate capital was the only thing that mattered. It wasn't until some 25 years later, when I no longer needed to amass capital in order to live my lifestyle, that I discovered that capital was not an end in itself. It was merely the measure of progress in only one department. Life, I learned, had many other, equally if not more important departments.

Even today, I hear people ask me about some of the things that I do now. The question comes up time and again in discussions of my efforts in support of Puerto Rican self-determination: "What's in it for you?" Anywhere else and this question would be pure cynicism. Here in the United States, I have found, people ask the question with a kind of cynicism that is anxious for idealistic reassurance. The question often means, "Please persuade me that there is some altruistic reason for your actions."

This book was written in response to that question. It seeks to answer whether there is an altruistic position on Puerto Rico's future and to urge people of goodwill to take that position and pursue it to its conclusion. My colleague Arthur Laffer and I have written these words with that aim in mind. In these pages the reader will learn some details about my early life and how I came to New York City and its Puerto Rican neighborhoods, and, through them, to a business career in San Juan and the Caribbean. This journey from wartime and tyranny, to sunshine and liberty, was not unique to me. Many others, from every corner of the globe, have made this trek. What compels me to write is that, because my destination was Puerto Rico, this journey is incomplete.

In the vignettes and chapters that follow, we lay out the essential nature of Puerto Rico's economy, status, character, and identity. Because we seek change (change with the goal of permanence), we write a great deal that is critical. Because human beings – Puerto Ricans, mainlanders, lawmakers and lobbyists, businessmen and politicos – are at the center of this drama, it is a tale of courage and conviction, of flaws and folly. The underlying theme here is not criticism, however, but love: of equality, prosperity, human fulfillment, and the blessings of freedom. We merely want to see these blessings secured for an island whose courageous though, like all of us, flawed people we have come to know and love.

The legal status of Puerto Rico lies at the physical center of this

Introduction 1

book, and it truly is the heart of the matter. We argue that the dependent notion of the current territorial status cannot last, that it is colonialism in modern dress. We make the case for what either independence or statehood, both of which are permanent forms of self-government, will accomplish for Puerto Rico. In fact, each of us has been making this case for many years, and in the course of our labors we have come across some of the best and the worst in our fellow citizens.

At this point, you may be asking yourself, "Why, as a resident of the U.S. mainland, should I care about these issues involving some distant island in the Caribbean?" My answer is simple: "Because this distant island is costing you, the American taxpayer, more than $22 billion a year to maintain." That's about $400 for every American tax-paying family. You are offering up this sum of money (which is growing every year), and the typical Puerto Rican is gladly receiving it, but neither you nor that average resident of Puerto Rico is likely to know all the adverse ways in which this transfer is affecting the well being of both parties to the transaction.

Bringing up the truth about U.S. dealings with Puerto Rico makes a great many people uncomfortable these days, whether they live on the mainland or on the island. Allow me to relate an example. I first met the plainspoken Congressman Dan Burton in the early 1990s. Burton, an Indiana Republican, was a key member of the House International Relations Committee. We had just begun our efforts to eliminate the obscenely expensive tax shelter called Section 936 that was funneling profits through Puerto Rico but doing precious little for its people. We were also working on the closely related matter of Rep. Don Young's bill to fashion the first real Puerto Rican plebiscite on its future status. Burton came down to Puerto Rico for a visit. I had heard he was an avid fisherman. I made arrangements for a fishing trip with Mike Benitez, a local deep sea fishing professional who was well known for his ability to deliver a solid catch for those who booked his services.

Before the fishing trip, which was to take place the day after Mr. Burton arrived, I had arranged for him to speak at the local Rotary club. These were the first days of our struggle to set the record straight on what Puerto Rico's status really was. We wanted our fellow business and community leaders in San Juan to know that we did have a problem and that it was in the best interest of Puerto Rico to have it resolved once and for all.

Up to this point, the majority of Puerto Ricans actually believed that the island had some kind of special status, that it was outside the territorial clause of the U.S. Constitution, and that it had some kind of "bilateral agreement" with the United States that made this status permanent and impossible to change without mutual consent.

During the luncheon, when Dan Burton began talking about a change in Puerto Rico status that could be initiated at any time by the U.S. Congress, there were a lot of exclamations of surprise among the audience. Tarring and feathering is out of fashion these days, but it wasn't hard to imagine bread rolls flying through the air at the visiting congressman.

During the question and answer period, one indignant attendee, who was visibly shaken by Mr. Burton's words, stood up and, in a voice bordering on panic, asked, "But isn't Puerto Rico an 'Associated Free State' of the United States and isn't that association based on an unbreakable 'compact'?" Mr. Burton, with his usual blunt honesty, blurted back, "I don't know of any 'compact' between Puerto Rico and the United States. All I know is that Puerto Rico is under the U.S. territorial clause, a possession of the United States, and that Congress can change that relationship any time it wants to and, besides, if there were any agreement between Puerto Rico and the United States passed by Congress that I do not know about, it is a simple fact that the acts of any one Congress do not bind the actions of any future Congress."

The audience was shocked by this reply. It was the first time that any member of the U.S. Congress had told the people of Puerto Rico the truth about their status. The next day, the local newspapers had a field day with Mr. Burton's comments. Some accused him of being uninformed. Others were outraged that a representative from Washington had dared to question Puerto Rico's "sovereignty." As events over the next few years bore out, Mr. Burton's plain talk was right on the mark. Congress could alter the terms of Puerto Rico's relationship with the United States by majority vote. In the end, the passage of Rep. Young's bill in the House of Representatives left no doubt about Puerto Rico's current status. Today Puerto Ricans are no longer kidding themselves about the bill of goods sold to them by Muñoz Marin.

The next day we went fishing as planned, and I brought along my son Michael to meet Mr. Burton. They got along very well because Mr. Burton was an Indiana State graduate and Michael graduated from Purdue, so that during the trip they were constantly razzing each other about their respective alma maters' football teams. I think that Mr. Burton must have won the arguments, not just with the people of Puerto Rico but with Michael, because, toward the end of the day, Michael got violently sick (which he never does, because he has been raised on boats) and emptied his stomach onto Mr. Burton's sneakers. It was the second day in a row that Mr. Burton had given some of his hosts a little nausea.

For the first time in history, Mike Benitez, the famous fisherman who guarantees every customer a catch, came back empty-handed. Our group didn't even get a strike. I guess all the fish in Puerto Rican waters that day must have been busy debating the status issues Mr. Burton had raised to the Rotary audience. Even they had lost some of their appetite.

A final word about the organization of this book. I am a semi-retired businessman who has lived and worked many years in Puerto Rico. Some of the chapters that follow tell the story of my transit from Eastern Europe to the States and finally to the Caribbean.

Other chapters tell the full story of the Young bill and those who worked for and against it, describe the dilemmas posed by Puerto Rico's massive role in the drug trade and money laundering, and ponder the meaning of Puerto Rican identity in our rapidly changing world. All of these chapters contain first-person narrative. The vignettes at the beginning of Chapters 13 and 14 are fiction, depictions of various aspects of Puerto Rico's social dilemmas. These vignettes are in third person.

Arthur Laffer, as he relates in his introduction has seen Puerto Rico as an adviser who has made a tremendous impact on both U.S. and Puerto Rican economic policy. His analysis is set forth in Chapters 4, 6 and 8, and he has given me excellent advice on the other chapters that touch upon Puerto Rico's economic well-being, specifically the chapters on the drug trade and money laundering. The remaining chapters and stories are all my own, and I am solely responsible for their content.

"What's in it for me?" My answer is: "If you have a couple of hours, let me tell you my story and perhaps then you might understand. But I will give you one clue; it is what America is all about. And it is about what all the Americas can be."

Alexander Odishelidze

Introduction 2

Alexander Odishelidze and I have reached similar conclusions about the future of Puerto Rico, about that island territory's best hopes and great promise, but we have done so with very different personal histories. Perhaps this lends some added authenticity to the confluence in our views.

Alex is a businessman who grew up in conditions of warfare and repression that most of us in the West have never faced. He came to Canada and then the United States because of the allure of freedom that has drawn millions of people to these shores to seek a better life for themselves and their families. Unlike the vast majority of those people, however, Alex took a second step that led from America's financial capital, New York City, to its economic nadir, the island territory of Puerto Rico. The ethnic connections that link these two places, at the top and bottom of the U.S. economic ladder, have formed a powerful bond that, examined as Alex has examined it, tells a compelling tale of a failed promise of opportunity for millions of our fellow citizens, the people of Puerto Rico.

It was not biography, but the history of ideas, that drew me to a less personal, but just as personally compelling examination of Puerto Rico's promise. The island has long been a political and economic curiosity. It is part of the United States, undeniably, but just as undeniably it is a creature of economic extremes and experiments that are unique in our hemisphere and perhaps in the world. For most of the past century, Puerto Rico has been torn between forces driving for independence and other forces driving, with growing vigor, for full integration with the United States. As part of the United States, it has lived inside the American tariff wall, as that wall has been, in turn, raised and lowered, and it has responded inevitably to economic events and cycles on the mainland. As a political commonwealth, however, it has developed a web of economic policies that have partially insulated the island from outside events, including those on the mainland. Unfortunately, that insulation, which is described in great detail in this book, has generally operated to depress Puerto Rico and to delay if not defeat its economic convergence with the mainland. A handful of mainland U.S. industries have profited, handsomely, under this regime; the vast majority of industries and individuals on the island have only suffered from the "insulation" that was designed to safeguard them.

Worldwide, a great revolution has taken place over the last few decades. Marxism has lost ground. Socialisms great and small have retained significant influence, but, in general, the maxims of high and progressive taxation and state-run economies are on the defensive. Trends toward the privatization of government-run corporations have moved sometimes fitfully, but with genuine progress toward the private sector in places as diverse as Russia, Eastern Europe, Great Britain, and Chile. Open trade policies have strengthened their foothold and the great debate at present, despite the antiglobalization demonstrations that have sprung up to bedevil international meetings, is not over whether such policies are to be pursued but over whether any or a few human rights, labor and environmental conditions should be attached to them.

Against this background, Puerto Rico's evolution is all the more striking for the way it continues to lag behind the economic systems with which the island is most closely associated. As 2004 begins, an election year on both the mainland and in Puerto Rico, the debate over tax policy and economic growth is suddenly, once more, intensifying. Not surprisingly, one of the first tremors in that debate is being felt in California, where Proposition 13, an economic event with which I have some deep familiarity, helped reshape the "landscape of the possible" for American tax policy in the 1970s. Today the issue is California's fiscal crisis, which led to a crisis of leadership, the first successful gubernatorial recall vote in the nation's history, and the installation of Republican Arnold Schwarzenegger as governor on November 17, 2003. California is once again proving a test case, as an administration promising tax relief comes into office facing a budget deficit that is a direct result of an omnipresent, progressive tax code.

As I have written elsewhere, the State of California, where I live, has a tax regime that is more burdensome than any other jurisdiction within 2,500 miles. Not only is that tax system oppressive and hostile to the creation of wealth, but it is also ingeniously detailed and pervasive. For a recent report, Laffer and Associates compiled a list of the manifold ways that California taxes its citizens at every turn; the list occupied an entire appendix of the report and even readers who *know* they are overtaxed were astonished to see gathered in one place the incredible variety of ways their state government punishes work and discourages entrepreneurship. As long as people and businesses have options (and may they always have options!), they will flee such regimes and look for places that allow them to build wealth and strengthen their communities.

Puerto Rico, of course, is more than 2,500 miles away from California, but even if it were next door, it would hold little attraction for the capital that has disappeared from and the people who have fled the Golden State. I was privileged to play a role in Puerto Rico in the 1970s when I visited there and helped the incoming Romero-Barcelo administration to begin the process of lifting the island's oppressive local tax burden. In April 1979 Laffer Associates delivered a comprehensive report to the governor that further detailed the steps needed to reverse the island's economic decline in that period and put it on a path of long-term economic growth. As I relate in more detail in Chapter 6, this process had a beneficent effect on the island, which was reeling under the weight of the Popular Democratic Party's central planning model.

No economic battle is ever finished, however, and the island, isolated in many ways in its complex political and economic struggle, has continued to veer in allegiance between its two major parties over the past two decades. In this book, we argue more than anything else for an end to the veering. Puerto Rico must dispense with the chimera of commonwealth, and become either an independent state along the lines of a model like South Korea, or finally welcome statehood and use that opportunity to overhaul its tax system and engineer it for growth and prosperity. The island can and should make improvements in local policy in the meantime, and the federal government can and should continue to move away from the system of tax subsidies for mainland corporations that is the focus of the discussion in Chapter 8, but these measures must not substitute for an ultimate resolution of the status issue.

The year to come will be an intensely exciting one. The tax rate reductions President George W. Bush has made the centerpiece of his economic policy are squarely on the table in 2004. His Democratic opponents are split between those who would repeal them immediately and those who would radically and swiftly alter them. As the ideas I have expounded for a lifetime predicted, the year 2003 is coming to a close with an impressive resumption and acceleration of national economic growth responding to the Bush tax cuts. Economics, after all, is a common language. This phenomenon of accelerated growth could be Puerto Rico's future as well, and its economic well-being (as well as its status) is squarely on the table in 2004. It is too soon to know whether the possibilities that exist for economic hope and opportunity will be seized, as the protagonists have promised from Sacramento to Washington, D.C., to San Juan, but these arguments are not being raised in the shadows. They are in the platforms and at the podiums, in the headlines and among the web blogs. In our political "world without walls," they are coursing through the heart of public discussion.

The road to serfdom still exists and any nation or people can travel it, but now it is lit by a billion spotlights. Puerto Rico, like California, like all of the United States, can see the avenues before it and choose the one that will lead to real freedom and economic vibrancy. It is the mission of this book to switch on a few more of those spotlights. Our aim is to add the illumination of the many roads we have already traveled as businessmen and theorists, as practitioners and policy makers, and as individuals who have witnessed the blessings of liberty in the land one of us adopted and into which the other, by the grace of God, was born.

To some, Puerto Rico may be a distant place unworthy of such attention. To us, this anomalous half-colony, indelibly part of the American scene, is another acid test of our national character. No

Introduction 2

---

man is an island, and no island should be another man's possession. The last century proved this truism once more. Let this century quickly become the one in which the phrase "American colony" finally passes into antiquity.

Arthur Laffer December 2003
San Diego, California

Section I

Economy

CHAPTER 1

My Odyssey to Freedom

The seeds of my passion for freedom were sown early, in wartime.

My first memory of this is neither a sight nor a sound. It is a sensation. It is possible that it is not a memory at all, but a recollection of what someone told me had happened. It was a death. My aunt was holding me in the garage of my grandfather's house in Belgrade. For some reason, the family regarded this dark, cramped space as safer than the house when the air raid sirens went off. It was 1945, the last year of the war and I was four years old. Wartime was all I knew. Freedom was not even an abstraction.

My aunt had scooped me up and carried me to the garage. I remember the neighbors there, along with other aunts, uncles and cousins. It was cramped. Some sat on the floor, others on low wooden stools. A goat was tied to the leg of one of the chairs. Dogs ran around among us, barking at the noise and confusion. I was a small child but I had already learned that when the bombing began one should listen for the whine and then the thump. The thump might be disaster to someone else, but to us it was word that we had not been hit. It was the whine you heard and the thump you did not that you learned to fear. That was a missile with your name on it.

Suddenly, this time, all was quiet. I remember looking up and there was open sky above us. I saw some people higher up and they were throwing ropes down to us, to raise us. Smoke and dust were everywhere. I could only move my head; the rest of my body was immobile. I felt a warm liquid pouring onto my face. I turned and saw my aunt's neck, her head torn away from it, veins protruding and spurting blood her blood all over me.

Somehow that day I was spared. That my life could have ended then and there is no less astonishing to me than that it has taken me to so many places so far removed from that garage and the city of my birth. A woman died in whose arms I was being cradled for safekeeping. Neither she nor I had any part in that war. If that were not irony enough, the bomb that killed my aunt was likely dropped by an airplane flown by men on a mission to liberate her and my family from Nazi domination. Here is a further irony: chances are that these American airmen were aided in some way by the information my dead father, an airplane parts manufacturer, had smuggled out of Yugoslavia to help the Allies understand and counter the capabilities of the Luftwaffe.

In that last year of World War II, liberation was still, for me, many years away. Before my 10th birthday, I had learned no firmer lesson than that devastation can come from any direction and tyranny can come in any form. The man or woman who lives life beginning to end in a single place, a town or address, and lives that life in peace and prosperity, is a person of great fortune. For most of us, certainly for most 20th century Europeans, life was a succession of dislocations and deaths, a session of fragmentation and fear. It was true that we yearned for freedom, but the definitions we gave it were limited. We were hungry even for crusts of freedom. My first definitions of liberty were always embodied in far-off places, even that place from which the bombs had come that killed half my family. But I knew this too: freedom comes from within. Most of us forge our own chains.

We Odishelidzes were Russians. Our roots were in what is now the Republic of Georgia and in old St. Petersburg. It was my maternal grandparents who began our family's journey to the west, a journey many generations would take in search of a better life. My father came west on his own, from Georgia, to escape the Bolsheviks. He died for freedom having had little chance to live for it. It fell to me and to my widowed mother to take the last phase of our family's journey, to the United States of America. But I am getting ahead of my story. Be forewarned that the United States is not the end of the story, but the place where the story of freedom, this story, awaits the beginning of a new chapter.

My grandparents on both sides were prominent Russian citizens, though in quite different senses. My mother's parents met as university students in St. Petersburg, before the Revolution. They were involved in the Bolshevik movement but became disillusioned and focused instead on their careers. They settled in Evpatoria, in the Crimea, where eventually my grandfather, a physician, opened a small hospital. He and my grandmother had five children. A few years after the Revolution, they decided to move the family out of Russia. My grandfather's family had gone to Russia in the mid-1800s from Serbia; they decided to return there because there were still relatives in the area.

The move tended to refute the proposition that you cannot go home again. They settled in Belgrade where my grandfather started a new practice. They enjoyed all the trappings of prosperity – a big house, live-in maids, a chauffeur. Their children also did well. Three of them, including the aunt killed in the Allied bombing, earned engineering degrees.

On my father Ilija's side adventure was added to the story of migration. My grandfather, I am told, was the Governor General of the Republic of Georgia in Tbilisi when the Revolution came. When the Bolsheviks seized power, they came after those who had been in charge. My father managed to escape (he was only 13 at the time) and he traveled first to Turkey. From there he went to Belgrade where his mother lived. She had left my grandfather shortly after my father was born and went to Belgrade with a young officer with ability and interest in aeronautics.

The Bolsheviks were ruthless, but the Georgian leaders they replaced were not provincial gentlemen. In the time of the Tsar, Georgia was a country like Afghanistan and the similar nations around it, predominantly Moslem. It was run by a tribe of Cossacks who maintained their independence from the Tsar by their willingness to be his storm troopers. Whenever a Russian village would get out of hand, the Tsar would send the Cossacks in to murder the men, rape the women, and steal everything they could carry. Through these pogroms, the Tsars managed to keep the villages in check without having to deploy any of their own soldiers.

Even if my grandfather was not the Governor General, he must have earned enemies, because that side of my family, apart from my father, was totally wiped out by the Bolsheviks. I still have a stamp from that era that bears my father's picture when he was six or seven; one can only conclude that my grandfather was, in the vernacular, a big shot. The family has also handed down from that era a collection of pictures and medals that were given to my murderous Georgian forebears by the grateful Tsars. Unfortunately, no one now alive can tell me what these mementoes signify. My pride in this side of the family, as you can gather, is not immense, but my father steered our heritage in a new and welcome direction.

When my father reached Belgrade, he located my grandmother and moved in with her and her husband. He attended one of the private Russian schools in Belgrade. There he met my mother. My father proceeded to become an engineer, a career path that now attracted both sides of my family tree. My mother was a musician, a concert pianist. Eventually, my father inherited the airplane parts business his stepfather had built up, and he made it very successful. My parents prospered anew, and before World War II they managed to travel all over Europe, leaving us many pictures of their travels in those days when the great excursions were taken by ordinary citizens and not the German Army.

I was born six months after Germany, Italy and other neighboring Axis Powers invaded and partitioned Yugoslavia. Our country was a stepping-stone for the Germans on their way to Greece. The killing field that Yugoslavia became has been compared to the carnage that ravaged Poland, and, as in Poland, much of the killing was carried out by the local population engaged in score settling. There was also a resistance movement, and it took different forms in various regions of the former nation that were now annexed to Germany, Italy and Bulgaria or under the domination of Nazi puppets. Marshal Tito led one band of partisans that represented an actual coalition of ethnic groups united against Nazi rule. Tito was a communist but not a Soviet communist and he detested the Nazis. The forces he led were willing to risk the savage reprisals the Nazis would visit upon the civilian population anytime their forces came under local attack.

During the occupation, my father quickly decided where he would cast his lot. Because of his business, he was a valuable commodity in wartime and he was presumed by the Germans to be loyal. Part of his business was to represent German airplane manufacturers in Yugoslavia and this gave him unusual access. He would make trips into Germany to visit the Reich's airplane factories and on these trips he would collect useful information, which he began to pass to the Allies. These actions marked him as a spy destined to summary execution if caught. He was also involved in the resistance in other ways, and in the summer of 1944 things became hot for him in Belgrade and he disappeared into the hills with the partisans. We not only had the Germans physically to fear, but also the American bombers. They would drop their ordinance on civilian sectors of Belgrade to hit the anti-aircraft guns the Germans had stationed outside the Americans' real targets, military installations.

It was in the early fall of 1944 that one of those bombs destroyed my grandfather's garage and killed my aunt. I suppose I should have resented the Americans ever after, even if there was military justification for this action. If I have learned nothing else in life, it is that the refusal to let go of even deep hurts and resentments not only is a futile dwelling on the past but a potent destroyer of the future. My surviving uncles concluded from these events that Belgrade was no longer safe. They decided to take the family into the countryside and they found us refuge with farmers. My cousin Lillian, seven years older than I and now living in Florida, recounts for me how she and I were walking through the cornfields when a German Stuka shot down an American plane. We ran through the fields and found the American, wounded but able to walk. We helped him to the house and he stayed there until the Partisans picked him up and hid him.

During the winter of 1944 my grandmother was taken to Dachau. Her crime was that she was not Aryan and for the Nazis, of course, that was enough. By 1945 my father had spent many years as a spy for the Allies. In gratitude the Allies arranged passage for our family to the United States. It had been agreed that we would reunite with him at the train station in Belgrade to begin our journey to freedom. The appointed hour came and my father did not appear. Only later did we learn that he had been caught on his way to the train station and murdered. Our hopes were crushed. We were later able only to retrieve bloody clothing he had worn. His body was never recovered.

In October 1945, with the help of the Partisans, the Red Army liberated Belgrade. I am an American of Russian ancestry so I may be forgiven for speaking frankly of this new occupying force. The Red Army's foot soldiers were fierce fighters, but they were a rabble of various extractions, including descendants of the Huns, Tartars, Siberian Chinese, and Arabs. They were a cruel, uncouth and uneducated lot, and they did not seem to know the difference between liberation and occupation. We hated them. They took whatever they wanted and shot people for so much as blinking the wrong way.

One joke that made the rounds during this time was that the Russian soldiers had never seen a watch. When they saw someone wearing a timepiece, they would say, "Davay, davay!" which means "Give, give!" They would walk around with 10 watches on each arm. The story had it that on one occasion a Russian got his hands on an alarm clock and took it to a watch repair shop, asking the owner if he could make him "10 little ones out of this one big one"!

Shortly after this, the Americans arrived and the difference was like night and day. I must have been like the little boy at the end of the movie Life Is Beautiful. The American G.I.s always had chocolates and other candy for the kids, and they were very respectful of the people. It was after I met these American soldiers and tasted my first marshmallow – I remember that moment like it was only yesterday – that I resolved on my own to go to America and eat marshmallows every day.

In postwar Belgrade we children had no toys to play with, so we invented games and found things to entertain us in the bombed-out buildings that filled the city. We picked up grenades, machine guns, rifles and the ammo that went with them. We would try to clean up the weapons and shoot them. Some of them didn't work, but some of them did, and some of our friends got killed or maimed. Our favorite sport was to take the gunpowder out of the bullets and pour it into a can, then stick a piece of paper into the can with one end sticking out, then light it and run like hell. Setting off these undoubtedly endeared us to everyone. A few of the explosions even managed to bring down walls. We thought this was especially exciting!

The transition to Tito's rule thrust the nation once again in a new direction. The Communists moved quickly in the wake of liberation to establish a provisional government, and, after the war's end, to establish a permanent government under Tito's lifetime rule. There was no doubt that the Partisans, having fought in a unified and often-effective way against Nazi rule, enjoyed a popularity that had little to do with their ideology under Tito. They quickly established a provisional government and moved to hold elections in November 1945. These elections pitted a single list of what was now called the People's Front versus a separate box for the opposition. Royalists connected with the provisional government had already resigned in protest over this state of affairs. Tito's People's Front scored a resounding victory.

I began my school years, therefore, as a young Communist, Yugoslavian-style. It was a very regimented system. The children were organized into military cells called "Pioneers." I must admit I was very gung-ho for this system. We were inculcated with the language of Marxism, with the importance of volunteering for all the things we were required to do, and with the plight of the proletariat. Over time, we saw how often the "proletariat" were dragged from their homes and made to disappear for no apparent reason. We saw the members of the Communist Party, by virtue of that fact alone and no merit that we could see, driving around in big cars, living in plush homes, and dining in luxury while the "proles" starved.

My father's involvement with the Partisans cost him his life, but it won for his family the privilege of keeping our grandfather's house. At first there were only eight of us to live in the house's six bedrooms. Despite our status, this was not the Communist way. Soon seven complete strangers were brought in (each accompanied by more relatives) and these new arrivals soon took over the house. Our family was squeezed into two bedrooms, all the while the party leadership lived like kings. Later, as an adult, I would learn how this aspect of Communism seemed to transcend all the variations that existed in Europe and around the world. Tito marched to his own drummer, and even though Yugoslavia modeled its first post-war constitution on the Soviet model of 1936, he pursued relationships with the West that irritated the Politburo in Moscow.

I was a good enough young Pioneer that I can recall being honored personally by Tito on May Day 1954. As he reviewed the day's parade, Tito summoned me to the platform where he personally presented me with a book written by a party leader. By this time I was 13 years old but, in truth, my mind was thriving on a literary tradition that spoke deeply to my heritage and my imagination. This real education had begun in a parallel universe outside the formal schools. My grandmother Cleopatra, one of the fortunate ones, survived Dachau and returned to Yugoslavia after the war. As one can imagine, she was a changed woman. She became very withdrawn and very religious. I became very close to her, and she would often take me to church, even though this practice was strongly discouraged by the regime. We were Russian Orthodox, and the ancient rites of the church were conducted in Old Russian. The anti-religious propaganda of the schools set up powerful currents of conflict, with the result that my interest in spiritual matters was piqued for a lifetime.

My real education in those days, however, came from my other grandmother, Eugenia. She had decided that my cousin Lillian and I were to be the intellectuals of the family, and so she taught us to read in Russian by the time we were four years old. We began with English adventure writer, Edgar Rice-Burroughs, and the first book I finished was *Tarzan*. Eugenia would not be content with that and she made me memorize the august Russian poets like Pushkin and Lermontov. She introduced me to Tolstoy, Dostoyevsky and even Zoschenko, a Soviet humorist who dared make fun of the system and not get sent to Siberia. At the age of five I had read all of Pushkin, memorizing long passages of the romantic poem "Ruslan and Ludmilla."

Pushkin's short stories were my favorite. I read them over and over again. One of the most important lessons this literature taught me was the proper way of letting go of baggage. If life is an Everest climb – if you are lucky, maybe it is only Annapurna – it's impossible to carry all your struggles and pain up the mountainside. Your friends can help you accomplish your goals, but so too can your enemies. I learned this lesson, most of all, from Pushkin's "The Captain's Daughter." It isn't just a matter of the saying, "What doesn't kill me, makes me stronger." We cannot walk through life sampling arsenic just so that we can survive the poisoner's attempt. This attitude is more a matter of avoiding the nursing of grievances that grow up around our hopes and our better natures like weeds, choking off our aspirations and our imagination.

Yugoslavia under Tito may have been one of the best places to live in the world of Communism, but the lives of the Odishelidzes there were uneasy. Tito pursued an independent brand of Marxism, and he valued his ties with the West and the economic aid from Britain and the United States that flowed, in the many millions, into his country. But he was jealous of control, and he cast a cold eye on the Soviet bloc to the East. He feared the Russians, quite reasonably, and this put Russian émigrés, even those who had been in the country for decades, under suspicion. Finally, one day in 1954, soldiers came to our house and loaded me and my mother into a truck. We were transferred to the railway and taken to Trieste, on the border between Italy and Yugoslavia and a place that had been disputed territory.

It was not that my family constituted a threat to Tito. He was under pressure to move firmly into the Soviet orbit. Our presence could become a pretext for a Soviet invasion to "protect" its citizens. To be a Communist leader one must be well versed in the matter of pretexts. Tito wanted all the Russians out of Yugoslavia. When we were placed on the train, the people around us were panicking. They knew the conditions in the DP (Displaced Persons) camps. Families lived in tents. Mud floors. Outside latrines and washing facilities. No hot water, no medical facilities, and no nutritious food. People sleeping in double bunks, with blankets hung down the side for privacy. Cold winds blowing from the side through the tent flaps. Tuberculosis rampant, easily caught and expensive and difficult to treat. We had heard the stories of people coughing all night and their bodies being carried out in the morning. No one survived more than five or six years.

It is amazing what political leaders can consider "humanitarian." The DP camps were an evil terminus almost as frightful to the passengers on the train as a concentration camp would be. There was another factor: if you caught TB, you knew for certain that no other country would accept you. At that point, you were stuck in the camp until you died. Sixty-five percent of those who were interned in DP camps died of disease or malnutrition, or both. I had to invent ways for my mother and me to get food that would sustain us.

My resolve was formed in the midst of the fearful crowd on the train trip to Trieste. I was only 13 years old and my life could not possibly be coming to an end. I was determined to go to America and to become a cowboy. There had to be a way.

As soon as you arrive at a DP camp, you make application to leave. Canada, Australia, Mexico, the United States, Venezuela, New Zealand, Argentina – just to name a few – were among the countries accepting application at that time. From then on, it was a race between admission and TB. Getting food outside the camp became the obsession. This was how I acquired my first taste of business and what a good commodity could do to open doors. I noticed that the guards' ears got cold under their helmets. I learned to knit and invented an earmuff that fit nicely under the helmet band. I scrounged for old sweaters and converted them into earmuffs, trading them into chocolates, milk and other survival goods.

In the summer I would sneak out of the camp and go down to where the cruise ships docked. It was not exactly summering on the Adriatic, but I would dive for the pennies that the passengers threw over the side just to see the scruffy ragamuffins dive for them and nearly die trying. It was cruel sport, but it worked and I am still here!

In truth, as I learned later, the camps were not intended to be anything more than rapid transit points. The goal was to move refugees through in 60 to 90 days, and this was the reason why no medical facilities had been set up for the internees. The camps, which dotted Europe (we were sent on from Trieste to Germany for a time), were run by the International Relief Organization, which was subsidized by many other organizations around the globe.

After two years of this uncertainty, my mother and I were accepted by Canada. It was the winter of 1956. I remember vividly the passage on the Scoubrin. We sailed up the St. Lawrence River and settled in Toronto. It was a long way to go for a 15-year-old boy and his widowed mother, but we were not unique during that tumultuous time. Once we reached Toronto, my mother, who had played the piano before appreciative audiences in Europe, took a job as a house-cleaning maid. She struggled and saved money so that she could buy a used piano and start giving lessons. We survived.

My three years of school in Canada were unremarkable and I left in 10th grade. I did not relate to the "normal" world of teenagers from protected environments. Canadians had served in the war and families grieved there, too, but their cities and their culture were unscathed. I spent some time with migrant farmers and in Canadian logging camps, then became a door-to-door salesman peddling pots and pans and sewing machines. I was still very shaken by the experiences of the war and the expulsion from our home. Witnessing death and misery had taken a silent toll on me, and focusing on the future was impossible.

Focus was thrust upon me when word came that my mother and I were now eligible to go to America. She had signed up for the U.S. admissions quota when we were in Trieste. In that desperate circumstance, one signed up for every option.

My life was about to take a radical turn for the better. It was the fall of 1960. A script was being written, with ink flowing from a source I could not see. Its font was freedom and the chance – another chance – to make something of a life that, until that time, had been driven by the rattle of war and TB. I did not yet know what freedom could do for me, but it beckoned, like a distant light on the horizon, and I stepped toward it.

CHAPTER 2

The Last Colony

The asterisk next to the name of Roger Maris may be the most famous punctuation mark in modern history. Until recent times, when the great Yankee slugger's name was superseded by those of McGwire, Sosa, and, finally, Bonds, the renowned asterisk in the baseball record book informed the reader to look more deeply. At the bottom of the page the reader would find the truth that Maris had hit his 61 home runs in a season that was eight games longer than the one that produced the Babe's legendary 60. Used this way, the asterisk meant, "More explanation needed."

In the year 2003, the name of the island territory nearly 1,000 miles to the southeast of the United States should always be written Puerto Rico*. Here, in this chain of islands spreading like a necklace of seashells from the Yucatan Channel to the tip of Venezuela, Puerto Rico is the ultimate anomaly, a place where things cannot be understood at a first, a second, or even a third glance. The economy, the form of democracy, the position in the Hemisphere. The past, the present, the future. Mark them all with an asterisk. More explanation is needed.

At the end of the warm, wet summer of 2003, the Robert Clemente Arena in San Juan, Puerto Rico, was filled to the rafters. Mark it with an asterisk. It was a merely a basketball game between two teams of American citizens. One was composed entirely of professionals representing the mainland United States. The opposition was composed of both professionals and amateurs, representing an unincorporated territory of the United States only 3,515 square miles in size, no bigger than the Los Angeles basin. But it was the mainland players who were looking for payback. *More explanation needed.*

The USA Team of NBA All-Stars in San Juan that late summer day was well aware that Puerto Rico had just weeks earlier scored an upset victory in the Pan Am games over a squad of U.S. college all stars. It was an earth-shaking event in San Juan, a kind of hardcourt Alamo, and the hostility of the San Juan crowd to a team of their fellow citizens from the mainland had been intense, according to the losing coach from recent NCAA champion Michigan State. Surely, the American pros would not repeat the disaster of the Pan Am games, or the shock of 2000, when they lost the Olympic gold to an upstart team from Yugoslavia.

Late in the first half, the spark that almost lit a bonfire occurred. Tracy McGrady of the U.S. team made a steal and knocked down Eddie Casiano, one of the Puerto Rican stars. McGrady scored. Casiano wanted the foul but none was called. When McGrady approached him as the buzzer sounded, hot words were exchanged. Both teams rushed the floor, the partisan crowd jeered, and a brawl nearly ensued. As the crowd pelted the floor with plastic cups and other objects, the teams finally retreated to their locker rooms. Sure, it was just basketball. Mark it with an asterisk.

That asterisk may mask a larger one. Why, indeed, if mainlanders are Americans and Puerto Ricans are Americans, are there two teams vying with each other for a place in the Olympic Games? Alaska does not field its own biathlon team. Colorado does not have its own slalom competitors. New York City does not seek a basketball gold, though it might have a good chance of winning one if the rules allowed. But Puerto Rico has an Olympic team, and that Olympic team has a basketball squad. And if, on a broiling Sunday afternoon, that squad could beat one featuring names like McGrady, Allen, Iverson, Duncan, and Carter, it would be as if the U.S. hockey team had skated out of the past and defeated the Russians all over again at Lake Placid.

Or would it? The truth is that, despite the peculiarities of the strangest relationship in the lexicon of American foreign/domestic policy, Puerto Rico* is very much a part of, and very much in love with, the rest of America. You only hurt the one you love, the saying goes, or, to put it a happier way, you only care about the hurts of the ones you love.

The story of Puerto Rico's unique and evolving relationship with the United States has all the elements of comedy and tragedy, of competition and cooperation. Chest-thumping on the basketball court or on a military firing range is about as contentious as it has gotten in a long while, even though previous eras of confrontation have seen gunfire outside Blair House, inside the House of Representatives in Washington, and outside the Governor's mansion, with lives lost, in Puerto Rico. All in all, the story of the dance between Puerto Rico and the mainland, more than a century long since the change of partners in 1898, has produced both exhilaration and exhaustion.

Today that relationship teeters more on the edge of exhaustion. Its very temperate nature, secured at the cost of billions in American taxpayer subsidies and Puerto Rican dependence, conceals the profound injustice that lies at its heart. A Latin people is very capable of tormenting an oppressor, or of following one. Like other peoples, it can produce a Simon Bolivar or a Trujillo, a Muñoz Marin or a Noriega. Perhaps the greatest injustice of all is that, given the passage of time in which Puerto Rico has been an American possession, the reaction of most of the island's people to their unequal yoke has been tempered and accepting. Somehow, in a world of violent revolution, where violence has been spurred by both just and unjust demands, Puerto Rico's lack of combustion should help to bring it the reward of a full measure of freedom. Today, in the fall of 2003, it is nowhere near that measure.

Instead, Puerto Rico has entered a state of economic and political hibernation called commonwealth. Ambiguous at its core, this status has increasingly allowed the island to claim the hallmarks of self-rule while barring it, under the U.S. Constitution, from the exercise of the sovereignty routinely available either to states in the American Union or to free nations. Every day the Congress of the United States is in session, its elected representatives can vote on and adopt laws over which the Puerto Rican people have no say. The House of Representatives can initiate a spending bill that includes the island to any degree or to no degree. The Senate of the United States can debate and ratify treaties to which Puerto Rico thereby becomes a party, with no vote or even presence of any person representing the perspective of the island on the issues at stake. That is the way it has been since 1898. No other U.S. territory, certainly no other cluster of 3.89 million Americans, is treated this way.

No one will ever know how truly expensive Puerto Rico's status is to itself and to the taxpayers across the 50 states who daily underwrite this experiment in disordered liberty. In the pages that follow, drawing from numerous sources, we attempt to calculate much of that expense, but it is all but impossible to summarize the diminution of human potential in dollar signs. The total cost was well past the $200 billion dollar mark over the past 20 years. The pace shows little sign of slackening. Even more important, the longer Puerto Rico's stultified status exists, the more the worst elements in both the Puerto Rican and mainland character come to the fore. If no long-term solution is at hand to a pressing problem, people logically reach for short-term advantage, or, worse still, cling to the narrowest prejudices.

Is racism a part of Puerto Rico's unusual story? Some evidence to the contrary exists. Alaska and Hawaii are the most two recent territories to join the Union. Both have now and had then native populations – Aleuts, Eskimos, and the Hawaiian people – who did not follow "American" ways and who spoke foreign languages. Yet these splendid places became the 49th and 50th states, and their representatives in Congress have included people of Western European as well as Polynesian and Japanese-American descent. Surely, the melting pot society that the United States has become is above every obtuse feeling? A nagging sense of doubt endures, however. Would Puerto Rico still be a territory and not a state or nation of its own if its people were half German and half Irish?

Ah, it's not the nationality, many say, it's the language. They speak Spanish there and want to preserve their culture.

But Spanish is also spoken in the United States, in Spanish Harlem and in the barrios of Los Angeles. In pockets of Wisconsin, German is the lingua franca, and in other parts of New York, Russian and other languages predominate. The local grocer speaks

Arabic to his cashier and the Chinese restaurateur rarely speaks anything but Chinese to his employees. They work hard and stick together for many purposes. The nation does not fall apart. Can it really be just language? Sometimes it is a champion of civil rights, a President Bill Clinton, or a senator less famed for his broadmindedness, a Trent Lott, who indirectly, even faintly, says or does something that suggests that a kind of prejudice, subtly racial, is at work in the hypocritical decisions that are made about the nature of Puerto Rico.

In his book about the Clinton presidency titled *The Agenda,* reporter Bob Woodward talks about a major debate in Congress over the repeal of special tax preferences for U.S. corporations that set up shop in Puerto Rico. The Clinton Administration had proposed a repeal of the preferences, based on its well-justified conclusion that they were benefiting certain well-heeled U.S. manufacturers and doing very little to boost employment and income for Puerto Ricans. The late Pat Moynihan, then-senator from New York, went to see Bill Clinton at the White House to complain about the President's economic plan. As chairman of the Senate Finance Committee, Moynihan felt he had not been sufficiently consulted. Moynihan, Woodward writes, focused on a part of the plan he insisted would have to be dropped, the President's proposal for Puerto Rico.

According to Woodward, Moynihan conceded to Clinton what every serious economist who had looked at these preferences had concluded: they were "indefensible." He then proceeded to defend them. Yes, one company had gotten tax breaks that amounted to about $500,000 per worker. The price tag for another's taxpayer giveaway was $150,000 per worker. Still, Moynihan "painted a doomsday scenario" for Clinton of what would happen if the preferences were repealed. The U.S. firms on the island would flee their tax haven and the unemployment rate on the island would double to 30 percent. A political crisis would follow. A plebiscite on the island's status – whether to remain a territory or seek admission to the Union or the path of independence – was imminent, and the panicked Puerto Ricans would approve statehood. Congress would reject it. It "would be a political nightmare. How would the United States look to the world?"[1]

None of these points could be made publicly (put an asterisk beside them). They were to be the private reasons for public actions. There was another point it would be indelicate to raise publicly, Moynihan noted. If the tax breaks went away, there would be "revolution in the Caribbean." Why, the loss of the preferences could even "vastly increase immigration to New York" from the island and, in Woodward's summation of Moynihan's message, "the increased welfare and other social service costs would outstrip the savings achieved from abolishing the tax [preferences]." Three liberal members of Congress, all of Puerto Rican heritage, one Chicagoan and two New Yorkers, agreed with Moynihan's analysis. They did not come away from the White House empty-handed. Watered-down but still generous, the tax breaks were preserved.2

Thus, for several more years, faulty public policy survived that helped, and in new forms still helps, to keep Puerto Rico shackled to something less than liberty. Had conservatives gone to a president of their party and made these arguments, warning that special tax breaks for big U.S. companies were needed to keep Puerto Ricans away from our shores, the cries of bigotry would be deafening, as would the complaints of corporate welfare and tax cuts for the rich. For decades, Puerto Ricans in New York City, Chicago and elsewhere across the country had voted reliably for the Democrats. Now here was their reward: to have their own presence, and the prospect that this presence might increase, used as an argument in favor of an "indefensible" tax gimmick that lined the pockets of the rich. Did it make sense for liberal Democrats to act this way about a reliable constituency? Is it "immigration" when American citizens move from one U.S. jurisdiction to another? Only if the place one is dealing with is Puerto Rico*.

In the fall of 2003, the United States of America is embarked on a project designed to bring democratic institutions and a functional constitution to Iraq. It is far too early to tell how that experiment will play out, but it is ironic indeed that our leaders believe they can bring the blessings of self-government to a nation that has no heritage of liberty. For 105 years now, we have been unable to bring about a permanent form of self-government in a place far closer to us, far more admiring of our way of life, a place that has such a heritage and surely has such a yearning.

The longer commonwealth lingers, the more difficult a permanent solution may be. The longer any person falls behind and fails to realize its dreams, the more fractious their politics becomes, and the less attractive their polity becomes to their fellow citizens. Substantive issues become symbolic and symbolic issues become substantive. A gubernatorial candidate who favors statehood can earn attention for a fracas involving proper display of the American flag. At a celebration in 2000 for the new Puerto Rican middleweight boxing champion, fans can force the organizers to remove the U.S. flags from the stage. A sitting governor can decamp to a hotel room in the Dominican Republic as she futilely awaits admission as an equal to a meeting of Latin American heads of state. The U.S. Navy can be tossed off a firing range it has used for decades to teach soldiers how to conduct themselves in battle. A heroin addict can see the sum total of his universe in the cost of a vial.

That last epiphany was reported in an article in *National Geographic* published in March 2003. The addict, Luis by name, complained to the writer about the high price of his fix relative to the cost of street drugs in New York. It was, he intoned, "another example of the unfair trade relations between Puerto Rico and the U.S."[3] Here, the words of the prophets echo off the walls of El Morro, the 17th century fort in Old San Juan where the shooting galleries hum in a zone the overmatched police seldom enter. What emotion resonates in the addict's bitter words? Resentment? Envy? A cruel joke? The dependency on drugs is perhaps the worst of all, but the dependency of 60 percent of a population eligible for welfare assistance is ultimately more debilitating.[4]

Puerto Rico has had less than full freedom within the American system for more than a century. Indeed, in that period, the Congress of the United States has not once passed legislation that would permit Puerto Rico to stage a clear, and consequential, vote on acceptable options for a permanent status. In fits and starts, the political parties on the island, shift their positions and their names, devising statuses of various definitions and seeking clarifications from Washington. They stage votes and some parties boycott them. They ponder the establishment of committees and assemblies, task forces and study groups, argue with one another, argue with the wind, looking for formulas that will satisfy the factions' desires and command the attention of Washington. It is the contradiction of Santayana's maxim: Puerto Ricans remember the past, and still they seem doomed to relive it.

Puerto Ricans are not exactly what an observer sees at first glance. More explanation is needed. The people of the island are part-Spaniard, part African American, and part Taino Indian. There is the blood of Corsicans and Irish in their midst, white Catholic settlers invited in at various periods. A handful were pirates, not invited in. Many were smugglers, self-taught in a craft born of dire necessity as first Spain and then the United States sought to limit what Puerto Ricans could buy and sell overseas, most of it legal goods, some of it contraband. Everything is not what it seems. Mark it with an asterisk.

Freedom House, in its annual report assessing the level of liberty enjoyed by various peoples, labels Puerto Rico "free." Relative to billions of other people around the world, this characterization is fair, the heated rhetoric of the island's *independentistas* to the contrary. Puerto Ricans hold effective elections for every local office. When they march in the streets, as 150,000 people did in February 2000 to protest the Navy exercises at Vieques, Washington, though reluctantly in many quarters, listens. Crowds of this size do not determine policies in China regarding the location of factories, much less military bases. In fact, crowds of this size do not form in China at all, unless it is to watch an official parade. No, Puerto Rico is assessed accurately as "free": it is as part of one of the freest countries on earth that its dearth of key liberties is incongruous.

Living in the shadow land between colonization and self-determination makes a people feel its way forward tentatively. A son complains of the "debilitating deference" many Puerto Ricans pay to the mainland United States, thinking that the island's association with the giant to the north has brought it prosperity. A father, a four-year veteran of the U.S. Navy, replies to his son, "If Puerto Rico ever became independent, I'd move to the U.S. This place would be bust in a minute – no more Social Security, no more checks every month." A generation gap does exist, with more older Puerto Ricans valuing their long-standing ties with the United States and the cash income they have earned in its service, and more young Puerto

Ricans, who have seen only the economic stagnation detailed in the pages that follow, willing to try something new.

In the fall of 2003, the mind of Washington is not focused on the populous island that bridges the Greater and Lesser Antilles. Looking toward its own wounds, from terrorism and several years of a cool economy, the American people and the Congress are paying little attention to the restiveness brewing in Puerto Rico. One in 70 of their fellow citizens lives there, but for most of us it might as well be one in 7,000. The average net transfer of taxpayer funds to each of those citizens now runs some $1,500, but the cost of rebuilding Iraq, $100 billion or more, is in the headlines. Per capita income in Puerto Rico is a national scandal, roughly $9,000, less than half that of Mississippi, the poorest state, but Americans are focused more on the 2.7 million jobs lost nationwide since the economy soured in 2000.

The lull in Washington is deceptive, however. The United States is a superpower and there is more to the world than Iraq. Changes are coming, swift and certain, across the whole terrain of national affairs. Domestically, the United States is "Hispanicizing," and African Americans have given up their place in the demographic pecking order as the nation's largest minority. California is the perennial political bellwether state, the home of future trends that usually overtake the rest of the country, Florida is the state that decided the last presidential election, and Texas is home to the nation's president. All of these states are seeing an influx of Hispanic Americans. Many of them cannot legally vote. Puerto Ricans can, and they are making their way in dramatic numbers to areas like Orlando, where the daily newspaper, *The Orlando Sentinel*, does some of the most thorough reporting in the states about Puerto Rico's condition.

In 2005, little more than a year away as this is written, the Section 936 tax that substituted so long for a development policy for Puerto Rico will sink at last into the sands of time. A new governor, likely the former two-term governor, Pedro Rossello, or the current pro-commonwealth Resident Commissioner, Anibal Acevedo Vila, will take office. The promises made by the Bush Administration in education and for Medicare, plus whatever promises are added on to these by the dynamics of the 2004 election season, will come due, and new taxpayer funds will begin to circulate, like some hurricane in reverse, from the mainland to the island. All the while, closer to home, an Hispanic nation that has always fascinated Americans, a long-captive nation whose capital is just 90 miles from our shores, may undergo a wrenching and epoch-making change.

One might soon be tempted to put an asterisk by the name Cuba as well. That "other island" has had a very predictable history for many decades, but the near future may bring it, too, into the realm of the not easily explained. If we are fortunate, our leaders will look beyond the policies and prejudices of the past and begin to perceive that a whole new era is about to begin in the Caribbean. How our president and our Congress handle that era may have more impact on the future of the entire Western Hemisphere, and much of the developing world, than any other factor on the scene today, save the threat of terrorism. The Caribbean has never had any success in avoiding the ancient Chinese curse of being compelled to live in interesting times.

Fifty years ago next June a band of Puerto Rican nationalists stood in the Visitors Gallery of the U.S. House of Representatives and fired shots, wounding five members of Congress. Five years ago, the real character of the Puerto Rican, our fellow Americans, was on display in the actions of one man in that same chamber. He was 100 years old, a veteran of the First World War, the war that induced Congress to make Puerto Ricans citizens of the United States. He had come to the House gallery to witness the first-ever extended debate and vote on legislation by which Congress would define the options it would accept for Puerto Rico's future. He witnessed a debate that was at once vigorous and principled, gnarled with petty politics and patent prejudices, ragged and messy, but democratic at its heart – the epitome of self-rule, the object of every civilized populace.

When at last, that debate was over and the amendments were all accepted or rejected, the House voted. By a margin of a single vote, the decision of one person in the chamber, the House approved a bill to set a date for Puerto Rico's rendezvous with self-determination. The centenarian had come, he said, "to see the values I fought for redeemed by Congress before I die." As one observer wrote, this gentleman was "just one of many with tears in their eyes that night after the deliberations ended with a nerve-crunching vote of 209 for the bill, and 208 against."[5] That bill died soon after in the United States Senate. The fate of that aged veteran is unknown to us. This we do know. Congress still has an act of redemption to perform.

CHAPTER 3

America Delivers

⇒◆⇐

It was September of 1960. I was looking forward to celebrating my 19th birthday that October in America. Few 18-year-olds know what life has in store for them. That life had Puerto Rico in store for me could not have been further from my mind.

Events had conspired at every turn to sharpen my appreciation for freedom. I had lived under Nazism as a toddler, under communism as a teenager, and with fear, disease, and uncertainty in the Displaced Persons camps of Italy and Germany. Coming to North America was for me, as it has been for millions of immigrants from war-torn Europe, an unimagined liberation. Belgrade was my birthplace, but it was more crucible than cradle. Half my friends did not escape the tides of terror that swept through the city from the west and then the east. They were either wiped out in the years of the German occupation, or "disappeared" as people had a habit of doing under Tito, or blown away, in a final irony, by the unexploded ordinance that still littered the streets and bombed-out buildings as late as the fifties.

My thoughts were on the future as I crossed the Canadian border at Niagara Falls in my 1955 Meteor (named for a combination of space and speed, the car was an emblem of its era, but it was really nothing more than the Canadian version of a Ford). As I got closer to New York City, flicking my radio from station to station, I suddenly picked up music that caught my attention. It was very different from the American popular music that had captivated me. I had been pushing the buttons for Elvis Presley, Jerry Lee Lewis, Bill Haley and the Comets, or Bobby Wilson. What I now heard was a silky rhythm, punctuated by percussion, that just grabbed me and kept me chained to the station for the rest of the trip.

For most of us, freedom has some kind of soundtrack. This was mine. I didn't know it at the time, but that seductive beat would help drive my life from that point on. Suddenly I forgot that after all this time I had finally made it to the land of my dreams. Here was my fortune, waiting for me just to reach out and take it. In Yugoslavia and the DP camps, I had imagined this moment, making it to America, and here I was, in the heart of Manhattan, listening to this strange music that just wouldn't let me go.

I had very few dollars in my pocket, but I had something more valuable. They were slips of paper with names and addresses of friends of my deceased parents. Some were Russians from Yugoslavia, like my parents, others were people I had met in the DP camps who had made it to New York a few years before me.

Sherwood Anderson once wrote that old age has arrived when you begin to take "the backward look at life." I had next to nothing to look back to, and that was why, basically penniless and with almost no formal education, I had all the optimism of youth. I believed at that moment that life had never been better. My schooling had been disrupted by the war and the camps and the death of my parents. I had no profession, no job prospects, no chance to go to college, but I was nearly nineteen and I had survived. Experience had made me feel more like forty-nine. Armed with confidence and a green card, I could move about as I pleased in America. What more did I need to sample its bounty? I had walked through the golden door, and there was nothing but opportunity and wealth on the other side.

Here at last I had made a shore where everyone, refugees and seekers from every other part of the globe, shared the same creed.

Gleb, my first friend in New York, was the son of an associate of my deceased father. It was he who told me that the music that mesmerized me was called "mambo" and that it was usually played in Puerto Rican and Cuban neighborhoods. He must have seen the excitement in my eyes. It was a red flag to him. As a white person, he said, I should stay away from those places.

There was a subtle difference in rhythms between the Cuban "mambo" and what I later learned was the Puerto Rican "salsa." The Puerto Rican version was just beginning at the time. It was played in nightspots like Club Caborojeno on Broadway and 145th Street and the Hunt's Point Casino in the Hunt's Point section of the Bronx. New Yorkers don't mince words. Hunt's Point was nicknamed Korea, because rumor had it that as many people had been killed in that neighborhood as there had been during the Korean War. Banking on the notion that this was probably pure exaggeration and that I was immortal anyway, I headed there first.

Enchantment and blindness are boon companions. I didn't notice that most of the people hanging around outside the casino had much darker skin than I did. Some had kinky hair. They stood around, fearless, smoking marijuana and drinking rum and coke from paper cups. I wasn't in Kansas anymore. This was "Korea." It didn't matter. All I heard was the music coming from the dark interior and it drew me in.

Inside it was near-pitch dark, and people were milling around the dance floor, the couples dancing in the middle. You could smell tobacco smoke mixed with the pungency of marijuana and human sweat. Most of the crowd was speaking Spanish. The conga player appeared to be in a trance, beating out the rhythm, and those who were not dancing as couples swayed to his cadence. Couples made out in the shrouded corners of the room. The dancers swam in the hypnotic stream of sexual chemistry. This was not the impersonal gyration of rock-and-roll or the formal cheek-to-cheek of ballroom. This was up close and very personal. The atmosphere was alive with exotic sensuality. I did not need to understand the words. I was hooked.

Gleb was not impressed with my sense of adventure. He refused to return with me to the real "salsa" clubs. "Alex, it's lunacy for a white person to go anywhere around there." In my heart I had to agree, but that, for me, was part of the allure.

Still, there were relatively safe places to go to hear similar music (never the kind of true "salsa" rhythm you heard in Club Caborojeno or the Hunt's Point Casino). Any truly popular music form eventually migrates, transmuted, into houses of respectability.

In the 1950s for mambo, these were places like the Palladium, the Taft Hotel or Roseland in midtown Manhattan. The music there was, by my standards, "tame" and so was the crowd, but it was passable, and I finally persuaded Gleb to accompany me there.

That is where I met Julie.

Julie was from Puerto Rico, and to me, she was everything a Latin lady was supposed to be. Straight out of West Side Story, "a beautiful Maria of my soul," as the Mambo Kings would sing it. She had just come to New York from Puerto Rico, possessed a college degree (which impressed me), and moved beautifully to that salsa rhythm. I was in paradise.

When I asked her if she had ever been to Club Caborojeno or the Hunt's Point Casino, she looked at me and snapped back, "Not my crowd!" That's when I first realized that there were two Puerto Rico's, and geography had nothing to do with it. In some ways, it was like every nationality's split about the "old country," but it had its own Latin twist of class and economic status. It was around November of 1960 when I met Julie. I had been in the United States but two short months. Revolutions, I learned, can be made in days.

It was not long after I discovered the United States that the United States discovered me.

In February of 1961 I received my draft notice. By that summer, I was in basic training and by the fall of '61 I was sent to Fairbanks. The direction of my life was hard to discern, but for the most part at least it was westward. Alaska had been a state but two years (joining the Union in January 1959 with Hawaii following seven months later, facts which will figure in this narrative later) and was an exciting frontier. In the summer of '62 Julie came up to Alaska and we got married. I was all of 20 at that time.

I spent my two years in the Army on the U.S. biathlon (skiing and shooting) team, which afforded me time to go to school. I received my high school equivalency diploma and completed about 32 college credits. Like the person who is starving, when given a plate with meat and potatoes, I skipped the potatoes and went for a second helping of the meat. I loaded up with courses in accounting, business law and economics. Having spent the better part of my life under the communist system, I did not want others to determine my economic fortunes. I had no desire to endure the vagaries of being an employee. I was going to be a businessman, and I wanted to get what I needed to be one.

The 1964 winter Olympics were to be held in Innsbruck, a few hundred miles from my birthplace. I was given an opportunity to reenlist in the Army with a chance to attend the Olympics as a substitute member of the U.S. biathlon team. Many people would have regarded this as a once-in-a-lifetime opportunity. My eyes were focused on other opportunities, however. The American business world was waiting for me. That is where I wanted to claim my medals.

I was discharged from the Army on July 1, 1963 and my son was born on July 3, 1963. Any illusions of instant wealth I had were tempered by immediate experience with the rules of the game. When my wife was in labor, I took her to the military hospital in Queens, New York for the delivery. The personnel there explained to me that if my son had decided to be born two days before, they could take care of the birth, but since I was officially out of the Army, my wife could no longer get medical care at a military hospital. "So where do I go?" I said. They suggested some taxi drivers could help out in a pinch. I wasn't amused at all, and Julie was even less so.

We made the best of it and returned to New York City. Reality set in like a mid-summer heat wave. I wanted to be a businessman. To go into business, you need capital. To get capital, if you are just starting out, you need to borrow it. To borrow it, you need a job. Try getting a job that will feed a family in New York City when all you have is a high school equivalency diploma and a year's worth of college education.

As others learned before me, when all else fails, there is always the insurance business. There, more than anything, you need contacts, circles of potential clients and referrals, and of these I had none. Thus I began my career at the lowest rung of the ladder, the one with the top that reaches the ground floor. I became a debit collector for Metropolitan Life in East New York, Brooklyn, working the tenements and low-income projects where many Puerto Ricans lived. Life has a way of keeping you focused in certain directions whether you like it or not.

I carried a lead pipe to make sure I got back to the office with the money I collected. Word got around quickly that the "Anglo"-

looking man on the elevator carried cash along with his ledger book. Later I found out that MetLife couldn't get anyone else to go into those neighborhoods. But I had had experience in "Korea," and Belgrade long before that, so the danger didn't bother me. Necessity is the mother of many things besides invention.

I sold more insurance than most other people, moved out of being a debit collector to selling "regular people," became a unit supervisor, and took all the insurance-related degrees I could get my hands on. America is more than a theory: the hard work paid off. I won a position as manager for Mutual of New York at a prestigious Manhattan location, became a training director for MONY at age 26, and took over a full agency in midtown at age 27. It was heady stuff, overseeing the operations of more than 20 salespeople, unit managers and clerical staff, being the youngest agency head in their history, in the nation's financial capital.

There was more to come. I became rookie manager of the year. It was like being the Walter Alston of insurance. I was invited to give a speech in Los Angeles about my overachievements to a couple of hundred insurance executives. A few insurance companies even started sending me serious offers to join their ranks as a Vice President.

God bless America. I was now 28 years old and there were no further questions about my high school equivalency diploma.

But I wasn't looking for a high salary with bonuses, perks, stock options and a corner office. Even though being in the life insurance business was as close to entrepreneurship as you could get because your income, whether you were a salesperson or a unit manger or a full agency manager was always dependent on the bottom line results that your area of responsibility produced, full entrepreneurship had eluded me up to this point.

This kind of success could have been the end of my story. I might have earned an excellent income and occupied a mahogany desk in an office tower in Hartford or Boston or one of the other insurance capitals. There would have been no island with a storm-swept past and uncertain future weighing on my thoughts and beckoning with its hurts and hopes. I would have seen all I know of Puerto Rico and its people in the dark clubs of the Bronx or in the dazzling eyes of my wife. Fate had a different plan.

Agency managers in the insurance business receive what is called an "override" on the business that their agents produce. Essentially, the manager receives a continuing cut of the premiums from every policy the agent sells. The bigger the agency, the bigger the manager's take, but the company, of course, still owns the operations. To me, the epitome of entrepreneurship in this business was to be a "General Agent." On this basis, the company grants a franchise for a certain geographical area and provides some start up money to hire salespeople and set up an office. The general agent, however, pays the expenses, keeps the profits, and owns the business. When he leaves, the company pays for the agency based on the amount of business put on the books during his tenure

That became my goal because, besides earning a high income, I could also create capital. In my immigrant's eyes, amassing capital was what the capitalist system was all about. Even in the late 1960's there weren't that many agency opportunities left, as most of the major companies were operating on the managerial system, a far more lucrative way for them to promote sales and funnel profits to the top. This was all perfectly natural in the business world. As I would come to learn, it was all perfectly natural in the realm of politics, where decisions are made not about insurance agents' territories but about real territories.

Life was about to teach me some major lessons about the realpolitik of real estate. All of my histories - personal, political and familial, were about to converge on a slab of tropical mountains and beach in the Tropic of Cancer. To Julie, it was the past. To me, it was the uncharted future.

CHAPTER 4

The Price of Dependence

───◆───

Some 8,500,000 travelers, most of them tourists, land every year at Puerto Rico's San Juan International Airport. Another 2,500,000 make the island a port of call on the cruise ships that ply Caribbean waters year-round. Millions of Americans have made this trip, some repeatedly. It is a romantic destination, sun-splashed, a place of beaches with a swatch of tropical rain forest, across the blue sea, yet still part of home, like some secret garden at the perimeter of a familiar park.

An advanced purchase, non-refundable air ticket from New York to San Juan on U.S. Airways could be had in the summer of 2003 for $188. Let us imagine that a desire has overwhelmed you, the reader, to become one of these 11 million annual visitors to one of the Caribbean's glamour spots, a shopping and beach-going Mecca for Americans and Europeans alike. It is the lure of Borinquen.

You and your spouse go on-line and, with a few keystrokes, select your dates and times of travel, enter your seat selections, and type in your credit card information, including the all-important expiration date. As a final warning, the web page informs you to be careful not to click "enter" more than once while you wait, as this will result in duplicate charges of $376.00 plus tax appearing on your statement. You are asked a final time to verify your information and confirm your decision to purchase twin airfares to your island destination.

You carefully click "enter" a single time and, after a minute's delay, this message appears:

> *Thank you for your contribution to the economy of the Commonwealth of Puerto Rico. Your funds have been transferred to the people of Puerto Rico in fulfillment of your annual allotment as an American citizen to the upkeep and progress of this territory.* **Please do not go to the airport in expectation of being permitted to take your flight.** *Your willingness to transfer these funds to your fellow citizens in the Commonwealth is deeply appreciated. We have taken the liberty of placing a cookie on your computer to assist you in making your automatic $400 contribution next year and every year thereafter, adjusted for inflation. Bon voyage! Or, as we say in the realm of economic subsidies for the needy few and the politically potent, "Thank you for paying up and staying put!"*

This is not a scenario under which any airline could stay in business. Nor is it a scenario under which any person would long keep his or her computer. But it is not a fanciful scenario in its essence, because the simple truth is that every middle-income American taxpayer forks over an average of $400 per year to subsidize the unique relationship between the United States and Puerto Rico. It has been this way a long time, and it may be this way for a long time to come. The unwholesome roots of this plot are not difficult to disentangle.

Puerto Rico is neither a nation nor a state. It occupies a shadowland, a kind of Limbo, where each and every aspect of its affairs, from law enforcement, to banking, to citizenship, to federal program eligibility, to taxation, is handled in a way peculiar to the island and its unique history. The keeping of African Americans as slaves was once referred to as the "peculiar institution." Today, the peculiar institution is that middle kingdom called a "commonwealth" territory, and in that kingdom, as in a Gilbert and Sullivan operetta, "nothing is as it seems."

The Price of Dependence

The heart of the imbalance consists in this: while, for the purposes of most programs that tap the federal Treasury, Puerto Ricans operate like other American citizens and receive benefits, the people of the island do not pay federal income tax. Moreover, through a series of decisions decades ago designed to spark Puerto Rico's tortured and flailing economy, industries on the island, particularly U.S. pharmaceutical companies, have enjoyed a targeted tax break that essentially relieved them of all U.S. corporate income tax on their earnings there. This tax giveaway, it turns out, and as we will describe in detail, no longer accomplishes any meaningful purpose for the Puerto Rican economy. Instead, it benefits a wealthy and well-connected few. Moreover, it punishes the many, not only the hypothetical tourists in our fictional example, but also the Puerto Rican people who suffer the fraud of dependency.

This mass injustice is perpetuated by an iron law that is well understood by the armed camps of lobbyists that surround Washington, D.C. like so many Confederate regiments. The I.R.S. code, thick as a Sequoia, is replete with sections, exemptions, and preferences that stand poorly, or not at all, on their own merits. Nonetheless, because they benefit a particular party, class of parties, or sector in very direct ways, and the parties they harm are diffuse or even uninformed about the existence of the special benefit, lobbying efforts invariably favor the status quo. This is especially true in a political scheme dominated by campaign money. Every member of Congress knows where the pharmaceutical industry sends its millions in political cash. Where does the "American taxpayer" send his or her political donations? Everywhere and nowhere. It is not difficult to see who will win the debate over an obscure spending program or tax break. It's the party that can focus its own efforts and deflect those of its opposition.

How do we derive the $400 figure used in the tale of the tourist? Simple! We take the total cost to U.S. taxpayers of maintaining Puerto Rico as a territory and divide it by the approximate number of middle and upper income, tax paying families in America. In some respects this is a very conservative number. It does not reflect the huge losses, for example, in productivity and individual health that flow from Puerto Rico's massive role in the narcotics trade. It does not include the costs, direct and indirect, of other crimes associated with drug abuse. Nearly a third of the most serious illegal narcotics that reach our shores transit Puerto Rico in some way on their journey north. The Office of National Drug Control Policy issued a study in September 2001 that estimated the overall cost to the United States of drug abuse in 1998 as $143.4 billion and likely to rise to as much as $160.7 billion in 2001.[1]

A figure this high is difficult to comprehend. Here is one scale of value. The *Canadian Journal of Cardiology* in February 2003 cited a Health Canada report that the direct and indirect cost of *all* illnesses in Canada was approximately $160 billion for 1998.[2] The drug "tax" alone on the American people rivals this amount. If Puerto Rican smugglers and dealers handle 30 percent or more of the major narcotics, it is not unreasonable to state that the island has a major role in imposing annual society-wide costs of some $50 billion or more on the United States. But the $400 figure does not include a penny of these costs.

Instead, look at a few sums that can be attributed to the major federal programs and special tax breaks Congress has, over time, made available to Puerto Rico. U.S. taxpayers foot the bill for $39,000,000 in fiscal year 2001 to build and maintain Puerto Rican highways. Puerto Rico has never been self-sufficient in foodstuffs, so it is no surprise that the 2001 federal budget saw $3.58 billion going to the island in the form of nutritional assistance for its poor. Medicare checked in at $1.32 billion, and the bill to Uncle Sam for housing assistance was $407 million.

To be sure, some of the estimated $17.8 billion that taxpayers spent on assistance to Puerto Rico in 2001 represents earned income (this figure does not include the value of business tax credits). As former soldiers whose physical and psychological battle scars are as real as every other citizen's, Puerto Rican veterans who have served the United States are eligible for veterans benefits and medical care. It is one mark of the extent of that service that these benefits cost the U.S. Treasury $379 million in 2001. Social Security benefits also flow to the island, totaling $4.56 billion that same year. This is technically an earned benefit, although under Social Security's pay-as-you-go structure both revenue-in and benefits paid out vary from year to year and are rarely balanced.

The Price of Dependence

Many individuals receive more than they paid into the system, even adjusted for inflation, as longevity has increased and the retirement age has gone unchanged.

The more one drills into the nature of the Puerto Rican relationship with the federal government, and thereby with the U.S. public, the more anomalous it seems. Disease, as outbreaks of Mad Cow Disease and SARS have potently reminded us, is no respecter of boundaries. The U.S. Centers for Disease Control, based in Atlanta, Georgia, has a series of regional offices that carry on administrative functions and perform surveillance on infectious diseases. One of the CDC's 10 area offices is located in San Juan. Congress, finding it difficult to deny U.S. responsibility for the well being of the Puerto Rican people even as it has been unable to resolve their status or include them on the tax rolls, has steadily included the island in one program after another. The table on page 65 lists a number of the most common federal programs and the status of Puerto Rico's participation.

Federal obligations to Puerto Rico are growing, and the cost of fighting the drug trade in the Caribbean will drive them up further. Between fiscal years 2000 and 2001, overall federal assistance to Puerto Rico grew more than 16 percent. From 1993 onward, the average annual increase in funding from Washington was a solid 3.6 percent.[3] Even so, measured on a per capita basis, as Table 1 notes, the level of federal funding of Puerto Rico ranks it among the lowest of the U.S. states and territories. That does not mean the money is modest.

In a special report for the American Alliance for Tax Equity, economist Robert J. Shapiro provided a detailed account of the cumulative cost of U.S. government expenditures and tax credits from 1981 to 2001. The combined cost of federal spending and tax preferences over this 20-year period was $192.8 billion, or an average of $9.64 billion per year. Table 2 on page 65 sets forth this spending and breaks down each major category by specific program. Note that this table excludes the amounts spent over this period on Social Security, Medicare and other programs that are financed, at least in theory, by employee contributions. Those "financed" payments totaled nearly $67 billion over this period. In addition, some of the categories in the table represent earned but not financed

Table 1

Leading Cultural and Economic Indicators: Puerto Rico and the 50 States	
Per capita income	52nd
Profits from manufacturing as a percentage of Gross Domestic Product	1st
Population	27th
Population Density	4th
Civilian Labor Force	33rd
Infant Mortality Rate	2nd
Percent of Persons on Disability	16th
Out-of-Wedlock Births (Percentage of All Births)	2nd
Death Rate	46th
Total Number of Food Stamp Recipients	4th
Local Income Tax Collections	1st
Total U.S. Direct Federal Transfer Payments Received	47th
Total Federal Expenditures, 2000	36th
High Energy Cost	4th *
High-Tech Employment	37th
Tech Exports	16th
Number of "suspicious activity reports" (SARs) filed with the U.S. Treasury regarding potentially criminal activity and/or money laundering in banks and financial institutions.	33rd
National Assessment of Education Progress	Experimental participation begins in 2003

- Base of comparison 60 U.S. power regions (includes cities and states)

(i.e., by individual contribution) benefits (e.g., veterans benefits), financed benefits (federal retirement), and benefits that are subsidized but must be repaid (student loans). Overall, federal grants produced about the same benefit for Puerto Rico as did the Section 936 tax gimmick, an average of just over $3 billion per year.

Chart 1 on page 67 shows the relative contribution to federal expenditures for Puerto Rico from each category of funding, including tax breaks. As the chart makes clear, this spending pie can be sliced into three fairly equal pieces: the special tax breaks from Section 936 and other measures; federal grants paid into Puerto Rico's operating budget; and "other," which includes insurance, defense contracts, and payments directly to individuals. As pies go, this one is neatly divided by the income characteristics of the recipients. The vast majority of the federal grants that make their way to the island go to its poor, through such programs as

Table 2. Federal Expenditures and Tax Credits for Puerto Rico, 1981-2001

Federal Program	Spending	Share of Spending
Federal Grants	**$62.01 billion**	**32.2%**
Nutritional Assistance (Food Stamps)	$19.25 billion	10.0%
Customs and ATF Rebates	$7.34 billion	3.8%
Educationally Deprived Children Program	$3.59 billion	1.9%
Disaster Relief	$2.36 billion	1.2%
Medicaid	$2.10 billion	1.1%
WIC Program (food for young mothers)	$1.98 billion	1.0%
Community Development	$1.79 billion	0.9%
Section 8 Housing	$1.59 billion	0.8%
Child Nutrition Program	$1.96 billion	1.0%
Family Support Payments (AFDC/TANF)	$1.48 billion	0.8%
Public Housing	$0.93 billion	0.5%
Low-Rent Housing Operating Assistance	$0.79 billion	0.4%
Community Development Block Grants	$0.57 billion	0.3%
Public and Indian Housing	$0.48 billion	0.2%
School Lunch program	$0.47 billion	0.2%
Highway Planning and Construction	$0.39 billion	0.2%
Other	$14.94 billion	7.8%
Federal Salaries	**$8.77 billion**	**4.6%**
Defense	$3.16 billion	1.6%
Postal Service	$1.99 billion	1.0%
Other Non-defense	$3.63 billion	1.9%
Federal Payments to Individuals	**$21.04 billion**	**10.9%**
Veterans Benefits	$6.32 billion	3.3%
Pell Grants	$5.48 billion	2.8%
Federal Retirement	$3.38 billion	1.8%
Housing Assistance	$3.00 billion	1.6%
Guaranteed Student Loan Interest Subsidy	$0.17 billion	0.1%
Other	$2.69 billion	1.4%
Federal Procurement Contracts	**$3.61 billion**	**1.9%**
Defense	$2.48 billion	1.3%
Non-defense	$1.13 billion	0.6%
Other Federal Assistance	**$32.61 billion**	**16.9%**
Direct Loans	$2.18 billion	1.1%
Guaranteed Loans	$11.55 billion	6.0%
Insurance	$18.88 billion	9.8%
Total Spending	**$129.59 billion**	**67.2%**
Section 936 Tax Credit	**$63.21 billion**	**32.8%**
TOTAL	**$192.80 billion**	**100.0%**

Source: Shapiro, et al., "The Costs of Puerto Rico's Status to American Taxpayers"[4]

Head Start, Title I education funding, the WIC program (which provides food for women taking care of newborn children), rental assistance, and school lunches. The tax third of the pie, as we will describe in detail in the next two chapters, benefits disproportionately some of the largest and richest companies in the United States. The remaining third, while it includes some spending (like Pell Grants) that is restricted by income level, is the only segment that is widely distributed across the Puerto Rican population.

As noted above, total federal assistance to Puerto Rico reached $17.8 billion in 2001, a sharp 16.3 percent increase from the previous year. This number is likely to climb sharply in the years ahead if Washington follows through on certain commitments, particularly in the area of education and health care, where prescription drug coverage under Medicare could provide new benefits to an estimated 500,000 senior citizens in Puerto Rico, roughly one of every eight people on the island. The numbers for FY 2002 show that federal spending, exclusive of business tax credits, totaled $18.5 billion, an increase of almost 4.0 percent from 2001. Add those business credits back in (the Section 936 credit is sunsetting, and companies are migrating to another tax benefit called Controlled Foreign Corporation status), and this federal transfer to Puerto Rico may be in the neighborhood of $22 billion for FY 2002. As we mentioned in the beginning of this chapter, our method of calculating the $400 it costs each American's family to maintain Puerto Rico involves merely dividing this sum by the estimated 50 million middle- and upper-income tax returns filed in the United States each year.

The typical Puerto Rican pays no federal income tax to buy into the baseline benefits included in these numbers. Even the U.S. family that does not have a son or daughter in uniform pays taxes to supply our Armed Forces with pay and equipment. While Puerto Ricans serve honorably and even courageously in the U.S. military as citizens, the typical Puerto Rican family has no one in uniform and enjoys the security umbrella of our missiles, planes, and naval forces, but pays not a penny to support that umbrella, even if our government gets something "in return" for the salaries and procurement dollars it pays to Puerto Ricans. Thus, while a significant amount of this $22 billion price tag is no outright gift to Puerto

Chart 1

Federal Spending by Category, Puerto Rico, 1981-2001

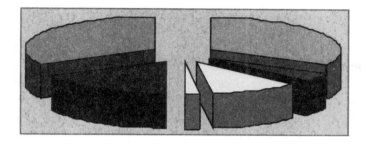

- Grants
- Salaries
- Individuals
- Contracts
- Loans/Insurance
- Tax Credits

Rico, and even if a portion of it returns to the mainland in the form of purchases of American goods, there is no doubt that the net loss involved in the current arrangement with Puerto Rico averages several hundred dollars per year for Mr. and Mrs. America.

Let's home in even more closely on that portion of this $22 billion annual cost that is targeted on Puerto Rico's poor, a near majority of the island's population even at the dawn of the 21st century. Here the dismal, and even declining, fortunes of the current commonwealth status of Puerto Rico stands in sharp relief against the trends at work in the 50 states. As noted above, roughly one-third of the federal transfer pie for Puerto Rico, exclusive of special tax gimmicks, is composed of grants designed to reach this target group. Over the years, while leaving the island's federal income tax exemption untouched, the U.S. Congress has made Puerto Rico eligible for more and more of the federal government's multitude of means-tested programs. With the exception of welfare, which was radically reformed in 1996, individual and household eligibility for many of these programs has been expanded over the years. Today (see Table 3 on page 69), Puerto Ricans have been made eligible for most, but not all, federal grant and cash transfer programs.

Chart 2 on this page shows the track of these grant programs over the last 10 federal fiscal years.5 The chart shows a significant spike in 1999 due to U.S. disaster relief after Hurricane Georges devastated the island. Still the overall trend in these numbers has been steadily upward, and there is nothing in sight to break the momentum. An estimated 80 percent of these grants will be applied to programs that assist impoverished and low-income Puerto Ricans. Washington in 2004 (Puerto Rican fiscal year, or PR-FY) is boosting the Puerto Rican General Fund by 49 percent and supplying 30 percent of the local government's operating budget. The percentage supplied by the mainland taxpayer varies

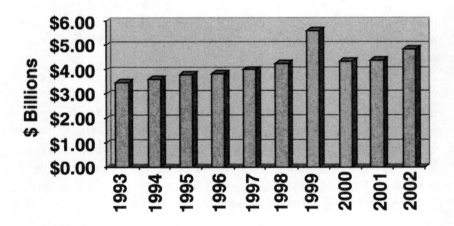

Chart 2

Federal Grants to Puerto Rico, 1993-2002

department by department, depending on the nature of the program and the history of the national government's responsibility for it.

The Price of Dependence

Here are some percentages for the federal component of various Puerto Rican education and social service agencies:

Table 3

Department	Federal Contribution	Percentage of Agency Budget
Public Housing Administration	$200 million	92.9%
Public Housing Administration (capital fund)	$151.2 million	98.7%
Education Department	$875.9 million	35%
Family Socioeconomic Administration	$1,350 million (USDA)	85.4%
Family Socioeconomic Administration	$129 million (TANF/Family Support)	8.2%
Adfan (Child Care)	$233.6 million	67%
Vocational and Rehabilitation Administration (Labor Department)	$67.0 million	75%
Health Department	$309.9 million	53.4%
Medicaid Allotment	-	15%

Source: Caribbean Business, August 2003

The grants enumerated here go to the core social service agencies that make up the Puerto Rican government. Overall, there are some 100 agencies of this kind that provide services to the public, helping to maintain Puerto Rico's extraordinarily high government share of Gross National Product. Clearly, agency after agency of the Puerto Rican government depends on the appropriations it receives from the federal government, and, therefore, from U.S. taxpayers. In a few instances, like the island's public housing authority, the program is a specifically federal creation and the federal share is likely to remain high as long as Puerto Rico's current relationship with the United States continues.

These grant totals omit a raft of money that Washington spends on Puerto Rico's public corporations. Uncle Sam will spend $183.4 million on Puerto Rican transportation infrastructure in 2004. Washington will buy 30 new buses for the Metropolitan Bus Authority. The Health Insurance Administration (if you are looking for it in the Puerto Rican budget, its acronym is ASES for its Spanish equivalent and it is found in the first place you would naturally look for it, the Puerto Rican Treasury Department) will receive

$189.2 million from U.S. taxpayers. This bureau negotiates and underwrites health plans for the needy. The total Washington tab for Puerto Rican public corporations will run an estimated $800 million in PR-FY 2004.[6]

Dependency always has a momentum of its own, a tendency to reinforce the very needs that stake a claim on the conscience. Franklin D. Roosevelt, though acting to the contrary, said it well when he called welfare "a narcotic, a subtle destroyer of the human spirit." Puerto Rico is a special case in this human drama, because its claim is reinforced by the denial to its people of full participation in the American story. Congress has not so much been a Hamlet to Puerto Rico, unable to make up its mind about what to do regarding this teeming island of U.S. citizens, as it has been a Pontius Pilate, washing its hands of Puerto Rico's ultimate fate, sending it ever larger sums of money but offering it no clear opportunity to choose a permanent status. The troubled conscience of Congress is likely only to drive these contribution numbers higher and higher.

Take the Medicaid figure cited above. Medicaid covers a wide variety of medical services for the indigent. States and territories must provide coverage for particular services up to a federally defined income level, which they can supplement with their own funds if they choose to do so. The matching rate for federal funding varies under the program, from 50 to 83 percent (higher for a handful of mandatory services that are more generously reimbursed), but for Puerto Rico's Medicaid program the federal contribution is capped at 15 percent. This is another Puerto Rican anomaly, and, over time, Congress has tended to notice such anomalies and address them, either by bringing Puerto Rico up to the funding level of the states (even though it pays no income taxes into the federal treasury) or providing stop-gap funds when the program gets in trouble. In the case of Medicaid, this was done in May 2003 with a $10 billion supplemental that will yield Puerto Rico an added $130 million over two years.

Education is another example. The quality of the Puerto Rican work force and the general education level of the populace has long been a source of pride. By 1990, according to the *Statistical Abstract of the United States* (yes, of course, Puerto Rico is not listed among the states but has its own data tables, along with other U.S. territories), the literacy level across Puerto Rico, defined as the percentage of the population above the age of 10 who are able to read and write, was 89.4%. The link between education level and future earnings is well-established as an economic fact of life. While it is true that Puerto Rico has always prized education (it was made compulsory in 1899, just after the cession of the island to the United States), it is also true that the pace at which Puerto Ricans are elevating their average level of completed education has slowed significantly.

Economists John Mueller and Marc Miles, who are strong advocates of a "human capital" model of economic development, have traced this deceleration of Puerto Rico's drive toward higher education for a greater proportion of its citizens. They write, "Labor compensation is the return on 'human capital' – the wage-earning ability resulting from the expenses of child-rearing, education, health, safety and mobility of Puerto Rico's workers." Under this form of analysis, times of economic weakness should follow diminishing investments in human capital, which is exactly what they found regarding schooling. "[B]etween 1940 and the mid-1970s, the median education level of Puerto Rico's workforce shot up from less than fourth-grade to almost twelfth-grade level: a tripling. Since then, the median education level has risen much more slowly (to about 13th grade today), and each extra year of education represents a smaller increase" in the ability to earn.[7] This economic truism, combined with the fact that the island's best minds continue to be drawn to better opportunities on the mainland – opportunities U.S. tax laws actually skew away from Puerto Rico! – represents a brain drain that translates into a steady leakage of human capital where it is needed most.

Mueller and Miles have produced an astonishing chart, reproduced as Chart 3 on page 72, that shows how closely the rise in median education level and annual growth in the Gross National Product of Puerto Rico have tracked one another over half a century. All investments in education are certainly not equal, but it is near-certain that the next decade of decisions in Washington, whether a Republican or Democratic administration holds sway, will mean a massive new infusion of education funds into Puerto Rico. George W. Bush has made education investments and education reforms, particularly testing combined with a limited experiment in school

Chart 3

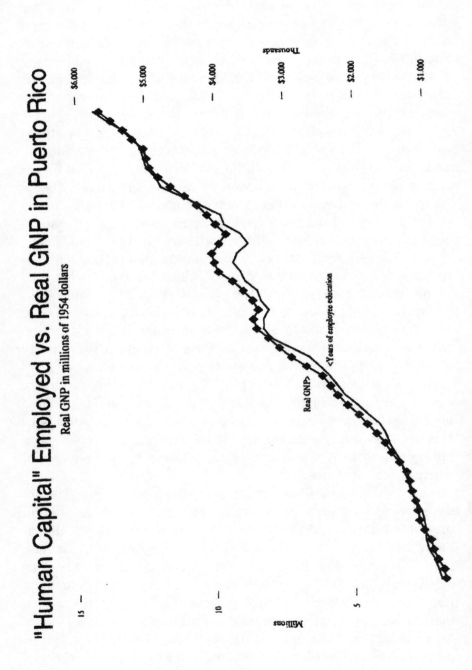

choice, one of the top priorities of his presidency. This fact, combined with the needy character of the vast majority of Puerto Rico's elementary schools, will exert yet another upward thrust on the percentage of the island budget that flows from the largesse of American taxpayers.

Already, new funds are set to go to Puerto Rico because of the No Child Left Behind legislation, the education funding and reform bill that President Bush signed in 2001 as his first domestic policy goal. This legislation aims fresh federal resources at the nation's poorest and least successful schools. Puerto Rico has an abundance of the former. The situation is partly a function of the island's poverty. As we discuss in the next chapter, nearly half the population of Puerto Rico remains below the poverty line, despite the pervasive government programs and tax preferences that have been established to meet the goal of development. Because those programs and preferences have not worked as they should, most of the 1,538 schools in the 84 school districts across Puerto Rico qualify for federal Title I funds. Private schools are eligible, too, and in 2002, some 219 of these schools accessed Title I.

The sum total of these funds was $270 million in fiscal year 2002. On an island of 3.88 million people, more than 533,000 students receive these benefits, an average of approximately $510. With all this, Puerto Rico could make a reasonable claim to being shortchanged (at least it could if its citizens paid federal income taxes). Prior to 2002, Congress had applied a separate funding formula to Puerto Rico that limited its Title I funds to 75 percent of what its allocation would be if the island were a state. Given the No Child Left Behind mood of largesse (no Puerto Rican child should in fact be left behind), Congress voted to increase Puerto Rico's allocation to 100 percent equivalence with the 50 states by 2006. This will mean an infusion of some $540 million in Title I for the 2006-2007 school year, assuming that Congress does not renege on its promises through the annual appropriations process.

By moving in this direction, Congress is merely behaving as its predecessors have done, taking note of the fact that Puerto Ricans are U.S. citizens and that Hispanics are a growing part of the U.S. electorate and that they live in key states like Florida, where the 2000 election was ultimately decided. The net cost to the United

States of Puerto Rico under commonwealth status is therefore high and likely only to rise. Health care costs are also likely to be a factor in pushing up the "cost of commonwealth" to the U.S. taxpayer. At one end of the spectrum is the prescription drug benefit that will be added, in one form or another, to the Medicare program. Puerto Rico's median age is three years younger (32.1 in 2000)[8] years than the rest of the United States, but in that same year there were 850,000 residents of the island age 65 or over, with another 812,000 more Baby Boomers age 45 to 65 who will reach their Medicare years before 2020.

Fairness requires acknowledgment that some portion, occasionally a significant portion of the federal grant money sent to Puerto Rico returns to our shores in the form of purchased goods. The simplest case is Puerto Rico's version of the food stamp program, known on the island as the Nutritional Assistance Program (PAN, under its Spanish acronym). This program has consumed 10 percent of all the federal grants and tax subsidies for Puerto Rico. The island has never been self-sufficient in foodstuffs and most of its produce is in the form of cash crops that it has bartered for the multitude of needs its natural resources cannot furnish. Between 1981 and 2001, the U.S. taxpayers sent $19.25 billion to Puerto Rico to provide food for its poorest residents. The program will cost about $1.35 billion in FY 2004. The average benefit was about $94 per month in 2001.[9]

Most of the dollars spent by food stamp recipients return to mainland food manufacturers. The program is both an anti-poverty measure and a domestic agricultural subsidy. James Dietz, an American economist who has sharply criticized various aspects of Puerto Rico's dependency model of development, has performed calculations, based on Puerto Rican Planning Board data, that show some 77 cents of every PAN dollar re-entered the United States as either a food purchase or as earnings to U.S. corporations operating on the island. This profit to American farmers does not diminish the fact that the program is a drain on American taxpayers to provide for people who do not pay any federal income taxes, even when they leave the program. Dietz calculates the *net cost* to American taxpayers of the PAN program as $20.466 billion from 1975-2000.[10]

Even here, Puerto Ricans have a claim of being shortchanged. Congress, in its eternal wisdom, has treated Puerto Rico at various times in different ways from the mainland with regard to food stamps. Congress extended the food stamp program to Puerto Rico in 1971, but funding did not flow until 1975. In 1983 the program was converted into a special block grant and funding was cut by 13 percent, though it was allowed to rise two years later. Nonetheless, the 1983 funding level was less than a comparable state (Kentucky and South Carolina are the closest in terms of population) would have received, and, most importantly, the income threshold for receipt of food stamps was set at 100 percent of the poverty line, not 130 percent as it is for the 50 states. Puerto Rico is treated differently and inequitably, and this practice, sometimes to Puerto Rico's harm, usually to its benefit, permeates U.S. policy. According to various sources, the net benefit to Puerto Rico of all the federal policies and programs applied to it is some $6 billion a year.[11]

By any definition, Puerto Rico is in a state of dependency. Its economic relationship with the United States involves a massive and widening drain on the taxpayer, with benefits flowing southward to a people not attaining their potential and northward to an array of U.S. corporations receiving earnings they have not merited. A condition of dependency, of course, is not objectionable solely or even primarily because of its economic effects. The current structure of U.S. policy for Puerto Rico, inextricably linked with and reinforcing the colonial status masked by the euphonic word "common-wealth," plays havoc with incentives to work, with the desire to gain additional education, with the structure and well-being of the family, with the propensity to drug abuse and crime, and with the prevalence of corruption and a general disordering of civil society.

All of these sad results are on display in Puerto Rico. In gross terms, look once again at Table 1, in many ways the heart of this book. The Leading Cultural and Economic Indicators for Puerto Rico, with a few interesting exceptions, show a society that ranks near the bottom of measurements of U.S. economic health and near the top of such sensitive measures of personal well-being as the out-of-wedlock childbearing rate, infant mortality, and the percentage of the population who are in prison. Contrast these rankings with the fact that Puerto Rico ranks number one against the 50 states in the percentage of U.S. corporate income that represents profit margin. It is an intolerable state of affairs that Congress and the Puerto Rico people must squarely face. Consider the lineaments of the social fracturing at work among our fellow citizens in Puerto Rico.

One of the linchpins of social stability is the presence of two parents in the home. Puerto Rico, however, ranks very high in both the percentage of children born out of wedlock and the percentage born to teenage mothers. Among the nation's political jurisdictions, Puerto Rico ranks second only to the District of Columbia in the percentage of births to single mothers: 49.7 percent of all births were to unmarried women in 2000. One immediate effect of this statistic is a persistent health deficit among Puerto Rican babies, who, despite receiving prenatal care to nearly the same extent as mainland American women, suffer from disproportionately high rates of low-birth-weight and its correlated mortality. In fact at 11 deaths per 1,000 births, Puerto Rico has the second highest infant mortality rate in the United States; again, only the rate for the District of Columbia is higher.

Interestingly enough, this high non-marital birth rate persists and is even higher for mainland Americans of Puerto Rican extraction. Chart 4 shows the prevailing rates for various U.S. ethnic subgroups. Puerto Ricans living in the United States are closer to the highest other ethnic group, African Americans (whose rate is falling), than they are to the American mainland average (which has been steadily rising, albeit more slowly in recent years). Marital status and the presence of both a mother and father in the home are positively related to a host of outcomes, most particularly educational achievement, household income, and the likelihood of forming a two-parent family in the next generation, and negatively correlated with welfare dependency, drug and alcohol abuse, sexual activity, and criminality.[12]

It is tempting to say that public policy can do little about such a personal issue. It is more accurate to say that public policy is one of the prime determinants of such personal issues. As long as government rewards the behaviors that lead to out-of-wedlock childbearing by creating financial incentives for single parenthood and homemaking, these phenomena will increase. The 1996 federal welfare reform law created a system of rewards for states and territories that

Chart 4

Unwed Births as a Percent of All Births, 2000, U.S. Ethnic Groups

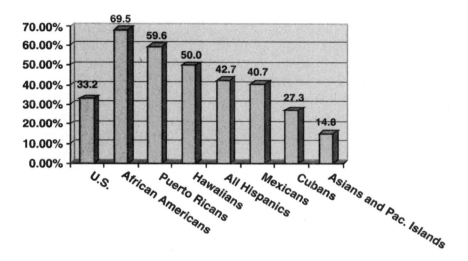

reduce their out-of-wedlock birth rate without accomplishing this result by increasing their abortion rate. The Secretary of Health and Human Services announced in September 2003 that the U.S. Virgin Islands was one of a handful of jurisdictions that would receive a large incentive grant for its success in this area. Evidently, it is not the Caribbean climate and its starlit nights that alone determine how often children are born to mothers without wedding rings.

The Puerto Rico family is in serious trouble, a disproportionate amount of trouble, in a Western world in which families are facing a new level of disintegration (or failure to form in the first place) from Mexico City to Moscow. Some of this trouble, as is well-known, is ideological, in the sense that while public policy increasingly supports marriage and family formation (encouraging marriage is an explicit goal of reforms adopted in 1996 under the Temporary Assistance to Needy Families program, in which Puerto Rico participates), cultural forces have driven cohabitation rates to an all-time high and are now moving public opinion toward complete redefinitions of the family that make either a father or mother expendable. The success of these cultural forces would do irreversible damage to Puerto Rico's long-term economic prospects.

For a time, Puerto Rico's educational level relative to its Caribbean neighbors helped sustained its leap forward under Operation Bootstrap. But the achievement curve is steeper now, and Puerto Rico must demonstrate its ability to climb higher. Doing so will not be easy, first of all, because insistence of results has been problematic in the unionized public school system of the United States, and second, because Spanish is the language of education and testing for Puerto Rican schoolchildren. The island has not participated in the National Assessment of Educational Progress, the U.S. Department of Education's sampling method for determining the relative performance of school systems and individual schools via their test scores. The NAEP has been in place since 1969, and it provides a variety of information for comparative evaluation of school systems, but, in deference to the decentralized system of U.S. education, the NAEP gives the states a great deal of authority regarding their participation and the release of the data gleaned from evaluations.

For example, the law mandates only that states take part in the NAEP testing for grades 4 and 8 in mathematics and reading. For the purposes of Title I of the Elementary and Secondary Education Act (ESEA), the source of the NAEP mandate, Puerto Rico is now defined as a state (yes, another legal anomaly in its variegated relationship with Washington). The 2001 amendments to the ESEA, in the No Child Left Behind legislation, required Puerto Rico for the first time to participate in the NAEP assessments, beginning in 2003 and continuing every other year after. These assessments will be used to trigger new funding for struggling schools and, if the schools fail to improve, to determine the eligibility of their pupils for limited school choice. The law is meant to provide means and incentives for schools to improve learning, with the ultimate leverage of aid to parents to put their children in other schools.

Despite the law, this will not be happening in Puerto Rico right away. On August 3, 2002, the National Assessment Governing Board adopted a resolution that noted this new mandate for Puerto Rico and then exempted the island. The Board, reasonably enough, concluded that the translation of standardized tests into Spanish, while achievable, raised legitimate issues of comparability with the English-language tests administered in the rest of the United States. Such translations, the Board affirmed, have "not previously been attempted as a part of the NAEP." As a consequence, though the Board will translate the tests and Puerto Rico will administer them, the results will not be used for comparison with the school systems of the 50 states and the District of Columbia. Rather, they will be used to evaluate the testing process itself and to determine when and if Puerto Rico's results can be compared to the rest of the country.

Naturally, the same concerns hold for testing in Puerto Rico's secondary schools. Puerto Rico does not report island-wide results for its students who take the primary college admissions tests, the SAT and the ACT. How will Puerto Rico then know how it is doing against national norms, and against its own norms year-in and year-out? At the dawn of the 21st century, when educational advantages matter more than ever, Puerto Rican and U.S. experts are some years away from having the answer. Both Spanish and English may be official languages of Puerto Rico (a brief enactment of Spanish as the official language was superseded by the local legislature in 1993 under the Rossello administration), and English may be the language of the business and governing class, but Spanish rules the classroom in the lower grades. This situation is a direct product of the commonwealth status. The first elected governor of Puerto Rico, Luis Muñoz Marin in 1954, changed the language of instruction in public schools from English (as it had been for almost 50 years) to Spanish. Yet he sent his own kids to English speaking private schools. He was sure where the future for his children lay, but he did not want that same future for the rest of Puerto Rico.

One of the popular expressions of that future may wind up playing a significant role in unknotting the NAEP's dilemma over Spanish-language testing. Increasingly, young Puerto Rican children are learning English from U.S. cable channels. There is a barbell in the graph of Puerto Ricans who speak English, as the grandparents of these children tend to speak it well because of the influence of U.S. efforts in the first half of the 20th century to impose English-language education on the populace. One of the legacies of Muñoz Marin was a renewed emphasis, once Puerto Rico acquired its own constitution, on restoring Spanish-language instruction in the classroom. That is still the policy today for the typical schoolchild, but popular culture, in both television and music, means that the classroom is not the only, and may not even be the primary, tutor.

Parenthetically, Muñoz Marin betrayed some of the same hypocrisy advocates of certain forms of education show in the United States. Despite his public posture on Spanish in the classroom, Muñoz Marin sent his own children to a private academy that conducted its instruction in English. In doing so, he was being realistic about the skills his own children would require in order to maximize their personal potential. In the United States, a similar phenomenon occurs when "champions" of the quality of public education routinely pass by the local public school and send their own sons and daughters to private academies.

At present, the numbers at the other end of the education cycle offer little more encouragement in Puerto Rico's drive to raise its GDP through advances in education. Here, Puerto Rico's status, and the tax system that has grown up around it, does promote the export of its best minds to high-tech and research-oriented opportunities on the mainland. Given the relative size of the two economies and the wealth of technical and engineering jobs in the United States, this is a long-term fact of life, but, as the next two chapters describe in detail, U.S. corporate tax policy disfavors the location of research facilities in Puerto Rico. Such centers not only employ Ph.D.'s but they also provide grounds for graduate training and internships that can coax young people into technical fields.

The U.S.-government funded National Science Foundation maintains an information service called EPSCOR, which tracks information on the research and scientific climate in various states. EPSCOR stands for Experimental Program to Stimulate Competitive Research. The tally for Puerto Rico in this area of endeavor shows a great deal of room for improvement, too. Puerto Rico has every reason, including the basic issue of population density, to envision its future as tied to the development of new technical prowess. Its climate and proximity to the United States and even Europe give it room to develop tourism further, but its limited landmass and continuing urbanization suggest that its best hopes lie in such areas as financial services and technology. Puerto Rico has the fourth highest population density among U.S. jurisdictions, third highest if one omits the city of Washington, D.C. (only New Jersey and Rhode Island have more people per square mile) and its slightly higher-than-average, though converging, birth rate will maintain that rank.

EPSCOR's data ranks Puerto Rico both in terms of the number of science and engineering graduate students and Ph.D.'s it has produced, and also in terms of the amount of federal funds committed by federal agencies for research and development performed on the island, whether by the government, private firms, nonprofits, or, the largest recipient, colleges and universities. Some of the general EPSCOR findings are shown below in Table 4. The findings for the

Table 4

Science and Engineering Profile

Characteristic	State**	U.S.	Rank
Doctoral scientists, 1999	1,120	518,670	50th
Doctoral engineers, 1999	200	107,100	46th
Science & Engineering Doctorates Awarded, 2000	84	25,979	41st
S & E postdoctorates in doctorate-granting institutions	12	41,548	50th
S & E graduate students in doctorate-granting institutions	3,928	435,612	31st
Federal R&D Obligations, 1999 (millions)	$73	$73,718	47th
Academic R & D, 1999 (millions)	$91	$27,036	39th
Public higher education current-fund expenditures, 1997 (millions)	$723	$125,236	38th
Number of Small Business innovative research (SBIR) grants	4	26,424	52nd
Patents issued	26	85,068	52nd

Source: **National Science Foundation, EPSCOR**

** Once again, Puerto Rico is a state for NSF data purposes.

top 10 federal departments engaged in underwriting research are shown in Table 5. Puerto Rico ranks 46th or even lower in six of the 10 categories reported in Table 4. The silver lining is that the better numbers are for current graduate students in engineering and science, and for expenditures for current academic research and development and for public higher education generally. These investments, if they can help keep highly skilled Puerto Ricans at home, will pay dividends for the island down the road. Even so, these better rankings merely put Puerto Rico closer to where it should be relative to other states in terms of the size of its population, where it ranks 27th.

Turning to the current funds Puerto Rico receives from the various U.S. departments, the figures are by and large discouraging, too. These figures may reflect the brain drain, but they probably reflect something else as well, a factor related to status. Because Puerto Rico has a non-voting delegate in Congress, this person has less than the typical influence of an elected official in the daily decisions of Congress. Where there ought to be seven votes cast on every bill before the House of Representatives, based on Puerto Rico's population, there is today one voice with no vote. This member of Congress cannot directly affect the outcome of debates, he cannot trade or sweeten his vote when a project of interest to Puerto Rico is at stake. The heads of federal departments know that, other than by indirect means, the delegate from Puerto Rico does not influence the U.S. Presidential election, and other members of Congress, whose constituents can, will precede him for appointments and perhaps for grants and contracts.

The Resident Commissioner of Puerto Rico, as he is called, leaves home, as it were, without a larder, and therefore comes back with less bacon. Thus, commonwealth status, even as it maintains a level of poverty that attracts support under mean-tested programs, helps to diminish it under discretionary authorities.

Of the federal departments and agencies shown in Table 5, only the National Science Foundation, which, ironically, compiled this data, conferred grants on Puerto Rico that moved its ranking as high as 31st, close to its population standing vis-à-vis the rest of the United States. The number for state and local government is particularly striking; it means that Puerto Rico received less in the way of science and engineering grants than the District of Columbia. Again, as with the number of graduate students in science and engineering and other academic indicators, Puerto Rico's prospects look a little better for the future. Raising these numbers, and accessing federal funds to assist the process, is one area where Puerto Rico could justifiably and profitably increase its draw on the federal treasury.

Table 5. Science and Engineering Grants, Puerto Rico, by Department and Type of Recipient, Fiscal Year 1999

Department	Amount*	Rank
Department of Agriculture	$9,542	40
Department of Commerce	$966	39
Department of Defense	$1,363	51
Department of Energy	$985	47
Department of Health and Human Services	$37,065	40
Department of the Interior	$1,847	49
Department of Transportation	$74	52
Environmental Protection Agency	$0	-
National Aeronautics and Space Administration (NASA)	$3,755	41
National Science Foundation	$17,112	31
Overall Rank, All Agencies	$72,709	47
Overall Rank, Grants to Industrial Firms	$4,193	48
Overall Rank, Universities and Colleges	$50,661	41
Overall Rank, State and Local Government	$548	52

* Amounts are in thousands.   Source: **National Science Foundation, EPSCOR**

It is no surprise that the weakness of Puerto Rico's overall economy, and the condition of dependency facing so many of its families, operates to promote the narcotics trade as well as political corruption. Ultimately, involvement in these practices is a question of personal character. The vast majority of poor people do not take part in crime waves. Even so, the lure of the incredible profits to be made as drug couriers and sellers draws many young men into an enterprise that requires little training and confers no small prestige in certain quarters. Chapters 7 and 8 of this book discuss Puerto Rico's role as the drug capital of the Caribbean. For the purposes of this chapter, we discuss only the impact of the drug problem on federal spending on Puerto Rico. Once again, the pressures of a social problem, one with particular impacts on the mainland, are driving up the dollars Washington is forced to spend in Puerto Rico and across the region.

Multiple federal agencies have a stake in various phases of the anti-drug battle. The new Department of Homeland Security brings together many, but not all of these agencies and functions, a process that itself will result in increased spending for a time. DHS houses the Coast Guard, the U.S. Customs Service, the Secret Service, and certain border security functions of the Immigration and Naturalization Service. The FBI, the Drug Enforcement Administration, the Bureau of Alcohol, Tobacco and Firearms, and the Department of Defense drug interdiction projects remain separate, and all of these assets, within and without DHS, are being deployed to counter Puerto Rican narco-trafficking. Anti-drug spending was a major reason why Department of Justice operating expenditures in Puerto Rico doubled between 1990 and 1995, from $23.7 million to $48.5 million, and rose sharply again, to $81.2 million by 2000.[13] Treasury Department spending also increased by nearly 150 percent during the decade.

As the new 21st century begins, the U.S. faces new challenges from terrorism that are taxing some of the very agencies that are engaged in the drug war. The federal budget deficit is soaring. The Congress faces an unpalatable choice between reallocating resources from one needy program to another, or seeing the deficit rise further. For now, Washington is trying to fight on both fronts. In April 2003 the Department of Justice announced that special funding from just two Department of Justice programs, including the community policing program instituted by the Clinton Administration, brought an additional $21.44 million to Puerto Rico in 2002. These funds included $7.53 million for substance abuse programs and a new, separate account in the amount of $7.28 million for counter-terrorism activity.[14]

This money is sorely needed. Puerto Rico's police face a daunting environment of increasing violence and insufficient resources. In 2002, there were 503 murders on the island, but by September 3, 2003, there were 526 and by the end of the next day there were 530. Gov. Sila Calderon claims that 70 percent of the murders are related to the island's burgeoning drug trade, but the Police Superintendent Victor Rivera claims that the real figure is 97 percent. It is hard to be reassured that progress is being made, or will be made, without a massive infusion of new funds. That was the message from the revolution in New York City achieved under former Mayor Rudy Giuliani, where a vast increase in police resources was allied with a revival of such measures as foot patrols and a new intolerance for nagging, open air street crime like the shakedown carried out by the so-called "squeegee men."

Puerto Ricans may be satisfied if the police are able to crack down on the increasingly brazen major crime rate on the island. According to the Public Broadcasting Service program *Frontline*, the San Juan area now sees an average of 10 carjackings a day, as thieves seize vehicles for one-time, untraceable use in transporting narcotics. Four people were murdered in one recent seven-hour period in the towns of Ciales, Guanica, Mayagüez, and Santurce. The latest step announced by the embattled police department was a decision to put its officers on 12-hour shifts in order to have 500 police on the streets at the most dangerous hours, between 11:00 p.m. and 4:00 a.m. Twelve hundred new police officers are expected to join the Puerto Rican force in January 2004.[15] The cost of maintaining these officers, who are critical to maintaining public safety, will undoubtedly come back, in some measure, to the federal government.

Crime is a feature of big city, or even just high-density living today, but Puerto Rico's mixture of economic futility, family breakdown, and a culture of dependency is a toxic brew. In the end, state dependency and individual dependency are inseparable matters. The lack of real data on this aspect of Puerto Rico's social turmoil only adds to the discouragement. Superintendent Rivera believes that violent crimes have recently decreased in Puerto Rico, but declines to offer numbers because, as a media source summarized his statement, "statistics prepared by the past administration are not trustworthy."[16] Numbers are also shaky for narcotics and alcohol addiction, with estimates of 38,000 drug addicts (1.4 percent of the population) and 130,000 alcoholics (4.8 percent of the population) in 2000. If these numbers are accurate, one of every 16 Puerto Ricans is addicted to narcotics or alcohol.[17] Another source, Iniciativa Comunitaria, estimates the number of drug addicts may be twice as high at 75,000.

Coordination among social welfare agencies is a problem everywhere (most families have multiple problems, and most government agencies deal with a problem or two at a time), but in Puerto Rico the problem is compounded by the sheer size of the government role. U.S. drug treatment and law enforcement funds flow through such entities as the Public and Indian Housing drug elimination program to the Puerto Rican police ($9.2 million in 2000) and to the chief mental health agency on the island, ASSMCA ($2.8 million in 2000). ASSMCA received some $24.5 million from seven different federal anti-drug programs in 2001;

the local health department received $33.1 million for HIV/AIDS programs, many of them drug-linked, from six different sources; and the police department $2.5 million more from two sources. Yet, as economist Emilio Pantojas-Garcia points out, despite these programs (15 in all), neither ASSMCA nor the health department can say how much drug addiction is costing either the island or the mainland.[18]

Wherever a community is awash in both drug money and in government funds, corruption is a perennial problem. Unfortunately for Puerto Rico's statehood party, the PNP, the latter half of the 1990s brought many instances of corruption in public office. The Rossello administration's Secretary of Education pleaded guilty to a kickback scheme in which he misappropriated more than $3 million. Island officials have been prosecuted in cases involving misuse of money from the Federal Emergency Management Agency meant for Hurricane Hugo reconstruction, from the Housing and Urban Renewal Corporation of Puerto Rico, and from the federally funded AIDS Institute. The practice of soliciting kickbacks for government contracts became so common during the Rossello Administration that it was generally referred to as the "tithe."[19]

The President and the Congress of the United States can continue to nurse this sick patient of commonwealth along, but his condition is deteriorating and decades of experience have shown that he cannot be cured by more of the same measures. If Puerto Rico's dependency is so costly – to U.S. taxpayers, to U.S. tourists, to Puerto Rican families, job seekers, and everyday citizens caught in literal crossfires between drug gangs – why does this situation persist? In many ways, the seeming intractability of Puerto Rico's problem is an illusion. It is not just that a growing number of Puerto Ricans are voting for change in the form of statehood, albeit that long-term trend is real enough. It is an even more compelling fact that next to no Puerto Rican is willing to vote to endorse Puerto Rico's territorial dependency as it truly and actually exists today. Nonetheless, another illusion has been built up, by politically motivated forces as well as by a handful of inaccurate reports, to suggest that any alternative to commonwealth would cause Puerto Rico to crash both economically and in terms of the fiscal aid it receives from Washington.

The first, and perhaps most important, of these reports is the one carried out by the Congressional Budget Office (CBO) in 1990. This report has had enduring influence, and it was even cited in the most detailed Congressional debate ever held on Puerto Rican status, the 1998 floor battle over the Young bill (see Chapters 9 and 10 for a full description of this key debate). CBO's model of the Puerto Rican economy caused it to project that the abandonment of commonwealth for statehood would result in a drop of 10 to 15 percent in the island's Gross Product and a reduction of two thirds or more in investments through special U.S. tax breaks for investment in Puerto Rico. The report also predicted an increase of between four and seven percent in Puerto Rico's unemployment rate.[20]

In a study prepared for the Citizens Education Foundation, J. Tomas Hexner and Glenn Jenkins used a Computable General Equilibrium model that is better suited to Puerto Rico's actual economy. It found that Gross Product would decline by much less (5.6 percent), special tax-spurred investment would decrease about the same (63.3 percent, the low end of CBO's range), and unemployment would rise by one half to one third the CBO estimate (2.3 percent).[21] The general difficulty with the CBO model is that it did not account for policy changes that Puerto Rico can, and indeed should, make to supplant what have become increasingly counterproductive tax and spending policies. If Puerto Rico did nothing and unemployment grew, then the cost of federal transfer payments to the nonworking population would indeed rise as the model depicts.

On closer examination, Hexner and Jenkins show persuasively that both the United States and Puerto Rico would benefit economically from a change of status that leads to statehood. Because their analysis was prepared in 1998 and relies on 1995 figures, we will omit most of the specific figures used in their calculations. With regard to changes in federal spending, Hexner and Jenkins found that there would be increases in Supplemental Security Income payments because this program for the aged, blind and disabled, an adjunct to Social Security, is not available to Puerto Ricans under current law. Puerto Ricans are already eligible for most other federal programs. Additionally, if Puerto Rico were a state, it would be eligible for the same Medicaid reimbursement level as the states, resulting in an almost fourfold increase in the cost of that program.

The per capita cost of the federal food stamp program is higher than Puerto Rico's current cost under the PAN program; thus, the cost of this program would increase, and an increase in unemployment might drive it up even further. Hexner and Jenkins then posited a modest increase in federal employment on the island under statehood (this is likely to happen in any case), and they calculated its cost based on bringing Puerto Rico into line with the average of the five states with the lowest per capita federal wage and benefits cost. Finally, Hexner and Jenkins excluded federal procurement spending from their analysis, inferring that Puerto Rico's status might impact where procurement dollars would be spent but would not affect the amount of such expenditures. These considerations prompted these authors to calculate an increase of some 14 percent in overall federal transfer payments to Puerto Rico.

Hexner and Jenkins then offset these transfer payments with calculations of the revenue gain to the U.S. Treasury from collection of both corporate and individual income taxes. The corporate taxes represent the lion's share of the increased revenue. Under statehood, corporations in Puerto Rico would have to be treated the same way as corporations in every other U.S. jurisdiction. Section 936, which is being phased out, could not be extended or reinstituted, and the Controlled Foreign Corporation status now being used by a growing number of Puerto Rico-based companies could not exist. As a consequence of these changes, Hexner and Jenkins conclude, new tax revenue flowing to the U.S. treasury from Puerto Rico would be roughly 2.5 times the amount of new federal transfers there. The result: a net gain in the range of $2.12 billion to $2.72 billion for the American taxpayer.

What about Puerto Rico? It, too, would gain under statehood, principally because the reversal of the funding flow to Washington would come from U.S. businesses that benefit disproportionately merely because of existing tax preferences. Hexner and Jenkins estimate that new corporate and individual taxes that would be paid by Puerto Ricans average only 18 to 21 percent of the new tax revenue that would flow northward as a result of statehood. The rest represents tax increases imposed on mainland companies that have their "legal residence" on the island. Using this figure, Hexner and Jenkins derive an estimate of $720 million for the amount of Puerto Rico's increased tax burden. With new federal transfer payments of

$1.4 billion, the net receipts for Puerto Rico in 1995 would have been $680 million. In short, Puerto Rico would be paying more due to its participation in the federal income tax system, but that system's yield for the island would actually increase by an even larger amount.

In truth, Puerto Rican fiscal policy operates, as all state or territorial policies do, in a dynamic environment. The current policy regime is replete with incentives that discourage individuals and families from working, saving and investing. Mueller and Miles have described especially well how the application of minimum wage laws to Puerto Rico, when combined with generous federal and commonwealth transfer payments, has contributed to its excessive unemployment levels by raising the "net cost of labor" to Puerto Rico's private sector. They point out that popular notions of labor cost, basically the cost of wages and benefits per person hired, have historically fallen short of explaining why chronic unemployment exists. It is also necessary to understand what a given worker will add to productivity, measured in terms of the worker's output per hour and the expected price of each unit produced. Moreover, employers must push against two factors, taxes on labor and transfer payments to the unemployed, that increase the price they must pay to lure workers out of idleness.

Concern about the impact of transfer payments, particularly welfare benefits, on the willingness of beneficiaries to seek paid employment was a linchpin of the adoption by Congress of the Temporary Assistance to Needy Families (TANF) program. The program imposed work requirements on TANF recipients, even single mothers after their child reaches its first birthday, and imposed a five-year lifetime limit on benefits. States were given new flexibility to design programs to promote work and marriage. Moving away from welfare's structure as a lifetime entitlement program restored the federal government's fiscal control and shifted the incentives for the unemployed poor in favor of seeking and holding jobs. Because Puerto Rico's scheme of benefits for the poor is so extensive, and also because it does not participate in the federal income tax program called the EITC, the effective "transition tax" on many families moving from dependence to independence is more than 100 percent.

Mueller and Miles offer the example of an intact (mother and father present) family with four school-age (below college-level) children. Because there are two parents at home, the family is not eligible for TANF money. However, they do qualify for the PAN food program and for rental assistance almost wholly paid for by Uncle Sam under the Section 8 public housing program. If one parent goes to work, the first $400 in gross income will net the family only $200 in take-home pay, for an effective "tax" rate of 50 percent on their decision to work. Mueller and Miles list the various ways in which this potent marginal tax rate accumulates:

> For every dollar earned, NAP [Spanish acronym PAN] benefits are reduced about 18 cents. Housing assistance falls about 27 cents, and Social Security and Medicare claim another 7.65 cents. The family also starts to pay [local] income tax at around $1000 per month of gross income. NAP subsidies end around $1300 per month. These two factors imply that the tax rate increases and then rises to over 100 percent in this range. Out of the first $1,000 per month of income, money available to the family rises by only about $460. At $1,400 per month the available money is only $490 more than with no income at all.[22]

When unemployment benefits are added to the mix (they are time-limited, of course, to 26 weeks) and they phase out with higher reemployment, the "marginal" tax rate on going to work can exceed 100 percent. Poor people are rational beings. If the government's treatment of labor provides severe initial penalties on the decisions to seek and hold low-wage work, many people will either delay accepting employment or defer it until benefits expire. Because these same effects were observed on the mainland, Congress made adjustments not only in welfare, but in the adoption and expansion of the Earned Income Tax Credit, a kind of wage subsidy or supplement for the working poor that reduces this "marginal" tax on decisions to work.

Under commonwealth status, the EITC does not exist because

Puerto Rican workers do not pay federal income tax. They do pay the Social Security and Medicare tax (7.65% of gross pay, plus, indirectly, the employer share of 7.65%), but the EITC cannot be credited against these taxes by law. If Puerto Rico were to become a state and be integrated into the federal tax system, the array of adjustments that Congress has made to bolster incentives for the working poor could be made for the island's population. Of course, the Puerto Rican government could adopt its own form of the EITC to apply against the local income tax, and the Congress could, as Mueller and Miles suggest, make the EITC available as a credit against payroll (Social Security/Medicare taxes) without resolving Puerto Rico's status, but the latter is a very expensive proposition and is unlikely to happen anytime soon.

The same could be said with respect to the unfunded federal mandate called the minimum wage. As Mueller and Miles note, the minimum wage makes it essentially illegal to hire a worker whose skills are worth less than the minimum – and it provides no alternative for that worker.23 If transfer payments are to lower, rather than raise, the net cost of labor and reduce unemployment, they must be conditioned upon keeping a job and not upon being out of the workforce. These principles are especially important in a lagging economy like Puerto Rico's, where a long history of unemployment and the use by nearly half the population of government anti-poverty programs dilutes any stigma associated with dependency.

Who is to blame for the continued bloat of government and blight of dependency in Puerto Rico? There is plenty to go around to explain this Partnership for Little Progress.

From one perspective, the Puerto Ricans might be the last people to blame for this situation, though for many residents of the island it has become a comfortable status quo. Puerto Ricans are American citizens, and they bear many of the same rights and duties as residents of the 50 states, but not all. They serve in our all-volunteer Armed Forces. If the draft is ever reinstated, young Puerto Rican men will be subject to it when they turn 18. At this age, they can also vote in U.S. Presidential elections, but only if they reside in one of the 50 states or have a mainland residence and vote by absentee ballot overseas. Every fourth November there are polling places open on the island to elect the Governor, the island legislature, and the "resident commissioner." But there is no ballot space for the President and Vice President of the United States, a slight even residents of the District of Columbia do not endure.24

Consistent with the territory's Limbo status, Puerto Ricans can be ordered into battle (and were so ordered as members of units in Iraq in 2003), but they cannot vote for or against the Commander-in-Chief who calls upon their heroism or may send them to their deaths. A similar conundrum applies to the non-voting representative Puerto Rico sends to Congress. He has all the rights of a member of Congress except the one that matters most, the right to vote on legislation on the floor of the House of Representatives. A parking pass, yes. The right to attend hearings and ask questions, yes. The right to introduce and cosponsor bills. The right to give speeches and appear on C-Span, yes. The right to represent the views of the people he represents when push comes to shove and cast his vote on whether a bill may become a law, no.

Thus, Puerto Ricans have not passed on the federal laws that apply to them, and, other than a brief period when the House of Representatives was in the control of the Democratic Party and the non-voting member's privileges were expanded under House rules to committee situations, their delegate can merely argue his case to U.S. elected officials, much as an ambassador would do. As a consequence, the federal funds that flow into Puerto Rico do so for a combination of reasons, which cannot rise to the level of a coherent public policy. Some of it is due to beneficence, some of it the desire of Congressional majorities to do the island a measure of justice, some of it to the portability of certain benefits that Puerto Ricans earn by virtue of their federal service in various roles.

From another perspective, the Puerto Rican people must bear the responsibility for the incomplete citizenship they possess and the excess benefits that reinforce it. The island is the "last colony" only because other U.S. territories found their uncertain status unendurable, and did something about it. It can hardly be said that Americans care less about Puerto Rico now than they did about Alaska and Hawaii before they became states, or at least before the second World War when events underscored the strategic value of those two territories (we learned to value them as our enemies showed how much they coveted them). Key issues move in

Congress all the time without widespread public interest or pressure. In the case of Puerto Rico, consensus interest and pressure from the people most directly involved (the governments of the two entities) should be enough to establish a routine and orderly process for the consideration of status. Given, as objective economic analysis has consistently shown, that the failure to resolve status hurts both the island and the mainland, the demands of self-interest and statesmanship coincide.

Those demands have converged in neither capital. Given the chance to address the Congress in a common voice, the Puerto Rican political leadership has failed time and again to draft a common position that frames the island's options realistically in terms of even the legal fundamentals at stake. With the gun of economic stagnation pointed at its back, many in the island continue only to plead for Congress to intervene and write a larger check for benefits and a blank check for Puerto Rico to exercise independence in the international sphere. Meanwhile, in Washington, statesmanship takes a back seat in a vehicle as long as a Greyhound coach, with every row of seats in-between filled with one special interest or another, here a drug company lobbyist, there a political hack looking for a temporary advantage with the Hispanic vote, here a "principled conservative" who thinks that language is destiny, and everywhere the free riders, drug lords and their minions who love the vulnerability of America's Achilles Heel in the Caribbean.

Who is driving the bus? While it is tempting to say that there is nobody at the wheel, the man in the blue cap most resembles a member of Congress. Every member of Congress. The people of Puerto Rico will continue to devise and vote upon definitions of the future that are so many mirages for just as long as the U.S. Congress allows them to do so. A handful of valiant Congressmen labored for years to convince their colleagues of the need for a status process that included definitions of the options consistent with the U.S. Constitution and acceptable to Washington. That effort, as we will see, survived by a single vote in the House of Representatives and failed to achieve a floor vote at all in the U.S. Senate in 1998. Five years later, no similar effort is in sight. Members of Congress are now twice shy of the Puerto Rican challenge. The cost of that position is evident in every one of the 13 appropriations bills that move through the Congress each year.

Which way is Puerto Rico itself headed? The worst of all worlds is on display. Domestically, the dependency is deepening. More federal involvement in and regulation of education are on their way. The Puerto Rican food stamp program has gone plastic, as beneficiaries are outfitted with debit cards to allow them to make their food purchases up to their benefit limit without having to handle coupons that other customers can see. Congress is poised to add a prescription drug benefit whose price tag for Puerto Rico will run into the billions of dollars (at least here the people will be receiving some benefit from the drugs the island has helped to produce and make profitable for the past three decades). Internationally, the local government yearns for Washington to look the other way and sign checks while it signs treaties and ejects the U.S. Navy from Vieques and Roosevelt Roads.

This, too, is the fruit of dependency. People bite the hand that feeds them because, at heart, they resent the conditions of subservience that make them hungry. It needn't have come to this, and it needn't stay this way. If change is to happen, statesmanship must refuse any longer to sit at the back of the bus.

CHAPTER 5

Pitorro and *Panas*
(Moonshine and Breadfruit)

Four hundred and seventy years after Columbus, I discovered and rediscovered Puerto Rico. In 1964, a little over a year after Sasha, my older son, was born, Julie and I decided to go to the island for Christmas so that I could meet her relatives. We stayed in her aunt's house on the southern coast in a small town called Patillas. Readers of *100 Years of Solitude*, the novel by the Nobel Prizewinning Gabriel Garcia Marquez, would immediately recognize Patillas as "Macondo."

The southern coast is far less developed than the north, where stand the ever-spreading concrete towers of San Juan. Patillas in 1964 felt more like the Puerto Rico of old. We slept under mosquito nets. We were awakened by roosters. We went to the market early to avoid the blistering sun and to buy groceries for the day's meals. In the afternoons, after all the men had come back from work, I would sit around with Julie's Uncle Victor, a local policeman, and his friends. We would drink "Pitorro," a homemade moonshine whisky, and get silly drunk by the time Julie's Aunt Hela had dinner ready.

What impressed me immediately was the total lack of awareness of the color of anyone's skin. Heritage in most parts of Puerto Rico is a complex and therefore almost irrelevant characteristic. The admixtures of many generations have produced nearly every hue. The family that lived across the street from Hela and Victor were not just black, they were blue. The father's name was Nin Plaud, and he and his wife had eleven kids. The rest of Victor's drinking buddies had skin tones across a taffeta range of colors and a similar array of hair textures.

The dinner table was always full of people. Even though I didn't understand the conversation, I could tune into the mood of the meal and the vibes were very upbeat, even in the face of the poverty that surrounded us. Strangers and guests were always welcome to join in, no special invitations necessary. The Puerto Ricans have a saying: "Donde comen dos, comen tres." Translated it means, "Where two people eat, three people can eat." There is always room for one more person at the table and whatever there is to eat can be shared. Like Hemingway's Paris, Patillas, in its own small way, was a movable feast.

Here is a story that reflects the prevailing attitude. One day during our visit, a man knocked on the door and handed Aunt Hela a live chicken. Naturally, she asked what it was for. The man replied that he had promised Victor he wouldn't tell her the reason for this present of poultry. Hela prodded him, made him a cup of coffee, and in due course he confessed. It seems that Victor had given the man a parking ticket. He hardly ever issued tickets, but the man had gotten drunk and parked in a spot that created a traffic jam. Victor had no choice but to write him the ticket.

When the man came to the police station to pay the $5 fine, he told Victor that he didn't have any money. He then asked Victor to lend him the $5! More Valjean than Javert, obviously, Victor lent him the $5 on the condition that he swear never to tell Hela about the loan. The man repaid the sum the following week, but his conscience did not let him rest. He felt a sense of obligation to Victor because of his kindness. The next time he had some extra chickens, he decided to go to Victor's house and offer up this cackling token of thanks. When Victor wasn't home the bird went to Hela. He was no match for her skill at prying secrets loose, a feminine ability inversely proportionate to their skill at keeping them.

Having spent a couple of years in New York, I could imagine myself asking the cop who gave me a ticket to lend me money for the fine. In 1964 the reply would have been, "What are you, a wise guy?" My guess is the answer wouldn't be half so pleasant today.

This is how I passed my first Christmas in the sun. This kind of relaxed courtesy and mutual respect among people of different backgrounds, features, and economic status was outside my experience. Nazism, of course, was the mortal enemy of ethnic and every other form of toleration. Communism was a hollow hymn to the workingman. In Puerto Rico, superficial differences did not matter, and neither did some deeper ones. In Europe at mid-century, such differences sent tanks smashing across borders and bombs crashing into apartment blocks.

For the first time in my life, I felt completely at home.

Six years later, by 1970, I had made my reputation and could pretty much write my own ticket in the life insurance and securities business. With my dream of entrepreneurship still alive, I turned my eyes to the "unincorporated territory" to the south. I made a deal with Aetna, one of the few firms still operating on the general agency system, to give me the franchise for Puerto Rico. They threw in the Virgin Islands to boot and some other parts of Latin America where incomes had finally begun to rise a little. I landed in San Juan ready to start an insurance operation from scratch, entering a Spanish-speaking territory with English as my own third language and no Spanish at all. I had learned English, I told myself, so this new tongue should come quickly. It was January 1971, and I had just turned 29.

When I was negotiating for my deal, everyone was saying: "Why do you want to go to some poverty-stricken banana republic when you can stay in New York where all the action in finance is?" I had no logical explanation, but later I learned that using only logic to make a decision, especially a business decision, is the kiss of death. As Joseph Campbell has written, "We must be willing to get rid of the life we've planned, so as to have the life that is waiting for us."[1] My plan had been to make it big in New York; like the song says, "if I can make it there, I can make it anywhere." No, I thought, I know I can make it in New York, but in Puerto Rico, the bruised heel of the Caribbean?

I rented a two-bedroom apartment in an area of San Juan called Hato Rey, in a building called El Monte and began making phone calls from the kitchen. That's how I started my business. I hired my first secretary, Yolanda, within a month and my first agent, within two months. Within three months I found approximately 600 square feet of office space in the most prestigious building in Hato Rey, the Banco Popular Center. I was in business.

Doing business in Puerto Rico is a lot different from doing business on the mainland. In the United States you could just start knocking on doors and pretty soon someone would say yes. In Puerto Rico, everything was done through contacts, influence, and what the locals call "pana." Literally, "pana" means breadfruit, but the word has nothing to do with breadfruit or any other plant for that matter. It had its origins with the U.S. soldiers who landed in Puerto Rico in 1898. They would call each other "partner." When the locals heard this, they assumed it applied to people who seem to take care of each other. But partner did not sound very Spanish, so they pronounced it "pana." The word came to denote a kind of "you scratch my back, I'll watch your back" friendship. "Oye Pana!" the Puerto Ricans say.

The American GI's imported other words. "Zafacon," for one. In Puerto Rico it means "garbage can," but if you say zafacon to anyone else in Latin America they won't know what you are talking about. It came from the U.S. military term "safety can," jargon for trashcan. The Puerto Ricans "Latinized" the term and made it "zafacon." These and other wartime gifts to linguistics are why Puerto Rican Spanish is sometimes referred to as "Spanglish."

To make a short story even shorter, if I were to survive in Puerto Rico, I very quickly had to find some panas or my business was headed for the zafacon. The most natural start is with people who need your products. We used a local law firm and a local CPA firm to open the office, so I pumped them for contacts. First, I got a cousin of my office landlord to get me into the "Banker's Club," the most prestigious luncheon spot in Puerto Rico. That put me in front of some important people in town. Next I joined the local Rotary and became a board member of a number of civic and charitable organizations. Planning to give back before you had received was not a bad thing to do.

One clear need was the large and growing youth population of the island. That led to my role in starting the "Boys Clubs of Puerto Rico." I called W. Clement Stone, a billionaire insurance tycoon, a champion of "positive mental attitude," the Bill Gates of his day.

Stone was an almost legendary figure who once roused the passengers on an overnight flight that landed in London by shouting, "Stand up. Raise your arms. Repeat after me: I feel healthy! I feel happy! I feel terrific!" Stone, I knew, was a major donor to Boys Clubs on the mainland. He put up some money to start the local club and even came down for a cocktail party to which I had invited San Juan's economic VIPs. These people later became board members and benefactors. Today, Puerto Rico has four Boys Clubs.

To get further funding for the Boys Clubs, I joined the board of the local United Fund and later became its campaign chairman. All this activity put me in touch with people who became my "panas" and helped me get business. They also helped with the peculiar regulatory issues on the island that helped my business survive and thrive. Despite my success in the states, survival in the Caribbean was not a given. The cultural and personal friendliness of the people was prodigious. Business was another story. Most Americans who come down here seeking their treasure either stay as alcoholics or flee as bankrupts. Puerto Rico becomes their Waterloo.

A certain notion of friendliness is part of the problem. Puerto Ricans, by nature, never want to offend anyone, and they would prefer to lie than to say no. They promise you anything you want but seldom follow through. Entrepreneurs from other shores need to develop both a sixth sense and a third eye to be able to distinguish an agreement from a desire to please.

Inviting someone for a business lunch was an experience. If you made the appointment for noon, your guest would arrive around 1.30 p.m., if he came at all. Usually I would take my invitees to the Banker's Club, where the bar was both the first stop and the last stop. You would sit around for two hours, talking about sports, politics, and women, and put away three or four drinks. Then the menu would come and you would place your order. Another round of drinks. Next, at last, the waiters would come and bring you to the table where your food was already served. Each guest had his own waiter to steady him to the table.

After lunch, it was time for more drinks to accompany the espresso. Now it was around 5.30 p.m. As you exited the dining room, a crowd of people had already gathered in the bar, playing "Generale." If you didn't join in, they would suspect you were a "gringo" and your guest would never do business with you again. Next came cocktail hour at the Banker's. Finally, you went out with some of the crowd to local joints so the serious drinking could begin. Around midnight you crawled home, never having discussed the essence of the business for which you had scheduled the lunch.

New York might be this way once in awhile on the weekend. This was the mid-week business lunch in Puerto Rico. Measured in paperwork, there was little output. But the Puerto Rico way produced "panas" by the dozen. And that was all you needed. If you ordered iced tea for lunch in those days, your bar tab would be manageable but your business career wouldn't last six months.

By 1974, I had the largest life insurance operation in Puerto Rico and one of the ten largest within the Aetna system. Aetna had some 200 agencies like mine nationwide. I now had some 5,000 square feet of office space in Banco Popular Center, housing 50 agents and clerical staff. I was 33. All this material success came at a high price. I was divorced from my wife Julie the previous year. My life had centered on business and prosperity. Personal life went on the back burner, and eventually there were ashes.

Life is not all roses, and business relationships in Puerto Rico were not all panas y cervesas. When I started my Aetna operation, I was resented by much of the local competition. Some did everything they could to derail me. They were irked by this New Yorker who spoke no Spanish (I am fluent today) and who had the nerve to beat them at their own game right in their backyard. Most insurance operations were started by Americans who came to Puerto Rico and, after a year or two, scampered back to the U.S. because they couldn't deal with the local customs and the language. Those operations were then taken over by Puerto Ricans, who continued to build them at their own comfortable pace.

The Odishelidze agency had long since warmed to local customs and I quickly learned the language, but I was still on New York time. The phrase "New York minute" had not yet been invented, but the reality existed. I wanted success quickly. My rivals used their panas to harass me with licensing and regulatory issues. My own panas fired back. This aspect of American mainlanders doing business in Puerto Rico has changed little. It was and is O.K. for the "gringos" to bring their capital and spend their money, but, sooner or later, the "gringo" had to retreat and cede control to a local.

I was something of a man without a country. What was local and what was foreign to me after three decades of migration from Eastern Europe to Canada to the Caribbean was an academic question. A better future had long been my true homeland, and the allure of Puerto Rico was the towline pulling me forward. I wasn't going to walk away from that future. The pressure increased, so I mingled even more with the locals. When they finally realized I wasn't going away, rivals became fast friends. They reinterpreted me. I was not a gringo, I was a Russian. It was no matter that I had never set foot inside my parents' Georgian homeland. Soon I was admitted to the local General Agents and Managers Association. They even elected me its president one year. I was a full-fledged pana, fighting off the real gringos.

The antagonism to the outside that I had overcome was not an anti-Americanism. True anti-Americanism in Puerto Rico is a rare, and usually organized event. There is, however, a feeling about the "outsider," and centuries of being under the control, direction, or influence of foreign forces have bred in most Puerto Ricans a sense that gaining and preserving an upper hand against the outsider is an event whose infrequency renders some excesses acceptable. A friend of mine, Peter, came into rather direct contact with this phenomenon.

Peter came to Puerto Rico from the States to run a small loan company. One day he caught a branch manager stealing from the company. He assembled all the proof and confronted the man, who admitted the theft. Peter fired him but did not press charges. The ex-employee came back and stabbed Peter seven times. When I heard what had happened, I went to the hospital and he told me the story. When Peter got well enough to return to work, he learned that he had been fired. The employee had filed a lawsuit against Peter and the company for wrongful termination. The man had three kids and he claimed he couldn't feed his family because of his dismissal. The local labor department found in his favor even though he admitted stealing the money. Peter's firing and the employee's reinstatement were part of the company's settlement. They put a Puerto Rican in Peter's place. I recruited Peter and he was an agent with me until 1985.

Another friend, Don, ran the Puerto Rican division of a U.S.-based auto supply company. One day a former employee, whose tenure preceded Don's, came in and asked for an employment recommendation. Since Don did not know the man, he called the home office in the States to find out who he was. They told him that he was a former store manager who had been caught stealing. Don's predecessor had fired him. The employee had come back and shot his boss three times, killing him. The murderer turned himself in and claimed he did it because he had "lost his head" and had five kids to support. He never spent a day in jail. The home office VP who was talking to Don told him to look on the wall behind him. Don saw a hole from one of the bullets that missed. He was instructed by headquarters to give the man anything he wanted. It was advice he swiftly took.

Bienvenidos a Puerto Rico!

My business grew and my friendships blossomed. Eventually, my wanderlust kicked in again. The first two decades of my life had been nothing but forced moves. Nesting wasn't my cure; choosing my moves was, or so it seemed. Puerto Rico is roughly three times the size of Rhode Island. I told myself I needed new challenges. In 1976, a friend of mine approached me about taking over a group of life insurance companies in Florida, Texas, California, Indiana and Ohio. We put a team together and made the acquisition.

Talk about "BigShot-itis." I had it in spades. Suddenly, I was president of a mid-size insurance company, with thousands of agents and employees, and reams of stock options that made me an instant multi-millionaire. I lived the life. Watching some of recent history's "dot.com" wizards get wildly rich through their IPO's and stock options and then come crashing down brought my exhilaration and despair back to me in a rush. There are no new business cycles, only new kinds of business.

When the balloon burst and the sun set on my newest adventure in personal wealth, it was 1978 and the shock wave of the Carter economy was about to hit its peak. It had taken me two years to come to the realization that I had finally reached my level of incompetence. I went back to the only place on Earth that spoke to me of home, sweet home. With my tail between my legs, I booked a flight to Puerto Rico.

CHAPTER 6

The American Taxpayer's Commonwealth Burden

[T]he incentives of government agencies are different than what the laws they were set up to administer were intended to accomplish. That may not sound very original in the James Buchanan era, when we know about "Public Choice" theory. But it was a revelation for me. You start thinking in those terms, and you no longer ask, what is the goal of that law, and do I agree with that goal? You start to ask instead: What are the incentives, what are the consequences of those incentives, and do I agree with those?

–Thomas Sowell

An encounter with economic policy in Puerto Rico turned the noted political philosopher Thomas Sowell away from Marxism. In an interview with *Slate* magazine in 1999, Sowell recounted how he reached the conclusion, as a young economist working for the federal government, that the minimum wage, as applied to Puerto Rico, was hurting lower wage workers rather than helping them, by raising unemployment. Liberals and labor unions had reached a different conclusion: unemployment was rising in

Puerto Rico because of the impact of hurricanes on sugar production. It wasn't public policy, it was the weather.

Logician that he was, Sowell came to the office one day and suggested a method to resolve the dispute. His government office should determine how much of the sugar cane crop had been destroyed by the weather. The proposal was met with disbelief and dejection. If pursued, it could unsettle the agency's favored theory excusing the role of the minimum wage in stoking unemployment. It was then that Sowell realized, as he recounts above, that the noble purposes of many laws and policies become ends in themselves, when the proper test is, what are the effects of the policy in question? In the case of Marxism, the effect of policy – ideology – was economic ruin.

Puerto Rico has been a test case now for more than five decades of a different kind of nobly intended ideology. That ideology, protected by powerful lobbies, turned an industrial outreach program into a long-term tax boondoggle. That boondoggle became, in turn, a cardinal principle of a political party wed to a particular form of government needed, naturally, to preserve that boondoggle. As a result, a dependent territory, half-filled with dependent individuals and families at or below the poverty line, has never approached the level of growth and freedom it might otherwise have obtained. Economic stagnation has gone hand in hand with political stalemate. Altogether, these factors have made modern Puerto Rico a less attractive partner to entrepreneurs than the fate of similar nations/territories suggests it should have been.

How much damage has continued commonwealth status done to the economy of Puerto Rico and to the aspirations of its people? There are different ways to measure this damage. Certainly, the most immediate and, in some ways, puzzling measurement is the poverty rate. As a Caribbean island, Puerto Rico could be compared to its near neighbors. As a Spanish-speaking former colony of a European power, it could be compared to other Latin American countries with a similar history. As an unincorporated territory of the United States with a diverse economy and a sizable population, it could be compared to the 50 states of the American Union. Under the first two standards of comparison, Puerto Rico fares somewhat better; compared to the U.S. states, the proper standard of measurement, its enduring poverty is dismal and disheartening.

Emilio Pantojas-Garcia is one of the deans of economic analysis of Puerto Rico and its status; he is a researcher in the Centro de Investigaciones Sociales and an adjunct professor at the University of Puerto Rico. In an April 2003 article he wrote for the American Alliance for Tax Equity, he prepared the data shown in Table 1.1 The Table compares the poverty rate for Puerto Rico with the poverty rates of six of the poorest U.S. states, as well as with the United States as a whole. The comparison covers a 30-year period from 1969 forward. Thus, as Chart 1 on page 106 shows, it covers the waning years of Operation Bootstrap (the first serious effort to industrialize the Puerto Rican economy) and the entire span of the Section 936 tax gimmick for U.S. pharmaceuticals and other corporations.

Table 1

	Percentage of the Population Below the Poverty Level			
	1969	1979	1989	1999
United States	12.6%	13.0%	13.5%	12.7%
Puerto Rico	**65.2%**	**62.4%**	**58.9%**	**48.2%**
Mississippi	35.4%	24.3%	25.7%	17.6%
West Virginia	22.2%	15.2%	18.1%	17.8%
New Mexico	22.8%	20.6%	20.9%	20.4%
Arkansas	27.8%	21.5%	19.6%	14.8%
Montana	13.6%	13.2%	16.3%	16.6%
Louisiana	26.3%	20.3%	23.6%	19.1%

First, the poverty level in Puerto Rico is appallingly high, especially for a territory that has enjoyed a special relationship with the United States. Today, nearly one of every two residents of Puerto Rico lives below the poverty line. That is a poverty rate nearly 2.4 times as high as that faced by any of the 50 states. Moreover, the gap, in proportionate terms, is increasing. Mississippi, which had the next highest poverty rate to Puerto Rico in 1969, has cut its rate by half; Puerto Rico has cut its poverty by less than a fourth. In economic terms, rather than converging (as most of the rest of the United States has done), Puerto Rico's economic profile is diverging from that of the mainland. As the table shows, the range of poverty among the states is collapsing somewhat, as they move closer to the U.S. average rate of 12.7 percent. That Puerto Rico's divergence from this norm is happening without federal income taxes on Puerto Ricans and with the availability of an enormously costly tax break is all the more striking.

Other factors make this trend even more disturbing than the poverty numbers suggest.

The first of these is the fact that Puerto Rico has been able to export a significant amount of its potential poverty over the years. This is due to its status as a territory of the United States. Since 1917 Puerto Ricans have held U.S. citizenship whether they live in Santurce, Puerto Rico, or the Bronx, New York, although U.S. citizenship has significantly different meaning in each place. In fact, during the 1950s and 1960s, the very period when the new Commonwealth government was finding some success in attracting

Chart 1

Stages of 20th Century Economic Development Puerto Rico	
Period	Policy
1900-1934	The era of King Sugar, characterized by: • Unrestricted, duty-free access to U.S. market • U.S. corporations and Puerto Rican landowners
1934-1947	New Deal Era, FDR and Rexford Tugwell, with: • Failed attempts at land reform • Extension of welfare programs to the island • Arrival of U.S. defense forces and spending
1948-1965 Operation Bootstrap	First period of rapid industrialization, with: • New local tax breaks and incentives • U.S. light manufacturing, including apparel • Puerto Rico an export platform to the U.S.

1965-1973
Operation Bootstrap
	Second stage of industrialization, with
	• Capital-intensive firms investing in Puerto Rico
	• Development of petrochemical sector, using
	   - corporate tax exemptions
	   - high quotas for Puerto Rican oil imports from and exports to the U.S.

1976-1996	The era of Section 936, characterized by: • Special tax breaks for capital intensive industry • Domination by pharmaceutical firms of Section 936 tax breaks
1996-2005	Phase-out of Section 936 and other tax breaks
2005-?	The Status Quo or Something More?

Adapted from: Pantojas-Garcia
The Cost of Puerto Rico's Commonwealth
Status to American Taxpayers

U.S. businesses to the island, the migration of Puerto Ricans from the island to U.S. cities was actively encouraged. Table 2 below shows the volume of this migration by decade, and obviously the numbers are substantial.[2]

Table 2

Net Out-Migration from Puerto Rico, 1950-2000		
Period	Net Out-Migration	NOM as Share of Population
1950-1960	470,000	20.9%
1960-1970	214,000	8.2%
1970-1980	65,817	2.2%
1980-1990	116,571	3.4%
1990-2000	-32,841	-
1950-2000	833,547	21.8%

Source: Dietz, "The Impact of Commonwealth Status on Puerto Rico's Economic Development"

Over the last century a net of more than one-fifth of the resident population of Puerto Rico (that population is in the neighborhood of 3.89 million individuals as of August 2003) departed the island. The actual figures for people leaving for the United States are higher, because a significant amount of the influx to Puerto Rico represents immigrants arriving from other Caribbean and South American countries. These immigrants include people seeking economic betterment (bad as conditions have been in Puerto Rico, they are better than in many other Caribbean Basin countries) and political refugees seeking relief in Puerto Rico's relative stability and security. Had Puerto Rico's unique status as part of the United States not permitted this free migration, the poverty and unemployment rates on the island would undoubtedly have been significantly higher throughout most of the past half-century.

Of course, every person who migrated from Puerto Rico to the United States was not poor. Education and business opportunities have always drawn people to the mainland United States. However, the Government of Puerto Rico consciously promoted such emigration in the 1950s and 1960s as a "safety valve." In fact, government policy was aimed at encouraging the poor, the unemployed, and women in their childbearing years to leave the island and seek their fortunes in the United States.[3] At least one analyst,

Stanley Friedlander, has ventured a figure for the impact this removal of population had on unemployment in Puerto Rico. Friedlander estimates that in 1960 the unemployment rate would have been 22.4 percent rather than the actual rate of 13.2 percent, some 70 percent higher.[4]

Temporarily, at least, especially when the emigration rate from Puerto Rico was high, the deficiencies in "Operation Bootstrap" could be masked to a certain degree. This is not to say that the industrialization of Puerto Rico did not produce gains in employment, per capita income and economic well being, because at first it did. The truth was that the reputation of the program, which was at its heart a government-led, New Deal-form of industrial development, was better than the reality. This reputation outlived the beginning of the era when the bottom dropped out and Puerto Rico's industrial growth began to stagnate, even as U.S. transfers to and tax benefits for the island began to take off.

In this sense, "Operation Bootstrap" can be seen as a second-stage New Deal approach to Puerto Rico's enduring economic challenges. The first stage, in the 1930s and '40s, involved land reform, the application of welfare state programs from Washington, and defense expenditures. The second stage, under Muñoz Marin and the Commonwealth model, involved special local and federal tax breaks designed to draw U.S. manufacturing interests to the island. What both stages have in common is that development is based not on local entrepreneurship and the operation of the free market, but rather on government institutions that create an artificial opportunity or haven that moves industry from one place to another without necessarily creating jobs.[5] The siphon, like the updraft in the core of a hurricane, that enabled Puerto Rico's second-stage New Deal to work well for a time was its extremely low wage costs. These costs, of course, rose over time, especially relative to other developing countries around the world, and the siphon lost its pull.

There are various ways to determine whether an economic program is working, but Puerto Rico's poverty rate is an especially appropriate gauge given the fact that New Deal programs in particular stress income redistribution and benefits for the poorest members of society. What then about unemployment? Was Puerto Rico's economic program at least putting large numbers of its citizens to work? Not surprisingly, the pattern here is an unkept promise as well. The most important point is again one of divergence: despite its close economic ties to the United States, despite the mobility of people, goods and services between the island and the mainland, Puerto Rico's unemployment picture is not tending to converge with that of the States. Table 3 below shows the fluctuations in Puerto Rican unemployment between 1950 and 2000.

By 1975, the unemployment rate in Puerto Rico, while high at 15.5 percent, was less than double that of the United States. By the year 2000, although the unemployment rate on the island was lower, at 11.0 percent, it was 2.75 times the rate in the United States. After 2000, the U.S. unemployment rate rose significantly, and Puerto Rico's followed suit, though the upward swing was much smaller on a percentage basis. The rate also moved in tandem in 2003, declining more rapidly on the island. This pattern shows how closely linked and, in may ways, integrated the economies of the United States and Puerto Rico really are, but it also shows how little effect the special tax breaks for Puerto Rico have had on altering the long-term relationship between the unemployment trends in these two places. The following chapter describes the history of these tax breaks, particularly Section 936 of the Internal Revenue

Table 3

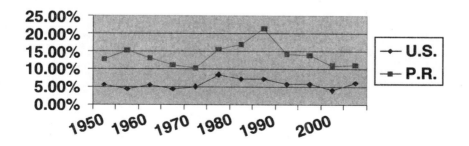

Code, in detail, but the key point to notice is that, based on total unemployment figures, the Congressional tax policies of the 1970s did nothing to put the Puerto Rican economy on the same glide path as the mainland economy.

In fact, during the 1970s and after, the Puerto Rican economy was outperformed even by a number of its neighbors in the region, for whom, naturally, no special tax breaks had been devised by Congress. In the 1960s, Puerto Rico had a real rate of growth in GNP (more precisely GP, since Puerto Rico is not a nation) of 3.7 percent, which was the third best among 22 Latin American and Caribbean countries tallied by the World Bank. From 1970 to 1980, half the countries the World Bank monitored had a higher rate of GDP growth than Puerto Rico, whose GDP growth rate fell by half from a decade earlier. Some of these countries had begun to develop their own resources, principally oil reserves, but for others it was their new ability to compete successfully with Puerto Rico in the area of inexpensive labor. The same was true for such countries as South Korea and Taiwan, whose growth also outstripped Puerto Rico's.

Dr. Joseph Pelzman, in a special report prepared in December 2002 for the European Union Research Center at George Washington University in Washington, D.C., highlighted the nondescript performance of the Puerto Rican economy relative to its near neighbors in the 1980s and 1990s. Table 4 allows comparison of the GDP growth rates over two decades for Puerto Rico, the Dominican Republic, Mexico and Costa Rica.

Table 4

GDP Growth, Selected Caribbean Countries, 1980s and 1990s				
Period	Puerto Rico	Mexico	Costa Rica	Dominican Republic
1980-1990	2.3%	2.3%	2.2%	3.8%
1990-2000	4.6%	3.5%	5.2%	5.8%

These figures are in the same range during a period dominated by growth in the United States and by rapid expansion in the value of the targeted tax benefits in Puerto Rico. While, as Pelzman points out, cross-country comparisons of GDP can be difficult given "a whole set of differing country characteristics and development approaches," any superiority of the Puerto Rican "dependency on imported capital" approach should be evident in these results.6 Clearly, the evidence is lacking.

This is an appropriate place to talk about the differences between GDP and GNP, because the two measurements speak volumes about the crippling effect of Commonwealth status and historical U.S. policy that has treated Puerto Rico as little more than a tax shelter covered with palm fronds. Gross Domestic Product, or GDP, refers to the total value of goods and services produced in Puerto Rico. GNP, or GP, means "gross national product/gross product," but it refers to what the residents of a given jurisdiction receive in terms of pre-tax income. The two numbers, GDP and GNP, can vary in a given locale for a number of reasons. In terms of the well being of the populace, GNP is the more precise indicator because of its emphasis on income.

In most countries and at most times, the difference between GDP and GNP is quite small; these calculations fall within 5 percent, plus or minus of each other. In the United States as a whole, GDP and GNP are quite close, even if, in certain jurisdictions, one or the other is higher because of a concentration of retirees, for example, or of businesses with out-of-state ownership. In Puerto Rico, the figures for GDP and GNP were close as recently as the early 1960s. Nonetheless, as economists John Mueller and Marc Miles uncovered, by 1997 GDP in Puerto Rico "was an astonishing 150 percent of its $32 billion GNP," a gap of $16 billion.7

Put another way, fully one third ($16 billion of $48 billion) of total GDP in Puerto Rico in 1997 did not make its way into the checking accounts, wallets, purses and cookie jars of the island's residents. Where did it go? The simple answer is the coffers of U.S. mainland companies, especially pharmaceutical firms, who were allowed for several decades to earn income tax-free on the island and transfer it, sometimes merely as a bookkeeping exercise, back to the United States for the benefit of residents here. The drama of Section 936 is described in full detail in the next chapter. For now, it is enough to note how this system of taxation worked in its latter decades in precisely the opposite of the manner its commonwealth advocates said it would: rather than build employment and raise per capita income on the island, it lowered mainland companies' federal tax burden and raised per capita income elsewhere.

Chart 2 on page 113 shows just how rapidly GDP and GNP diverged in Puerto Rico over the 35-year existence of the local and federal tax incentives established under Operation Bootstrap. Now, certainly some portion of that $32 billion in GNP is attributable to the operation of the Section 936 companies. They did indeed have to open and maintain manufacturing enterprises on the island in order to qualify for special tax treatment, and these enterprises employed workers (we will discuss the figures in a moment) and paid them wages that, arguably, were higher than those same workers might have otherwise been able to earn in the commonwealth marketplace. Even so, Section 936 had minimal effects in producing employment because, with changes in tax rules over time, it gave manufacturers leeway to locate intangible assets in Puerto Rico and research and development (intellectual capital) in the United States.

Intangibles are items like patents and brand names, which have real marketplace value and can thus be the source of significant profits for a firm. The sale of these assets to the Puerto Rican subsidiary makes compelling financial sense for the American parent company, but results in little or no additional employment on the island. At the same time, research and development can be very high costs in certain firms, particularly firms drawn to Section 936 like drug companies and electronics manufacturers, and Section 936 only adds to the incentive these firms have to build or keep their research costs on the mainland where they can be deducted from profits and reduce tax liability further. Some would describe this as a form of double dipping. It is clearly a brain drain on Puerto Rico in these fields, as the best minds in high-tech arenas like biochemistry and computer development locate with the U.S. parent company.

For drug firms, the combination of these effects can be particularly potent. Research, development, and testing of a significant new drug in the United States is an unusually expensive and time-consuming proposition. Pharmaceutical companies must file New Drug Applications (NDAs) with the Food and Drug Administration and overcome high hurdles that address safety, efficacy and suitability for use in particular populations, including children. These steps all take time. In the meanwhile, the companies' patents are time limited, and the longer FDA review takes, the fewer years that the company will

The American Taxpayer's Commonwealth Burden

Chart 2

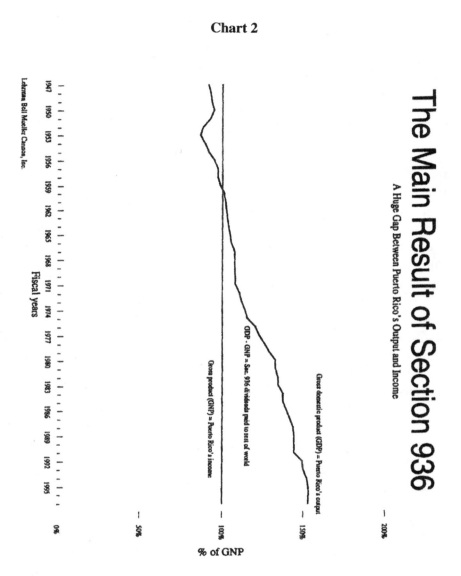

The Main Result of Section 936
A Huge Gap Between Puerto Rico's Output and Income

be able to market the drug free of price competition from generic versions manufactured by rival producers when the patent expires. The ability to move the intangible part of this process to Puerto Rico is highly prized as the window of maximum profits on new drugs is relatively narrow. This is yet another factor that makes Section 936 unsuitable as a long-term strategy for job creation.

Table 5 below examines the role of manufacturing in the modern Puerto Rican economy at four discrete points in time, expressed both in terms of total jobs and as a percentage of the island economy. The first column underscores the fact that manufacturing's share of GDP (which includes profits shifted to the United States) has continued to rise steadily for the past 30 years, even as the share of the Puerto Rican job market devoted to manufacturing continues to decline. This decline is a fact of economic life in Puerto Rico, and it has occurred during both the rising and falling cycles in the value of the Section 936 tax breaks. The total number of manufacturing jobs on the island peaked at 172,000 in 1995, according to the Junta de Planificacion. While obviously there has been some decline in the number of such jobs since the beginning of the phase-out of Section 936, that decline has not been dramatic. While manufacturing jobs declined by some 13,000 between 1995 and 2000, retail jobs increased by 24,000 and service-oriented jobs increased by 58,000.

Table 5 Manufacturing in the Puerto Rican Economy, Selected Years

Year	Percent of GDP	Percent of Jobs	Total Jobs	Net Change Over 10 Years
1970	30.5%	19.2%	-	-
1980	36.8%	19.0%	143,000	-
1990	39.6%	17.5%	168,000	+17.5%
2000	43.5%	13.7%	159,000	-5.4%

It could be argued that the new jobs created in retail and services are not as good as the jobs lost in manufacturing. Job for job, this may well be true, but more than six such jobs have been created for every one in manufacturing that has been lost. The Puerto Rican economy is clearly more resilient than the disastrous picture painted by the doom-saying defenders of Section 936. In line with the comments of Thomas Sowell at the head of this chapter, the proper question to ask in the context of Puerto Rican manufacturing is not, "What was the intention of the policy?" but "What are the incentives that the policy creates?" and "What are the consequences of those incentives?" In the case of Section 936, the incentive was for U.S. manufacturers to locate certain kinds of enterprises in Puerto Rico that produce merchandise of high value, with their associated intangibles, while retaining as much as possible of the real research and production costs in the higher-taxed environment back home.

In the first five years of the phase-out of the Section 936 boondoggle, Puerto Rico lost manufacturing jobs but gained jobs overall. The loss in any event was hardly the kind of "flight" or "investment strike" that Section 936 companies had used to threaten Congress when the idea of repealing the provision first surfaced in the 1970s. It is even possible that the decline in manufacturing jobs is temporary. As James L. Dietz, Professor of Economic and Latin American Studies at Cal State-Fullerton, has pointed out, Puerto Rico experienced real losses in manufacturing jobs in 1980-83, 1985, 1990 and 1991,[8] when the credit was in place. The decline is even less dramatic after a review of the changes in the number of companies claiming the Section 936 exemption and the tax revenues the phase-out has yielded for the U.S. Treasury.

The peak year in terms of the number of companies claiming Section 936 tax benefits was 1978, when almost 600 companies claimed the credit. The peak year in terms of the dollar value (revenue lost to the U.S. Treasury) for the Puerto Rican 936 companies was 1993, right on the eve of the major Congressional reform, when the annual cost of Section 936 to U.S. taxpayers was an astounding $4.6 billion. A subsidy of this magnitude can be measured in many ways, but all of those ways underscore just how inefficient Section 936 was as an economic development program. Pantojas-Garcia has aptly described the situation, "Puerto Rico has been the most important tax haven for many U.S. transnational corporations producing high-tech and knowledge-intensive patented goods[.]"[9] The same author has been even more categorical, describing the "unique political and economic arrangements of Commonwealth" status for Puerto Rico as "the largest tax shelter in United States history."[10]

If that assertion seems preposterous, look at Table 6 below. It lists the U.S. income on direct investment overseas (for our purposes here, and because of its unique tax-preferred status, Puerto Rico is listed as a nation) in 1986 and 1996 and the global share of all such income earned in the top five countries. Shouldn't Canada be the top income producer for U.S. direct investment? After all, we share a common border several thousand miles long, with major cities on both sides of the border and an excellent road system connecting the two countries. How about the United Kingdom? The U.S. and Great Britain fought two wars with each other two centuries ago, but have enjoyed a "special relationship" ever since that has seen each country risk its soldiers' lives in the service of the other. How about Japan, where American manufacturers went in the 1980s to relearn the art of high-quality mass production?

Yet none of these countries has generated more income for the United States than Puerto Rico, whose global share of such income ranked first among all the world's "overseas entities" in both 1986 and 1996. In fact, Puerto Rico's contribution to U.S. global income was the same at both slices of time, at 13.8 percent – roughly one in seven dollars generated overseas. It is a very potent tax break indeed that can produce such a percentage and maintain it over time, even as other countries rise and fall on the list.

Table 6

**U.S. Global Income on Direct Investment:
Top 10 Nations, 1986 and 1996**

Year	Rank	Country	Global Share (%)
1986	1	Puerto Rico	13.8%
	2	Canada	12.2%
	3	Germany	10.9%
	4	Netherlands	7.8%
	5	Japan	7.7%
1996	1	Puerto Rico	13.8%
	2	United Kingdom	12.4%
	3	Canada	7.7%
	4	Netherlands	7.1%
	5	Switzerland	4.2%

Adapted from: Pantojas-Garcia
The Cost of Puerto Rico's Commonwealth
Status to American Taxpayers

Moreover, the economies that fall behind in this measurement of U.S. investment are dramatically larger than Puerto Rico's. The economy of the United Kingdom was 26 times larger than that of Puerto Rico in 1996, and Canada's was 13 times larger in that same year, yet Puerto Rico generated profits on U.S. investment that were twice those generated by all of Canada and 11 percent more than those of the UK. To paraphrase a well-known American television commercial, "Can your tax shelter do this?"

Again, however, this largesse was not even spread across a panoply of American businesses that "discovered" Puerto Rico – let us say, found gold there in places Columbus could not have imagined. The result of the Commonwealth strategy was not a diverse manufacturing economy that might have offered workers a greater variety of jobs in different industries. The result, year after year, was a distorted and artificial manufacturing base that could, at least plausibly, threaten to leave the island if its tax shelter was shredded by the high winds of change. Likewise, it was a manufacturing base that, in the tax sense, was *continually in the process of leaving the island* as income flowed northward and was not reinvested in new plant and new jobs in Puerto Rico. This reality can be seen in government figures describing the narrow way in which Section 936 tax benefits were distributed.

To put the numbers in perspective, look at Chart 3, which shows the trend line for the cost to the Internal Revenue Service of the Section 936 tax credit. This credit is available to all U.S. corporations operating in American possessions, but more than 90 percent of it is attributable to operations in Puerto Rico. Over the 20-year period from 1976 to 1996, the credit brought its beneficiaries $51.7 billion in total tax breaks, an average of more than $2.7 billion per year. At least one school of economic conservatism will argue that tax relief is a rare bird and any form of reduced taxation on business - given that there are so many examples of over-taxation of business income, including the double taxation of dividends - is a good thing. The bad thing that Section 936 turned out to be is clear not only in how costly it is in terms of job creation, but also in how high a proportion of the benefits go to a handful of industries and how much it has done to prevent a real development policy from taking root.

Chart 3

Value of 936 Credits 1976-1998

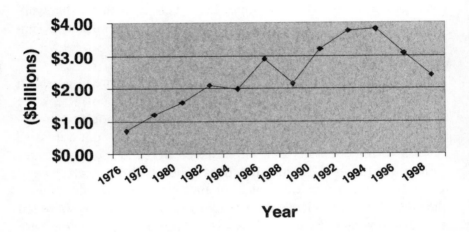

Some tax credits are difficult to measure in terms of their economic effectiveness. The child tax credit, for example, now provides qualifying families with a $1,000 per child credit against their federal income taxes for each child under the age of 17. The credit is very popular, and the Bush Administration has recently expanded it. Its value is hotly contested by economists who argue that it does not stimulate economic growth, or, conversely, that it facilitates the purchase of destructive items like beer and cigarettes. The credit's defenders argue in turn with great force that tax policy should trust the vast majority of parents (or, analogously, businesses) and that the credit represents an investment in human capital whose long-term "dividends" are extremely remunerative, in fact, they argue, the key to true growth through human creativity and productivity.

The Section 936 credit presents far fewer analytical obstacles. Over the years the IRS has examined the credit, in general terms and in terms of specific industries, to determine how much in the way of tax savings flows to companies for each job the credit creates. To begin with, a case can be made that this tax credit determines not whether jobs are created, but only *where* they are created. A pharmaceutical company that makes a popular prescription drug is unlikely to cease production in the absence of a tax credit, but it is quite likely to locate that production in Puerto Rico because of Section 936. Indeed, one source states that fully half of all drugs prescribed in the United States are physically manufactured in Puerto Rico. This goes to the question of whether the government needed to make any specific concession at all for a particular job to exist.

In any event, the average dollar amount of tax benefits per worker for the possessions corporations (all types) was $18,736 in 1995. The average compensation paid to the workers in these corporations (again, all types) was $23,835 in that same year. In essence, then, for the average 936 company, the U.S. taxpayer paid 80 percent of his gross wages and benefits. That is a significant subsidy, but IRS figures go further and allow us to look at the amount of tax benefits provided for workers in each sector. The companies that create relatively few jobs but enjoy magnificent tax cuts because of their passive investments and patent holdings in Puerto Rico will naturally have a much higher ratio of benefits to dollars of compensation paid.

Table 7

Ratio of 936 Benefits to Compensation, Specific Sectors, 1995				
Sector	Average Compensation	Average Tax Benefit Per Worker	Ratio of Benefits to Compensation	Number of Jobs in Sector
Pharmaceuticals	$39,404	$56,040	1.42	21,113
Apparel and Textiles	$12,307	$2,393	.19	16,222
Electrical and Electronic Equipment	$21,572	$10,036	.46	19,531

Adapted from James Dietz, "The Impact of Commonwealth Status on Puerto Rico's Economic Development"

After 1995, of course, as Chart 3 shows, the value of the Section 936 tax credit declined (although many of the corporations involved converted to controlled foreign corporation status to claim its deferred tax benefits), so that these ratios have undoubtedly declined. Even so, it's important to note just how distortive the 936 approach was; the higher-paying the job, the higher the ratio of the tax benefits, to the point where it would have been cheaper for the U.S. government to hire pharmaceutical workers directly and, for example, have them learn about the pharmaceutical industry at the Food and Drug Administration. The tax benefits for the electronics industry were far more reasonable, and the jobs produced paid nearly twice as well as those in the textile and apparel sectors. For this reason, the drug companies were the most vociferous defenders of Section 936 and, as we will see in the next chapter, the electronics firms were far more open to compromise on tax reform.

Just to cut the numbers one more way, the total tax savings for pharmaceutical companies from Section 936 jobs in 1995 was the product of the number of jobs subsidized times the tax benefits per job. In other words, producing 21,113 jobs in the pharmaceutical industry in Puerto Rico cost taxpayers a hefty $1.2 billion in 1995. Creation of nearly as many electronics manufacturing jobs cost the U.S. taxpayer approximately $196 million – less than one-sixth what the pharmaceutical jobs funneled out of the U.S. Treasury. That this kind of highway robbery persisted as long as it did is a tribute to the way in which focused lobbying and political spending can overcome, for a significant period of time at least, the more diffuse public interest.

As we will describe in subsequent chapters, the hold of the "Commonwealth" form of government, which has evolved really into a neo-industrial colonialism, has begun to slip over the past few decades as its political inconsistencies and economic shortcomings are laid bare. So, too, has Section 936 lost much of its grip, and the economic events of the past seven or eight years are worth discussing further. While, as we have demonstrated, Puerto Rico's economic development has misfired and, in key areas, continues to diverge from the norm for American political units (that is, the 50 states), the predictions of disaster emanating from the drug company lobbyists and PPD leaders in Puerto Rico have not come true. The fact of continuing U.S. economic growth for most of the 1990s, the resourcefulness of the Puerto Rican people, and the need to pursue more promising long-term growth strategies have all played a role in averting the shipwreck some had forecast.

First, despite the anchor of Commonwealth, there exists enough integration of the United States and Puerto Rican economies that the cycles of boom and bust send riptides through the island (medications may be one industry that is exempt from this cycle – as the Section 936 numbers suggest – because the variety and costliness of pharmaceuticals, and people's need and willingness to use them, have steadily grown in our Baby Boomer, biochemical society). Between 1995 and 2000, Puerto Rican economic indicators improved in a number of areas, including unemployment (declined from 13.8 percent to 11.0 percent), labor force participation (increased from 45.9 percent to 46.2 percent), share of GDP from federal transfer payments (declined from 20.8 percent to 19.2 percent), food stamps as a share of such transfer payments (down from 18.2 percent to 15.2 percent), and poverty (from 1989 to 1999 the percentage of the population below the poverty threshold dropped from 58.9 percent to 48.2 percent).[11]

After 2000, as the U.S. economy slipped into a recession that was accelerated by the aftershocks of the terrorist attacks of September 11, 2001, the Puerto Rican economy suffered in tandem with the overall U.S. outlook. Unemployment ticked back upward to 13 percent, and personal and corporate debt and bankruptcies rose significantly. In Puerto Rico's Fiscal Year 2002 alone, the manufacturing sector lost 5,542 jobs. It is important to note that this job loss was more than halved the following year, and that, in September 2003, with the U.S. economy showing signs of life, average manufacturing wages in Puerto Rico are reportedly up 1.4 percent with predictions for a much better year in fiscal 2004. Company openings (71) nearly doubled the number of closings (38) in 2003, according to the Puerto Rico Industrial Development Co. (PRIDCO).[12]

The more recent the data, obviously, the more cautiously conclusions must be drawn. It seems fairly clear, however, that the economic course of recent years for Puerto Rico parallels the course of the U.S. economy, both good and bad. As Mueller and

Miles put it regarding just one indicator, "unemployment in Puerto Rico is . . . explained by unemployment in the United States."13 Under these circumstances, it seems reasonable to conclude that Section 936 has not been the linchpin of the Puerto Rico economy and its removal, though incomplete (and with the option of Controlled Foreign Corporation status standing behind it), has not precipitated a collapse of the island economy. Instead, the factors that move the Puerto Rican economy are far larger forces that influence domestic and international economies everywhere. These factors include the size of government, the size and complexity of the tax code in general, international rules affecting free trade and the wages workers earn - in short, the whole array of policies that mark an economy as free and that sustain it in competition with other national economies that are either more or less free.

In all of these areas, Puerto Rico faces a great challenge, perhaps a crossroads, even a crisis, where it must choose whether to stake its economic fortunes on the tax ploys of the past, or to plot a new course that recognizes the island's real position and tremendous potential in the global economy. The temptation of the past is plain enough. In 2003, five years after the last abortive attempt in Congress to address Puerto Rico's ambiguous legal status, the pro-Commonwealth party is agitating for the creation of new options for CFCs that move back in the direction of the failed policies of the 1970s and 1980s. It's instructive to look at where Puerto Rico might be today if it could rewrite that past, if, that is, it had introduced balanced pro-growth policies 30 years ago rather than the whitewashed wealth policies it pursued in the last quarter of the 20th century.

A number of economists have taken exactly this approach and sketched out exactly how far behind Puerto Rico has fallen because of the Section 936 boondoggle and the Commonwealth status quo on which it has depended. The economic term for this phenomenon is *opportunity cost*. The real financial cost of "the road not taken" is not just the losses sustained on the path less traveled by but the riches foregone on the route forsaken. A man who drinks rotgut rather than tomato juice sustains both the liver damage of the alcohol and the effects of the lost vitamins from the alternative beverage. The opportunity cost of his decision is in both glasses. The same is true for the Puerto Rican economy as a whole. On the one hand, it has made a transition from a predominantly agricultural society to a society with modern sectors in services, manufacturing, government, and financial institutions. It has done so in a way, however, that is neither ripe nor balanced, and much of the fruit of that transition has been left hanging too high for the island to pluck.

Different approaches have been taken to this opportunity cost analysis for Puerto Rico, but they point to a similar conclusion: the island is slipping further behind the comparable state jurisdictions in the United States, and this needn't have happened. Dietz developed data, shown below as Table 8, that shows what would have happened to per capita GNP in Puerto Rico if the island had been able to maintain either the 9.2 percent growth rate established in the 1960s (the boom years of Operation Bootstrap) or the still robust 7.2 percent growth rate of the 1970s. To those who would suggest that these numbers were either artificially high or unsustainable, Dietz points out that both South Korea and Taiwan maintained per person income growth of more than 11 percent for more than 30 years. It's worth noting that both of these countries thrived under adverse political conditions with nothing like the stability and security of Puerto Rico.

Table 8

Year	Actual Annual Growth	Actual GNP Per Person	7.3% Growth Scenario 1980-2000		9.2% Growth Scenario 1970-2000	
			GNP/ Person	Increase Over Actual	GNP/ Person	Increase Over Actual
1960	-	$716	$716	-	$716	-
1970	9.2%	$1,729	$1,729	-	$1,729	-
1980	7.3%	$3,491	$3,491	-	$4,169	19.4%
1990	5.8%	$6,155	$7,062	14.7%	$10,052	63.3%
2000	5.6%	$10,906	$14,287	31.0%	$24,237	122.2%

Adapted from James Dietz, "The Impact of Commonwealth Status on Puerto Rico's Economic Development"

Like compound interest, the gains in income these scenarios illustrate are cumulative. This is lost ground that Puerto Ricans who have lived through their productive years will not make up. The intermediate growth rate would have meant an average of $4,287 more in income to each Puerto Rico resident; the high-growth scenario (remember, it would still be short of what South Korea and Taiwan achieved) would have meant more than a doubling of the per capita share of GNP. Under the intermediate growth scenario, the proportion of families below the poverty threshold would have dropped well below 50 percent by 1989. Under the high-growth scenario, the proportion of families in poverty in 1989 would have been in the 35 to 37 percent range, rather than the 55.3 percent actual incidence of poverty. Thus, a third of the island's nominal poverty would have been eliminated *before the growth decade of the 1990s began.* That the status which denied this result is called "commonwealth" is truly ironic. "Commonpenury" would be more appropriate.

The economists J. Tomas Hexner and Glenn Jenkins used another mode of analysis in their examination of the opportunity cost of Puerto Rico's misdirected economic policies. In their 1998 report for the Citizens Education Foundation, a group that advocates self-determination and permanent status for Puerto Rico, Hexner and Jenkins use the 50 states as a standard of comparison as well as the other U.S. territories. They note, first of all, that the states as a group have experienced an average annual growth rate 2 percent higher than that of the territories, including Puerto Rico.[14] Next they examine the wide disparity in economic standing among the states themselves and how those disparities have behaved over the course of recent U.S. economic history.

Put simply, the states have tended, over significant periods of time, to cluster more closely together in terms of their relative economic well-being. Liberal politicians like to charge that the rich are getting richer, and the poor are getting poorer, but in terms of the "fate of the states," the distance between the richest and the poorest has tended to shrink over time. This can only happen if, on average, the poorest states are growing faster than the richest ones and are thereby catching up with their stronger neighbors. This, in fact, is what has happened, and the rate at which it has been happening can be quantified. From 1940 to the present, Mississippi has grown twice as fast as the wealthier states of the Northeast (Connecticut is the wealthiest today), and earnings there are now 50 percent of the wealthiest state, up from 22 percent. This has happened with the help of all sorts of federal benefits for Mississippi (interstate highways, defense installations) from its integration with the U.S. economy, but not, of course, with any unusual tax benefits unavailable to other states.[15]

Mississippi has access to the Gulf of Mexico, low taxes, and warmer weather, but these advantages are either natural or non-industry specific. In essence, no gimmick has been at work in the catch-up to the rest of the American economy that has taken place in the state. Puerto Rico has most of the same benefits (it benefits from U.S. highway funds and defense installations, for example, and it has access to vital sea lanes and good weather), but it has only lost ground relative to Mississippi in the economic sweepstakes from 1940 to the present. We compared poverty rates earlier in this chapter. The phenomenon holds up for the broader measurement of per capita income as well. In 1949, Puerto Rico's per capita income was 60 percent of Mississippi's; in 1999 it was 52 percent. Relative to the entire mainland, Puerto Rico reached 38 percent of the U.S. per capita income in 1959. Forty years later it was stuck at the same figure.[16]

Well, a critic might point out, this comparison is between apples and oranges, or at least between an orange and a former apple. A better comparison would be one that looks at how the Puerto Rican economy has performed against an economically challenged entity that became a state. The comparison will be strengthened if that entity is a tropical island, if it has a population many of whose members spoke a different language, if it had a love-hate relationship with the rest of the United States, if it was of strategic military value to the United States, if it had tourist potential, and if it was largely agricultural when the change occurred. Fortunately, there is just such an entity, and it is called Hawaii. To aid the comparison further, this entity became a state in precisely the year (1959) that Puerto Rico reached the modern peak in its per capita income ratio to the United States as a whole.

Again, Puerto Rico suffers by comparison. In fact, Hawaii's development course after statehood has been described as probably setting "an all-time record for sustained high-level expansion for any state or region in the nation."[17] From 1949 to 1958, as Hexner and Jenkins, note, Hawaii experienced an average annual growth rate of four percent; from 1958 to 1973, the growth rate jumped to seven percent per year in what economists call the "Great Hawaiian Boom." As everyone knows, the years cited here were good ones overall for the U.S. economy (they were good to Puerto Rico as well), but Hawaii's growth outstripped even the strong U.S. overall growth rate (real growth of 6.31 percent versus 4.4 percent for the United States).

Unaided by the possessions corporation system of taxation, external investment in Hawaii soared after the declaration of statehood. A cloud of immense concern to any major business (political turmoil and uncertainty) had been removed from Hawaii's horizon. It is one thing to sell bread; quite another to build a plant to bake it. The number of companies doing business in Hawaii grew sixfold between 1955 and 1971. Tourism went through the thatched roof. Between 1958 and 1973, the annual number of visitors to Hawaii increased fifteenfold to more than 2.6 million, an average annual increase of 20 percent. Hawaii offers spectacular beauty, and it might be said that its reputation is better than the reality. Puerto Rico, on the other hand, has more natural beauty than its reputation admits ("you ugly island," repeats the Puerto Rican chorus in *West Side Story*).

Today tourism amounts to nearly one-fourth of Hawaiian income. Puerto Rico's ratio of tourism income to GDP stands at only six percent, despite the fact that it is much more accessible to East Coast population centers (that is, it is closer and far cheaper), has beautiful beaches and variegated terrain, offers a more familiar history, and is part of a region world-renowned for the variety of its vacation offerings. To underscore this point, and another Puerto Rican statistical oddity, the Caribbean region *as a whole* derives 29.5 percent of its GDP from tourism. Yes, Puerto Rico's numbers are lower in part because its unique relationship with the United States elevates its GDP with income to Section 936 companies, but it remains the case that the island's tourism industry is a fraction of what it could be. Moreover, that fraction has the potential to be frozen as factors like the crime rate, and other residues of dependency, continue to deflate what could be a reputation for inexpensive vacations in an exotic spot close to home.

We have discussed the phase-out of Section 936 and demonstrated its near irrelevance to the real economic well being of Puerto Rico. Indeed, we have underscored just how intertwined this failed economic strategy is with the persistence of Puerto Rico's current commonwealth status. We give this topic more attention in Chapters 5 and 6, which deal directly with the status debate and how it has evolved and accelerated over the past quarter-century. As complex as the status question makes both internal politics and U.S.-Puerto Rican politics, its linkage with a Section 936 and a faltering economy can be boiled down to a few simple points. Either of the two major forms of permanent status, independence (either as a sovereign neighbor or freely associated state) or statehood, would bring Puerto Rico's "imported capital dependency," in Pelzman's pithy phrase, to a halt. Federal corporate income tax treatment of U.S. corporations or multinationals would have to be uniform under either permanent status: none of the 50 states could constitutionally receive such a preference to the exclusion of the others, and all U.S. companies with foreign partners or subsidiaries are treated alike under separate provisions of the Internal Revenue Code.

As long as Commonwealth status is allowed to persist, the strong potential exists for a reversion to form and the resurrection of something akin to Section 936 at the height of its folly. That truth has already become evident with the latest wrinkle to enter the U.S.-Puerto Rican economic relationship, Section 956, or the Controlled Foreign Corporation. As the phase-out of Section 936 moves toward its conclusion in 2005, the number of companies on the island that have elected to convert to CFCs has continued to rise. The juridical anomaly here is readily apparent: Puerto Rico, its people citizens of the United States eligible for most federal aid programs, is now, for U.S. corporate income tax purposes, a foreign country.

The CFC conversion option was included in the 1995 reform of Section 936 as a safety valve for U.S. businesses that operate manufacturing plants on the island. In order to qualify as a CFC, as defined by a 1962 tax law, a company must be majority owned by U.S. shareholders. There are various ways to define this ownership, and CFC rules and limitations have changed over time, but essentially, a company qualifies today as a CFC if U.S. shareholders either own more than 50 percent of the value of all the company's outstanding stock or control more than 50 percent of the total combined voting power of that stock. The original goals of CFC status were to ensure that U.S. partners and subsidiaries overseas were competitive with the foreign holdings of other nations and that these entities were not used to park or shield personal wealth from proper taxation.

The chief mechanism for accomplishing these goals is tax deferral, whereby these corporations pay U.S. taxes on their income only when those funds are repatriated to the United States, typically many years after the income is earned. Thus, CFC status, while it gives multinational companies many options for deferring taxes and continuing to expand earnings, delays but does not avoid taxation altogether, as Section 936 does. In the case of Puerto Rico, however, commonwealth advocates and their economic cronies, the drug companies, CFC conversion is not only economically attractive as a short-term proposition but also politically attractive as a potential wedge for reinstatement of something that mimics Section 936. Since CFC status makes little sense in the first place for an unincorporated territory of the United States, an "enhanced" or super-CFC status does not strike these parties as any more senseless. With the 1995 option to convert, these companies bought time, and with that, they hope to buy favor in Congress.

The process of conversion to CFCs for former Section 936 companies in Puerto Rico is now virtually complete. As Pelzman notes in his December 2002 paper, "With the phasing out of Section 936, multinational companies started to take advantage of the CFC umbrella." Billions of dollars are earned every year by CFCs. Worldwide, in 1996, the 7,500 largest active foreign corporations controlled by U.S. multinationals held $2.7 trillion in assets, an increase of 35.4 percent in just two years. Their earnings and profits before taxes were $141 billion, an increase of 44 percent over 1992. In the year before the Pelzman study was released, some 80 U.S.-owned businesses in Puerto Rico converted all or part of their operations to CFC status, a 19 percent increase from the previous year's conversions.

Merely converting to CFC status does not require a Puerto Rico-based manufacturer to defer income tax. In theory, at least, a company could conclude that paying income tax in a given year offers the best hope for minimizing their liability (if, for example, it foresaw imminent or certain tax increases in coming years). In truth, these companies, like most individuals, desire to hold on to their earnings and find current or fresh ways to shelter them from taxes. They are not passive actors in the drama either, as they hire lobbyists and make campaign contributions, steps designed to persuade lawmakers to hear them out and give them new tax breaks down the road. Statistics on tax receipts are the first indicators that the Puerto Rican CFCs are indeed deferring their repatriation of offshore income, looking for a blue-sky opportunity to bring that money home.

The specific numbers for Puerto Rico tell a simple story. Repatriation of capital back to the mainland occurs in the form of distributions to stockholders. Between 1992 and 1996, Pelzman shows, total distributions as a percentage of total assets from Puerto Rico-incorporated CFCs declined from 1.72 percent to 0.14 percent, a 91.8 percent decrease. How much money, in current dollars, did this CFC conversion cost the U.S. Treasury? A June 1999 estimate from the Congressional Joint Committee on Taxation found that the tax deferral would cost the federal government $7.2 billion between 1999 and 2003, an average of $1.8 billion per year (not quite in the same league as the Section 936 break, which peaked at some $3.8 billion in revenue losses in 1994, but still a huge sum).

A fairly precise method of checking this calculation was used by Pelzman for Puerto Rican CFCs in 1999. He began with the fact that Puerto Rico taxes CFCs on their current-year income, even if U.S. corporate income tax is deferred. In 1999 ten of the then-existing 45 CFCs paid the sum of $431 million into the Puerto Rican treasury. This revenue was generated by the "Flat Tax on Industrial Development Income," which is set by law for CFCs at seven percent. Working backward, we can determine that these CFCs must have had taxable income in the range of $6.15 billion in 1999. Now let's suppose that this income had been subject to the then-current U.S. corporate income tax rate of 35 percent. Multiplication of these last two figures yields U.S. corporate income tax revenue of $2.15 billion. The difference between the potential U.S. and actual Puerto Rican tax payments is $1.72 billion ($2.15 billion minus $431 million, or $.431 billion). This is the net figure for "missing revenue" due to the CFCs' ability to defer taxation.[18] The actual figure is somewhat smaller because some CFCs do repatriate a portion of their profits in the year in which they are earned.

CFC status does not defy long-term taxability the way the former Section 936 did, but its present and potential value to firms that elect the status are fairly clear from the example. An attempt to revive Section 936 on Capitol Hill today, especially with high federal deficits occasioned by the impact of terrorism and the costly war against it, would face major hurdles. Enacting it in some other form is a distinct possibility, however, and the linkage between "enhanced CFC" proposals and the island's ruling party, the PPD, assure that attempts to do so will continue to be made with regularity, until the resolution of Puerto Rico's status takes this bad idea off the table, as statehood would, or converts America's interest in Puerto Rico from a witch's brew of domestic policy issues into a foreign policy concern, as independence would.

In the next chapter, which relates the history of the lobbying efforts to preserve the Section 936 gimmick, the latest maneuvers to expand the CFC option in Puerto Rico are described in detail. It is important to realize that these maneuvers are not just the proto-typical operations that surround the preservation of a generous tax subsidy. For the past 30 years, the Section 936/CFC drama has become the sum and substance of Puerto Rico's economic policy and the economic engine that has sustained a mode of governing that has produced both stagnation and corruption. The time and energy devoted by both Puerto Rican officials and U.S. political leaders to this tax gimmick have crowded out, time and again, the adoption of a credible, long-term economic policy for Puerto Rico. Considered in a vacuum, Section 936/CFC breaks for Puerto Rico are bad policy. In terms of what they displace, they are actually the obstacle to good policy.

Puerto Rico potentially has a bright economic future, and that future must begin with its natural assets and with what it has done right over the past century. On the positive side are its fair climate and location at a shipping crossroads in the South Atlantic, with good access to the Panama Canal and with the seaports of South America's Eastern Seaboard. Puerto Rico, as Mueller and Miles point out, has completed a transition from its agricultural, low-wage past to an incipient high-tech economy and has done so in roughly half the time this process took in many U.S. states. The island, moreover, has wisely maintained its close ties with the United States, giving it a fading, though still real, advantage over its Caribbean neighbors in securing access to American capital. Finally, it has an educated populace that shows a greater willingness to stay at home and make the island a success story.

Fresh ideas abound to tap into these resources. Hexner and Jenkins offer a series of ideas that, they argue, would be put into play if the alternative Puerto Rico chose were statehood. Overarching these ideas is the political stability that would ensue if the underlying relationship between Puerto Rico and the mainland were no longer an issue. Businesses worldwide look for and value political and economic conditions that afford them predictability regarding their holdings and profitability. This is not always, of course, an admirable characteristic, as predictable conditions are sometimes accompanied by dictatorial or authoritarian governance. Nonetheless, democratic governance offers the ultimate stability, particularly when it is alloyed with an enduring power like the United States.

Advocates of commonwealth or "enhanced commonwealth" status for Puerto Rico recognize this yearning for stability as the key to investment. It is the reason they insist on words like "compact" to describe the current Puerto Rico-United States relationship, because it lends an air of legal permanence. This is little more than public relations, and both the Puerto Rican government and business must know it. The history of U.S. tax preferences for Puerto Rico tells a tale of impermanence. The turmoil over the Vieques firing range only underscores the volatility. Businesses hear Puerto Rico's blandishments, but they heed not what San Juan says but what Washington does. Interestingly, the governor of Puerto Rico, Sila Calderon, gave an address on Puerto Rico's future at Princeton University in April 2002 in which she referred to the failure of the U.S. government "to develop the promises of the commonwealth." Her address, and another delivered the next day at Rutgers University, linked this failed promise to federal business tax preferences.[19] It was the only specific policy issued mentioned in published reports of her speeches.

For Hexner and Jenkins, such thinking is a dead end, but the explicit linkage of commonwealth and a discredited tax scheme is at least honest. They propose a different course. Under statehood, to begin with, the Section 936 and CFC tax regimes could not exist. Puerto Rican business enterprises would face the same tax policies and schedules as any other U.S. business. A Congress desiring to encourage economic growth in Puerto Rico would do so only as a subset of the general task of creating policies that foster economic growth across the board. As the recent example of California shows, there remains ample room for the states, regardless of their economic resources, to enact pro- or anti-business policies and to encourage or discourage growth, regardless of federal policies.

Thus, Hexner and Jenkins propose reforms that require actions both by the federal government and by any future State of Puerto Rico. Their plan has five major parts:

- Privatization of inefficient public sector corporations
- Increasing investment in infrastructure from the private sector
- Improvements in government efficiency
- Enhancing natural competitive advantages in education and tourism, and
- Reforming the tax system[20]

Obviously, some of these reforms can be undertaken right away, and they should be. Any completed path to permanent status for Puerto Rico will be a multi-year, perhaps as much as a decade-long process. In fact, several of these ideas have been on the table for a while in Puerto Rico, with local partisan divisions and debates. The ruling PPD has been strongly opposed to privatization and has pursued a course of government-funded infrastructure development that, most concede, has had mixed results with more projects promised than delivered. The full implementation of any of these ideas rests upon resolution of the status question and an understanding of island and mainland policy as a comprehensive whole.

Privatization themes have permeated modern political discussions in various countries, including Margaret Thatcher's Great Britain, the United States (where the Bush Administration is aggressively seeking to expand out-sourcing of government functions), and the former Communist Bloc countries, where central governments have rapidly depressurized. Puerto Rico has had government-led economic policy for decades and the local government manages a wide variety of services that could be handled in the private sector. In 1972, the Puerto Rican government took over the island's privately owned telephone company and the privately owned shipping company.21 In fact, government of all kinds (federal, island-wide and municipal) consumes an astonishing three-fifths of the Gross Domestic Product of Puerto Rico, twice the percentage in the United States and considerably more than our poorest state. This percentage changed little even in the growth period of 1992 to 1997 (see Chart 4 below) under the Rossello administration.

Chart 4

Percentage of GDP Devoted to Government

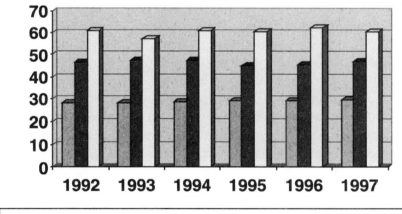

Adapted from Hunter, Institute for Policy Innovation, July 2003

Rossello and the pro-statehood NPP pursued privatization with some significant successes in the 1990s. Navieras, the government shipping line obtained in 1972, was sold to private investors in 1995 for cash and stock. It was resold to the Holt Group, Inc. in 1997, and its history immediately afterward underscored the inefficiency of continued government ownership of enterprises with private sector potential. Within the first three years after its purchase, according to its president Thomas Holt, Navieras "refurbished and remodeled its ocean-going vessels, containers and information technology" with an infusion of $1 billion. Navieras maintained a 98 percent on-time arrival record and found that it could reduce its government-padded employment rolls by 40 percent without impacting its service level. Moves like this helped to fuel the shipping boom that Puerto Rico enjoyed in the 1990s.[22]

Already a world-class hub for the transshipment of ocean-going cargo, Puerto Rico increased its maritime trade at an average annual rate of 6.2 percent. Exports increased at an average annual rate of 7.4 percent and imports at an average annual rate of 4.7 percent. The total value of Puerto Rico's domestic and foreign trade in the fiscal year 2000 was $65.5 billion, with exports valued at $38.5 billion, yielding a favorable trade balance of $11.5 billion. The United States as a whole has faced a chronic trade imbalance, fueled by huge imports from such low-wage economies as the People's Republic of China. This only underscores the power of Puerto Rico's natural asset, its strategically located and spacious harbors, when fueled by investment in infrastructure and privatization of bloated government-run corporations.[23]

An even more significant act of privatization occurred in 1999 with the sale of a controlling share of the government-run telephone company, Puerto Rico Telephone (PRT) to the private sector. The buyer was a consortium led by the Texas-based communications company GTE, which included the leading island financial institution Banco Popular. As Jose Martinez wrote for the publication *Caribbean Business*, the sale transformed the local carrier into a "lean, customer-oriented, technology-driven company."[24] The new, private PRT established as its goal to become the telecommunications hub of the Caribbean. It invested its first $20 million in training and service improvements, and, in a little more than a year, it had reduced installation back orders by 20 percent and increased the percentage of repairs made within 24 hours by 50 percent. It did all this with fewer employees, as 1,200 employees of the government-owned PRT took early retirement offers and were not replaced.

PRT President Jon Slater emphasized how the changes implemented at the company had everything to do with a new mindset and exposure to a competitive market. "We are not trying to change the local culture of our employees," he told *Caribbean Business*, "just the way business is conducted. We need to be customer and market sensitive in order to succeed . . . We're not the only game in town anymore."[25] Sensitivity to competition in the marketplace is also the reason why the new PRT planned to expend $1 billion over five years to improve its communications infrastructure and increase the quality and reliability of its service. It is a portrait of the rippling success that can come with the end of unjustified and inefficient government monopolies.

Finally, like other jurisdictions in the United States, Puerto Rico has made some efforts to privatize, either in whole or in part, its overcrowded prison system. Puerto Rico's poverty and high crime rate has caused the building of a prison system that, in the fiscal year 2000 alone cost the government a record $471 million. This number represented an increase of some $274 million just since 1992. The average daily cost of housing a prisoner on the island in 2000 was $76, about the same as "a night in a country inn," according to one commentator.[26] By the year 2000, Puerto Rico had four privatized prisons in operation, with an average per-prisoner cost of $64 per day. These prisons were still owned by the government, but operated by private companies under government contracts. Legal issues regarding facilities standards and political factors continue to hamper this form of privatization, but Puerto Rico's high costs justify continued efforts to explore the alternatives.

Further privatization of public companies essentially halted in 2001 with the inauguration of Governor Calderon. The Calderon administration, constrained by the power of labor unions on the island, a key base of support, is wedded to this big-government approach. For example, Puerto Rico, as noted in the previous chapter, has some of the highest energy prices in the United States. Efforts to privatize the system, even partially, have met with strong resistance from the PPD, amid promises from Calderon that, in uncertain times, no one who works for the Puerto Electric Power Authority (Prepa) would lose their job. Reacting to a new local law that gave Prepa more operating flexibility, Calderon told a reporter in August 2003. "My government has a specific public policy against the privatization of public services."[27]

As Dr. Lawrence A. Hunter of the Institute for Policy Innovation in Washington, D.C., describes this stance, "It is an almost inevitable consequence of elected politicians' not knowing how to revive economic growth and [finding] it difficult to resist using the public payroll as a means to provide voters financial support they cannot secure for themselves[.]"[28] Big government and stagnant economy become a vicious cycle.

Hexner and Jenkins next suggest increasing private investment in infrastructure. Here, too, the current PPD government, fierce defender of commonwealth status, resists change. Nearing the last year of Calderon's four-year term, the government is promising to accelerate public works projects, including the building of two high-tech industrial parks in Dorado and Aguadilla. This version of Puerto Rican industrial policy continues to vest in government planning alone the role of picking winners and losers. It goes hand in hand with efforts to resurrect federal tax preferences for mainland companies. Businesses on the island may be more pleased by the government's recently announced plans to streamline the permit process for construction and operations in the country. Calderon announced that her Administration, with the blessing of its powerful Environmental Advisory Council, would reduce a complex nine-step permit process at the Environmental Quality Board to a three-step process.[29] Baby steps perhaps, but progress.

Regarding their third plank, improvements in government efficiency, Hexner and Jenkins stress the need for performance-based budgeting. They cite the example of New Zealand, a locale with some similarities to Puerto Rico. New Zealand is a collection of islands, has a population of 3.95 million in 2003 (Puerto Rico's is estimated at 3.89 million), has a colonial history that mixed a European power with a native population, and has made a recent transition from an agricultural society to a technology-services-tourism economy. New Zealand has established production targets for its government employees, and these targets are included in job descriptions and reviews and in budget requests. Diligently setting and striving to meet these targets guides agency's decisions about necessary staffing levels. Combined with retirement incentives and limits on new hiring, Hexner and Jenkins state, these measures can reduce the size of government while improving its output.

Enhancing Puerto Rico's natural advantages in education and tourism is also within reach. Controlling local crime will be one key to increasing tourism, which has suffered in Puerto Rico as elsewhere since the terrorist hijackings of 2001. Despite its urbanization and high population density, Puerto Rico remains a significant draw for American and European tourists who seek a foreign flavor with a domestic base. The island offers ecological variety in a compact format, with no point on the island more than three hours' drive time, on good roads, from San Juan. Education, as touched upon in the previous chapter, is a much more complex issue that, in economic terms, can powerfully influence Puerto Rico's future course.

Over the course of the 20th century, Puerto Rico invested in widespread education and enjoyed, as a result, significant labor force advantages over many of its Caribbean neighbors. Those investments have lagged behind the mainland standard, however. In 1990, Hexner and Jenkins note, education spending accounted for only 18.3 percent of general fund spending on the island, slightly more than half the 35 percent of total expenditures devoted to education by U.S. governmental units that same year. State by state spending data on education does not generally correlate with educational success, though it is clearly a factor. Family composition, study habits, and school size all seem to bear a stronger direct relationship with educational achievement than does per-pupil spending. In another of its anomalies, Puerto Rico does not participate in the National Assessment of Educational Progress. More accountability and more school choice could work productively with Puerto Rico's existing devotion to family to enhance its investment in human capital.

Mueller and Miles are emphatic in their argument that such investments have been vital to past periods of Puerto Rican economic growth. Given the reliance on the shifting sand of Section 936 and the turmoil over cultural heritage and political status, it might even be said that human capital investments have represented Puerto Rico's only true long-term investment over the centuries. As Mueller and Miles write, "Puerto Ricans are probably the best educated Hispanic population in the world, clearly so with respect to technology and modern business. In fact, the median education of the Puerto Rican labor force is almost identical to that on the mainland. Education therefore is an established strength in Puerto

Rico."[30] These authors argue persuasively in favor of the education decentralization program (the Community-Based School Program) carried out by the Rossello administration. They note that each year of completed education raises Puerto Rico's net income per person by at least $2,100 per year.[31]

Hexner and Jenkins' final plank involves an overhaul of Puerto Rico's tax system. This is a much greater challenge than merely recognizing the failure of the Section 936 tax gimmick and allowing it to expire on schedule, without some kind of CFC-oriented rescue. Our focus on the Possessions Corporation Tax System, and its exploitation by capital-intensive U.S. mainland companies, might foster the impression that Puerto Rico is, overall, a low-tax jurisdiction. It is anything but. Its out-sized government needs operating revenue. Dr. Hunter's July 2003 study for the Institute for Policy Innovation identifies seven "layers" of taxation that plague and retard the Puerto Rican economy. These include: business income and capital gains taxes, individual income taxes and capital gains taxes, death taxes, real and personal property taxes imposed at the municipal level, excise taxes, municipal business licensing fees, and employment taxes (including Social Security, Medicare, and unemployment insurance, from which Puerto Ricans are not exempt).[32]

First, the existence of so many tax layers only further underlines the inequity of the Section 936 tax scheme, whose benefits go disproportionately to very large enterprises. Job creation in most economies, including Puerto Rico's, is accomplished by small businesses and entrepreneurs. In fact, U.S. Census Bureau data and a study by the research firm Estudios Technicos in 1999 showed that small businesses on the island generate 63 percent of all new jobs and account for 48 percent of the gross national product.[33] For many *potential* businesses, however, the mere existence of a costly web of taxation means not just reduced profits, but an inability to form. Add to this the potent mix of a fully applicable (since 1981) U.S. minimum wage law, generous welfare benefits and subsidized government services, and the economic rationality of taking a low-wage job is destroyed for many entry-level Puerto Rican workers.

As Thomas Sowell would observe, the question here is what kinds of incentives and consequences are at work in Puerto Rico's tax system? We have shown that the current system, relying on imported capital that returns as tax-free revenue to the mainland, has produced all kinds of incentives for the perpetuation of the neo-colonial status called commonwealth. The option of statehood would end this status forever and eliminate all variants of Section 936 and CFC law from the scene. Independence, on the other hand, would expose the harsh reality of Puerto Rico's oppressive local tax and spending regime and force the government to find ways to eliminate its disincentives for Puerto Ricans to found businesses and to seek and hold jobs. The adverse impact of minimum wage laws will not, of course, go away with statehood, but they could be addressed under independence, as Puerto Rico would find itself in even more intense competition with other nations.

Hexner and Jenkins, like Hunter, devote a major portion of their criticism to Puerto Rico's excise tax. Because it is part of the United States, Puerto Rico is inside the U.S. tariff wall, so that any policy or practice applied by Washington to foreign-source goods applies to Puerto Rico in the same way as it does to the 50 states. Puerto Rico trades with the United States freely and benefits from this "interstate" access to U.S. markets. Conversely, economists estimate that U.S. goods shipped to Puerto Rico sustain roughly 320,000 jobs on the mainland. The excise tax, which is imposed on most goods used or consumed in Puerto Rico, is imposed differently depending on whether the goods originate in Puerto Rico or enter from the outside. The "outside" includes the mainland United States, so that, in effect, there is something of a tariff on goods entering Puerto Rico from the rest of the country. Put bluntly, U.S. taxpayers are subsidizing a protectionist dependency in the Caribbean!

The excise tax is set at 5 percent, and the valuation of goods is based on 72 percent of the expected sales price for locally produced goods and 132 percent of the sales price for goods entering from outside. Thus, the local excise tax is basically 3.6 percent and the "overseas" excise tax is 6.6 percent. No matter what the source of the goods, these excise taxes are collected and paid into the Puerto Rican treasury. The Hunter study points out that these taxes are collected in a cumbersome and inefficient manner. Because the manufacturer must collect the tax and, in theory, as the product moves from wholesale to retail, so must every other purchaser-reseller along the chain, the tax can cascade into multiple taxation of the same item. Enforcement of the tax presents significant problems, and, of course, goods often fail to sell at MSRP (as automobile dealers like to style it). Tax avoidance is a problem and, perhaps most important of all, the ultimate impact of the tax on what a consumer buys is invisible at the endpoint when the purchase is made; this shields the tax from public scrutiny and criticism.

Naturally, Puerto Rico takes advantage of two peculiar twitches even in the excise tax law. These twitches came into the spotlight in 2002 when the Government of Puerto Rico increased the excise tax on beer by 78 percent. Miller, Budweiser and Coors and other American beers were all hit with the additional tax, but the government found a way to basically exempt the lone local Puerto Rican brewery Medalla. The senator from the capital of Colorado, Ben Nighthorse Campbell, threatened to retaliate against this protectionist act by repealing Puerto Rico's rum tax rebate. For many Americans, this was the first news they had received that any such tax rebate exists.

The rebate, it turns out, is a species of the general spectrum of U.S. excise taxes on goods imported into the mainland from Puerto Rico. Under existing law, all the revenue collected by the United States on these imports is sent to the Puerto Rican treasury! In short the federal government collects a tariff, which it then deposits into the treasury of the territory from which the import came. Not surprisingly, this is the only intergovernmental arrangement of its kind permitted by the U.S. government. But the second half of the policy is even more astonishing. This second rebate – or "cover over" as it is sometimes called – involved the U.S. collection of an excise tax of $13.25 per proof gallon on imported rum. Call it the Tanqueray Tax. Like the other excise taxes it collects, the federal government takes the rum proceeds and rebates them to Puerto Rico and the Virgin Islands. Here's the kicker. The rum tax is "covered over" to these two jurisdictions *no matter where the rum is produced.*[34] Americans who drink Venezuelan rum are providing a subsidy to the governments of Puerto Rico and the Virgin Islands. It's enough to make a man order a daiquiri.

Like so many other elements of the U.S.-Puerto Rican relationship, the rum rebate has little logic but much political momentum behind it. It will play out in the political arena as a battle between

American and Puerto Rican distillers. It is actually a battle between Puerto Rico's past and its future. All of this only reinforces the views of economists that the excise tax system – hidden from public view, difficult to enforce, regressive in the sense that it is paid by the poor and the wealthy alike – cries out for reform, as so much else of the Puerto Rican tax system does. Hexner and Jenkins have proposed that the excise tax be replaced with a consumption tax that shifts the collection point to the final sale. In response to those who argue that Puerto Rico's many small, family-run businesses would avoid collecting this tax, they point to a 1994 government study that revenues would actually increase under this approach. They note that an estimated 90 percent of Puerto Rico's retail sales occur in large, high-profile shopping areas.

The Hunter study also recommends that these excise taxes, which yield an estimated $320 million to Puerto Rico, be phased out. He, too, recommends movement toward consumption taxes, which have the benefit of being transparent and are sensitive to political conditions. Mueller and Miles offer an appropriate caution about such a shift, noting that sales taxes can represent a tax on investments in human capital. They locate some two-thirds of Puerto Rico's modern growth in the investments that have been made in developing human capital through education and other measures to improve the learning and earning capacity of the people. Consumption taxes can, however, be structured to take human capital concerns into account, excluding taxes, as some American states do, on necessities like food, clothing and medicines.

The Calderon administration, to say the least, has not taken such recommendations to heart. Between 1970 and 1990, with a pause and even decline during the years of the Barcelo Administration, government grew more than three times faster than the private sector, a period when the two major parties in Puerto Rico split possession of the governorship. From 2001-2002, under Governor Calderon, privatization efforts ceased and the number of government employees grew. Excise taxes were increased and the reduction of income taxes has been postponed. Moreover, one of the "reforms" heralded by the Calderon administration was its decision to expand the hours of "service" at the island's treasury offices so that the excise tax could be collected more expeditiously. The implementation of bad policy will now only cost the economy more as a shortsighted effort to raise revenues will only reduce consumption.

The far more sensible course would be for Puerto Rico to simplify its web of taxation and cut taxes across the board. Such a step, as has been shown elsewhere, will increase both revenues and tax compliance. Limited as its experience has been with tax-cutting (apart from the Section 936 tax boondoggle), Puerto Rico has documented the truth of this axiom several times in recent decades. The focus of this chapter, in fact, of this entire book, is the impact commonwealth status, and its linchpin, Section 936, have had on draining the U.S. taxpayer without lifting the Puerto Rican economy. The prohibitive rates that characterized the local income tax on the island for the duration of "Operation Bootstrap" actually interacted with the U.S. tax law not only to stifle growth further but to help drive the island's best and brightest to seek their careers and fortunes on the mainland. This perverse policy matrix brought U.S. factories to the island, exported their profits to the mainland, while simultaneously driving Puerto Rico's intellectual capital offshore.

In the 1970s when Laffer Associates entered the picture in Puerto Rico, Operation Bootstrap had lost momentum and the island had launched a search for fresh policy ideas. In a misguided attempt to inject growth into the economy by growing government, a Keynesian path of fiscal stimulus was chosen. Under this regime, total government spending increased an astonishing amount, from 30 percent of gross product in 1969 to 47 percent in 1975. Current government expenditures as a percentage of gross product began the decade at 22 percent and had risen to 35 percent by 1978. All kinds of predictable results, uniformly negative, had ensued. In 1975-76 the Puerto Rican economy experienced the first fall in output since 1947. Private investment, crowded out by government borrowing, fell to little more than half its peak in 1970. Unemployment rose, employment participation rates declined, and the private savings rate plummeted.

The island's own Keynesian approach was matched by a similar thrust from Washington. As mentioned throughout the course of this book, Puerto Ricans pay no U.S. income tax and yet, over time, the amount and variety of benefits they receive from Washington have steadily increased. The first half of the 1970s was one of the periods of most rapid expansion of such transfer payments. Overall in Puerto Rico, transfer payments, primarily financed from Washington, grew sixfold between 1969 and 1977. At mid-decade Puerto Rico was added to the food stamp program and 70 percent of the island's population was eligible to purchase subsidized food. Just as the capital available to the private sector to invest in, start and expand businesses was decreasing, the average Puerto Rican worker was being offered incentives not to work or to increase his earned income. As the 1979 Laffer Associates report to the governor phrased it, both federal and local Puerto Rican government policy dramatically increased the "wedge," that is, the difference between the cost of employing a worker and the amount of income that worker actually receives from employment.

The wedge consists of income, payroll, excise, sales and property taxes, business licenses, plus an assortment of costs associated with the hiring of tax lawyers and accountants who help the company maintain compliance with government regulations. In the 1980s the term "unfunded mandates" was developed to describe the cost of such regulations when imposed on the states by the federal government. Such mandates can be imposed on the private sector as well (environmental regulations are an example), and they represent a form of taxation that imposes a cost of doing business that is not reflected in higher income earned by workers. These are all parts of the "wedge" and a significant percentage of that wedge is missing income a worker may never realize he has forfeited. Raise the wedge high enough, and the job offer does not materialize. Combine the wedge with generous transfer payments and it becomes a rational decision for a worker to leave the labor force or for a potential second wage earner in a family to remain idle.

The dynamic could hardly have been more efficient in limiting Puerto Rico's long-term economic horizon if it had been designed with this purpose in mind. Ironically, when Puerto Rico pondered the deterioration of its economic fortunes in the mid-1970s as Operation Bootstrap's program of industrial incentives lost steam, a coterie of U.S. intellectuals, certainly well-intentioned, proposed a series of policy ideas that rejected tax rate cuts in favor of measures they thought would increase taxpayer compliance and spur government revenues. Public savings would accomplish what private investment was unable to achieve. This episode in Puerto Rico's economic history is worth discussing in more detail, because it is what first brought the author[*] of this chapter into direct contact with the unique policy experiment taking place in America's semi-colony in the Caribbean.

Puerto Rico's generosity to the American manufacturers it sought to attract to the island under Muñoz Marin's administration was mirrored in local tax policies that had the opposite effect on the population's motivation and ability to accumulate wealth. For the vast majority of Puerto Ricans during this era (1948-1977), the benefit of having no federal income tax to pay was more than offset by draconian local tax laws that featured high income taxes, punitive estate and gift taxes, and a form of marriage tax that penalized couples for wedding and having the second earner remain in the labor force. For a time the magnet of Section 936 worked its magic to bring new enterprises to the island and the destructive effect of local tax policy was masked by this good news, but events on the mainland, especially John F. Kennedy's program of tax rate reductions in the 1960s, soon put Puerto Rico at a severe disadvantage.

Muñoz Marin and his PDP had increased the progressivity of Puerto Rico's income tax in the 1940s, setting a top rate of 72 percent at $200,000 of income with an additional "Victory Tax" of 5 percent (military victory was secured in 1945, but this tax, certain as death, went on for many decades). When the Kennedy rate cuts took effect, the 70 percent marginal rate in the United States was not reached until the taxpayer had $100,000 of income. In Puerto Rico, this high rate was triggered at $60,000. A second cut in 1969 moved the top federal marginal rate on earned (wage) income to 50 percent. People with high wage-earning capacity in Puerto Rico had a fresh, sharp incentive to move that capacity to the mainland. Initially, the lessons of these long-overdue rate reductions was lost on the Popular Democratic Party, still wedded as it was to the Operation Bootstrap formula.

By the 1970s Puerto Rico's highly progressive structure for income taxes stood in even starker contrast to mainland rates. In

---

[*] Arthur Laffer, see Introduction

1974 under the Popular Democrats, with the Victory Tax still in place, the local government imposed a graduated surtax, beginning at an annual income of only $10,000. At this income level, both individuals and married couples with combined income entered a 32.45 percent tax bracket. When income reached the threshold of $22,000, the marginal tax rate rose to 51.82 percent. Finally, at $200,000 of income, the marginal tax rate reached 87.10 percent. Not surprisingly, with marginal rates this high there was relatively little government revenue from the highest bracket relative to the total. In fact, in 1977, tax returns reporting income of $22,000 or less provided some 75 percent of local income tax revenue.

Puerto Rico in this period also punished married couples (or couples contemplating marriage) by refusing to allow them to choose whether to file jointly or separately, as they could on the mainland. A manager earning $32,000 a year in Puerto Rico would pay local taxes at a top marginal rate above 50 percent. If he married a woman who was making $12,000 a year and paying the much lower marginal rate for an income of that size, he would immediately convert all of her income to the 58 percent marginal rate, increasing the couple's tax bill by nearly $3,500 dollars, a very expensive honeymoon. A couple facing this situation would either forgo the second income or move to the mainland, since their U.S. citizenship made this option just a plane ride (costing much less than $3,500) away from realization. It is easy to see how few motivated, upwardly mobile professional couples would remain in Puerto Rico under this regime.

Conversely, as immigration data from this period showed, the rapid rise in transfer payments on the island actually operated as a magnet to draw nonworking individuals back to the island. Net immigration back to Puerto Rico exceeded 1 percent in 1972 and remained there through 1977. The evidence suggested that this net immigration did not represent retirees but rather younger, working-age people. Unemployment rates for males rose rapidly and topped 22 percent by 1977.

Estate and gift taxes made matters worse. Local law actually sharply limited the amount of money a parent could transfer to a child, taxing any amount gifted in excess of $500 per year. This tax applied even to tuition paid for the child's private education, operating, therefore, as a tax both on the parent's accumulated financial capital and the child's heritable intellectual capital. The exemption on personal estates disappeared at a mere $60,000 in value, and the tax reached 70 percent for estates valued at $6 million or more. Worst of all, perhaps, there was no charitable deduction under the local income tax, a feature that only increased the pressure on government to be the provider of social services on which the people rely. Missionary groups, including religious charities, had traditionally opened hospitals and other social assistance agencies in Puerto Rico, but local tax law did nothing to bolster local contributions to their efforts.

How Puerto Rico came to impose and repeal the graduated surtax of 1974 is worth further description, because it is a microcosm of what can pass for economic wisdom and of the speed with which government can, when it has the will to do so, change course. The U.S. economy sailed into difficult waters in the early 1970s and the temptation to pursue bad policy choices in Washington and San Juan proved impossible to resist. The 1970's was the decade of stagflation, an unprecedented situation that Keynesian economics had not prepared the nation's leaders to address. The appearance of low growth and inflation (not yet approaching the double-digit level of the Carter years, but high enough to panic otherwise sensible men) led both to counterproductive intervention in the economy (President Nixon's wage and price controls) and useless symbolic gestures (President Ford's campaign-style "Whip Inflation Now" buttons and paraphernalia in 1974). Consistent with its long history of trailing the U.S. economy, Puerto Rico's fortunes ran parallel with those of the mainland economy in the summer of 1974, with unemployment, as usual, twice as high.

In September 1974 Ford responded to the advice he received from the Keynesian advisers gathered at his Economic Summit Meeting and proposed a five percent income surtax as a putative means to control inflation – this, while the Dow Jones Industrials were sagging below 600. As a former House Republican leader and as a fiscal conservative, Ford should have recognized the danger to which this proposed tax hike was exposing his party in Congress, with the elections but weeks away. The people have their own way of providing government with sound economic wisdom, and fortunately, in the United States, the people get this chance every two years when they choose the entire membership of one chamber of Congress. The Republicans lost three dozen seats in November 1974 (Watergate and ethics certainly played a role in the GOP defeat), and Ford's team was reeling.

At this point, at the risk of self-flattery, let Jude Wanniski describe the turn the Ford Administration took on taxes:

> *In the days immediately following the GOP debacle, White House Chief of Staff Donald Rumsfeld was persuaded by Laffer that the correct policy was tax reduction, not tax increase. It was for Rumsfeld's assistant, Richard Cheney, that Laffer drew his Curve for the first time on the back of a paper napkin in the Two Continents Restaurant a block from the White House. The stock market stopped its decline and began a serious advance in December 1974 with the first hints that Ford was turning on tax policy. And while the "tax cuts" announced by Ford in February* [of 1975] *were inefficiently designed by the administration's conservative Keynesians, it made a great deal of difference to the economy that there would be some movement down the Laffer Curve instead of a leap upwards.*35

Congress signed the Ford income tax rebates into law in March 1975. Electoral forces and a change in economic advisers had produced a change in course. As many others have found, however, changing course in Puerto Rico is a much more challenging proposition. First of all, the island holds its "national" elections every four years. PDP Governor Hernandez Colon, drawing on the same Keynesian advice that had led Ford down the garden path, had proposed a 5 percent income surtax to counter stagflation on the island. Colon's PDP controlled the general assembly and its members did not face the electorate until November 1976, when Colon's second term would end. There was no opportunity to draw the same Curve and the same conclusion about tax hikes for Colon's people, so these ideas were taken by the author of this chapter to Colon's opposition, Carlos Romero-Barcelo of the pro-statehood New Progressive Party (an ironic name in this context, since one goal of these cuts was to lessen the punitive progressivity of the Puerto Rican tax code!).

To the everyday Puerto Rican citizen, the Colon surtax was one more bit of toxic public policy, and it was quickly dubbed *La Vamparita*, or the "Little Vampire." Colon went even further in the direction of policies to extract the lifeblood from the Puerto Rican economy, naming a Committee to Study Puerto Rico's finances that was studded with conservative Keynesian superstars from the mainland, among them the late James Tobin, the Sterling Professor of Economics at Yale; William Donaldson, founder and dean of the School of Organization and Management at Yale (Donaldson is now chairman of the Securities and Exchange Commission); and Kermit Gordon, then-president of the Brookings Institution. The Tobin team spent $120,000 in public money to produce a report in December 1975 that proposed additional ways to harness revenue for the Puerto Rican government so that it could continue to fund infrastructure projects.

La Vamparita had plenty of fresh nighttime companions among these proposals. The report recommended the elimination of Puerto Rico's existing tax exemption for land and real property, including personal residences. Second, it urged tighter enforcement of the existing code and more aggressive collection practices. One of the more obvious results of Puerto Rico's anti-wealth-creation tax regime had been the perpetuation and strengthening of its underground economy and its informal system of bartered services. Third, the report argued for increased taxes on consumer durables, even adopting an early environmentalist idea of taxing automobiles at a higher rate if they had poor gasoline mileage. Another proposal targeted the deductibility of interest charges on individual consumer debt.

The PDP government had paid for these ideas, but their real cost was to be charged at the polls in the November 1976 elections. The author of this chapter gave Romero-Barcelo the same advice he had offered to the Ford administration after its 1974 embarrassment at the polls. The PDP could have observed these effects on its own and perhaps made the right decision to fight stagflation with strict monetary policy and tax relief. Instead, it went in the opposite direction, extending the economic grief of the first half of the decade. The overall Puerto Rican unemployment rate topped 20 percent, even as the economy picked up on the mainland and the U.S. unemployment rate dropped to seven percent. Puerto Rico's joblessness was now nearly three times that of the mainland. The situation was untenable for the PDP, and the 1976 election denied them control of the island's legislature for the first time since 1940.

The electorate reached up and pulled the fangs of *La Vamparita* from its neck, rejecting the PDP with a firmness that Ferre's breakthrough in 1968 had not embodied, and inaugurating a period of real political competition in Puerto Rico that persists to this day. The election drove a knife into the heart of La Vamparita and it expired in January 1977 as Barcelo took office.

In a sense, the Reagan revolution, delayed by the four-year election cycle on the island, reached Puerto Rico two years before it ripened on the mainland, even if its effect on "national" politics there over the next 20 years proved to be less pervasive. The Romero-Barcelo administration (1977-1985) cut the local income tax and lifted the 5 percent Victory Tax in 1978. The result was an increase in tax revenues of $15 million by the following year. Inflation slowed and the unemployment rate dropped by 1.2 percent. Another round of reductions was implemented in 1979, leading to a 13.5 percent increase in tax revenues and 100,000 more taxpayers appearing on the rolls. The value of tax cuts as a way of stimulating tax compliance was once again vindicated. On an island where an estimated one-third of the population files no tax return at all, these developments demonstrated an untapped potential for growing the economy without starving the legitimate needs of government.

As helpful as these steps were, a more extensive reformation of Puerto Rico's tax structure was needed. Laffer Associates carried out an analysis to this end and delivered a landmark report to Governor Barcelo in April 1979. The report noted the advantages Puerto Rico enjoyed as a result of its legal relationship with the United States: a common currency, a customs union, and unrestricted movements of capital and labor. These factors helped to bolster the island's economy in the 1950s and 1960s, but the unprecedented climb in government taxes and spending in the 1970s had contributed significantly to the reversal of the island's fortunes. The elimination of La Vamparita and the repeal of the Victory Tax represented sound steps, the first in many years, in the right direction, but more was needed. The Puerto Rican economy was still high on the Laffer Curve in at least three areas that our report was able to identify.

The first one was the tax on corporate-held capital, which during this era may have been effectively taxed at 90 percent or higher when one accounts for under-reporting of depreciation, inventory expense, capital gains taxes, excise and sales taxes, and the cost of those ever-present accountants and lawyers mentioned above. The second group taxed near what our report called the prohibitive range (the level at which the activity taxed disappears and a rate reduction will result in a real increase in the activity and increased revenue to government) was the high personal income group, who still faced marginal tax rates that reached nearly 83 percent even excluding excise taxes. The third, and just as important, was the low-income group whose decisions not to increase their work effort or to acquire training (which sometimes requires forgoing current income) hurt both their own and the island's long-term economic prospects.

Our report urged an economic revolution whose primary theme was the termination of confiscatory tax rates that hurt every sector of the Puerto Rican economy, including the government sector. In a real sense, the Reagan Revolution, at least in its economic aspects, was conceived in the United States but born offshore in the final 18 months of the decade of the '70s. Our 1979 report recommended a phased, four-year reduction in personal income tax rates. The first year, the elimination of the Victory Tax, had already been accomplished the previous year. For the second year, the report recommended that the top tax rate be further reduced from 79 percent to 70 percent with all the other rates reduced proportionately. For the third year, the rate should be lowered further still, to 60 percent, and for the fourth year, to 50 percent, again with all other rates reduced proportionately. This phased reduction would give different sectors of the economy time to adjust and would allow the Barcelo Administration to monitor the effect of the cuts and to assure that they matched expectations.

Others reforms were just as urgently needed, as our report underscored. We recommended a widening of the tax brackets for married couples to minimize the tax penalty they faced when two wage earners combined income. The corporate tax rate should be reduced from 45 percent to 25 percent and the Section 931/936 tax exemptions for foreign and mainland corporations should be phased out gradually in the interest of equal treatment of corporate entities under the tax code. Government expenditures as a percent of the gross product should be allowed to fall, without alarm, as this would reflect only an expanding economy and a reduced demand (through increased private employment and earnings) for government assistance and other spending programs. The report also urged an examination of opportunities for privatization of publicly owned corporations (a process that gained some genuine momentum in the 1990s) and a requirement for corporations that remained under government control to earn a market rate of return on invested capital.

Finally, the Laffer Associates report called for a narrowing or abandonment of the island's micro-managing minimum wage law, which set different minimums for different sectors of the economy based on their putative "ability to pay." This economy-distorting policy not only kept the least-skilled workers off the lowest rung of the ladder by denying them opportunities priced at their ability to perform, but it also had the perverse effect of punishing companies for being successful. Ultimately, wage supplements, when fiscal conditions permitted, would be preferable to minimum wage laws of any kind because such supplements increase the attractiveness of work for the laborer while adding nothing to the wedge experienced by employers in making a decision to hire. Our last recommendation was directed at Puerto Rico's import duties and at mitigating the differences in effective tax rates among different imported goods, as well as between imported and home-produced goods.

The theme here for Puerto Rico's economic well being is simple. Economically speaking, no island is an island. Historic relations between the United States and its last semi-colony have resulted in a pseudo-benefit to the Puerto Rican of being exempt from federal income taxation. What would seem to have been a great blessing actually led to a detachment of the Puerto Rican people from feeling the sting of federal policies that drew income from them while delivering the mixed blessings of government that provides for some legitimate needs while delivering transfers that actually stifle personal initiative and productivity. Worse, the absence of federal income taxation distracted attention, for a time, from the fact that Puerto Rico had steadily built a system of local taxation that was also stifling personal initiative and productivity. The federal portion of this double jeopardy was politically immune from the feelings of the Puerto Rican people, even if they perceived the overall effect of government policies on their economic well-being.

The Section 931/936 debacle, discussed in Chapter 8, was for Puerto Ricans truly a last straw event. It provided an illusion of growth that was in fact a massive subsidy to a handful of industries that employed an unimpressive number of local people and transferred profits and intellectual capital to the mainland. In sum, the federal and local policies actively discriminated against and overtaxed Puerto Rico's domestic manufacturers, to support a self-feeding and expanding government that viewed itself as the only force in the commonwealth able to manage savings, investment and infrastructure development. Because that is a false picture of any citizenry, including the people of Puerto Rico, it was a policy mix certain to fail. The Barcelo Administration was the first in the modern history of Puerto Rico to take on this policy mix. It did so before the same revolution in tax rate reductions reached the mainland, and our report played a key role. No island is an island, and the ideas that captured the attention of political leaders in San Juan soon played themselves out in the remarkable economic turnaround in the United States in the 1980s.

Because of the continuing status issues, however, and the dependency of both the local government and the people on U.S. generosity (Washington's apology for Puerto Rico's diminished share of freedom), the reform process on the island remains incomplete to this day. Still, the basic facts are worth reciting again and again. In 1987 Puerto Rico cut the marginal rate on personal income taxes, reducing the top rate, for example, from 67.6 percent to 41 percent. The results repeated the lessons of 1978-79. As the Hunter report notes:

- Puerto Rican taxpayers declared 50 percent more income than in 1986;

- The total number of registered taxpayers rose by a third;
- Total tax revenues increased by 28 percent;
- The percentage of the personal income tax paid by the highest-income bracket ($30,000 and above) rose from 45 percent in 1986 to 62 percent in 1987; and
- Lower-income taxpayers not only paid a lower proportion of total tax revenues, but the dollar amount they paid actually declined in real terms.36

In the wake of the phase-out of Section 936 and in lieu of any extension of CFC preferences, Puerto Rico needs more of the medicine that will come with real tax reform and pro-growth and pro-work policies at home. The combination of the transfer payments described in the previous chapter and the warping tax preferences described in the next chapter have produced the economic stagnation described in this chapter. The ultimate factor that the United States and Puerto Rico must contend with is the spread of free trade in a globalized economy. The worries about Japan, Inc. that dominated U.S. economic weeklies a scant 15 years ago now seem quaint. There are rivals everywhere and the rising influence of the World Trade Organization (WTO) and of area agreements like NAFTA, MERCOSUR and the European Union bar the way back. The Hunter report even argues that WTO precedents may doom any revival of Section 936 as an illegal export subsidy.

Far from the present situation being all Puerto Rico's fault, Washington has sometimes tried to have at least its cake crumbs and eat them, too. Puerto Rico enjoys great advantages from its relationship with the mainland, but that has not prevented other concerns from making the most of that relationship. One clear example is the cabotage laws. The mainland United States consumes the vast majority of Puerto Rico's exports. Under the Jones Act of 1920, goods and produce shipped by water within the United States can only be transported on U.S.-built, -manned, -flagged, and –citizen-owned vessels. This law makes sense in the context of a barge shipping coal from West Virginia to St. Louis. Americans would not expect to see a Norwegian tug and Chinese crew handling this shipment down the Ohio to the Mississippi River.

Nonetheless, the same law applies to goods and produce

shipped between San Juan and Miami, as well as from Juneau and Honolulu to Seattle or Los Angeles. After the adoption of the North American Free Trade Agreement, our own non-contiguous territories, Puerto Rico, Hawaii and Alaska alike, have suffered an enormous disadvantage vis-à-vis Mexico and Canada, which are closer to the United States and under no requirement to use anything but the least expensive shipping method to get their goods and produce to our shores. Protecting the American shipping industry is a valid concern, and its national security value cannot be discounted. The Puerto Rican economy would be greatly helped, however, if Congress could find ways to support the competitiveness of U.S. flag vessels that does not rely on penalizing the 49th and 50th state, as well as, potentially the 51st.

Puerto Rico would be better served in this area if it were an independent nation and joined NAFTA. It would then, ironically, have a freedom that Alaska and Hawaii do not possess. Rather than face this issue and others squarely, Puerto Rico's government today is wrestling with its multiple identities and seeking to join as many international organizations as will permit it to enter, or as the U.S. State Department will tolerate its trying. The recent tension between Secretary of State Colin Powell and the Calderon administration is likely to continue as Puerto Rico attempts to maximize the benefits of international independence while maintaining its various draws on the U.S. Treasury. This tendency is both rationally and emotionally satisfying for the island's psyche. However, it is also relentlessly short-term in its application. Perhaps tension will be, as it often is, the midwife of positive change. This is not inevitable.

In the meantime, amidst the maneuverings in San Juan and Washington, the long-term goal of economic growth continues to elude Puerto Rico. It is a sad commentary on the lack of statesmanship both in the north and the south. A transition either to independence or to statehood would cause dislocations and pain to various sectors both in Puerto Rico and on the mainland. Like a stern exercise regime, real gain would entail real pain for many people who have come to rely on the existing, mutually harmful regime. Congress has, however, become more adept (too adept, some would say) at writing generous transition rules that eliminate the cliffs in policy change that sometimes force public officials to draw back from needed reforms. From Capitol Hill to La Fortaleza, the power exists to shape policy changes that smooth the descent from the current precipice and lead the way to a road that can carry its passengers to the summit.

The statistics with which this chapter began, the appalling poverty rate, an unemployment level 2.75 times that of the mainland, per capita income that is barely half of the poorest American state – all of this more than a century after the people of Puerto Rico rushed into the arms of their American liberators – these are conclusive arguments for action that rises above narrow self-interest. Even boldness would be appropriate. The Hunter report concludes with a bold idea of its own, a recommendation that the entire island of Puerto Rico be designated as a national enterprise zone. This idea has been advanced by the Institute for Policy Innovation, and its leaders, including, most notably, William Bennett and Jack Kemp, as a cure for the economic woes of various sections of the United States. The idea begins, as it should, with recognition that current policy frameworks for blighted areas are not working.

In order to qualify as national enterprise zones, the locality or territory would have to have a minimum (say, 5,000) number of residents and have an elevated poverty rate or depressed median household income, specified as some ratio to the national average – no need to worry, Puerto Rico would qualify under almost any definition. Hunter adds that the qualifying area would also have to demonstrate compliance with the educational standards of the No Child Left Behind Act of 2001. Within the zone, businesses would have the choice of two federal tax regimes: 1) the current law with an enhanced research and experimentation tax credit, or 2) a flat tax for income actively generated in the zone. Hunter suggests that, with a properly defined tax baseline, the federal rate could be 20 percent or lower. Residents of the zone would also get a choice of tax regimes, either the current federal system or some variant of a flat tax that would be sensitive to family size and/or reward savings.

Hunter leaves many details, and even the entire question of status, unresolved in sketching out this plan for a better future for depressed economic zones. The important point is that the era of Puerto Rican special privileges is over and new ways of building pro-growth and pro-family economies must be found, tested and perfected. The rest of the world is moving ahead and growth rates are besting those of Puerto Rico. The thinking that delivers this kind of result will not be bound by the mistaken development models of the past, and certainly not by that unique Edsel model that ran out of gas in San Juan in the early 1970s.

Had Puerto Rico won its independence in 1994, it might be speculated that it would enjoy good relations with the United States, have established its own membership in MERCOSUR and NAFTA, reduced the cost of government and reformed its tax system in order to extend a welcome to businesses that could go anywhere but see the value of locating in the warm-weather gateway to the Americas, the Panama Canal, and even, in this age of space exploration, the planets and stars. Had Puerto Rico become a state in 1994, it can be calculated that it would now enjoy an even higher degree of integration into the U.S. economy, a significant voice of in Congress, a reliable political climate to reassure business, and an acceleration of growth that would have, by 2000, produced an additional $1,343 in per capita income.[37]

Puerto Rico has come halfway along these paths, but it is now standing still. Its capability and its future can be glimpsed in various ways through the present fog. It can be seen in the magnificent ports whose promise is echoed in its name. It can be felt in the cosmopolitan flavor of its capital, a city that is the product of the confluence of many cultures and peoples. It reverberates in the roar of a crowd at a major league baseball game at Hiram Bithorn Stadium. It can be heard in the restaurant and café chatter of a populace, who love both their island home and the great United States whose uniform their sons have worn in battle. It can be glimpsed, finally, in an awesome structure at Arecibo that peers into the far corners of the universe.

The radio telescope maintained near this north coastal town in Puerto Rico is the most sensitive in the world. It is also one of the most visually impressive structures on the planet, a spherical dish more than three football fields across surmounted by a 900-ton platform. Its antennae are cooled in liquid helium, to dampen the noise of electron vibration, and it is said that this telescope can pick up the sound of a telephone conversation on Mars. Perhaps that conversation will happen someday, thanks, in part, to the work of a

Puerto Rican named Orlando Figueroa, a graduate of the University of Puerto Rico at Mayaguez who heads NASA's Martian exploration project.

Arecibo and gifted scientists like Figueroa are not the public image of Puerto Rico in many quarters, even in some quarters of the U.S. Congress. Still, this image offers a vision of a future for the island that marries technological prowess with human talent and unfolds new possibilities. Even ears far less sensitive than those aimed skyward at Arecibo can pick up the murmurs of these possibilities. At the dawn of the 21st century, we can turn our back on these murmurs or amplify them into a symphony of hope for our neighbors in the last American colony.

CHAPTER 7

Making Lemons into Lemonade

Broke and feeling sorry for myself, I once again touched down on Puerto Rican soil. I did not know if I had it in me to begin all over again. The agency operation that I built into an insurance powerhouse was now in shambles. I was starting almost from scratch, territory that was no more comforting because it was familiar.

Somehow, once again, this drubbing became the best thing that had ever happened to me. My failure taught me the most important lesson in personal finance, which was learning to tell the difference between real money and funny money. It was 1978, and I was 37 years old.

I could not have picked a worse time to start over again. The United States was in a serious recession. The misery index, the sum of the unemployment rate and the prime interest rate, was soaring. Market lending rates were as high as 20%. Unemployment in the U.S. was at 10% and in Puerto Rico it was at 24% (unemployment peaked near 25 percent during the Great Depression). The great industrial boom, which had begun in the late 1950s in Puerto Rico and continued to the mid-1970s, had come to a screeching halt. The tax breaks that had fueled Puerto Rico's economic breakout two decades earlier were powerless in the face of the Carter recession and their job-producing capacities had been shown to be largely illusory.

Of course, when times are tough, they are not equally tough on everybody. I saw an opportunity. The Puerto Rican Treasury had never recognized the concept of Non-Qualified Deferred Compensation, and the maximum local income tax rate stood at a hefty 67%. With the help of a pana, I sought and obtained a ruling through the Puerto Rican Treasury that accepted the deferred compensation concept. Next, I got licensed with a variable annuity and mutual fund company and set up a broker-dealership to sell securities. I bypassed the National Association of Securities Dealers (NASD) and was regulated directly by the Securities and Exchange Commission (SECO). I had more brass than brains, because no one told me that it was good to seek the shade of the NASD umbrella. I took the opportunity to hire every stockbroker in town as a part-time producer for me, while each of them kept his office with Merrill-Lynch or Paine-Webber. It was an offer they couldn't refuse.

My variable annuity had a 17 percent, four-year, front-end load and paid the broker a first-year commission of 30 percent. I signed up all the universities, hospitals and even the U.S. 936 companies that were tax exempt. Non-Qualified Deferred Compensation was an idea whose time had definitely come in Puerto Rico. The stockbrokers were anxious to sell my product because they were starving. It was the depth of a bear market and nobody was investing in common stocks. The variable annuity sold itself because of the system I put in place. Suppose, for example, a professor made $30,000 per year and her spouse was a doctor or lawyer who made $100,000. She would pay $20,000 in income taxes on her earnings alone. By putting all her income into my plan, she saved $20,000 in taxes and the broker made a $9,000 commission.

The stockbrokers were lining up at the front door to sell my product. My life insurance agents would go with them to sell the life insurance, too. Every stockbroker in town and every insurance agent wanted to work for me.

Another great thing happened. After I returned to Puerto Rico in 1978, my former wife and I had a conversation and we decided it might be a good idea if our two sons, Michael and Sasha, lived with me for a while. Sasha was 14 and Michael was 10. We didn't go to court to arrange this, we just decided between the two of us and did it. Julie and I settled most of our problems that way, without court interference. But that's another story.

The best thing that ever happened to me was becoming both mother and father to my kids for a time. It was poetic justice of a sort that I took two roles where previously I had less than one. When you are a Master of the Universe, but not the master of your sons' household, you are an orphan in reverse. It wasn't as if Julie disappeared from the boys' lives. She was always there, but when your kids live with you and you become a single parent, you create a bond that is very difficult to duplicate. My return to Puerto Rico was a second chance in more ways than one.

By 1982, I had one of the top three insurance/broker-dealer operations in the Aetna system, which was 200 strong. It was both the largest insurance and largest broker dealer operation in Puerto Rico. Actually, my operation sold more life insurance than any other within Aetna. A few operations did more securities business. All told, I had half a floor in Banco Popular Center (10,000 square feet) in San Juan, offices in two other Puerto Rican cities, and offices in the Virgin Islands with more than 200 producers, sales staff and clerical people.

That year Aetna decided to transform its distribution system into company-owned offices, rather than independent franchisees or general agents. They bought me out. As part of the deal, I stayed on for three years, but no longer, because being an employee was of no more interest to me than it had been a quarter century earlier.

By 1985, I was out of the insurance and securities business and had enough real money (not funny money, like stock options) to live modestly for the rest of my life. I was 44 years old.

What now? Business no longer beckoned to me, despite the many offers I was getting in the financial services industry. Piling millions on top of more millions was an irresistible summons for many business people my age, but those sirens were not singing to me. I had no desire to live lavishly. I was comfortable, with no financial pressures. Even so, there was a vacuum in my existence. It was time for a new career, a career that was about something more than the next brass ring on tomorrow's carousel.

I started writing a newspaper column, did some consulting, bought a house in Vail, Colorado, and started spending four or five months a year there. Hearkening back to my days in the Army in Alaska, I became a ski instructor. As long as I earned enough to maintain my lifestyle and preserve my capital, I would be fine. I realized that working six months per year was more than enough to accomplish my goals. If I had continued to build my fortune in business, instead of eventually leaving this world with a net worth of a few million dollars, it might have been a few hundred million. I have friends who took this, the road more traveled by. They have had heart attacks, strokes, and other health crises. Some of them are my age and they don't see the light of day during their 60-hour workweeks. What does it profit them? And for whom? We kid ourselves and say we are "doing it for our families." Nonsense. It is our great grandchildren's ex-husbands and ex-wives that will reap the benefit.

My column became quite popular because there were two things that I could contribute. Having spent over 20 years in the insurance and securities business, I had learned all the inside baseball and could advise my readers on how to keep them from being hoodwinked by the industry. Every insurance agent and stockbroker now hated me. The other thing was that I was financially independent, unlike many finance gurus and self-help advisors whose work is designed to end their own financial dependence by tapping that of their audience.

Since Scripps-Howard owned the local newspaper, I was asked if I wanted to have the column syndicated. I said yes, and within a couple of years my prose was going out to roughly 350 newspapers nationwide. It was very rewarding to get dozens of letters every week from people all over the country thanking me for the insights they got from my column. That prompted me to write a book and launch a newsletter, "Money Mastery," which I published for seven years.

All this occurred in the 1980s, the "decade of greed" as the Democratic Party christened it. Republicans called it the Reagan Revolution. In a crucial way it was neither of those things. It was, instead, a decade of rediscovery of first principles, for which Ronald Reagan could justly take credit. The power of free enterprise, grounded in a system of personal and political freedom, has been demonstrated time and again. As for greed, certainly there are men and women motivated by the power of gold in every era, as the history of Section 936 shows, but the engines of economic growth in the 1980s and 1990s only proved how mysterious a process real economic progress is.

In the 1990s, political figures discovered Silicon Valley – as a source of campaign contributions. With that discovery came all the speeches and the talk of government subsidies and public-private partnerships to identify and support the next generation of cutting-edge industries. It's not a matter of the chicken and the egg. Government can neither predict nor produce creative genius. Given a chance to pick economic winners and losers, Leviathan is rarely going to choose a Stephen Jobs, a high school dropout tinkering with computer circuits in his garage. Ten years later, after the inventor-geniuses have rewritten the rules and helped develop businesses the world has never seen before, government can sit up and take notice. Ask Puerto Ricans if Columbus discovered their island. Like government in most eras, the Admiral of the Ocean Sea did not create the places where he landed, but rather he passed through them, with mixed consequences.

The dogmas of central economic planning played themselves out to their inevitable conclusion in the Soviet Union in the early 1990s. The seeds of that collapse were present at the beginning, and people like me who were able to flee the planting were fortunate. In the West, the distortions of well intentioned central government policy are more subtle, but no less real. They are at their worst when they lead not to collapse, where renewal can finally take place, but to a deadlocked status quo, where a powerful minority benefits at the expense of the majority and blocks all reform. This happens daily under the communist system, where the minority is composed of personal and family networks masquerading as ideologies. It happens in a quite different way in democracies, where, as in the case of Puerto Rico, the minority is a group that benefits from programs or tax breaks that are not available to everyone and that favor a select few.

As I made my own fortune in New York and Puerto Rico, I was dimly aware of the havoc public policy wreaks when it preys upon the worst in human nature. Only when I had the time to write my column and examine U.S. economic policy toward Puerto Rico did I clearly see just how much damage the dogmas of the stormy past could do. Once again, my path, formerly as an entrepreneur, now as an analyst and advocate, pointed me back to the island territory whose quiet present belied the bands of steel that held it captive.

I was now 48 years old. Part of my consulting practice was giving personal finance seminars to groups of top corporate executives. My contacts for this enterprise came from my days selling Non-Qualified Deferred Compensation programs to the Fortune 500 companies that operated in Puerto Rico under that targeted tax provision we discussed in previous chapters called Section 936.

This part of the story begins with my meeting a brilliant young lady. Inez was in her late twenties and was the head of human resources for a mid-sized company in Boston that hired my services. We started dating, and she introduced me to a friend of hers who was a tenured professor of international law at Northeastern University. Since my column appeared in the Boston Globe from time to time, he had been a reader of mine and wanted to meet me. We became instant friends.

Manuel Rodriguez Orellana was and is a Puerto Rican independence party leader. This fact led to very vivid political discussions. Manuel is one of the most brilliant individuals I have ever met. Our discussions have always been enjoyable and challenging.

Up to the point of our meeting, I was just a businessman, totally oblivious to the political situation in Puerto Rico. No one should underestimate the tunnel vision of the average citizen meeting the travails of daily life, and business people may have the narrowest tunnel vision of all. I was all but clueless about the impact of Puerto Rico's status on the island's economy and on U.S. taxpayers. Manuel opened my eyes and showed me how totally out of whack Puerto Rico's current status really is. In a nutshell, the island is an impoverished U.S. colony whose maintenance requires our nation's taxpayers to fork over billions of dollars. As the previous chapters examined this issue in some detail, much of this goes to support a welfare system that only reinforces this poverty and dependency.

As we stated previously, the real reason for this tragedy, the tragedy of the last American colony, is grotesquely simple: Puerto Rico is what it is and not what it could be because of the influence of a select few U.S. companies that pocket billions of dollars through such targeted tax breaks as Sec. 936. This fact is as simple as an oak tree, but its roots and branches now radiate in all directions. One way or another, a portion of the excessive profits generated for these companies by this tax preference makes its way back into the political system, as gifts not only to the Puerto Rican political parties but also to U.S. members of Congress and the Republican and Democratic parties. Money has been called the "mother's milk of politics." That money has been the fuel of Puerto Rican servitude as well.

The corollary of being a man without a country is to be a man of many countries.

Since I was both an American taxpayer (I had properties and other investments on the mainland on which I paid federal taxes) and a Puerto Rico resident (where I paid local Puerto Rican taxes), not to mention a European immigrant who had lived under repressions of both the right and left, this subtle tyranny by tax gimmickry riled my Russian soul.

My friend Manuel was an "independentista" and I loved America. His arguments at first provoked me, because I was a believer in the ability of the individual to rise above his circumstances. America had been good to me. It became clear to me, however, with my friend's persistence, that a nation can be yoked, even if some or even many of its citizens toss off that yoke. It was some point like this that Gerald Ford was grasping for when he made his gaffe in the 1976 presidential debates about Eastern Europe being free. Puerto Rico is not a Captive Nation in the sense that Hungary and Romania were, but it does occupy a halfway house of freedom and conditions there are deplorable.

My friend and I shared ideas as to how Puerto Rico's status could be changed and it could achieve some form of sovereignty. My friend was committed to independence, and he persuaded me that this status would be better for both Puerto Ricans and mainland Americans. Statehood would be better as well, and the common enemy of both statehood and independence was the status quo.

At about the same time as I was making the acquaintance of Rodriguez Orellana, I was on a flight from Newark to San Juan where I sat next to the vice president of finance of a New Jersey-based pharmaceutical firm. He had attended one of my seminars and began to tell me how much he enjoyed the presentation. We started talking about Section 936. By this time, he had had a couple of drinks, and he confessed to me that his firm didn't need this tax break to operate in Puerto Rico. Tax break or no tax break, the company would still be there. He told me that their operation was capital intensive and they hired mostly engineers. The same engineer who earned $50 an hour in New Jersey got paid $25 an hour in Puerto Rico, so that their productivity (cost per unit of production) in Puerto Rico was much higher than on the mainland. As to the question of going elsewhere in the world, that might be an option for such things as garments and shoes, but not for pharmaceuticals. FDA rules all but guarantee that drugs made for the U.S. market are manufactured domestically. Puerto Rico is under the U.S. flag. South Korea and India are not.

This was fascinating because this same company was publicly claiming that if Sec. 936 were phased out, it would leave the island and thus create long unemployment lines in Puerto Rico. I asked him about those public claims and he assured me that they were "pure bullshit. We just want the tax credits for as long as we can get them. It's just good business, and we will say anything we need to say to keep them."

As a devout capitalist, that made all the sense in the world to me. Logic and ethics are two different branches of knowledge and, all too often, two divergent courses of action. As a U.S. taxpayer, however, this logic really angered me. "Why should I and other Americans subsidize a Fortune 500 company just because it has the political influence to make me do it?" My sense of justice impelled me to ponder ways to counter that political influence.

First, it occurred to me that one man's tax break is another man's tax burden. I counted among my friends and clients in Puerto Rico some very wealthy people. Those whose capital was generated and maintained in Puerto Rico had every reason to desire more control over the destiny of that capital. They might be fierce allies in a fight to change Puerto Rico's status. If nothing else, it would be clear to them that the tax preferences enjoyed by U.S. companies doing business on the island were reflected in excessive taxes on locally owned businesses.

As motivation for local capital to get involved in the debate over status change, status had to be positioned as a drain on local capital. Fortunately for the argument, and unfortunately for the island, this is the reality. In essence, economically, if the present status continues, the divergence, which began in the mid-seventies, between the U.S. economy and the Puerto Rican economy will make assets on the island worth cumulatively less than the comparable assets on the mainland. If Puerto Rico were to be fully integrated into the U.S. economy and have political self-determination through representation in Congress, capital assets in Puerto Rico should grow at the same rate as those in the average state.

This analysis made good financial sense as a means to encourage local capitalists to weigh in on the status issues. To do so they would have to buck the local political parties and what they were proposing. This required both an intellectual and a social leap, grounded in the recognition that the local party interests were financed by U.S. capital, which resisted change in order to continue pocketing billions in tax credits every year.

We formed a small and loosely knit network and started getting together and planning strategies. We were total neophytes when it came to the political hunt and chase. One of the Washington lobbyists who gave us a presentation framed the issue in the starkest terms. "Here is how it works," he said. "You find yourself a member of congress and you give his campaign some money. Then you give the campaign some more money and he starts to listen to you. Then when he sees that you are helping him, he becomes a champion for your cause, provided it does not hurt him politically with his voters." This was a jaded view of the American political system, but sadly it has proved to be all too accurate in many cases.

The first objective was to kill the tax boondoggle that was keeping the island a captive "welfare territory." The new effort at Puerto Rican status change of which I was a part took its first shot not at a physical place like Concord Bridge but at a place in the Internal Revenue Code called Section 936. That is where I first saw this lobbyist's axioms about campaign cash in action, at the White House and among many members of Congress, and it was not a pretty sight.

My first move was to send a letter to all the pharmaceutical companies that benefited from the provision, inviting them to a seminar where we would discuss the importance of Section 936 in keeping their operation in Puerto Rico. This was nothing new because I often held seminars, either on my own or sponsored by financial institutions or law firms, that dealt with a mix of personal finance and general business and economic conditions. I even invited Peter Holmes to attend. He was the head of the pharmaceutical industry lobbying office in Washington. The idea was that since many of these companies were my clients anyway, and since they knew who I was and they all read my column, we might examine, objectively, what Section 936 meant to the drug companies. If there was a good economic case for these preferences, I wanted to know what it was.

It is not difficult for an active consultant to find his potential conflicts of interest multiplying in such a context. Section 936 was of disproportionate importance to a modest-sized island economy. To make matters more intricate, I had become involved, as an employee benefits consultant, in helping relocate labor-intensive portions of the Puerto Rican economy to other nations in the region, like Haiti and the Dominican Republic, where education levels were far lower and economic conditions far poorer. The bottom line for the pharmaceutical companies was this: as long as a certain portion of their manufacturing process was done in Puerto Rico, they still qualified for the Section 936 tax credit and the CFC, even if 90 percent of the product assembly was done by workers bringing home wages of $1 per day (in those days) on nearby islands.

At first, some of my colleagues considered me a "traitor" because I was perceived to be taking jobs away from Puerto Rico. When President Reagan established his Caribbean Basin Initiative, it required U.S. companies to make certain investments in the Caribbean if they were to continue enjoying the benefits of Section 936. Job creation among Puerto Rico's poorer neighbors qualified for this purpose. Overnight, I became the savior of Section 936 for some of these companies and an agent in helping them reduce their labor costs and boost productivity.

Having an enlightening discussion about the value of tax preferences to Puerto Rico's economy during my seminar would have afforded me an opportunity to write about the subject. As it turned out, my seminar was totally ignored. Perhaps the invitees thought it would become some kind of "gotcha," but I believe the reality was that these pharmaceutical giants felt very confident in their position because of their inroads into the two main political parties locally and their influence with members of Congress in Washington. They had no need to explain or defend their position publicly. They were over-confident to the point of arrogance.

What was most important for me was that I had found a new windmill to charge against.

Given my reputation and existing work relationship with these companies, and believing in the public spiritedness of the topic we had proposed, I took this rejection hard. Had the pharmaceutical companies merely sent a lowly clerk or bureaucrat to sit-in on our seminar to offer reasons why Section 936 was vital to their presence in Puerto Rico, I might have been less zealous about this issue. Instead, this rebuff gave me a clear green light to hit them with both barrels.

About the same time, a Puerto Rican economics professor, Dr. Rivera Ruiz of Interamerican University, did a study of the effect of Section 936 on the island economy. The results were eye opening. The study showed not only that Section 936 was doing nothing positive for our economy, but also that it was actually causing it harm. Prof. Ruiz presented the study in an academic forum, but the orchestrated voices of the pharmaceutical firms drowned out his core message. The local papers made it appear as if the study proved that Section 936 was good for the Puerto Rican economy. Of course, local media were dependent upon paid advertising from these companies and their suppliers and distributors, so they did everything they could to please "the hands that fed them."

We had our work cut out for us.

I then wrote a column in the San Juan Star that summarized the negative effects of Section 936. The furor that this piece produced was incredible. No one had ever spoken out publicly against Section 936 for fear of what the pharmaceutical lions would do to them and their livelihoods. The editor of the paper invited me to lunch and showed me a file of dozens of letters that had been sent to the paper threatening to pull all their advertising if they continued to run such articles.

My next step was to produce a special section of my newsletter that delved into the subject in depth. Essentially, I offered my readers a detailed analysis of the Ruiz report. Dozens of letters went to the local newspaper asking it to run a more detailed article than the one they had already published. The editor took a chance and had me produce a special, two-full-page section with graphs and charts, based on my newsletter piece, which detailed the effect of Section 936 on the Puerto Rico economy.

Once again there was a flood of threatening letters to the editor, but there were also many letters that praised the article. Many prominent local people began writing special columns in other newspapers as well, claiming that my articles had challenged their assumptions and that they, too, were re-examining the benefits of Section 936. For a tax provision, this one was treated as mighty personal. My answering machine was filled with threatening phone calls to the point where I no longer answered the phone.

I was undeterred and wanted to keep the buzz on the issue going. Next I produced an eight-page insert in the San Juan Star in the summer of 1995 that promoted my newsletter locally, offering as a sample a complete reprint of the back-issue that had dealt with Section 936. It was called "Puerto Rico at the Crossroads." Again, there were more phone calls, letters, editorials, and opinion pieces by local business, civic and political leaders. I had overcome the first round of the battle, indeed the first round of any policy battle. I had spoken the unspeakable and surmounted the barrier of isolation, and I was still standing. The threats to cut off advertising to newspapers were no longer effective, because everyone was talking about the issue, and such a cut-off would only have been a self-inflicted wound for the advertisers.

Emboldened, I converted "Puerto Rico at the Crossroads" into booklet form in 1996, had it translated into Spanish, and saw to it that thousands of copies were circulated locally in both languages, even sending a few thousand copies to Washington for members and staff of the U.S. Congress to digest. I was relishing my newfound career as a pamphleteer, with all its resonance of Tom Paine and "Common Sense." We had begun to reach around the gatekeepers of information, the "official sources" who dominate what most of us read and hear. We had a subject with a life of its own, and we had something more: a movement.

The issue gained such notoriety that even the then-current governor of Puerto Rico, Pedro Rossello, had to take a position against Section 936 (despite the heavy support he enjoyed from Section 936 companies). By this time our ad hoc coalition had found and established our champions in Congress, and soon there were hearings in the tax-writing bodies of both chambers of Congress, the House Ways and Means Committee and the Senate Finance Committee.

That year, Congress decided to phase-out Section 936 over a 10-year period. Attempts to phase-out the Puerto Rico counterpart to the credit had been made, though unsuccessfully, in the past, as the government kept adding extensions and exceptions. The biggest tax giveaway, the income approach to tax credits, was now to be eliminated within two years. As time wore on during the phase-out, more and more of the firms losing Section 936 would abandon it for CFC status, which would allow them to defer their tax liability as if they were operating in a foreign land. For now, we had won the first leg of our battle and were now ready for the second. The heart of the injustice wrought by Section 936 was not just the economically futile benefits it conferred on a handful of companies that did not need them. The essence of the problem remained the long-standing and unresolved nature of Puerto Rico's status within the U. S. legal system. Section 936 was a gourd growing on the tree of a false doctrine.

In the near-century that Puerto Rico had been a U.S. territory, Congress had never passed a bill to authorize its people to hold a referendum on their preferred political status. Wave after wave of national liberation movements had passed over the modern world, releasing long-time colonies in South America, Africa and Asia. The ideological gods of fascism and communism had come and gone, though a few convulsive outposts of these dogmas remained. Tyrannies of personality had risen and fallen. The path of the modern world was toward greater freedom and self-determination. Moreover, the epicenter of this change was the political West and, in particular, the United States. One prominent political scientist even optimistically proclaimed this evolutionary progress "the end of history."

By some means, however, each of these waves passed through the Caribbean and left untouched two near neighbors. One, of course, is Cuba, the last vestige of communist hegemony in the hemisphere. The other is the last American colony, Puerto Rico. The hollow excuse of the apologists for the status quo was that Puerto Rico somehow had it better than a nation or a mere state. It was a Commonwealth and no bill of improvement was needed. Tying the future of nearly 4,000,000 people to the survival of their tax haven, the pharmaceutical companies and other Section 936 and CFC beneficiaries spent millions of dollars to promote this misconception. The reality of Puerto Rican life under the U.S. territorial clause was never allowed to come to the surface. Events nonetheless have a way of lifting the truth before our eyes.

CHAPTER 8

Biography of a Tax Gimmick[1]

No one will ever know how many revolutions are made or broken in boardrooms and hearing rooms, around conference tables where glass containers hold spring water not Molotov cocktails. Historians who subscribe to "great man" theories of events and look for epic struggles in the tide of human affairs often have little patience for the click of time's economic balance wheels. The fervor of the Puerto Rican drive for independence, a drive that led to death but not mass death, to famous men wounded but not killed in assassination attempts, to fiery political speeches but not street conflagrations – that fervor faded not under the heel of police actions but the gavel of legislators manipulating the tax code.

On the whole, and for their time, Section 931 of the U.S. tax code and its antecedents and successors, as applied to Puerto Rico, were no fool's bargain. They played a vital role in jump-starting an economy that had languished for centuries, a land subjected to deadly assaults from wandering Caribs, harsh measures from a monarchy in Madrid, attacks from French and English seafarers, a beneficent invasion in 1898, and aggressive land acquisition from foreign agricultural corporations. Tax policy was a lever that had gone unused until it became a major component of social engineering in the 20th century. Indeed, the potential of this new lever went unrecognized for nearly half a century as Puerto Rico sorted out its unique economic identity.

Puerto Rico and U.S. Tax Law
Biography of a Gimmick

1921 — Congress enacts the Possessions Corporation System of Taxation as Section 262 of the Revenue Act of 1921, which eventually becomes Section 931 of the Internal Revenue Code. The provision exempts from federal taxes all income of individuals and corporations that originates in U.S. possessions, including Puerto Rico, subject to certain key limitations. To qualify for this exemption, the individual or corporation must derive 80 percent or more of the income from the possession (e.g., Puerto Rico) and at least 50 percent of the income must be from active involvement in commerce. Advocates for the legislation focused on arguments about double taxation and the competitiveness of U.S. firms against foreign companies in the territories. The Philippines, and not Puerto Rico, was the focus of debate.

1930s — New Deal projects and programs are applied to Puerto Rico by the Roosevelt Administration, without success. By the end of the decade, the island's economy remained dominated by agricultural production, primarily sugar cane. More than four in 10 Puerto Ricans were employed in farming, and only one in four worked in manufacturing.

1940s — The Popular Democratic Party, led by Luis Muñoz Marin, wins control of the local Puerto Rican legislature, and works with the U.S.-appointed governor of Puerto Rico, New Dealer Rexford Tugwell. Tugwell and the "Populares" embark on a failed experiment to stoke the Puerto Rican economy by focusing on small farmers and new profit-sharing arrangements.

Biography of a Tax Gimmick

1948   Operation Bootstrap begins. Recognizing the failure of liberal land reform, the Puerto Rican legislature passes the Industrial Tax Exemption Act, which mirrors the tax relief offered to mainland U.S. corporations under the Revenue Tax Act of 1921. The goal is to attract labor-intensive manufacturing employers to the island with a potent blend of local and national tax relief. Puerto Rico emphasizes its abundance of low-wage local labor relative to the mainland. Over the next few years, more than 100 new factories will open their gates on the island.

1954   The Puerto Rican legislature expands the Industrial Tax Exemption Act and makes it more generous. Originally, the exemption was phased out over time. When Puerto Rican officials concluded that this phase-out was a disincentive for companies to relocate, they provided that certain businesses would be exempt a full 10 years until 1964. In this same year, an overhaul of the Internal Revenue Code redesignates the federal tax breaks for Puerto Rico and other U.S. possessions as Section 931.

1950s   The Internal Revenue Service uses Section 482 of the Internal Revenue Code and begins to investigate a potential tax avoidance scheme used by corporations with common ownership. Section 931 corporations are part of the investigation. The IRS's concern is that these corporations may be illegally moving expenses from one corporation to the other to reduce their tax liability.

1959   Puerto Rican Governor Muñoz Marin asks the IRS to suspend these Section 482 investigations because they are "hurting Puerto Rico's ability to attract U.S. investment." The IRS complies and suspends the investigations until 1963.

1963	The Puerto Rican legislature amends the Industrial Tax Exemption Act yet again and offers exemptions that vary in length. Industries that located plants in the most under-developed areas of Puerto Rico receive exemptions for up to 30 years.
1963	New IRS rules to allow enforcement of Section 482 create fresh incentive for mainland corporations to transfer their industrial property, including "intangible" properties like trademarks and patents, to their Puerto Rican affiliates. This step allows more and more of these companies' profits to be attributed to the tax-free Puerto Rican affiliate.
1966	Despite its tax advantages, the Puerto Rican economy continues to be vulnerable to the normal fluctuations of the business cycle. To alleviate this problem, the Puerto Rican economic development authority, FOMENTO, decides to focus new energy on attracting capital-intensive, rather than labor-intensive, companies to the island. The new emphasis targets big corporations such as pharmaceutical and petrochemical companies.
1973	Labor unions led by the AFL-CIO launch complaints about the flight of U.S. manufacturers from the mainland United States and call on Congress to act. The House Ways and Means Committee holds hearings on an overhaul of the U.S. tax code and signals its intent to review the Possessions Corporation System of Taxation.
1974	By this date, some 20 major U.S. pharmaceutical companies have established manufacturing operations in Puerto Rico, responding to the enormous tax benefits of relocation there.
1976	Congress enacts the Tax Reform Act of 1976 and

Biography of a Tax Gimmick

preserves Section 931, modified and renumbered as Section 936 for corporations (individuals may continue to use Section 931 until 1986). The government of Puerto Rico leads the fight for the tax break by arguing that an "investment strike" will occur if the break is repealed. The House Ways and Means Committee capitulates to the argument that repeal will cripple the Puerto Rican economy and lead to mass migration to the mainland. The value of the tax break is even enhanced for U.S. corporations because it allows profits earned on the island to be repatriated to the mainland immediately rather than only when the Puerto Rican affiliate is liquidated. This change diminishes investment in Puerto Rico. Moreover, Congress allows island manufacturers to claim the exemption for profits earned passively, that is, through company investments and not the active conduct of the business, as the law had required since 1921. The drain on the federal Treasury from the tax gimmick increases.

1980　For three consecutive years the U.S. Treasury Department issues reports on the impact of Section 936 that critique it sharply as an ineffective development tool that enriches a narrow group of capital-intensive, not labor-intensive, industries and that costs the Treasury $3 for every $1 paid in wages to working Puerto Ricans.

1981　The Reagan Administration pursues and wins passage of the Economic Recovery Tax Act (ERTA), which features the Kemp-Roth 25 percent across-the-board income tax rate reductions.

1982　Deficit worries prompt the Reagan Administration to begin a search for nearly $100 billion in new tax revenues in the budget resolution. The Treasury Department turns once more to Section 936 and recommends to Sen. Robert Dole (R-Kan.) that its repeal be included in his Tax Equity and Fiscal Responsibility Tax Act (TEFRA). Pharmaceutical companies and other beneficiaries of Section 936 rally in opposition. They succeed in saving Section 936 but lose the 100% tax credit it provides for their profits in Puerto Rico. Instead, they are left with options that legally permit but limit their ability to attribute costs and profits to intangible assets held by their Puerto Rican affiliates. They view the result as only a partial victory because the benefit of the tax break is significantly reduced.

1984   A coalition of U.S. businesses with affiliates in Puerto Rico forms the Puerto-Rico-USA Foundation (PRUSA) in Washington to wage a full-time battle to protect Section 936 and its generous benefits from future erosion in the deficit politics of the 1980s.

1986   PRUSA concentrates its efforts and successfully blocks the Treasury Department from proposing repeal of Section 936 in the Reagan tax reform plan. Pharmaceutical companies benefiting from the tax law dominate PRUSA. The blocked reform proposals from the Treasury Department focused on gradually replacing Section 936 with a wage-based system of tax credits that would have cost less and rewarded job creation. The final bill signed by President Reagan did shift the tax burden from individuals to corporations and included a "super royalty" that made it harder for companies to move profits around and shield them from taxes.

1993   President Clinton's first budget plan proposes the elimination of Section 936, seeking to raise $7 billion in new revenue over five years. Taken by surprise, PRUSA and other supporters of Section 936 find themselves on the defensive as Hillary

Biography of a Tax Gimmick

Rodham Clinton devises a national health proposal that threatens pharmaceutical companies' freedom to set prices for their products.

Recognizing that the Section 936 break is incredibly expensive and no longer serving the interest of job creation and building the Puerto Rican economy, Congress revamps it. The existing credit was reduced to 60 percent, declining gradually to 40 percent in 1998 and beyond. The credit is made available only for income earned in the active conduct of a business. However, companies are given an alternative: they can claim a new credit for 60 percent of the wages they pay in Puerto Rico, as well as enjoy another credit for capital depreciation and part of their Puerto Rico income taxes. The new scheme does little to boost economic growth and job creation as it preserves the tax exemption for "passive" income and income derived from intangible assets.

1996   Congress finally enacts a 10-year phase out of Section 936. From tax year 1995 to 2005, corporations use a scaled-back version of Section 936 or choose, in the alternative, to deduct 60 percent of their capital investment and wage costs. The cost of this new scheme to the Treasury is smaller, and more targeted to job creation.

Throughout the phase-out period, however, companies with factories in Puerto Rico can convert these entities into "controlled foreign corporations," or CFCs. These CFCs can then enjoy the same tax status as the subsidiaries of U.S.-owned or controlled corporations operating in foreign countries, like Mexico or China. Under CFC law, the income from these enterprises is not subject to federal tax as long as the profits are not returned to the United States. In essence, allowing the CFC option, which most of the U.S. operations remaining in Puerto Rico elect to take, returns the tax situation in Puerto Rico to its original commonwealth status.

The CFC option differs from the original commonwealth arrangement, which spurred a period of high growth in the 1950s and 1960s, because it applies to corporations' passive and intangible assets. Thus, Puerto Rico once again serves not as a model for development but as an industrialist's model tax haven.

2002 The pro-commonwealth government of Puerto Rico proposes Legislation to allow CFCs to repatriate their profits to the United States and receive a 90 percent tax exemption. Sen. John Breaux of Louisiana introduces a bill in September 2001 that would allow an 85 percent tax exemption on these repatriated CFC profits. The bill dies in the 107th Congress.

2003 The pro-commonwealth government continues to press for a new repatriation option for CFC's. Sen. Gordon Smith, Republican of Oregon, introduces an amendment to the Bush Administration's stimulus package to allow all CFCs worldwide to repatriate income to the United States with an 85 percent exemption. Breaux successfully amends Smith's amendment to add Puerto Rican based firms to do the same. The Senate Finance Committee narrowly rejects the new Smith amendment, averting, for now, a full-scale re-enactment of the boondoggle called Section 936.

Biography of a Tax Gimmick

Tax policy, much like other aspects of public policy, tends to follow the law of unintended, foreseeable if unforeseen, consequences. It could hardly be otherwise for Puerto Rico and its unique history of unresolved status and unparalleled tax preferences. As the 20th century began, the potent mix of politics and profits that would dominate the island's economic picture at the end of the century had scarcely taken form. Puerto Rico in 1900 was just released from the grip of the Spanish Empire. The electronics industry did not exist. Pharmaceuticals were in their infancy, more a branch of botany than of biochemistry, and the practice of manufacturing and distributing medications to accepted standards of purity and efficacy had yet to be born. The U.S. federal income tax was still more than a decade and a constitutional amendment away from reality, and international economic policy was dominated by disputes over trade and tariffs, not comparative tax rates.

The shape of the modern dilemma over U.S. tax policy and its territorial possessions was determined, therefore, by a chain of events that involved little long-range planning and had their own sequential logic. One constant of U.S. intentions was expressed well by Calvin Coolidge's assertion in the 1920s that America's "business was business." This was as true of Puerto Rico as it was anywhere else. A mere two weeks after the U.S. flag was hoisted over Puerto Rico, a delegation of businessmen arrived from the mainland to assess investment opportunities on the island.2 Nonetheless, the establishment of special tax breaks, formally known as the "possessions corporations system of taxation," was not done at the behest of industries wishing to invest in Puerto Rico. That system instead operated like a saucer of milk left on the back porch of the U.S. economy: it appealed and offered sustenance to any number of potential visitors, some of whom were quite unanticipated when the saucer was set.

The first form of this tax break was enacted by Congress in 1921. Its underlying rationale had more to do with notions of tax equity and competitiveness for U.S. businesses operating overseas than it did with any desire to encourage development in the sense of nation-building. The prime advocates for this tax relief were U.S. business interests in the Philippines, and there is little evidence either that the legislation's sponsors gave much thought to Puerto

Rico or that the island made much use of the final provision to attract new industry in the first few decades after its adoption. U.S. businesses in the Philippines were concerned that they were losing ground to their British rivals because the Crown deferred any tax liability on income earned by foreign subsidiaries until that income was repatriated to Britain. Then as now, keeping up with the Lord Joneses was a key argument for U.S. industries pleading their cause before Congress. They insisted that to do otherwise was to subject U.S. firms with foreign operations to double taxation, as the Philippines did indeed levy taxes on their earnings there.

The first version of what became Section 246 of the U.S. tax code, as introduced in Congress, would have exempted from U.S. federal income tax all foreign source income, regardless of the country in which it was earned. Rep. Nicholas Longworth, later Speaker of the House, led an effort to save this expansive and expensive proposal by proposing limitations that would reserve its benefits for active businesses and deny them to wealthy investors in the U.S. who were merely passive investors. The Senate version of the idea won the opposition of Wisconsin Robert La Follette, who contended that it made little sense for the United States to subsidize the export of capital when it was needed at home.

The combined effect of these and other arguments was to doom the broad version of Section 246 and spawn what was called the Possessions Corporations System of Taxation. Keeping capital "at home" would be accomplished by restricting the tax break on foreign-source income solely to U.S. possessions. The Virgins Islands was the only exception. From this point on, a U.S. corporation doing business through a subsidiary in Puerto Rico would be treated as if it were operating in a foreign country, albeit one with workers who, since 1917, had been citizens of the United States. The restrictions Longworth had proposed were kept in this special tax break for U.S. possessions: the individual or corporation who benefited from it was required to receive at least 80 percent of his income from that possession source and at least 50 percent of the income must be from active engagement in the business. Just parking assets in Puerto Rico as a pastime was never intended by Congress to receive any tax rewards.

To the early 21st century mind, the idea that a tax break of the value of Section 246 could exist for decades like a Penelope without suitors is hard to accept. There were simple reasons why this tax preference mattered little to Puerto Rico until the 1940s. The industrial transformation that it would eventually spawn had not fully happened on the mainland. Before industries could be moved to a tax haven offshore, they first had to be created. Take just one example, the pharmaceutical company Hoffman-La Roche. The company was founded in 1896 in Basel, Switzerland by a 28-year-old man named Fritz Hoffman. Hoffman, along with his wife Adele La Roche, had a vision for the worldwide manufacture and distribution of medicines of uniform strength and quality.

The company opened a Chemical Works in Manhattan in 1905 and formed a branch dedicated to discovering new pharmaceutical compounds in 1910. By 1929 Hoffman-La Roche was large enough to need a new campus, and it relocated that year to Nutley, New Jersey. In doing so, the company was following a pattern that many pharmaceutical companies established in the 20th century, including in the geographical sense. A high percentage of America's home-grown and European-branch pharmaceutical companies are located in just five northeastern states. It was not, however, until the 1930s that Hoffman-La Roche introduced the nation's first commercially manufactured vitamins. In the 1940s the company introduced antimicrobials to the market. Section 246 was not originally written with Puerto Rico or any such industry in mind, but it would prove to be tailor-made for the pharmaceutical companies as they came into their own at mid-century.

Puerto Rico, in the meantime, was working its way very slowly through economic experiments that had one element in common: they relied on the island's colonial history as the source of cash crops produced for export. In the first half of the 20th century the primary crop was sugar cane, which displaced coffee as the island's leading export in the late 1800s. There were also smaller exports of tobacco, and, of course, of the distilled spirits that sugar cane made possible. The chief effect of American engagement in the Puerto Rican economy in these years lay in the development of larger producing plantations with absentee ownership. The relaxation of American tariffs on Puerto Rico's exports to the mainland under the Foraker Act of 1900 (free trade was not implemented until 1902 under this law) was desired by all, U.S. investors and Puerto Rican farmers alike. In an effort to resist the transformation of Puerto Rico's small-farm economy into a plantation economy, mainland corporations were limited to holding 500 acres of land; but this stricture was widely ignored.

Sugar flowed north and so too did the economic benefits of these investments. Puerto Rico had a low-wage economy that made this form of investment profitable. One source describes the average *campesino's* daily wage as 12 cents per child, four cents less than the contemporaneous average cost of daily hog feed in the United States. There was job creation with little wealth creation for the island. As one leading figure in Puerto Rican history put it during this period, "Puerto Rico was being treated as a factory, not as a free society."[3] Superficially, as would happen in the second half of the century under even more favorable tax preferences, Puerto Rico's economy appeared to prosper under this regime. In the first decade after its acquisition by the United States, Puerto Rico increased its export of sugar almost four-fold. The total value of articles traded between Puerto Rico, the United States and European countries rose 400 percent. The era of King Sugar began, but for the working farmers, the *peones*, conditions did not markedly improve.

A few statistics suffice to show how concentrated wealth had become by the late 1920s. In terms of land, notwithstanding the legislative maximum, by 1917 there were 477 corporations, individuals, and partnerships that owned more than 500 acres. Combined, these individuals and entities owned more than a quarter of the island's arable acreage. By 1925 three corporations alone controlled almost 44 percent of Puerto Rico's sugar production. That production totaled an astounding 660,000 tons. The absentee corporations, the "sugar trusts," controlled 59 percent of the wealth on the eve of the Great Depression. Wage increases had occurred, but they failed to keep up with the cost of living, and it was no coincidence that this period gave rise to more nationalism and stronger calls for Puerto Rican independence.

In the late summer of 1928, this monocrop reliance collided with a mono-event common to the Caribbean. Its name was *San Felipe*. In Puerto Rico hurricanes carried the names of the saint's feast day on which they made landfall. *San Felipe* hit on September 13, 1928 and its toll of devastation was enormous. The hurricane's winds may have reached as high as 200 miles per hour. Miraculously, only 300 people died in that storm, a tenth of the number killed three decades earlier by the probably weaker *San Ciriaco*. Economically, however, *San Felipe* was a killer, destroying 250,000 homes, one third of the island's sugar cane, and one half of the coffee crop. Half a million people were thrust into poverty overnight.4

San Felipe proved to be the first of three destructive blows that came in rapid succession. A year later the tropical depression of most import was the Great Depression. Finally, in 1932, another massive hurricane, *San Ciprian*, struck. Beyond the physical havoc, these events played havoc with Puerto Rican self-confidence, or, more precisely, with the mainland self-confidence that its colonial possession could thrive by its loose association with its patron to the north. Laissez-faire economics was in trouble all over the Hemisphere, and it was inevitable that the administration of Franklin Delano Roosevelt would bring New Deal philosophies to bear on the economic challenges in Puerto Rico. But that experiment did not happen right away.

The brief, ironic tenure of Theodore Roosevelt, Jr. as the appointed governor of Puerto Rico under Herbert Hoover deserves some mention. Roosevelt's father, Teddy, had led the effort to turn the Monroe Doctrine into an offensive policy and drive Spain out of the Caribbean. In the years that followed, Teddy generally resisted the forces of more rapid evolution to self-rule in Puerto Rico. The son shared his father's admiration for the American role in accelerating Puerto Rico's economic growth, and especially its advances in health, education, and road building. Even so, Teddy Roosevelt, Jr. was disturbed at the refusal of American officials in Puerto Rico to speak Spanish, at the assumption of racial and cultural superiority in his fellow Americans, and in the sway of American capital.

Roosevelt advocated a dominion status for Puerto Rico that would have mimicked the strong self-government exercised by nations like Canada and Australian loyal to Great Britain. By 1931, however, Roosevelt had tired of the island's tortuous politics and chose to devote his attention to a new assignment as governor of the Philippines, a possession that was headed for an earlier and happier resolution of its status. In the younger Roosevelt's view of Puerto

Rico, the intellectual struggle between bearer of the "white man's burden" and the trustbuster was won by the latter, but the politics of the island were tending toward more polarization and even violence. Roosevelt's service, short as it was, represented one of the few efforts by any American administration to place the island's future on a higher plane of concern.

The next decade in Puerto Rico was a time of tremendous turmoil, of shifting alliances among the island's political parties, and of the birth of a Nationalist Party willing to seek violent change and test the will of the American governors. The 1930s were a dismal era in the relationship between the United States and Puerto Rico, as a series of governors appointed by FDR – Robert Hayes Gore, Blanton Winship, Admiral William D. Leahy, and Guy Swope – struggled to implement policies of relief and reconstruction of the devastated Puerto Rican economy. None of the four proved adept at what was likely a hopeless task, to make New Deal policies of land reform work in a territory with the population density of New Jersey. Moreover, neither Gore nor Winship had a feel for the character of the island's people or their history. Gore's program in particular was premised, as one historian put it, on "trade with Florida, cockfighting, and statehood." His "100 percent Americanism" helped to fuel the radicalism of the U.S.-educated Pedro Albizu Campos, founder of the Nationalist, or independentista, Party.

As the New Deal economic measures failed, Albizu and the Nationalists chose a course of confrontation. Stymied electorally, they pursued a theme of anti-Americanism that, despite all the historic tensions in the relationship, had never been the predominant view of Puerto Ricans. Albizu's arrest and conviction in 1936 on charges of conspiring to overthrow the federal government in Puerto Rico sparked a chain reaction of attempted assassinations of government officials that culminated in a massacre of Nationalist Party marchers in Ponce on Palm Sunday 1937. In this atmosphere, the more nuanced messages of other Puerto Rican leaders, like the Liberal Party spokesman Luis Muñoz Marin, who worked for self-determination and economic reform, were stifled.

Muñoz's temporary retreat from the national political scene coincided with the run-up to World War II, when Puerto Rico's strategic value in repelling Nazi submarines came to the fore. Like those submarines, changes happening underneath the surface of both Puerto Rican and mainland society had begun to operate in the late 1930s. The decade ended with the demonstration of the failure of both the era of King Sugar and the idea of colonial tutelage, indeed of any form of top-down solutions from Washington. The next phase of Puerto Rican economic history revolved around the interplay of fresh steps in self-rule and industrialization that mobilized the talents of new political leaders and veterans like Muñoz who remembered the lessons of the past and were thereby not doomed to repeat them.

It has been said that the power to tax is the power to destroy. In the 1940s the political leadership of Puerto Rico applied the corollary principle that the power *not* to tax is the power to create — or at least it is the power to attract. Muñoz spent the last years of the 1930s creating a new grassroots movement, the *Partido Popular Democratico* (PPD, or now, the PPD), nicknamed the *Populares*. The PPD inherited much of the economic legacy of the Liberal Party that had been dissipated in the failure of the first round of New Deal initiatives. Muñoz's PPD climbed into prominence with a revamped platform that finessed the issue of independence and focused on social reforms. In 1940 the need was as acute as ever. The typical Puerto Rican had per capita monthly income of $122, one-fifth the average per capita income on the mainland. The number had not changed since 1930.

The PPD program was in the right place at the right time. By deferring the explosive question of independence at a time when popular resentment against America's handling of its colony was peaking, the PPD soared past its rivals and won an historic electoral sweep in 1944. Its proposals for the local legislature included land reform (the PPD supported the purchase and redistribution of parcels of land that exceeded the 500-acre limit), a national budget office, two agencies for economic development, and a program of industrialization that was more suited to the populous and still-growing island. Like many American communities, Puerto Rico grew steadily, if not dramatically, during the war years, as it enjoyed new advantages in trade with the mainland and national defense dollars were spent in recognition of the island's strategic importance as a gateway to the Panama Canal and to the Gulf

States. Puerto Ricans' disdain for a totalitarian threat from Europe was natural and intense.

In 1947 Puerto Rico began the experimentation in tax relief that became the dominant economic reality of the second half of the 20th century. Section 262 and its promise of relief from the federal corporate and personal income tax already existed. Now Muñoz and other Puerto Rican leaders were prepared to match that extremely generous policy with an exemption from Puerto Rico's own income tax on corporate profits. The goal was explicit: to lure capital to the island in the post-war period and to accelerate the transformation of Puerto Rico's economy from its agrarian past to a technocratic future. Education had made steady progress throughout the island in the colonial period, and the University of Puerto Rico had been a bright star in the Caribbean with capable leadership since its organization in 1925. Puerto Rican leaders believed, with good reason, that industrialization was the pathway to higher wages and the retention of skilled workers.

The key step in this era of rapid change was the Puerto Rican legislature's adoption of the Industrial Exemption Tax Act in 1948. This law gave qualified firms relocating or expanding from the mainland exemptions from various levies, including income taxes, property taxes and municipal license fees. The corporations were encouraged to come south by additional acts of largesse, for example, the offer of buildings and low-interest loans through the Government Development Bank. The focal point of this activity was a governmental organization called FOMENTO, the Economic Development Administration set up by the *Populares* when they came to power. FOMENTO took the step of actively advertising Puerto Rico's reduced labor costs. One item that appeared in the *Detroit Free Press* in May 1953 romanticized this aspect of the island's appeal:

> *Investors dreaming of paradise might visualize a place where a factory owner doesn't have to pay any taxes or rent. If their imagination were working overtime they might daydream of workers happy to toil for as little as 17½ cents an hour. Actually there is no reason for such dreaming ... for such a place – Puerto Rico – exists in reality.*[5]

"Happy to toil" was a somewhat suspect appraisal of workers' psychological status, but in all other respects this description of the Puerto Rican advantage to U.S. corporations was accurate. The combination of no local taxes, relocation incentives, and the non-taxability of earnings attributable to manufacture on the island proved to be a powerful, if distorting, magnet. Puerto Rican officials were not unaware of the exorbitant cost of these tax preferences. At first, the tax exemptions were designed to be phased out, beginning in 1959. For the corporations, however, there could not be too much of a good thing. The industrial portion of the Puerto Rican economy grew some 25% from 1948 to 1954, but by the end of that period Puerto Rican officials recognized that the coming phase-out was easing the rate at which new manufacturing concerns were moving to or expanding there.

The Industrial Tax Exemption Act was therefore amended in 1954 to allow qualified businesses the full exemption for 10 years from that date. In 1961, the Act was amended a third time and adopted in its most generous form. Businesses could obtain an exemption ranging from 10 to 30 years, with companies locating in the most underdeveloped areas receiving the lengthiest exemption. These maneuvers brought a variety of enterprises to the island, including firms specializing in apparel and shoes, textiles, electronics and mechanical products. Even so, none of these measures could succeed in abolishing the business cycle, and, thus, while these factories brought jobs, they were vulnerable to the ups and downs of the American economy.

The planners at FOMENTO hit on an alternative strategy of attempting to attract industries to Puerto Rico that tended to do well regardless of macro economic conditions. This led to a new favoritism for capital-intensive, as opposed to labor-intensive, companies. This scheme was well suited to industries like petrochemicals and pharmaceuticals, and later it would be similarly attractive to the semi-conductor industry. For these companies, and for others that relied on highly automated production facilities, the comprehensive tax preferences on which Puerto Rico embarked offered a chance to maximize profits without necessarily incurring major new expenses for wages.

In the short run, the transformation this industrial policy worked was the source of dramatic economic growth. The postwar era was a time of rapid expansion across the U.S. economy, but growth rates in Puerto Rico were impressive by any measure. Per capita Gross National Product rose by 4.7 percent in the 1950s and an even more rapid 5.5 percent in the 1960s. The comparable figure for the mainland economy during these same time periods was not as good. Over the same 20-year period, per capita GNP in the United States rose only 2.2 percent. As early as 1958, per capita income in Puerto Rico was the highest in Latin America. The "poorhouse of the Caribbean" was not yet a treasure house, but the sense of progress and an incipient prosperity was palpable.

Underneath this apparent growth, however, the distorting effects of the Section 931-inspired tax regime (a re-codification of the Internal Revenue Code in 1954 had renamed Section 262 as Section 931) were apparent. First, although the manufacturing influx brought better jobs, the sheer numbers were not enough to offset the simultaneous losses in agriculture. The total gain in manufacturing jobs from 1950 to 1974 was 92,000. The island would have experienced net job losses were it not for migration to urban America and the growth in non-manufacturing jobs during this period, including government jobs and the service industries.

Dramatic shifts took place in the kinds of manufacturing represented in Puerto Rico's industrial mix. The "capital-intensive" industries showed the greatest increase. An analysis reported by Sandra Suarez-Lasa at Yale University in 1994 discussed the changes in the make-up of the Puerto Rico manufacturing sector between 1947 and 1976. Over those nearly three decades, the proportion of the island's Gross Domestic Product contributed by apparel, for example, declined from 15 percent to just under nine percent. Food production declined even more steeply, from nearly 40 percent of GDP to under 10 percent. At the same time petrochemicals increased more than fivefold (to just under nine percent of GDP) and pharmaceuticals grew from a negligible percentage to more than 23 percent of total GDP.

Thanks to the nature of these manufacturing entities, these numbers do not translate into jobs. Despite the decline in apparel, for example, by 1976 the percentage of factory workers employed in the apparel industry was still over 25 percent. The relatively low

Biography of a Tax Gimmick

capital content of the goods produced, and the need for hands-on manufacture for many products, kept this industry employing workers far in excess of the dollar value of its contribution to the island economy. Pharmaceuticals, on the other hand, may have created nearly one fourth of the manufacturing wealth, but they employed, in 1976, only one of every 20 workers in the industrial sector.

Where, then, was this wealth creation going? As in the days of King Sugar, and with the assistance and inducements of the federal and local tax codes, these profits were being repatriated to the mainland. Not only did the tax code facilitate such transfers, but it also made possible several practices that maximized the ability of the U.S. corporations to attribute their income to Puerto Rican sources. If they could do this, all such income was essentially tax-free earnings to the parent corporation.

One method involved intercompany transfers of finished products. For example, the U.S. pharmaceutical manufacturer would either relocate or build a new pill production plant in Puerto Rico. If it did so in a zone on the island designated as underdeveloped, it enjoyed all sorts of immediate tax breaks in addition to the prospective income exemptions. The company could then arrange purchase agreements with its island manufacturer that maximized the price of the drug as it was shipped to the mainland. Reduced to its simplest terms, a prescription that might sell for $105 in the United States could be priced so that $100 was paid to the Puerto Rican manufacturing arm before it left the island. All of the profits for the product were located in the intercompany transfer and reported as income to the Puerto Rican entity, and, thus, virtually tax-free to the company as a whole.

A second method of shifting profits to the island was subtler and more difficult for the Internal Revenue Service to monitor and regulate. This tactic involved the shift of "intangible assets" of U.S. corporations to the island. The cost of building a manufacturing plant and purchasing production machinery was easy to calculate. A major part of a company's value is found not in these "plant and equipment" items, however, but in such intellectual and marketing properties as patents and trademarks. U.S. corporations learned quickly that if they could assign or sell these intangibles to their Puerto Rican subsidiaries, profits and royalties attributable to these activities could also be attributed to the island, resulting in an even more valuable shelter from the U.S. corporate income tax.

These "benefits" to the Puerto Rican economy were equally intangible, in quite a different sense. Few jobs emerged from such practices. Operating in this manner, with the Internal Revenue Service struggling to enforce rules against business practices that had little purpose other than tax avoidance, the development "miracle " spawned by Section 931 and the Industrial Tax Exemption Act came more and more to be seen as sleight-of-hand. At the same time as capital-intensive industry was being drawn to the island, Puerto Rico's reputation as a land full of people "happy to toil" began to erode. Under the Fair Labor Standards Act, modified for Puerto Rico, the minimum wage on the island rose to equal the U.S. figure by 1982. Economic progress on the island changed attitudes as well, and the wage rate at which the typical Puerto Rico would accept employment also rose. The addition of more and more transfer payments, especially food stamps, made it easier on unemployed laborers not to work.

In all of this period, U.S. corporations behaved with a sterling and perfectly understandable rational self-interest. Very few corporations and individuals relish April 15 every year, and most of us seek to minimize what we are legally required to give to the government. In the case of Puerto Rico, this instinct was married to what had begun as a noble public purpose: the transformation of an impoverished, storm-wracked U.S. territory from its status as a dependent, cash crop economy into a modern industrial zone. The results for U.S. corporations, particularly the pharmaceutical companies that would mount an aggressive defense of Section 931 and its successor, Section 936, in the 1970s, were overwhelmingly positive from their point of view.

Investments in Puerto Rico, tangible and intangible, came to represent a high percentage of the net income of these corporations worldwide. Just how high a percentage can be seen in the earnings statements of the several dozen pharmaceutical companies that moved or set up operations in Puerto Rico during these robust years of economic transition. Citing these particular companies here is not to allege that they used any of the income shifting tactics just described. That kind of analysis is beyond the scope of this book.

For some enterprises, it was just a matter of moving massive amounts of production capacity to Puerto Rico. Even so, the concentration of profits in the Puerto Rican subsidiaries was tremendous. In 1975 some 68.7 percent of all of G. D. Searle's after-tax earnings derived from its tax-free income in Puerto Rico. That was the highest percentage reported, but others like SmithKline (45.2 percent) and Baxter Laboratories (46.4 percent) also relied on their outposts in the Caribbean for much of their companies' profitability.

Good tax news, of course, travels fast. In 1960 there were no pharmaceutical concerns operating on the island. By 1974 twenty major pharmaceutical companies had begun to operate there. Plants – for some companies, multiple manufacturing units – were opening all over Puerto Rico. None of this was lost on the bean counters in the U.S. Treasury, for whom the impact of Section 931 in creating, in combination with local relief, a corporate tax haven became a matter of increasing concern. The Treasury noted that between 1973 and 1975, fully one half of all the tax relief provided by Section 931 was concentrated in a single industry: pharmaceuticals. During the 1970s and 1980s, regardless of whichever political party was dominant in Washington, Section 931 and its successor, Section 936, became the object of increasing professional criticism from Treasury staff.

The dollars lost to the Treasury under the provision were significant, but the most sustained criticism revolved, appropriately, around the lack of meaningful benefit to the Puerto Rican economy. Section 931 moved profits for tax purposes to Puerto Rico but it did little to keep those dollars recycling in new investment in the island, especially after 1976, when companies were allowed to move their profits tax free to the mainland. This imbalance can be measured in various ways, but Treasury used one that resonated with the ideas that had motivated the whole campaign for industrialization in the first place: job creation. Treasury developed figures that measured the amount of tax relief provided to each manufacturing sector in terms of the average compensation paid to that sector's employees. For the electronics and electrical components industry, Section 931 provided roughly a dollar in tax relief for every dollar paid to an employee. For the pharmaceutical industry, on the other hand,

Section 931 provided more than *three dollars in tax breaks for every dollar paid to a Puerto Rico worker.*

Obviously, these retained dollars were heading somewhere else, and that somewhere was at the beck and call of the senior executives of these U.S. corporations. In the early 1970s the U.S. trade deficit became a political issue and American labor, historically friendly to free-trade policies, changed its stance. Labor leaders began to support tariffs and "buy American" policies and they concluded that U.S. tax policy toward Puerto Rico had the effect of shifting jobs from higher-paid American workers to lower-wage labor on the island. Combined with Treasury's hostility, these efforts put reform of Section 931 on the table just as House Ways and Means Chairman Wilbur Mills began to carry out his 1972 promise for a major review of the tax code.

In May 1973 Ways and Means adopted provisional changes in Section 931 that would have resulted in the taxing of this income at the moment it was repatriated to the United States. Had this change been put into law, Puerto Rican profits of these parent companies would have been favored so long as they circulated in Puerto Rico, and, for all intents and purposes, income earned by U.S. corporations on the island would have had the same tax treatment as income produced in any foreign country. The nature of Puerto Rico, a Commonwealth, whose residents were American citizens, was always a subtext of the developing debate. Puerto Rican officials had long supported Section 931, and this first move in Congress to dilute or eliminate it elicited immediate opposition from the island's elected officials, particularly the Popular Democrats.

In fact, Puerto Rico's governor at the time, Rafael Hernandez Colon, the Treasury Secretary Salvador Casellas and FOMENTO head Teodoro Moscoso took the lead in insisting to the House Committee that Section 931 should be preserved in the midst of the tax overhaul. The U.S. beneficiaries of this tax gimmick were content, and probably politically wise at this early stage, to let the Commonwealth government carry their water. The corporations quietly endorsed the idea, articulated by the Puerto Ricans, that substantially weakening or repealing Section 931 would lead to an "investment strike" and further industrialization of the local economy would halt. Chairman Mills was almost apologetic in receiving the testimony of these officials and his Committee backed off its reform proposal.

A raft of related arguments were made that also played a role not only in preserving the tax break, but also in strengthening it. The special relationship between the island and the mainland, and the issue of keeping Puerto Rico as a model for democratic development in a region that included Cuba and other countries engaged in undemocratic experiments, had emotional appeal. So, too, did the idea that an "investment strike" would have residual effects in decreasing Puerto Rican imports from the United States, swelling the island's welfare rolls, and, just as important, as Governor Colon, put it in a memorandum to the Committee, causing "net inward migration" [to Puerto Rico] to "reverse and again flow heavily toward the mainland."[6] The investment strike, he implied, would be accompanied by a "migration strike" upon the mainland, a kind of Puerto Rican Mariel. There was no federal budget deficit at this time, so there was no external pressure on the tax writers to raise revenue.

When the tax reform bill finally passed the House in 1975, Section 931 had been renumbered as Section 936 for its corporate beneficiaries (individuals were to rely on Section 931 until 1986). It had been changed substantively as well. Companies were given some latitude, for example, to decide whether to be treated as Section 936 corporations under the law, although their decision to do so would be irrevocable for 10 years. Most important, in a change the mainland corporations regarded as an improvement over Section 931, the new law permitted the American parent corporations to receive dividends from their Puerto Rican subsidiaries tax-free. No longer would the U.S. parent have to wait and liquidate the producing arm in Puerto Rico in order to return the proceeds tax-free to the States. The goose that laid the golden egg no longer needed to be slain to be harvested. President Gerald Ford signed the Tax Reform Act in October 1976, four years after the process began.

Treasury was adamantly opposed to the new Section 936, but it had one victory in the reform battle. The law authorized the department to issue annual reports on the operation of the tax preference over the next three years. It was an opportunity not to be missed. For three consecutive years the Treasury Department issued assessments of Section 936 that raked it over the fiscal coals. Policy makers at the department were concerned about the excessive profits and income-shifting the tax break seemed to encourage and reward. The analyses they produced only reinforced these findings. Treasury argued that the revenue loss associated with the new Section 936 increased rather than decreased after 1976. The transfer of capital-intensive, rather than job-creating, industries to Puerto Rico also continued. As a result, successful businesses became more successful, without more Puerto Ricans finding work.

Increasingly, the language of policy makers seemed to migrate from categorizing Section 936 as ineffective or excessive to describing it as an abuse. For these reasons, the Treasury reports did not favor a regulatory or enforcement-oriented fix. The political history that underlay Section 936 was, of course, beyond the scope of the Carter Administration careerists who wrote these reports. In truth, the whole development model Section 936 represented for Puerto Rico was intertwined with the confused state of its political existence and links with the mainland. It was a Limbo law for a Limbo nation. Had Puerto Rico been a state, it could not have enjoyed the Possessions Corporations System of Taxation. Had it been an independent country, the United States might have all sorts of reasons to foster trade in the region and with the island, in particular, but Congress would have been extremely unlikely ever to write a law as Puerto-Rico-specific and generous as this special tax break proved to be.

The vague, hybrid nature of Commonwealth status harmonized well with the now vaguely purposed Section 936. Other events intervened in the U.S. economy as the 1970s came to a close, however, that put this hybrid law at risk. Chief among these were the chaos in the financial markets that occurred under President Carter as the 1970s came to a close and the convergence of forces that drove the federal budget deficit upward in President Reagan's first term. Reagan campaigned with enormous success on themes of economic recovery, tax relief, restoration of American military might, and smaller government. His national security agenda called for defense expenditures designed to put pressure on the Soviet Union to curb its expansionist ambitions and recognize the futility of an arms race with the United States.

In 1981 Congress responded to Reagan's smashing electoral

victory and adopted the Economic Recovery Tax Act (ERTA), legislation that reduced corporate and income tax rates with the goal of restoring economic growth and, thereby, increasing government revenues indirectly. ERTA was designed as a broad-based stimulus measure, but the economy Reagan inherited was plagued with record-high interest rates and soaring unemployment. Reversing the economy's momentum proved to be difficult, indeed, and in 1982 the country experienced recession. Thus, only a year after ERTA's passage, Congress embarked on a search for reform measures that would deal with the deficit and public spending without choking off the long-term course correction Reagan was seeking.

In this environment, with revenue needs very much on the radar screen and Congress seeking to be both pro-business and anti-corporate welfare, Section 936 found itself back on the policy makers' chopping block. This time, the U.S. corporations proved not to be resilient enough to protect their tax haven in Puerto Rico from the reformist spirit. Treasury kept up its pressure to reform Section 936, raising particularly piquant concerns about the way U.S. corporations handled intangible property and shifted profits to their Puerto Rican holdings. Puerto Rican officials tried to head off radical rewriting or repeal of Section 936 by meeting with Treasury staff and proposing regulatory changes that would establish standards for allocating certain costs between the U.S parent corporations and their Puerto Rican partners. This approach promised to correct what Treasury regarded as an abuse, to bring in new revenue, and to preserve the system of credits that was the heart of the tax break.

In late 1981 talks between the Puerto Rican leadership and Treasury broke down. This event brought the Section 936 U.S. corporations off the sidelines, but it did so at a time when the pro-corporation "solution" to the threat to Section 936 was not altogether obvious. The Reagan Administration, restive Congressional committees, political appointees at Treasury, and the department's career staff were all in the mix as potential focal points of, and fomenters for, a range of proposed actions. The Section 936 corporations found themselves in an open lobbying contest where the renewed threat of an "investment strike" had little or no force. As in most lobbying situations, pragmatists and idealists (those who wanted to keep Section 936 untouched) pulled in different directions. The pharmaceutical companies in particular, which had the lion's share of the tax benefits at stake, were resistant to the idea of compromise and allowing Section 936 to be dragged into the arena of debate.

The new bill that emerged in 1982 was called TEFRA, which stood for the Tax Equity and Fiscal Responsibility Act. The name contrasted suitably, and meaningfully, with that of the Economic Recovery Tax Act. As 1982 began, budding concerns about the deficit blossomed when the Congressional Budget Office estimated that it would reach $157 billion in fiscal year 1983 (the year beginning September 30, 1982). The pressure on Congress grew and in June a budget resolution was passed, with White House support for the compromise, that called for $98.3 billion in new taxes between 1983 and 1985. The Treasury Department under Reagan maintained its traditional doubts about Section 936 and it persuaded then-Sen. Robert Dole of Kansas to include a major contraction of the credit in the Senate bill.

The pharmaceutical companies and Senate Finance Committee Democrats, alerted by Puerto Rican officials, fruitlessly opposed the changes to Section 936. The pharmaceutical companies apparently believed their ill fortune was due to the fact that Senate Republicans on the tax-writing committee hailed from western states, and not from the northeastern states that were home to their corporate headquarters. The Democrats believed that their ill fortune was due to the Senate Republican majority, period. This breakthrough against Section 936's largesse drove its U.S. beneficiaries, led by the pharmaceutical group, to organize a complete lobbying campaign premised on visits to members of Congress, political action contributions, and other traditional tactics. By this time, some 80 percent of the tax savings from Section 936 that were held in Puerto Rican banks emanated from the drug companies' activities.

This fact left the drug companies unwilling to make significant compromises with Dole's overhaul. They opted, instead, with the Puerto Rican government's help, to try to convince the Treasury Department to take up again the limited reforms it had discussed with Puerto Rican elected officials in 1981. The idea was to get the Reagan Administration on board a less-drastic change and to use that as leverage against the Dole bill. This effort showed some early success when Treasury Secretary Don Regan publicly criticized the Finance Committee's product. The lobbying campaign continued in an effort to obtain Treasury's stamp of approval on a substitute, but, to Treasury's dismay, the new drug company-Puerto Rican alliance looked for new allies on Capitol Hill. They ultimately found them in Democratic Senators J. Bennett Johnston and Pat Moynihan and in House Ways and Means Chairman Charles Rangel.

The geographic background of these members was no accident. Moynihan and Rangel represented New York State and a Harlem Congressional District, respectively. There were numerous Puerto Ricans among their constituents, and a number of drug companies called the Empire State home. Johnston, moreover, represented Louisiana, which, as a Gulf State with petrochemical companies, enjoyed benefits not only from Section 936 but also from active trade with the island. These legislators worked to support a brokered compromise that would block Dole. The Kansas Republican was reportedly shocked by the size of the benefits select U.S. corporations were enjoying, however. He took to the Senate floor in July 1982 and denounced the companies' practice of shifting patents and other intangible property to the island, saying, "A clearer case of having your cake and eating it too has seldom existed in U.S. tax law."[7]

That any of these members of Congress took completely irrational positions based on their constituents' views could not be said. For Moynihan, however, the endorsement of tax measures that offered such out-sized benefits to big business while helping to maintain Puerto Rico in an exceptional and dependent status was philosophically out-of-kilter. Dole was certainly a business advocate, but he found Section 936 unconscionable. This was not the first time, of course, that the oddities and intricacies of Puerto Rico's contradictory status caused political figures to dance to some unusual tunes. The drug companies' political contributions only clouded the picture further. Generally speaking, corporate PACs founded in the wake of the post-Watergate ethics reforms tended to give money to whoever was in power, regardless of political affiliation.

Cash put in the pocket of a member of Congress to change his or her opinion can be considered a bribe, an illegal act. A contribution given in accordance with the law to the re-election committee of a member of Congress is a perfectly legal act. The giving patterns of most corporations in the political arena include both their traditional friends and traditional opponents, but the complexity of the tax and regulatory agendas of American corporations makes assertions about their motives no easy task. Generally, corporations want to guarantee access for their representatives and for their arguments. In the case of Section 936, the pharmaceutical companies had begun to make PAC expenditures well before TEFRA came to a head. Between the 1979-1980 and 1981-82 election cycles, PAC gifts from the drug companies to members of the House and Senate tax-writing committees increased 86 percent.

Dole had his way in the Senate, ultimately, and his reform of Section 936 passed intact. That proved to be the high-water mark for the reform. The House Ways and Means Committee elected to bypass floor action and go directly to a conference committee with the Senate. This step shortened the timetable for action, but it also focused the pharmaceutical companies' efforts. Lacking a grass-roots presence other than what they could stir up on the island through their alliance with Puerto Rican officials, they turned to Rangel, a high-ranking Democrat on Ways and Means. Rangel took up the cause of preserving Section 936 by advancing the Treasury compromise that the Puerto Rican government had been seeking since 1981. Reluctantly, the pharmaceutical companies went along and Dole found himself pincered between the Reagan Administration and Rangel's shrewd politics.

That high principle does not decide most questions on Capitol Hill is no surprise to any Congress-watcher. As noted above, Rep. Rangel's position on Section 936 was not incongruous with the nature of his district nor with his belief, since reaffirmed, in using selective tax breaks and "empowerment zone" concepts as ways to target economic development. Even so, the brokering of political money in the preservation of Section 936 in 1982 was blatant. One Puerto Rican official who met with Rangel in this period later gave an account of what happened in the time between the Dole amendment's passage in the Senate and the climactic conference committee rescue of Section 936:

> *When he went to see Rangel, the congressman was very straightforward. Rangel said "What can you do for me?" What supporters of 936 did was give the congressman a fund raiser in Puerto Rico. According to a Puerto Rico official in that fund raiser, given to the congressman after the "Dole amendment" passed the Senate, but before it was being discussed in conference, Rangel raised $141,000. The fund raiser was attended mostly by company officials from the island affiliates.*[8]

In the long history of Section 936, the TEFRA "rescue," although incomplete, was one of the clearest examples of self-interested political maneuvering.

If nothing else, the 1982 debate saw the introduction of an alternative by the Congressional Joint Tax Committee staff to replace Section 936 with a wage credit. This idea, which resurfaced as the debate continued, was designed to return the tax break to its original job creating purpose.

Despite their victory, the Section 936 corporations and Puerto Rican leaders were displeased with the outcome. They had hoped only for new regulatory policies on the income-shifting issue, and instead they had new, harder to amend legislative mandates. However, the ability of the drug companies and others to transfer intangible assets to Puerto Rico, though limited, had at least been legally recognized and permitted. The alliance sensed that there was blood in the water on Section 936 reform, and that a new level of activity was needed. Moreover, the 1981-1982 debate had been sullied for them by the lack of unity among Section 936 advocates. The danger always existed that one or more of the parties involved, the Puerto Rican government, the pharmaceutical giants, or the electronics firms, would negotiate their own "separate peace" with the Congressional and Treasury reformers.

To address these concerns, a new organization was established in Washington to lobby full-time for Section 936. A single tax break that has a full-time lobbying operation working to defend it is one lucrative tax deal, indeed. The drug company lobbyists and their Puerto Rican government allies called the new entity the

Puerto Rico-U.S.A. Foundation. Like the Nationalist assassins who fired shots in the U.S. House chamber in 1954, reformists had taken aim at the Golden Goose of Section 936 and barely missed killing it. The drug lobby was determined not to allow this to happen again. For a standard sign-up fee ranging from $3,000 to $25,000 annually, corporations could join the partnership and, if they paid the maximum fee, help to direct its program. This fee was pocket change given the tens of millions of dollars at stake. The Treasury Department's fourth annual report on Section 936 estimated that TEFRA would reduce the companies' tax benefits by a hefty 30 percent.

The PRUSA Foundation was set up in 1984 and it girded for battle. No longer content to let the Puerto Rican government lead in arguing that changes in the law would precipitate an "investment strike," no longer willing to let disparate members of its coalition seek their own deals with the various federal actors in the drama, the U.S. corporations, chiefly the drug companies, aimed to build a cohesive, unitary lobby. The continued size of the federal deficit and the Reagan Administration's sustained desire to simplify the mammoth U.S. tax code led to another round of tax reform in 1986. This time, the Section 936 companies, through PRUSA, devised a successful policy of pre-emption. They secured enough advance commitments in Congress to defeat Treasury's reform ideas before they were even sent to Congress.

By January 1985 PRUSA had more than 50 member companies. The pharmaceutical firms had the highest rate of participation, but they were joined not just by electronics manufacturing companies but also by banks and investment firms who handled the tax-free profits in Puerto Rico. This united front conducted all the traditional lobbying activities associated with public policy, including a generous practice of fact-finding tours (junkets, in the plainer phrase) for targeted members of Congress. Later, both the House and Senate would crack down on such expenditures and limit them, but in the 1980s it was possible to make the most of Puerto Rico's attractiveness as a quasi Club Med of tax shelters.

Charlie Rangel wanted company this time around in the defense of Section 936. The PRUSA developed some improved arguments, stressing the related jobs in the mainland that might be lost with repeal of Section 936. The drug companies noted, as a matter of national pride, how their rate of research and discovery rendered the industry the undisputed world leader. They attempted to bolster the Puerto Rican government's erstwhile assertions about investment losses by commissioning studies that, unsurprisingly, found the island could not maintain its prosperity without tax preferences. The best way for Congress to understand this prosperity, PRUSA concluded, was for the Foundation to take members and their staffs to the island to see it for themselves. It was a brilliant stroke, because the physical operations on the island would be obvious and the location of the capital attributable to Section 936 would be invisible.

Since common sense dictates that it was easier to get a member of Congress to go in the winter than in the summer, PRUSA reportedly sponsored two trips a year for six to eight staff members of the House Ways and Means Committee. One participant acknowledged that it was "very effective" for PRUSA to take House employees to play golf in Puerto Rico. He noted that the trips did include a "business" component as the hosts would discuss Section 936 over dinner with the Congressional staff members. The visits were, he admitted, "heavy duty lobbying."[9] It might better be described as light duty for the staff members who were its target. Overall, eight U.S. senators and 15 House members were treated to these "working vacations" in Puerto Rico.

All these efforts ultimately paid off, and the Tax Reform Act of 1986 as signed by President Reagan contained only minor changes in Section 936. The extent of the success of the PRUSA lobbying campaign can be seen in the fact that Treasury's first draft of the Tax Reform Act contained an outright repeal of Section 936. To ease its impact, Administration policy makers once again surfaced the idea of replacing the income credit with a credit against a percentage of wages paid to the island's workers. Even this break would be phased out, but it would cost the Treasury less and reward only that portion of industrialization that was directly linked to job creation in Puerto Rico. Treasury estimated that limiting Section 936 this way would bring $3.7 billion into the government's coffers over five years.

The Puerto Rican government made a brief attempt to rescue Section 936 on its own by linking it to President Reagan's Caribbean

Basin Initiative and promising to use $700 million of the corporations' island profits in Puerto Rican banks to finance regional development projects. The pharmaceutical companies were cool to this approach and unconvinced it was necessary. They trained their educational resources on the Hill tax-writing committees. Neither approach envisioned any underlying change to Section 936. In that sense, the actions of the Puerto Rican government and the corporations were completely coherent. In any event, by the time the second version of Treasury's proposal was prepared and sent to the White House in 1985, the repeal of Section 936 had been watered down, though it was still to be replaced with a credit that targeted wages paid and not corporate income.

The PRUSA kept up its intense lobbying, focusing more and more of its argument on domestic grounds for preserving the tax break. Rep. Rangel was more than willing to help, using his time with one of the group's witnesses before the Ways and Means Committee to elicit information on which Congressional Districts were home to plants owned by the Section 936 corporations. This was not testimony but rather tutored lobbying. By the time the process was over and the Tax Reform Act of 1986 became law, reforms to Section 936 were tailored to yield the Treasury only $300 million over five years. This was a dramatic improvement for the corporations over the 30 percent slash in the value of this tax gimmick they had suffered in 1982. All that Congress had done was to use a concept called a "super-royalty" to require the mainland corporations to attribute less of their income from intangibles to their tax-free subsidiary in Puerto Rico.

Legally, Section 936 lost ground in the 1980s, though the pace of its erosion slowed thanks to the stepped-up pressure of the drug companies and their allies. Politically, given the deficit politics of most of the decade, PRUSA could conclude that it had done better than other targets of reform in the area of corporate welfare. It had friends in both political parties, even if the basis for that friendship varied from a general hostility to federal taxes to a desire to serve U.S. constituencies with either business or family ties to the island. Oddly, despite its corporate image, the Republican Party had more members who seemed willing to entertain repeal. That would change in the 1990s, however, as the incoming Clinton Administration, determined to demonstrate its "third way" in public policy, focused on eliminating the budget deficit and paying down the national debt.

The drug lobby and its allies were taken by surprise when the Clinton Administration proposed the repeal of Section 936 just after taking office. Despite their continuing contributions to Charlie Rangel's re-election campaigns, the New York congressman was unwilling this time to expend his political capital to protect the pharmaceutical companies' financial capital. To make matters more difficult, other Section 936 beneficiaries, such as the electronics manufacturers, had less at stake in preserving the tax break and were open to compromise, as was the Puerto Rican government. Moreover, after a few decades of being treated as glamour industries, the drug companies found themselves under new pressure from a liberal administration determined to enact a national health care plan. That effort would require some villains, and the Clintons and some of their Democratic allies were willing to cite the soaring cost of prescriptions as an example of the need for reform.

The Clinton Section 936 proposal made its way into H.R. 2264, which was enacted as the Omnibus Budget Reconciliation Act (OBRA) of 1993 on August 10.[10] The Clinton budget reached back to ideas that had been advanced by the Carter and Reagan Treasury staff and the Joint Tax Committee in different forms: a wage-based tax credit. This was inserted into the final legislation as a 60 percent credit against wages paid on the island. In addition, the companies could take another credit for capital depreciation and part of the income taxes they paid in Puerto Rico. These credits were only an alternative; the 1993 bill left the U.S. companies on the island free to choose an abridged form of Section 936, under which the credit was reduced to 60 percent of its former value in the first year and gradually declined to 40 percent for 1998 and beyond.

This was the largest blow to date for the profit-based tax credit, and it did have the effect of offering a wage-directed alternative, but this version of Section 936 did not last long. In any event, it is likely that it would have done little to correct the distortions created by the favoritism that drug companies and others were capitalizing on. First, the wage credit was only an alternative; a capital-intensive business was unlikely to use it, and perhaps more unlikely to create jobs because of its existence. Second, the 1993 reform left the U.S. operations in Puerto Rico free to enjoy tax exemptions for their passive activity and for profits attributable to their intangible assets.

After the 1994 Congressional elections, the Republican Party had the upper hand in the House of Representatives, thanks to the over-reaching of the Clinton Administration on social issues, like homosexuals in the military, and the development, under Newt Gingrich (R-Ga.), of the GOP's Contract with America. The Ways and Means Committee Chairman Bill Archer guided to passage the Small Business Job Protection Act of 1996. This law gave the Clinton Administration its desired step increases in the minimum wage, offered small businesses an off-setting tax credit to help pay for the increase, and used the demise of Section 936 to pay for the new credit. This would have marked real progress for Puerto Rican economic development, but for the length of the phase-out and the option that was left in federal law for the Puerto Rican companies to convert to Controlled Foreign Corporations for tax purposes under Section 956.

Like an addict withdrawing from a narcotic, the existing Section 936 companies were given a period of years by Archer's bill to taper off reliance on the credit. The passive income portion of Section 936 was ended immediately. The income-based tax credit was phased out by 1998 and the wage-based credit was set to end in 2005. By converting to CFC's under Section 956, the U.S. subsidiaries in Puerto Rico could adopt a tax regime that had been designed for U.S. companies operating in foreign countries. Once more, the confusion over the political status of Puerto Rico was being employed to the benefit of U.S. companies employing U.S. citizens. In the tax code, Puerto Rico might as well have been Malaysia. For the food stamp program, it might as well have been Milwaukee. For payment of the individual federal income tax, it might as well have been Munich.

With the adoption of the 1996 reform, the pharmaceutical firms, petrochemical companies and their allies could bide their time. As CFC's they could not repatriate their profits tax free without dissolving the entities that had earned them, but there were ways and means (the House Committee is appropriately named) to get around that problem and the cash-flushed pharmaceutical lobby, as will be described in a moment, set about to get those ways and means into law.

It is hard to deny that, in its early years under the masterful political balancing act of Muñoz Marin, Section 931 and its complementary local tax breaks drew industry to the island and perhaps prevented some of them from moving outside the United States altogether. While the overall gain to the U.S. economy was doubtful, the shift of thousands of jobs from the mainland to Puerto Rico certainly benefited workers and families on the island.

The premise, however, of Section 931/936 was deeply flawed, and only astute and well-heeled lobbying preserved this albatross long after its utility disappeared. In the final decades of its existence, Section 936 functioned mostly to pad the income of wealthy pharmaceutical companies to the tune of some $4 billion per year. The threats of an exodus from Puerto Rico if their special tax haven were shut down were put to the test with the reduction of Section 936 that began in 1993. As critics of the credits had predicted, the exodus did not happen. Section 936 was not intimately connected with economic progress in Puerto Rico after the 1960s, and the evidence suggests that, by building an artificial and distorted prosperity that distracted from the island's real problems and needs, the special tax breaks have delayed Puerto Rico's rendezvous with reality.

A few final statistics will illustrate this point. After the Section 936 tax credit was cut from 100 percent to 60 percent in 1993, the number of Puerto Rican employees of Section 936 drug companies in 1994 was actually higher than it had been in 1992. Dr. Rivera Ruiz updated his study and demonstrated that the elimination of Section 936 would actually bring down the island's unemployment rate. Capital-intensive manufacturing like the drug companies, with their patents and brand names, had not been the real source of the island's net gains in employment. The real story of Puerto Rico's economic growth and improvements in such areas as life expectancy had been investments in human beings in the form of education and training. Puerto Rico had seen employment growth in the modern era in such areas as construction, financial services, tourism and government services. Incomplete as it was, its modernization was broad-based, not a gift of "foreign" capital from a handful of mainland industrial giants.

As we have seen, much of that capital only "visited" Puerto Rico to establish a business address and a tax haven. It was a kind of economic tourism, with profits inuring to the benefit of parent companies, not to Puerto Rico, America's stepchild in the Caribbean. Section 936 long over-stayed its welcome and its usefulness. Freedom, and a natural economy capable of sustained growth that would benefit Puerto Rico over the long haul, would continue to elude the island so long as it remained dependent on tax breaks that existed nowhere else in the Americas.

Political forces in Puerto Rico continue to press for the revival of some form of special tax-induced mainland investment in the island. Ironically, the most strenuous efforts in this direction are coming in the 21st century from the PPD, the same party that is devising new ways to challenge the United States over putative Puerto Rican autonomy in foreign affairs. Consistency is clearly not the hobgoblin of some large parties. Led by Governor Sila M. Calderon, the PPD proposed in 2001 that Congress amend Section 956 of the Internal Revenue Code in two ways. The first would have allowed Controlled Foreign Corporations in Puerto Rico to return 90 percent of their island profits tax-free to their sister companies on the mainland. The theory here was that these profits would benefit the U.S. economy by circulating there rather than remaining offshore or being invested in other foreign holdings of the U.S. affiliate.

The second part of the Calderon proposal was by far the more expensive. It would have allowed U.S. companies (limited to those companies already benefiting from Section 936 preferences as of the date of enactment) a way around the Treasury rules that barred many of them from transferring their intangible property – patents and branding – to their Puerto Rican operation. This would have allowed these companies once more to attribute a high percentage of their overall profits to the more or less tax-free activity in Puerto Rico. In advancing these arguments, the PPD appealed to the desire of Congress to keep U.S. corporations operating in U.S. territory with presumed benefit, somewhere down the line, to the U.S. economy. Puerto Rico was offering itself as an alternative to relocation of U.S. subsidiaries and affiliates to low-wage destinations like Singapore and Ireland.

Economist Lawrence A. Hunter of the Institute for Policy

Innovation has offered an example of how this latter idea might actual work as a kind of Puerto Rican "laundry" for profits generated elsewhere. He offers the example of a CFC incorporated in Ireland that has the bulk of its employees there but a sales office in Puerto Rico. Because a significant amount of the company's profits could reasonably be attributed to its sales and marketing efforts out of Puerto Rico, those profits could be shielded from U.S. taxation under the Calderon proposal. Moreover, he notes, if the product thus advertised and marketed from Puerto Rico was never actually shipped from or through the island, the profits from its sale could be shielded from Puerto Rican taxation as well.[11] It is hard to get more "intangible" than that.

Calderon attempted to pitch Congress on the idea that these changes to Section 956 would result in at least some money flowing into the U.S. Treasury as the CFC's repatriated profits rather than shifting them around overseas. Sen. John Breaux, a Louisiana Democrat whose state had major petrochemical interests in Puerto Rico, introduced a bill, S. 1475, on September 26, 2001, that included both of Calderon's proposals. The bill gave the CFCs an option: they could either exempt 90 percent of the Puerto-Rican source income that was invested in "U.S. property" on the mainland, or they could enjoy an 85 percent deduction of dividends received by the domestic (non-Puerto Rican) corporation. A nearly identical companion bill, H.R. 2550, was introduced in the House by a senior Ways and Means Committee Republican, Phil Crane of Illinois. Neither of the bills made it to the floor, but the House version had a respectable 51 cosponsors and the Senate alternative had two. Crane, as befit his advocacy role for continued tax dependency legislation for Puerto Rico, had voted against the 1998 legislation designed to give Puerto Rico Congressional guidance and a meaningful referendum on status.

Sen. Breaux's approach, on the other hand, seemed somewhat opportunistic and disingenuous. His bill was introduced just two weeks after the Al-Qaeda terrorists' attacks in Washington and New York. He described it as a means to stimulate the Puerto Rican economy and to create jobs in the United States. In a floor statement printed in the *Congressional Record* on September 26, Breaux asserted that S. 1475 "would provide a new tax regime to encourage

American companies to retain their Puerto Rican operations and to reinvest profits earned in Puerto Rico and the U.S. possessions in the United States on a tax preferred basis."[12] This argument was something of a revival of the "investment strike" idea the Section 936 manufacturers had floated to rescue their tax break in the 1970s: Adopt the bill and Puerto Rico would keep its operations and the tax benefit would come back to the mainland and stimulate job creation. Reject the bill, and who knows where these companies might go?

It was opportunistic not only because of the timing, but also because the pressured atmosphere in Congress might have persuaded some members not to look very closely into what H.R. 2550/S. 1475 would actually have done. Very little of it had anything at all to do with producing jobs in Puerto Rico or even the United States; Section 936 in its heyday had not done so, and there was little reason to believe that the Crane and Breaux bills would perform any better.

Then came the estimates of the bill's cost. The Calderon Administration had paid hundreds of thousands of dollars for a cost estimate of its own that came in at $1.3 billion in lost revenue to the U.S. Treasury over 11 years. The Joint Committee on Taxation of the Congress begged to differ. Its estimate of the bill was some 25 times higher than the Calderon Administration's, $32.1 billion over 11 years. The intangible property proposal was the larger of the two drains on the public purse, coming in at an estimated $20.8 billion over that time frame. These figures were consistent with previous Treasury estimates of the full-blown cost of Section 936, which had been pegged at some $3.2 billion per year from 1981 to 2001.[13]

This dose of reality forced the PPD Resident Commissioner, Anibal Acevedo-Vila, to suggest that the second, more expensive part of the proposal could be dropped. Recriminations began between the Calderon administration and Congressional officials, as well as Price Waterhouse Coopers, which had prepared the initial estimate. Despite Breaux's effort to link the legislation to the World Trade Center-Pentagon attacks, the measure was not included in the economic stimulus package that was passed swiftly and sent to President Bush.

It is instructive to remember that the pharmaceutical companies' first efforts to prevent Section 936 from being weakened in the early

1980s foundered not only because of their over-reliance on an "investment strike," but because deficit concerns loomed high on everyone's radar screens in Congress. That challenge is even more formidable as annual deficit projections soar toward the $500 billion range for 2004. Moreover, as a columnist for the *San Juan Star* put it shortly after the Joint Committee on Taxation cost estimates were released, "[S]pecial deals for Puerto Rico are simply out of tune with the current realities of globalization and free trade."[14]

Even so, this "enhanced CFC" measure came a little closer in May 2003 when the Congressional tax-writing committees considered a fresh economic stimulus bill. Reps. Charlie Rangel, longtime friend of the Puerto Rican tax breaks and Crane favored the Calderon proposal, but did not offer it when Ways and Means Chairman Bill Thomas, Republican of California, opposed it. In the Senate, this indirect revival of Section 956 had the support of Trent Lott, the former Republican Majority Leader, Orrin Hatch, Republican of Utah and Breaux. An effort was made by another supporter, Republican Gordon Smith of Oregon, to cut taxes on all CFC income by 85 percent. This gave Breaux an opening, and he successfully added language including Puerto Rico in the Smith amendment. The contradictions ever present in Puerto Rico's status were once again, however briefly, on display. Tax-wise, Puerto Rico would once more be a foreign land, populated by U.S. citizens.

Breaux's stratagem ended, however, when the Smith amendment, with Breaux's language, was voted down 11 to 10 in the Finance Committee. During the debate, Sen. Rick Santorum, a Pennsylvania Republican, objected to Breaux's proposal to treat Puerto Rico in the context of a future committee hearing on foreign taxation. Republican Don Nickles of Oklahoma replied that, as chairman of the Senate Budget Committee, he was open to discussions of Puerto Rico's difficulties, but not in the stimulus bill. He made the case that had doomed Section 936 to begin with: that is, it had little to do with job creation or improving the lives of the typical Puerto Rican. He cited Treasury figures that the earlier Section 936 had cost the government more than $300,000 per job created, and that the new version offered by Breaux would cost even more. Obviously, the money involved in the tax break would not go to workers; it almost never had. It was meant to line the pockets of some of most prominent corporations in the country.

Many of those corporations, especially the pharmaceutical firms, had fully adjusted to the new political realities of campaign finance. According to one source, the drug companies alone made $40 million in campaign contributions between 1999 and 2003. Few entities have this kind of political cash to spare. In 2003 the drug firms hired some 600 lobbyists to help the industry deal with an "overseas" threat of a different kind, a legislative proposal to allow Americans to buy drug prescriptions overseas and have them shipped into the United States. The battle was fueled by the stark price differentials between foreign-source prescriptions and the same drug in the United States (example, sixty tablets of the breast cancer drug tamoxifen cost $60 in Germany, $360 in America). To preserve their market, the drug companies and their lobbyists stressed their concern about the safety of imports and, incongruously, threatened to sharply limit supplies of their drugs to Canada.[15]

Most political observers in Washington believe that the free-spending pharmaceutical companies will win the reimportation fight. The good news in this situation for opponents of the boondoggle that was Section 936, and that threatens to become the new boondoggle of an amended Section 956 for CFCs, is that the drug companies are occupied for a while in 2003 with an issue they regard as more urgent. Moreover, the U.S. public is getting another firsthand taste of the intimidation tactics of the drug lobby, which has even added to its repertoire by creating a religious front group, the Christian Seniors Association, to lobby for high drug prices. No one doubts that the Congressional fight over the "possessions corporation system of taxation" has a few more rounds left to be fought.

The merry-go-round in the U.S. Capitol never stops. Unfortunately, it continues to spin at the expense of sound long-term public policy, and, as a result, Puerto Rico was and still is but a shadow of its future self.

Section II

Status

CHAPTER 9

The Young Bill: The Roar of the Coqui

I grew up living in a territory – my state of Alaska. We had taxation without representation. Many people in the state of Alaska, filing their income tax returns, used to write in red. "filed in protest." It made them feel a little better. It didn't do any good. But the point is these people living in Puerto Rico are entitled to certainty, and it is the obligation of Congress to address a final resolution. I think our committee has a moral and constitutional responsibility to address the situation in Puerto Rico, but we don't want to get involved in the politics of Puerto Rico. That is not our business.

– Senator Frank Murkowski (R-Alaska)
Floor of the U.S. Senate
July 31, 1998

Let us talk about history again. This is the last territory of the greatest democracy, America. A territory where no one has a true voice, although our government does an excellent job, but there are approximately 4 million Puerto Ricans that have one voice that cannot vote. This is not America as I know it. This is an America that talks one thing and walks another thing. This is an America that is saying, if Members do not accept this legislation, "no" to who I think are some of the greatest Americans that have ever served in our armed forces and are proud to be Americans but do not have the representation that they need.

This legislation is just the beginning. It is one small step of many steps. It is a step for freedom, it is a small step for justice, it is a small step for America. But collectively it is a great stride for democracy and for justice.

– Rep. Don Young (R-Alaska, At-Large)
Floor of the U.S. House of Representatives
March 4, 1998

We have not come to make war upon the people of a country that for centuries has been oppressed, but, on the contrary, to bring you protection, not only to yourselves but to your property, to promote your prosperity, and to bestow upon you the immunities and blessings of the liberal institutions of our government. It is not our purpose to interfere with any existing laws and customs that are wholesome and beneficial to your people as long as they conform to the rules of military administration, of order and justice. This is not a war of devastation, but one to give to all within the control of its military and naval forces the advantages and blessings of enlightened civilization.

– General Nelson A. Miles
Ponce, Puerto Rico
July 28, 1898

Five score and five more years after the commander of the American fleet that landed on their southern coast uttered the above words, the people of Puerto Rico are still wrangling with the liberal institutions of the U.S. government. The blessings of those institutions have flowed in their direction, in the form of billions of dollars if not in "enlightened civilization," and immunities have come as well, though perhaps most saliently from federal taxation, if not from military service. An observer from space, reading General Miles' words, and the speeches of the two representatives from Alaska who played key roles in the most recent round of Puerto Rican referenda, could be forgiven for his confusion. Given so many high-sounding promises, and such eloquence in the service of Puerto Rican self-determination, why is Puerto Rico's status so muddled?

In my own speeches over the years about the "last colony" of Puerto Rico, I used the example of the coqui, the little tree frog found on the island that has become the symbol of Puerto Rico. The status of this creature sums up the status of Puerto Rico perfectly. Frogs are amphibians and live, most of us like to think, in and around the water. They make deep-throated sounds that sound, well, frog-like. Not the coqui. He spends his time in a tree and the high-pitched noises he makes sound exactly like a chirping bird. Only in Puerto Rico, where even the local fauna have no idea exactly where they should be in the grand scheme of life!

Confusion aside, there is good news in the speeches being made on the floor of Congress and in the halls of government in San Juan and in municipalities across the island. The intensity of the Puerto Rican/U.S. relationship is increasing. Fifty-four years passed from annexation to the adoption of a Puerto Rican constitution. Fifteen years passed between the adoption of that constitution and the first advisory referendum in Puerto Rico on its future status. Twenty-six years later a second referendum occurred, and five years later a third, while in that same year a bill was approved by one House of Congress pledging a referendum every 10 years until the status question is resolved. Chairmen and ranking members of the relevant Congressional committees and subcommittees have cosigned letters signaling their agreement on the underlying nature of Puerto Rico's current status as an unincorporated territory and reasserting their determination to present options that represent "full self-government" in votes that will recur "within a certain number of years" and be "realistic" about the alternatives.

This acceleration of the debate over Puerto Rico's future, both within and without the island, is beset with all manner of political overtones and undertows. Entwined within it is the new and intensely competitive posture of the Democratic and Republican Parties as they vie for the support of Hispanic-Americans from Puerto Rico and from Mexico, El Salvador, Guatemala and other Latin nations. The election of a Republican President in 2000 who speaks Spanish and hails from Texas, George W. Bush, puts a new premium on GOP efforts to win the percentage of Hispanics votes nationally that Bush as governor won in Texas. In California, in October 2003, the first statewide Hispanic office-holder, Democrat Cruz Bustamante, came in second in his bid to succeed Gov. Gray Davis when the people of the state voted to recall him. The resolution of the 2000 election in the state of Florida, almost two months after the polls closed, further intensifies the thrall in which the parties find themselves to the demographically rising Hispanic population: Cuban-Americans in Southern Florida saw their leverage increase, as did, potentially, the 117,000-some Puerto Ricans who have settled around Orlando in recent years.

Entwined within the debate as well is the frequently contentious and seldom enlightening feud over English as the official language of the United States. Classical education, handed down in America through secular and sectarian institutions alike, had always hailed bilingual and multi-lingual capability as the hallmarks of superior education. At one time this included grammar-school study of Latin and Greek, and undergraduate and graduate requirements to be able to read and research in academically relevant languages, from French to German to Spanish. With the ascension of identity group politics and continuing tensions over immigration issues, language issues have become explosive, sometimes sincerely so, sometimes as cover for racial and ethnocentric ideologies. In the case of Puerto Rico, they have proved polarizing and thereby tended to reinforce the status quo, as the island's commonwealth advocates hint darkly of the submersion of Puerto Rican culture by the United States and conservatives in Congress hint just as darkly of the reverse.

Overall, it seems, illusions that have endured for decades are losing their hold, and a conscious desire for clarification, certainty, permanence and real self-determination is gaining strength both in San Juan and in Washington. Meanwhile, the *status quo* has its hired guns and vested interests, but, as was the case with the weakening and final repeal of the Section 936 tax gimmick, the forces of Puerto Rican inertia and special pleading have lost some of their steam, like a tropical storm fighting the steep slopes of a resistant headland.

Once Congress had decided to change Puerto Rico's "tax status" as a haven extraordinaire, trimming the special manufacturing tax breaks in 1993, it was primed, we hoped, to focus on the root of the problem: the cruel contradiction known as "commonwealth." Our goal was to persuade the House and Senate of their responsibility to frame the options in legal terms that would be both clear to the Puerto Rican voter and acceptable to the Congress, which means acceptable under the U.S. Constitution. This sounds like it should be something of an easy task, but it had proved to be anything but. As the 104th Congress began in 1995, appeals by Puerto Rican leaders for Congress to define the terms of a plebiscite had not borne fruit.

I learned a great deal about the political realities in Washington as we looked for members of Congress willing to take up and advocate real self-determination legislation for Puerto Rico. Over the course of this lobbying effort, and in the years that followed right up to the present, I met and personally engaged in conversations with dozens of members of Congress relating to the referendum bill that we had going in both houses. What amazed me most was that, initially, participation in the bill was mainly limited to cosponsorship, and it was done solely to placate certain insiders. However, once the issues became clear to these cosponsors, they became champions of the issue straight from their hearts. They came to believe that they were doing the right thing for 4 million disenfranchised people.

The passion that those legislators exhibited in promoting the issue frequently came at a high cost to them politically, yet their integrity drove them forward. It is this kind of passion to "do the right thing" that most impresses me about many members of Congress and reinforces my faith in our democratic system. Without it, "insider influence" would win every debate. Money would always talk, and "we the people" would be forced just to listen.

Like gumshoe detectives, we walked the halls of Congress looking for any members of the House and Senate who could be convinced of the justice of our cause. The first House version of the referendum bill we championed was introduced by Rep. Don Young, Republican of Alaska, in March 1996. I came to know Don very well over the course of the fight for Puerto-Rican self-determination, and I admire him greatly. Puerto Rico was six to seven time zones away from his home state and Alaska, to say the least, was not a favorite destination for Puerto Rican immigrants. Don derived all his feeling for the issue from human empathy and a sense of history. He knew what consistency and fidelity to freedom required of America's elected leaders.

The measure we launched ultimately became known not by its various bill numbers, but by the shorthand phrase, the "Young bill," so named for this 16-term, at-large congressman. Like most Alaskans, Young is a rugged individualist. He is a former riverboat captain whose home state politics and personal inclinations led him to membership on the House Interior Committee, later to become the House Resources Committee. Some individualists care very little for the freedom of others as long as they have their own. Others have as much passion for the freedom of their neighbors as they do for themselves. Only a few have passion for the freedom of people far away. Young's passion took the form of legislation to allow the people of Puerto Rico to show a preference for statehood or independence, then to ask Congress to honor this preference and proceed to transition and implementation, if needed. He wanted a mechanism established whereby Puerto Rico could routinely vote on clear options, so that Congress could regularly gauge the sentiments of the Puerto Rican people and commit itself at the outset to honor those sentiments.

The bill's findings provided a capsule history of the whole status debate and the actions taken to date, culminating with a proposal for Congressionally defined options for continuation of Puerto Rico's territorial status (commonwealth), independence and statehood. Any attempt to untangle the modern twists and turns of the fight over Puerto Rico's legal relationship with the mainland requires some in-depth understanding of the island's history and place in the Caribbean. Most of what I had learned about this history came from discussions across a dinner table or over drinks with my Puerto Rican friends in business, philanthropy, and the academic world. One does not have to study the issues long to understand how keenly disappointed Puerto Ricans are about their dealings with the United States.

Originally, the American role in Puerto Rico was something of an act of opportunism. It came as Spain was loosening its grip on its struggling colony, not increasing it. In 1897 excitement had spread over the island because Madrid had granted an "Autonomic Charter" that, among other things, permitted Puerto Rico to create its own bicameral legislature. This experiment proved ephemeral, however, as Puerto Rico, like the Philippines, became an object of attention when the United States intervened in the Cuban rebellion against Spain. Different men in power had somewhat different motives for pushing a U.S. move on Puerto Rico. The assistant secretary of the navy, Theodore Roosevelt, viewed war as inevitable and welcomed the chance to expel Spain from the Western Hemisphere. Henry Cabot Lodge responded to a blunt Roosevelt letter in May 1897 and assured him, "Porto Rico is not forgotten and we mean to have it."[1]

Have it we did, as General Miles' delicately balanced proclamation, quoted above, makes plain. American soldiers, contrary to some politically motivated histories, were largely welcomed to the island. The vast majority of residents viewed U.S. forces, among them a young Carl Sandburg, as liberators. The Treaty of Paris ended hostilities with Spain in December 1898. Guam, Puerto Rico and the Philippines were included in the treaty, with the United States basically buying these three countries for $20 million. The idea of colonial exploitation acquired a new wrinkle in the case of Puerto Rico when some of the prime advocates for acquisition of the island turned out not to be rapacious industrialists but textbook publishers! The situation developed this way. Many in Congress were balking at Spain's asking price for its former possessions. The yellow journalist William Randolph Hearst stepped forward and offered to buy the three countries himself. Some people thought that private ownership of a few nations would be, well, unseemly.

The textbook publishers entered the fray and urged Congress to spend the money. Look, they said, there is a great deal of profit to be made in selling textbooks to Puerto Rico's schools once they institute the study of English as part of the United States! They argued that the mainland would get excellent return on its investment from this step alone. Congress ultimately concurred and the $20 million appropriation was approved, clearing the way for the inclusion of Puerto Rico and the other two territories in the treaty.

Article IX of the Treaty of Paris recognized the supremacy of the American Congress in determining the civil rights and legal status of the island's people. Congress, however, moved only tentatively to exercise this power (at least relative to the speed with which it recognized Cuban independence, subject to the severe restriction of the Platt Amendment, in 1902). The Foraker Act in 1900 began the period historians describe as "colonial tutelage," deferring questions about U.S. citizenship for Puerto Rico's inhabitants and establishing the idea of the "unincorporated territory." The only advantage of the idea was the flexibility it granted in shaping overall economic and fiscal relations between the island and the mainland.

In 1906, as U.S. president, Roosevelt paid a visit to San Juan and enthused, consistent with his naturalistic bent, over the island's beauty and variety of plant life. Although he spoke patronizingly of the "childlike" character of the Puerto Rican people, he called in December of that year for U.S. citizenship for Puerto Ricans. That would not occur until the adoption of the Jones Act in 1917, which coincided with the U.S. engagement in World War I and the beginning of the century-long involvement of Puerto Ricans in the U.S. Armed Forces. The Jones Act also made provision for an elective Insular Senate, whose enactments were subject to approval by the appointed governor (a mainlander until the 1940s) and, of course, in principle, the U.S. Congress. The Act's leading sponsor was Democratic Congressman William H. Jones of Virginia, who had strongly criticized the U.S. retention of colonial power embodied in the Foraker Act.

It may oversimplify matters a bit, but for the most part the next 30 years of Puerto Rican history were dominated by economic rather than political, particularly status-related, issues. These developments are described in the context of U.S. investment and tax policy in the previous chapter. From the time of the Treaty of Paris, the island had political parties and activists who made the case for variants of the major status options that exist today – independence (including free association), continued dependence with expansion and elaboration of Puerto Rican self-government, and statehood. The Federal party, led by Muñoz Rivera, the father of Muñoz Marin, the great patron of common-wealth, was sharply dismayed by the Foraker Act. Muñoz Rivera's deepest sentiments rested with independence, but he was practical and realistic in seeking the expansion of self-rule. It was he who prodded Rep. Jones to add such items as an elective Puerto Rican Senate to his reform proposals.

Muñoz Rivera was concerned that the granting of citizenship might mean a stalling of progress in the direction he favored. The U.S. Congress might grant this favor and believe it had done enough. In most respects, he was proved right over time, and nothing decisive happened to change the features of Puerto Rico's status until the arrival on the scene of Muñoz Marin. Like his father, a combination of idealist and practical politician, Muñoz Marin focused on rescuing Puerto Rico's economic plight after the Great Depression and World War II, and on winning evermore levers of self-rule. Another step was taken in this direction in 1946 when President Truman, bowing to deep sentiment on the island and an advisory vote of the Puerto Rican Senate, appointed the first Puerto-Rican born governor, Jesus T. Pinero. The U.S. Senate confirmed the choice six days later.

In form, this was consistent with the old procedure for the selection of governors; in substance, it was a shift in power. While tempests swirled in Congress for both statehood and independence, Muñoz Marin and his popular Democrats, or PPD, lobbied Washington successfully in 1947 for an elective governorship. The Butler-Crawford bill, its way paved by the appointment of Pinero at the Puerto Rican Senate's overwhelming insistence, sailed through Congress. The elective governorship was another sign of Puerto Rico's uniqueness in the American territorial scheme. Having done the work necessary to bring about this step toward self-rule, Muñoz Marin and the PPD won a resounding victory in the first gubernatorial election in 1948. The PPD's plan for economic development also had popular appeal, and it was at this time that the idea of an evolving commonwealth, matched with tax policies to attract investment to the island, took hold in the public mind.

The next task was the writing of a Puerto Rican constitution and the creation of the "commonwealth." While this task was fully achieved in 1952, giving Puerto Rico another hallmark of a full-fledged state in the American Union, the process by which it occurred underscored the reality of Congressional and U.S. Constitutional supremacy under which Puerto Rico lived then and still lives today. The sequence involved five discrete steps that, in sum, increased home rule dramatically in Puerto Rico but did not achieve a permanent result. The first step began in March 1950 and ended in July of that year with action in the U.S. Congress. A bill, H.R. 7674, was introduced in the House by the non-voting resident commissioner, Dr. Antonio Fernos-Isern. This bill was necessary so that Congress could authorize Puerto Rico to organize a government under the design of a constitution of its own making. The bill won bipartisan support and President Truman signed it into law on July 5, 1950 as Public Law 81-600, also known as the Federal Relations Act.

Next came an 18-month period in which the consent of the people of Puerto Rico was sought for the holding of a constitutional convention. This required public discussion, the scheduling of a referendum, the registration of voters, and finally the vote itself. This proved to be the bloodiest period in Puerto Rico's history vis-à-vis the United States. A radical band of nationalists, opposed to a process they saw as leading to deeper ties with the mainland, organized an attack on the governor's mansion in San Juan. Two other nationalists fired shots in an attempt to assassinate Truman outside Blair House in Washington. These actions did not block the vote, which ultimately, on June 4, 1951, delivered a ringing endorsement of the process laid out in Public Law 81-600. The terms were set for a Puerto Rican constitutional convention, and in August 1951 the pro-commonwealth PPD won the vast majority of delegates to the convention. The convention itself met from September 17, 1951, to February 6, 1952. The result was a document that uses the term *Estado Libre Asociado* (Associated Free State), but that also has been referred to as the Commonwealth, or "compact." The use of *Estado Libre Asociado* proved profoundly confusing in the long run because Puerto Rico's status did not meet the international meaning of that phrase, which connotes sovereignty and the ability to act unilaterally.

The convention on February 4, 1952 adopted a resolution asking the governor of Puerto Rico to hold another referendum, this time to accept or reject the convention's work. The people of Puerto Rico did so on March 3, 1952, overwhelmingly approving the draft constitution. The constitution was then forwarded to President Truman in April, and on April 22 he inaugurated the next phase of consideration by sending it to Congress for its approval. Truman praised it wholeheartedly for its embodiment of the principle of "government by consent." Members of the House and Senate argued with certain of the draft's provisions, especially its social guarantees in the areas of education and living standards. The House ultimately approved the constitution without amendment, but a much more serious challenge to it, indeed to the entire process, was repelled in the Senate only when Fernos-Isern offered an amendment that provided for changes to the Puerto Rican constitution only if they were consistent with applicable U.S. constitutional and statutory provisions. With this deft nod to sensibilities on both the Congressional and Puerto Rican side, Congress adopted Public Law 447 on July 7, 1952.

In step four, the Puerto Rican constitutional convention accepted the Congressional amendments, after making provision for their ultimate approval in the island's next general election. With this accomplished, step five, a day of jubilation, arrived. Governor Muñoz Marin proclaimed the Puerto Rican constitution on July 25, 1952. In a symbolic gesture, he had the flag of Puerto Rico raised side-by-side with the Stars and Stripes atop the ancient Spanish fortress of El Morro. In the euphoria of the time, many Puerto Rico activists and scholars actually believed and argued that a new day had dawned on the island, that its colonial status was at an end, and that it was no longer a possession of the United States under the Territorial Clause of the U.S. Constitution. Certainly, a significant expansion and elevation of Puerto Rico's status had occurred. Like a state (and nothing in the process of adopting Public Law 81-600 had undone the possibility of eventual statehood), Puerto Rico would elect its own officials and adopt its own laws.

As Fernos-Isern's saving amendment implied, however, nothing in the adoption or amendment of the Puerto Rican Constitution did or could undo the reality of the island's obligation to conform both to the U.S. Constitution and to Congressional statutes. This included both bills adopted by Congress that bore specifically on status and those other laws, as Congress could choose at its discretion, to apply to the island. In many cases, as subsequent history would show, it would be the Puerto Rican government itself that would seek to have a law applied, desiring to participate in federal programs, to enjoy the benefit of U.S. law enforcement, or to work at U.S. military bases, to name just a few examples. The new relationship, had then, and has now, practical power as an expression, ratified on multiple occasions, of the preferences of the Puerto Rican people, U.S. citizens all. Successive presidents of both parties and the Congress have paid homage to Puerto Rican self-determination, even if their actions have sometimes impeded its realization. Frustration with Puerto Rico (for example, over Vieques) is a permissible political feeling in Washington today; hostility toward it is not.

Nonetheless, the legal and juridical reality is that this status or structure, and each of its elements, exists at the discretion of Congress and can be unilaterally changed by Congress in the exercise of its prerogatives under the Constitution. That this is very unlikely to happen in any radical sense does not alter the basic fact that Puerto Rico remained, and remains, under commonwealth status an unequal partner in its relationship with the United States. Over the past half century, this core ambiguity has sometimes worked in favor of the local government's aims on the island, as when it sought to increase or preserve tax benefits for industry while maintaining the unique fact of not having to pay federal income tax in most situations. It has more often worked as a factory of illusion, however, as a dwindling number of Puerto Rican residents opt to endorse a concept of "enhanced commonwealth" that is, in reality, a contradiction in terms, a way of espousing full self-determination while claiming benefits that flow only from concrete dependency.

This brings us, then, to the current era, beginning in the 1960s, in which Puerto Ricans have voted three times, in deeply flawed plebiscites, on the question of status. The result of those votes has been a perpetuation of impermanence. Nonetheless, an undercurrent has formed and flowed, albeit slowly, from illusion to realism. As this is written, Puerto Rico knows with increasing clarity that it is attempting to have its cake and eat it, too; that the cake has been baked on what is, in part, a false recipe with a stale outcome; and that the future belongs to those who are willing to take on all the risks of freedom and not just savor its rewards.

The first flawed plebiscite on Puerto Rico's long-term future took place in 1967. Economically and politically, it occurred at, and accelerated in certain ways, a time of transition. Muñoz Marin had passed on the leadership of the *populares* to a new governor, Robert Sanchez-Vilella, elected in 1964. The new governor had difficulty wearing the mantle of the beloved Muñoz Marin, and statehood advocates were able to cite the increase in dependency that was coming through LBJ's Great Society as a source of concern. The Republican Statehood Party (PER) did not officially endorse the statehood option under the 1967 initiative, but its leader, Luis Ferre, did so, heading a group called the *Estadistas Unidos,* or United Statehooders. The *independentistas* sat out the plebiscite and Muñoz and the *populares* rallied their forces to sustain the commonwealth option. It's important to note that, as with the later 1993 plebiscite, the options identified in 1967 were framed by Puerto Rico, in a local law adopted in December 1966, and not by the U.S. Congress. Non-binding to begin with, the actual scope and details of the options were not "reality-checked" against what Congress would allow.

Consistent with the large turnouts that have long characterized Puerto Rican democracy, two thirds of registered voters went to the polls on July 23, 1967. Of these, more than 60 percent endorsed the continuation of commonwealth status, described on the ballot in the language of *estado libre asociado*. The wording of this option included the highly contestable words *autonoma* (autonomy) and *permanentemente* (permanence) that had been falsely ascribed to commonwealth from the beginning. The second provision of the commonwealth option referred to the bond thus created as "inviolable." People of goodwill may have intended this to be the case, but legally it was meaningless. The other options, statehood and independence, were simply stated, without adjectives or other elaboration. Each option acknowledged the role of Congress in accepting and acting upon the expressed will of the people.

Thus, the Puerto Rican majority voted in favor of something that was and is an illusion. Some have called it "enhanced commonwealth" status, to distinguish it from the actually existing arrangement. First of all, this status is "enhanced" for what it does *not* mention, that is, that Puerto Rico is a territory of the United States and any element of its arrangements with Washington can be altered by Congress and the President acting on their own volition. Second, implicit in the words "autonomy" and "permanence" are ideas that are mutually contradictory under the American system and exceptional in almost every way imaginable. The vision set forth is that Puerto Ricans are irrevocably citizens of the United States, that Puerto Rico and the United States are permanently joined, that federal benefits can and will flow to the island, and that federal income taxes will not be paid. Moreover, enhanced commonwealth envisions a sovereign Puerto Rico that can make its own treaties with other nations, and even exercise a selective veto over which federal laws do and do not apply to it.

Given such options, who would not be sorely tempted to vote for them? It can be hazarded that, presented with such an opportunity, each of the existing 50 states would deliver strong majorities for "enhanced statehood." In fact, within the American constitutional ideal of a federal system, other than acting to leave the Union (a small war between the states settled that question for the foreseeable future), each of the 50 states retains a certain sphere of sovereignty over its own affairs. Numerous examples exist of individual states following statutory or constitutional imperatives unique to their jurisdictions. As one authority puts it, however, Puerto Rico's notion of "enhanced commonwealth" would provide it with greater sovereignty than a state while denying its residents representation at the federal level. This is not a formula that anything but a New Age Congress would consider, much less approve.

Even historians sympathetic to Puerto Rico's circumstances through the centuries candidly admit that it operates under federal laws that have been enacted and amended, and that can, in fact and in principle, be repealed or amended again. The only true path to "enhanced commonwealth" status would be a U.S. constitutional amendment that, by its express terms, carved out exception after exception to U.S. law and practice in both the domestic and international arenas. It is not likely that one will ever see a plebiscite option that acknowledges this fact, and that asks Puerto Ricans to support the introduction of such an amendment to the federal Constitution. Nonetheless, it would be an honestly worded approach.

Despite winning just two-fifths of the popular vote in the 1967 plebiscite, the United Statehooders were ecstatic. They had done better than they had thought possible against the increasingly divided ruling party, and the returns from San Juan and Ponce were especially encouraging. Emboldened, the PER regrouped as the New Progressive Party (PNP) and took its cause and its leader, Ferre, into the 1968 gubernatorial election with a new confidence. There Ferre scored a major upset, winning by 23,000 votes. Just as Ronald Reagan benefited in 1980 from the presence of John Anderson on the ballot, and Bill Clinton from the presence of Ross Perot and his short-lived Reform Party in 1992, Ferre benefited from Sanchez-Vilella's decision to abandon the *populares* and form his own New People's Party. The new party captured more than three times the number of votes needed by the PPD to deny Ferre the governorship.

Ferre served a single term, and his election did not translate into immediate gains for the statehooders. The period of rapid transfer of U.S. capital-intensive industries to Puerto Rico was just cresting under Ferre, and Puerto Rico's economic transformation, incomplete but nonetheless significant, was still underway. The growth of the welfare state in this era was rapid, and the belief that U.S. tax policies were hurting the Puerto Rican economy, or at least only artificially helping it, was turning up in U.S. Treasury documents but not registering in public. Just as Section 936 of the tax code first came under political question in a period of high federal budget deficits, so too did questions about Puerto Rican status gain piquancy as residents worried about their future.

The PNP and the PPD traded places in the governor's mansion in San Juan with regularity after Ferre's breakthrough. The PNP maintained its strong advocacy of statehood and won the governorship again in 1976, 1980, and 1992. The 1992 election saw the PNP win just over 50 percent of the vote, to 45.6 percent for the PPD and a scant (and typical) 4.1 percent for the independence party. The election was even more favorable for the PNP at the municipal level, as the party won 54 of the 78 mayoralties at stake.

Rough parity between the two major parties in Puerto Rico bred more intense competition, but one offshoot of that competition has been an approach to the status question by all parties that is more serious and more focused. The defects in previous efforts to resolve the issue were gradually recognized. In 1989 all three parties (the PPD, PNP and the PIP) united in asking the U.S. Congress to formally consult with Puerto Rico regarding the status options and complaining that this had not happened since the Treaty of Paris in 1898. This petition led to a round of Congressional hearings and to the introduction of a bill, setting forth the options, in the 101st Congress. As would happen again later, this bill became deadlocked in the U.S. Senate, where it died. Finally, in 1993, Puerto Rico took up the status question again, once more on its own initiative and with wording clouded by unrealistic and utopian impulses.

After the passage of 26 years and the surge of the PNP, the enhanced commonwealth option had lost significant ground. For the first time, this option, which could be called the "status quo plus a wish list," commanded the votes of fewer than half (48.6 percent) of those who participated. Statehood received 46.3 percent of the vote, with independence, as always, lagging far behind at 4.4 percent. The Commonwealth position prevailed by a mere 38,000 votes, or roughly 1,000 votes for every seat in the Puerto Rican House of Representatives. The statehood option captured three of the island's eight Senate districts and 16 of its 40 House districts. At last, a race was on.

This is a good place to underscore how fundamental the status question is in the alignment of Puerto Rico's political parties. Even when the issue is not directly on the table, or even when economic or other issues dominate voters' minds (as they do in every democracy), the status issue is inscribed in the grain of each political party that operates on the island. The PPD and the PNP are not mirror images of the Democrats and the Republicans in the United States. These Puerto Rican parties represent poles on the status question that attract or repel the typical voter. The most important impact of this phenomenon is that, in the votes on status, political parties have their very existence at stake. To choose independence or statehood would, for members of the PPD, for example, be to choose to dismantle the structure of the party to which they belong. In American elections, some degree of patronage is usually at stake, but the number of people affected is not usually enough to tip the outcome. In Puerto Rico, the dislocations caused by a change in status could uproot an entire party's machinery. Activists on all sides fight much harder under this circumstance.

Writing two years later about what happened in 1993, in response to a resolution adopted by Puerto Rico in December 1994, four chairmen of House committees and subcommittees with jurisdiction over Puerto Rico issues diagnosed the difficulty this skewed plebiscite presented. They told the House Speaker and Senate President in Puerto Rico that the United States and the Congress respected the process by which the plebiscite took place and that Congress would "take cognizance" of the results of this "orderly," "lawful and democratic election." Even so, they noted that Congress had not addressed itself beforehand to the feasibility of each option and the manner in which it would be implemented. There was an even deeper problem with the Commonwealth option, because, the chairmen wrote, this option, as presented, would actually "profoundly change rather than continue the current Commonwealth of Puerto Rico government structure."[2] The chairmen went on to enumerate the changes that would be required, compiling a list remarkably close to those that would have been needed to realize the Commonwealth option as it had been phrased in 1967.

The chairmen then stated, in language that was not meant to be blunt but merely truthful, "that Puerto Rico's present status is that of an unincorporated territory subject in all respects to the authority of the United States Congress under the Territorial Clause of the Constitution."[3] Rejecting the illusion of enhanced Commonwealth (Dan Burton, chairman of the Western Hemisphere Subcommittee of the International Relations Committee, *was* blunt on a separate occasion, labeling the Commonwealth option "bogus"), the letter affirmed that Puerto Rico had only three options to pursue if full self-government was the goal. These were "separate sovereignty and national independence" (e.g., France, Venezuela); "separate sovereignty in free association with the United States" (e.g., the Marshall Islands,

Micronesia); and statehood (e.g., Ohio). They noted that none of these options need be taken by Puerto Rico; legally speaking, it could remain an unincorporated territory indefinitely.

About this last option, nothing would be permanent, nor, the chairmen wrote, would the island's desired goal of equal treatment under federal programs be achieved. For that to happen, the island would first have to submit to federal tax laws. The enhanced Commonwealth option had not been written with this sequence of events in mind. Indeed, some critics of Commonwealth have pointed out how the one-way street it would preserve in federal tax benefits toward Puerto Rico was our government's way of apologizing to Puerto Ricans for denying them self-rule. Keeping or extending that policy has been Puerto Ricans' way of accepting the apology. The letter closed with these Republican leaders pledging to take the next steps to ensure that a future plebiscite would contain options that were accurately and fully described, and that could, in fact, be implemented by Congress with the final consent of the Puerto Rican people.

This was a watershed in the entire debate. Just two years before the centenary of the U.S. acquisition of Puerto Rico, a Caribbean "roadmap," to use a term that would later be applied to the Middle East conflict, had been laid out by Congressional leaders with the authority to turn their words into action. Four months later, not to be outdone, four House Democrats, including ranking International Relations Committee member Lee Hamilton, weighed in with a letter of their own on the 1993 vote. Using more diplomatic language, they acknowledged that the wording of the Commonwealth option on the ballot had been "difficult." Their brief letter continued by concurring with the Republican majority on the depiction of Puerto Rico as an unincorporated territory subject to U.S. law. The letter called for "sound options" to be presented to the Puerto Rican people and for the adoption, by Congress, of legislation that would guide these votes and ensure that they regularly took place.

By this time, of course, Congress, under the Clinton Administration, had already moved to trim the tax gimmick known as Section 936. Even so, U.S. companies that had benefited from it had not given up hope of rescuing their pot of gold at the end of the commonwealth rainbow. Members of the House on both sides of the aisle distinguished themselves in these public letters by adopting a stance that took a candid and long-term view of self-determination for the Puerto Rican people. The potential economic dislocations and adjustments that would follow any change in Puerto Rico's status were very much on the members' minds. The thrust of the Democrats' letter was to state their support for H.R. 3024 in the 104th Congress, and to stress their concern about the island's economic fate. Both letters showed largeness of spirit; the industrial groups bent on preserving their tax advantages and opposing a clear vote showed something else.

This was the state of the battle as we began our fresh drive for a *Congressionally defined* status bill. As helpful as the 1967 and 1993 votes were (they showed, beyond the shadow of a doubt, that the Puerto Rican people were very unhappy with the contemporary state of affairs), the options presented in these referenda were written as Puerto Ricans understood them, or, more precisely, as they imagined they could be. Congress had stood back from the raging debate and washed its hands of the outcome. It had not committed itself to do anything in response even to the clearest statement of Puerto Rico's preferences. We wanted this indifference and ambiguity to end.

The "Young bill" of 1996 was designed to achieve this goal. Our search for House cosponsors, as I mentioned earlier, took us all over Capitol Hill and through the doorways of member after member in the House office buildings south of the Capitol. Like most lobbyists, we wanted the support of the Congressional leadership, the relevant committee chairs, and rank-and-file members, in that order. One particularly important segment of the latter, naturally, was the Puerto Rican contingent. By this I mean the voting members of the Congress of Puerto Rican extraction. At the time of our efforts, there were three House members who fit this description, Luis Gutierrez of Chicago and Nydia Velazquez and Jose Serrano of New York. All three were liberal Democrats.

Of these three, Congressman Serrano was probably the deepest thinker and the one who was truly interested in Puerto Rico's well being. Velazquez and Gutierrez preferred to echo the sales pitch of the multinational drug companies, although Gutierrez developed and mastered a technique that managed to wrap the pharmaceutical firms' tax breaks in the Puerto Rican flag. I approached Serrano to ask him to become a cosponsor of the Young bill. At first he was suspicious and reluctant because he thought I was another "gringo" trying to milk something from the island of his birthplace that he loved so much. It took a lot of exhorting on my part and the help of Manuel Rodriguez Orellana, the *independentista* leader, to make Serrano feel comfortable that I was acting in the best interest of Puerto Rico and not representing another scheme to exploit the island.

The clincher came, I believe, when we talked about how I first came to America, a penniless Eastern European, and been drawn to Salsa and to places like Club Caborojeno. With a big smile Serrano confessed to me that, at one time, he was an emcee at Club Caborojeno. At that moment, I saw that the ice was finally broken. He became a big and faithful supporter of the Young bill from that point on. This was another event along the way that confirmed the advice of Joseph Campbell to "follow your bliss." All logic (and a few of my friends) told me to stay away from those "Salsa" places when I was 19 years old and a new arrival in a strange country, but I followed what made me happy. The seed that I planted there bore fruit, many years later, under circumstances I could never have imagined.

With the House bill sponsorship moving ahead, our search then began for a Senate sponsor, but this proved to be much more difficult. We had more than a few fruitful as well as comical meetings with senators. All of the meetings were illuminating. When we first went to see Sen. Larry Craig, an Idaho Republican, about being the bill's prime sponsor, he was reluctant. Sen. Craig fit the definition of "unlikely prospect" for becoming a champion of Puerto Rico. Like Don Young, he hailed from a conservative, GOP-oriented state that had a small population and few Puerto Ricans. On top of this, his business approval rating was high (80 percent from the U.S. Chamber of Commerce), and he had a 100 percent rating from the American Conservative Union. But I soon found out again how careful one has to be with stereotypes in Washington. U.S. history is full of small-state legislators who have taken outsized leadership roles in surprising areas like military issues and foreign affairs.

Sen. Craig's relationship with some of the people that were our friends steered him in the direction of helping us. When the bill was drafted and we went to see him, the first question he asked our lobbyist was, "Are you sure this is not going anywhere?" Our lobbyist assured him that this was "dead in the water." Craig replied, "Then I am going out on the floor this afternoon and make one hell of a splash with this bill." On our way back from the Senate Office Buildings, I asked the lobbyist, "What do you mean the bill isn't going anywhere? Aren't we trying to get a real referendum bill in Congress?" He said, "Yes, we are, but senators do not like to take on issues that could potentially hurt them, and," he added, "the pharmaceutical companies can create an awful lot of hurt for someone who opposes them."

As Sen. Craig got more and more involved with the bill, however, he developed a passion for it that was memorable, especially given his reaction to it in the beginning. The bill was ultimately introduced as S. 2019 on August 2, 1996, on the eve of the annual late-summer recess. It was referred to committee, with six cosponsors. We realized that it was already late in the session and that we needed more senators with us. One of our stops was to see Sen. Joseph Biden, a Delaware Democrat. Biden was a member of the Judiciary Committee and he prided himself on his subtle understanding of the law and the Constitution.

Biden listened intently to our group presentation on the bill and then proceeded to ask some basic questions about Puerto Rico's relationship with the United States and the status of Puerto Rican residents as U.S. citizens. After our briefing, he smiled as if he had received a private revelation. He said: "You know, this has been the most informative session about Puerto Rico that I have ever had. The most amazing thing is how uninformed many of my colleagues in Congress are about Puerto Rico. I'll bet that half of the people in Congress don't even know that Puerto Ricans are U.S. citizens, and I'll bet that if they found out, they would try to vote to take that citizenship away."

It was very obvious that Sen. Biden was making a joke about the widespread ignorance regarding Puerto Rican issues in Congress. I am sure, however, that if a vote on Puerto Rican citizenship were taken, it would win a resounding majority. But the fact that such a joke could even be made told us just how much work remained to be done to educate Congress about Puerto Rico. Biden ultimately did not sponsor our bill, either in the 104th Congress or the next. In fact, our high-water mark for Senate sponsors was only 17 (in 1998). Despite our best efforts, our Senate cosponsors remained stuck at six that year, and S. 2019 did not see the light of day. Nonetheless, we had gained a toehold in the "upper chamber," as its proud members call it, and a Mountain State senator who might have been expected to do the bidding of big business was gradually being transformed into a passionate advocate for people who were never going to be a significant part of his constituency. It is heartening developments like this that have kept me and others in this arduous fight.

Meanwhile, our efforts to get a floor vote on the Young bill (its formal title was H.R. 3024, the Puerto Rico Self-Determination Act) also faltered that year. It was not without some initial success, however. H.R. 3024 was approved by the House Resources Committee, by voice vote, a sign of virtually unanimous support. This was quite an accomplishment. But, by this time, it was June of 1996 and it would take until September for the House Rules Committee to devise a rule for debate and get the bill cleared for consideration in the full House. By this time the pharmaceutical firms were in the thick of things. It was not that they cared about the niceties of constitutional law, and they certainly were not deeply attuned to the aspirations of ordinary Puerto Ricans. It was the simple fact that for them the best outcome was a continuation of the current confusion about Puerto Rico's colonial nature.

The pharmaceutical lobbyists came to the debate loaded, politically speaking, for bear. They had learned a great deal from their campaign over the previous two decades to fight off the direct efforts by the Treasury Department and members of Congress to repeal their tax gimmick. On the status question, they knew they would have to fight indirectly, because a straight-on argument about the need for commonwealth as a means of preserving tax preferences would carry no weight at all. They became adept at deploying all kinds of surrogate arguments, from the "English-First" issue, to the threat of a flood of new Puerto Rican immigration, to the loss of a Republican Congress, in their drive to delay action on self-determination.

The English language argument, spurious as it was, became one of the most potent.

The Young Bill: The Roar of the Coqui

As we weighed our strategy on H.R. 3024 in the fall of 1996, I went to a fundraiser for Don Young held at a private home. The pharmaceutical companies had signaled their plan to put an amendment on the bill that would make English the official language of Puerto Rico. Don was in a quandary. He wanted to get a vote on the bill the next day, but he knew that its passage would be held hostage to the "English" amendment. That night, he asked me, "Do you guys want this bill or not?" My answer was yes, but the English amendment would be political suicide for our governor, Pedro Rossello, because the Puerto Rican elections were just around the corner. Since the governor, along with his pro-statehood party, backed the Young bill, his opponents could allege that he and the PNP no longer wanted Spanish to be spoken in Puerto Rico, a deadly accusation. We debated the issue for a long time, and, finally, the next morning we decided to pull the bill.

As we walked out into the hallway flanking the House chamber, Don Young was on one side of me and Dan Burton was on the other, with his arm around my shoulder. Dan said to me: "Don't worry, Alex, next year we will stick this bill to them."

On the plane ride back to San Juan shortly thereafter, I sat next to Ramon Luis Lugo, the lobbyist for the PPD, the commonwealth party. Ramon is a very intelligent and competent local strategist for the PPD. He had recruited Charlie Black's powerhouse lobbying company, with its strong GOP leadership connections, and had helped orchestrate much of the PPD strategy in Washington. He said to me: "Why did you guys pull the bill? This was your big chance. You may not get another chance again." He was angry. I didn't say anything but, inside, I knew that if the Young bill passed with that "English" provision, the PPD could say Rossello was in favor of making English the official language of Puerto Rico. I suspected that they felt the issue could have turned the election.

Fortunately, Rossello won reelection handily. Cynicism had killed H.R. 3024, but it did not take Rossello down with it. We would live to fight another day.

There is one more story to tell from this first round of the status battle in 1996. This one involved the Clinton White House and it nearly converted me into a permanent cynic. Shortly after Don Young pulled H.R. 3024 off the floor because of the "English Only" poison pill planted there by the pharmaceutical firms, and right after the November elections, I was in Washington, D.C. for a black tie affair. I had flown up that afternoon from San Juan and my plan was to fly back to Puerto Rico on the 7 am flight from Dulles the next day.

When I got back to the Hotel Mayflower from the black tie event, I had an urgent message to call one of our lobbyists. I did, and the lobbyist told me that arrangements had been made for me to have breakfast with Vice President Gore the next morning at the White House. I told the lobbyist that the only clothes I had with me were my tux and my jeans and that all the stores were closed and they did not reopen until after the breakfast. The lobbyist told me that he could get one of his people to lend me a suit and a tie. I said OK. The next morning, Wayne, one of the associates of the lobbying firm, showed up with a suit of his own clothes that was to be my outfit.

Everything was in order except that Wayne was 5'9" tall and I am 6'1".

What to do? It was 7 a.m. and the breakfast was scheduled for nine o'clock. I quickly whipped out the sewing kit supplied by the hotel and extended the trouser-length by putting in a new cuff (a trick I learned when I was a sewing machine salesman). Then I ironed out the cuff. It looked passable. The sleeves were a little short, but fortunately Wayne was about the same chest size as I and had long arms, so the shirt and the jacket were also passable (if you call looking like Charlie Chaplin passable). Since my appearance wasn't bad enough to send me back to the DP camps, everything would be just fine, I thought. By 8:30 a.m. we were out of the hotel room. At the breakfast there were about eight other people, mostly from the pharmaceutical companies. The issue of Section 936 was heating up again and they were all out to convince the Vice President that Puerto Rico desperately needed this tax provision.

After the pharmaceutical pitchmen made their case for half an hour, it was my turn to speak. I was seated right next to the Vice President. I proceeded to tell our side of the story, which involved how Section 936 was a tax boondoggle and how it really hurt our economy and was a colossal waste of money for U.S. taxpayers. Mr. Gore, who had already been very well briefed by my opponents, smiled and thought he would throw me a curveball. He asked: "You make a very convincing argument, but how do the people of Puerto Rico feel about this issue?"

I answered: "Ending Section 936 is a very complex issue, and if the people of Puerto Rico understood it as you seem to have understood it, they would be all for it." At that point I heard laughter around the table and the Vice President now had that famous smile on his face, like the one he had when he said he invented the Internet — the smile that said, "Who do you think you are kidding? I know everything and no one can tell me anything I don't know." My next response was, "On the other hand, Gov. Rossello is in total agreement with my viewpoint, and his opponent made it his campaign slogan that a vote for Mr. Rossello was a vote against Section 936. Mr. Rossello just won his election by the widest margin in Puerto Rico's electoral history."

A few days later, at another breakfast with the Vice President, some proponents of Section 936 were caught on videotape waving a campaign contribution check right in the White House and asking to whom they had to give this check. That was the famous scandal of the White House being used for campaign contributions. As the reader will guess, I never did make it to the Lincoln Bedroom.

With a clearer understanding than ever of what we were up against, we prepared our game plan for the 105th Congress in 1997. In January 1997, the Puerto Rican legislature adopted a resolution asking Congress to approve legislation that would authorize a plebiscite, this time "sponsored by the Federal Government," that would be held no later than 1998. The plebiscite bill was reintroduced as H.R. 856. The spirit of bipartisanship was continued and even strengthened. H.R. 3024 was cosponsored by 59 House members. H.R. 856 was ultimately cosponsored by 87 members. Both the Republican Speaker of the House and the Democratic Minority Leader endorsed the bill.

Our key leaders in the House of Representatives were once again Don Young and Dan Burton of Indiana. We were joined as well by two of the GOP's strongest and ablest leaders in the House, Tom DeLay of Texas and Newt Gingrich of Georgia. They saw the wisdom of reducing the burden on U.S. taxpayers and giving the people of Puerto Rico self-determination (how ironic that, more than two centuries after Marshal Alejandro O'Reilly wrote his famous Memoria to the Spanish crown that we could still speak accurately, as O'Reilly did, of the need for a measure to relieve Puerto Rico's "perpetual and heavy burden to the . . . Treasury"[4]). This stance required vision on the part of these key members of the House of Representatives, because, like Sen. Craig's, their respective constituencies could not be said to be clamoring for action on behalf of an island hundreds or thousands of miles away from their cities, their farms and their forests.

I had this point underscored for me during this period by a close colleague of Rep. Don Young's. He had worked for Don in various capacities. He also had a house in Colorado near a ski area, and since I spent so much time in Vail, which is less than one hour from where he lived, he invited me for dinner one night. When I got there, he had the barbecue going and had seasoned a couple of steaks to throw on the fire.

After a bottle of wine, he began plying me with questions about my role in the Puerto Rico debate. They went mostly like this. "Why are you guys doing this?" "What's in it for your people?" "What's your angle?" When I tried to explain to him our concepts of self-determination, disenfranchisement, true citizenship and sovereignty through either statehood or independence, his response was: "But what's in it for you personally?"

Those questions, I learned later, were very natural questions for Washington people. Everyone had to have an "angle." There always had to be personal self-interest to motivate any action. Ideology was a dirty word in that town (the disparaging term "true believer" is used to deride the "ideologue"), and if someone talked the talk and walked that walk, he was looked on with suspicion. I was a neophyte and had a lot to learn about what made the wheels turn in Washington. I still believed in Santa Claus.

Finally, after the second bottle of wine, he said: " Look, what I am saying is that Don Young is not going to fall on his sword for this bill because it would be political suicide. So we both know it is not going anywhere. So why are you doing what you are doing?"

I had no answer. But in the end, this fellow was no Don Young. Don had put so much of his time, effort and political career on the line for the Puerto Rico Self-Determination Act that he ignored the bruises he repeatedly suffered in the battle. Perhaps, in 1961, when he was a boat captain on the Chena River in Fairbanks and I lived just a stone's throw away from where his boat was docked, we imbibed something of the same independent Alaskan spirit. Frontiers have a way of doing that to their inhabitants. Moose used to come around and pick on the garbage and when the ice fog set in at 60 degrees below zero and the street dogs got vicious, all you wanted to do was curl up by a hot stove and wait for a morning that turned out to be as dark as the night before. Perhaps some of those common experiences (even though we didn't know each other at the time) had sparked something in both of us to fight for Puerto Rico under adverse conditions.

Don Young went out of his way to accommodate concerns about the wording of H.R. 3024. While the thrust of the two bills was the same, H.R. 856 featured simplified language and did away with the complicated, two-stage voting under the 1996 bill that would have required Puerto Rican voters to choose "sovereignty" first and then mark the ballot a second time to choose between statehood and independence. Negative language about commonwealth status was also eliminated, so that the ballot would not emphasize that the "free association" available under this bill was not what that phrase meant as understood in international law. Moreover, in its "policy" section, H.R. 856 deftly mentioned and balanced the English language issue, making it clear that the Spanish language heritage of Puerto Rico was worthy of honor but that, if the statehood option were chosen, any official English language policies under federal law would be applied by Congress to Puerto Rico as they would be to any other U.S. jurisdiction.

The new bill got a much earlier start in the 105th Congress, and once again it passed the House Resources Committee with only one dissenting vote. The bill was ready for floor consideration in October 1997, with the contemplated Puerto Rican referendum to be held in the next 14 months. Remember that this bill did not merely authorize another symbolic vote on status in Puerto Rico. It authorized what would be, in fact, the first meaningful vote on the island's status, articulating the legal reality and setting forth a mandatory process for implementing the preferences of the Puerto Rican people. H.R. 856 represented careful thinking, not wishful thinking. It included no inducements or pressures upon Puerto Rico to choose one option over the other. The available alternatives were clear. Puerto Rico could:

1. Choose sovereignty and **independence** from the United States. Under this alternative, Puerto Rico would follow the path initiated for Cuba in 1902 and the Philippines in 1946, both of which had been war booty and become possessions of the United States in 1898. The meaning of independence could not be illustrated more clearly than it has been by the contrasting fates of these latter two countries.
2. Choose sovereignty as a **freely associated state or associated republic**. This might be described as "Canada without the crown." Under this status, Puerto Rico would establish treaty relations with the United States that would preserve friendship and mutually beneficial arrangements — open immigration for example — while maintaining real sovereignty and enjoying the right to unilaterally revoke prior agreements.
3. Opt for **statehood**, setting in motion a process for Puerto Rico's admission to the Union as the 51st state, with permanent guarantees of citizenship and equality with other states.
4. **Continuation of its current status as an unincorporated territory** of the United States, enjoying the substantial measure of self-rule that had been achieved over time but acknowledging the ultimate discretion of the U.S. Congress, consistent with the U.S. Constitution, to determine the parameters of that rule.

Ninety-nine years after the U.S. occupation of Puerto Rico began with cheers and hopes, the Congress of the United States finally seemed to have a formula that would permit the Puerto Rican people to choose a way forward. Then came the landslide on the high road. Whatever else might be said about Puerto Rico's self-initiated plebiscites in 1967 and 1993, they were fought out in terms of ideas and motivations that represented real strains of thinking on the island. Passions ranged high, and weak and misleading arguments were made and believed. At no time, however, did these earlier measurements of island sentiment descend to harsh partisan characterizations and overtones of racial prejudice. The same cannot be said for what transpired in the U.S. House of Representatives in 1997-1998. The battle over status became the partial property of hired guns, employed by manufacturing interests who had short-term aims. Partisan considerations, particularly the charge by some very conservative Republicans that the Young bill would cost the GOP its majority, dominated the aisles, hallways, and cloakrooms of Congress. The "English card" was played, out of all proportion to its significance.

Very little of this, of course, happened on the surface. Instead, the GOP rear guard that most effectively opposed H.R. 856 chose to focus on another issue that was equally bogus, but nowhere near as loaded: the "cost of statehood." This initiative, carried out partly through a paid advertising campaign, was deceptive on two primary grounds. Consider an ad that was placed in *The Washington Times* on September 24, 1997. The ad bore the headline, "H.R. 856, The Budget Buster," and the bold subscript, "Are you willing to pay this price? H.R. 856: Making Puerto Rico Our 51st State." First, the bill did no such thing. As described above, it set forth, in accurate terms, the available options for the resolution of Puerto Rico's century-long limbo. Statehood was but one of the four options. Second, the idea that statehood for Puerto Rico would cost the U.S. Treasury money was completely false and premised on incomplete information.

The ad was sponsored by an entity called Puerto Rico First, Inc. It was not a very informative descriptor. The chief Washington strategist against the bill was once again Charlie Black, Jr. Black represented Puerto Rico's PPD and led the stateside campaign against H.R. 856. In the strange-bedfellow world of Washington, it was a "normal" alliance: a Republican lobbyist with conservative credentials working with self-interested manufacturers in tandem with a political party whose roots were nourished by socialism. The relationship, by the way, would ultimately pay off handsomely. When the PPD returned to power with Sila M. Calderon as Governor of Puerto Rico in 2001, Black's current firm, BKSH, Inc., was reportedly awarded a contract to represent the PPD in Washington for as much as $1,020,000 in the first full year.[5]

Who was behind Puerto Rico First? One of our allies was

curious, since the ad contained no other real identifying information about its sponsors. Dr. Miriam Ramirez de Ferrer, a physician and a very energetic lady who had been a political activist for many years, had formed an organization called Puerto Ricans in Civic Action. Her group had collected 350,000 signatures and delivered them to Congress demanding that Puerto Rico become a state. She was later elected to the Puerto Rican Senate and is now running for Resident Commissioner. Miriam got very angry at this advertising and started investigating the organization. Her trail led her to an address in a poor and drug-infested island neighborhood called Barrio Obrero where the executive director of the sponsoring organization had lived. Her trail also led her to some prominent Republicans in Puerto Rico who were, oddly enough, staunch statehooders. Her research is well documented in local newspapers.

One of those Republicans, it turned out, was a friend of mine whom I have a lot of respect for and whose name I would not reveal in this book if they pulled out my fingernails. I invited him to lunch and asked him: "How, could you, of all people, get involved in such a rotten scheme to discredit Puerto Rico statehood and hurt our cause when you have been such a staunch supporter of statehood?" His answer was simple, "You know how the system works, Alex. When someone you trust calls you and asks you to write a check or lend your name to an organization, you don't ask any questions. You simply write the check and ask to whom and how much or sign where you are asked to sign because you trust the person you are dealing with. That is how we have been able to come as far as we have on this road to self-determination." I did not pry any more.

Instead, we did all we could to counter the ad's message. It was clear that it grossly distorted the pending legislation and the likely impact of only one of the four options it framed. The ad quoted information from a 1996 General Accounting Office (GAO) report on Tax Policy and a 1990 Congressional Budget Office (CBO) report that purported to tally the cost to the federal treasury should Puerto Rico become a state. Leave aside for the moment the fact that any of the poorer American states could be portrayed as net drains on the U.S. economy. Leave aside as well the fact that Puerto Rico's per capita income, although it had grown rapidly, reflected to a significant degree the century of colonial control that the United

States had exercised. The reports cited in the ads simply left out most of the important factors that would determine the fiscal impact of Puerto Rican status change on the U.S. Treasury.

For example, the CBO model was primarily premised on the removal of Section 936 of the Internal Revenue Code and changes in federal transfer payments. The report did not take into account the unnatural shape of Puerto Rico's various economic sectors, where manufacturing had expanded (without major job creation) well beyond the normal potential of the island and other sectors remained underfed from an investment perspective. The CBO also ignored the fact that, with the phase-out of Section 936 and the advent of statehood, locally implemented decisions based on long-term needs would lead to more, and more reliable, economic growth for the island. The most important point of all, ignored by the CBO, was that the disappearance of Section 936 would end a grossly generous tax gimmick and return revenues to the Treasury.

Instead, the ad focused on what expanded use of the Earned Income Tax Credit would cost the United States. The EITC is a device Congress created with the aim of helping the working poor. The structure of the tax code, including social security taxes, was such that, under the pre-1996 welfare law, a welfare family that moved from dependency to work found itself striving against a very steep marginal tax rate as it moved through lower-wage jobs to middle-income status. Policy makers concluded that this high marginal tax was a huge work disincentive, and they devised the EITC as a way to rebate taxes to low-income workers. EITC fraud became a serious concern, the low wage-earner's kissing cousin to welfare fraud. Whatever merits this argument had, the problem was slowly being ameliorated by enforcement actions and by welfare reform itself, which put stringent time limits on the receipt of benefits.

The ad was not meant, of course, to stimulate discussion of the dynamic economic effects of any of the options facing Puerto Rico under H.R. 856. It was even carefully crafted not to take a formal position on the bill or to urge the reader to take action. It was placed in the national capital's conservative paper to be read by conservative Republicans who were looking for reinforcement in resisting a bill whose actual premise was human rights, self-determination, and a realistic hope for a dynamic Puerto Rico. H.R. 856 had cleared the House Resource Committee on May 21, 1997 by vote of 44 to 1. This was a vote by sometimes-contending legislators who did not often agree on issues of such magnitude. They had traveled that spring to Mayaguez and San Juan, held public hearings, and listened to the voices of the people most directly affected by the bill. Now a stick had been thrust into the axle of deliberation.

With the committee report filed, the next step was for the House Rules Committee, an often-overlooked body with tremendous power, to set forth the terms of debate and decide which amendments and counter-amendments to the bill would be in order. The pace of lobbying intensified and delay became the partner of defeat. Nineteen-ninety-seven came and went without a vote on H.R. 856. The chairman of the Rules Committee at this time was Rep. Gerald Solomon of New York. Solomon was a tough-minded conservative who hailed from an upstate New York district. He served 10 terms in Congress and the 105th was his last. That several of the chief advocates of H.R. 856 were tough-minded conservatives, too, did not seem to matter to him. He was determined to make use of the English language a major part of the debate over a bill that only set forth the first stage of the process for moving toward resolution of the status issue. H.R. 856 was an historic first step, not a heroic last stand.

As the bill finally neared floor debate in March 1998, I found myself in a new and, as I would soon prove, unaccustomed media role. I had been a newsletter writer and columnist, and these tools figured in the outcome, but more and more the public policy world is shaped by radio and television. I had to learn to operate in every media forum there was as the issue came to a head. I soon found myself debating clever ad writers, butting heads with interest group leaders on issues that seemed tangential to Puerto Rican status, and even going jaw-to-jaw with members of Congress, who had a lot more debate experience than I did.

It was the night before the bill was supposed to go to the House floor. My scheduled opponent was an official of one of the organizations that promoted English as America's official language, and the venue was a popular syndicated radio show that went to over 400 radio stations nationwide. The issue was whether Puerto Rico should be forced to adopt English as its official language, even though no other state was under that requirement.

This was the first time that I had met this gentleman and he seemed like a nice fellow. He gave the usual party line for his point of view, that English should be the official language of the United States and that if Puerto Rico wanted to be a state it had to adopt English as its official language. He did not have an answer when I asked him why Puerto Rico should be asked to submit to this requirement if no existing state was forced to do so. When I asked him if he would still be against H.R. 856 if the bill stipulated that Puerto Rico would follow suit if all the other states adopted English as their official language, he said "yes." It was obvious to me that the position of his organization in opposing H.R. 856 had nothing to do with language but with something else. I wanted to find out what that was.

Since the Show's radio studio was in Virginia and I was staying across the river in the District of Columbia, he offered me a ride and I accepted. We stopped along the way and had a beer and talked. He told me that his organization had more than 250,000 members and that each one paid $10 in annual dues to be a member. As publisher of a newsletter, I knew that the economics in this case did not make sense. There is no way you can maintain membership and publish a monthly or even a quarterly newsletter and solicit new members and all on just $10 per year. When I asked him that question, he told me that many of the members were individuals who paid their dues with sponsorship from corporations. I asked him if any of the corporations were pharmaceutical firms. His reply was a candid: "Yes"

Bingo!

It was all very simple. If you are the corporate president, you tell all your employees that they will get a $10 raise, which will be deducted from their paycheck, in order for them to become members of an organization that promoted English as the official language – a perfect vehicle to oppose Puerto Rico's change of status and to keep billions of tax credits rolling in to the pharmaceuticals.

During our conversation, it came out that the next morning he was scheduled to appear on a national cable TV talk show and that we would spend another hour together talking about these issues, only this time in living color. The next day he still couldn't tell me or the audience why Puerto Rico should be required to make English its official language if no other state had that requirement. He added that he would still be opposed to the Young bill if the requirement for Puerto Rico were the same as that for any other state. At the end of the debate, I asked him if he were so much in favor of "Anglicizing" America, why did he pronounce his name in a foreign (European way) and not in an Anglicized way (as his name has obvious European origins). The last camera shot was of his face as he struggled with the answer to that question which told the whole story.

I was quickly learning that the shortest distance between two points in the great city of Washington was not necessarily a straight line. Sometimes a punch line worked better.

My radio and T.V. debates were just a prelude to the crashing cymbals of debate on the House floor. That daylong debate brought all the passions about Puerto Rico to the surface, dividing both parties, especially the Republicans, driving a few of the most polarizing members of the House to the fore, and mixing high-minded and politically jaundiced arguments in a clash of great historic import. Appropriately enough, the debate on the floor began at high noon. Rep. Solomon's Rules Committee had made a number of amendments in order, including his own, which would have made English the official language of the United States. The Young bill, as noted earlier, handled this issue in a delicate and balancing way. It described English, accurately, as "the common language of mutual understanding in the United States" and recognized the already existing use of English in Federal courts on the island, but noted that Spanish is the predominant language in everyday use there. Rather than single out Puerto Rico, the Young bill made it clear that, if the island chose statehood, it would be subject to all laws governing English usage that then applied to other jurisdictions.

The debate opened with several hours of exchanges between advocates and opponents of the bill. The basic arguments were laid out. Opponents of H.R. 856 charged that Young's English language amendment was vague, that the bill was just a stalking horse for statehood, that the commonwealth option, unlike statehood and independence, was not worded as its political advocates on the island would like, and that it was not the business of Congress to tell Puerto Rico how often to vote on the status issue. The advocates met these arguments head on. They said that the Young bill treated Puerto Rico exactly the same way the 50 states were treated with respect to English. They pointed out that H.R. 856 was neutral among the options, using nonpartisan language, describing each with its actual legal effect as agreed upon by legal scholars across the political spectrum. They lamented the Popular Democrats' decision to oppose the bill because it did not contain their fanciful conception of commonwealth. Finally, they noted that the bill set out the first real framework for Puerto Rico to hold meaningful referenda on the status issue, with assurance by Congress that the procedures used to conduct the referenda would follow Puerto Rico's previous and exemplary electoral standards.

Opponents of the bill raised one other argument, and it was related to the charge that the bill was a statehood measure in disguise. Several opponents argued that it would be illegitimate for the President and Congress to move ahead with statehood if only a bare majority of voters approved it. This was probably the strongest argument against H.R. 856, but it was not pressed with as much vigor as some of the weaker objections. What lent it some strength was that rather than having several options dividing the vote equally, the dominant options (and political parties) on the island were built around two primary ideas, statehood and continued commonwealth. Implementing statehood with a near majority strongly opposed, especially with high voter turnout, raises the possibility of antagonizing a large body of public opinion on an emotional issue. The commonwealth advocates, distorting its meaning as they were, could always point to the fact that the existing status could be altered in the future; once Puerto Rico chose statehood and Congress admitted it to the Union, further change would be impossible.

Rep. Young and his colleagues anticipated these objections, however, and stressed several points. The proposed referendum would, for the first time in Puerto Rican history, give voters a choice of three futures that were legally realistic. In other words, they said, commonwealth as it really is – an arrangement that Congress had agreed to and could amend – had never been voted on in the context of a modern plebiscite. Second, even if Puerto Rico voted for statehood and this result was certified to the President, the next steps involving transition and implementation were not automatic and would require subsequent review and approval by the Puerto Rican electorate. Finally, however, statehood advocate Dan Burton was willing to concede that a bare majority vote would weigh on the minds of many in Congress who favored this direction. "If they [Puerto Rican voters] come back and only 51 percent say that they want statehood . . . we decide in this body whether we want to proceed any further. I think if it was that close, we probably would not."[6]

This was the debate as it largely appeared on the surface, restrained and, for the most part, reasoned. Beneath the surface, a different political drama was being carried out, with partisan appeals being made to members and strategies being employed that were far from the statesmanlike discussion occurring on the House floor. One of the strategies involved a skillful attack from the left on H.R. 856, implicating the other side of the English-only coin. Rep. Luis Gutierrez, an Illinois Democrat, joined the fray in opposition to the bill by offering an amendment not to enshrine English as the official language of a future State of Puerto Rico, but to define Spanish as the island's official language now. Like Solomon, Gutierrez was aiming for a poison pill, an amendment that, if adopted, would only ensure that the coalition behind the bill would collapse. Gutierrez was one of the most left-wing members of the House. He had been a '60s radical who had allied himself with the island's pro-independence terrorists. He insisted on calling Puerto Rico a "nation." He was, in short, a very unlikely person to receive any of Solomon's precious debate time, but the aim was to torpedo the bill, not refine it.

The conservative counterpart to the "nation" argument was the "Quebec argument." Solomon introduced his ally, Rep. Steve Horn of California, calling him "the least partisan of all on both sides of the aisle." Horn quickly undid that description. He proceeded to describe the U.S. error in not leaving Puerto Rico independent, as Cuba and the Philippines were, saying it was not too late to correct that error. He compared the island to Cambodians in the City of Long Beach asking him if Cambodia could become a state. He tweaked small-state legislators about the impact of Puerto Rican representatives coming to Congress – "those who have small States and want the second representative [under reapportionment], just forget about it if six representatives come in from anywhere, Puerto Rico or any other territory that seeks statehood."7 He closed his remarks by urging his colleagues to support Solomon, complaining that Puerto Rico "will be another Quebec, no matter how much we teach the English language."

Horn's speech had the virtue that it was laying bare the key points that were being made in the hallways and the cloakrooms, and even on the House floor, according to observers who watched Solomon's arm-twisting of his GOP colleagues. Lamenting that Puerto Rico had not been left independent 100 years earlier had all the practical relevance of a complaint in 1876 that the U.S. should not have fought a war of independence against Great Britain. Moreover, it ignored the fact that a genuine independence movement had always existed on Puerto Rico and that it had frequently been radical and never been popular. Second, the comparison to Cambodia was ludicrous. Cambodia already was a nation. The Cambodians who resided in Long Beach were refugees from a war zone comparable to the worst the world has ever seen. Cambodia was halfway around the globe. It was not U.S. territory and its people were not U.S. citizens.

The third and fourth arguments Horn used were the real ones, in modified form, making their way around and just outside the House chamber. Solomon was busily warning his colleagues that allowing Puerto Rico to choose statehood would mean six more Democrats in the House and two more Democrats in the Senate. The precarious new GOP majority would be jeopardized. Neither party could disenfranchise an existing Congressional district that elected members from the other party, but they could sure keep new ones from coming into the Union, never mind if the people of that district were U.S. citizens without voting representation in Congress or even the White House.

Finally, there was the Quebec canard. Horn's argument conveniently overlooked the political fact that the most ardent advocate for the maintenance of a unique Puerto Rican culture, and for official Spanish language policies, was the commonwealth party. Neither independence nor full integration via statehood would produce a Quebec-like outcome; commonwealth was preserving a

Quebec-like present. Worse, as his last sentence pointed out, the determination to maintain a "nation within a nation" reality was sure to persist "no matter how much we teach the English language." Horn might as well have said, "Oh, these Puerto Ricans will never learn." The truth has long been otherwise. English has been the language of Federal Government business in Puerto Rico since 1902. Bilingualism is common. The third largest newspaper on the island, *The San Juan Star*, is printed entirely in English. Literacy is high. Most important, love for the United States and desire for long-term attachment to it (as three of the four status options would signify) is nearly pervasive on the island.

Another congressman, Republican Bob Barr of Georgia, made a related argument, meant to show that this attachment of Puerto Ricans to the mainland was tenuous at best. "Mr. Chairman," Barr said, "63% of Puerto Ricans can't recite the Pledge of Allegiance. Sixty-six percent do not know the words to the Star Spangled Banner. This makes sense when you consider that only 16% of Puerto Ricans consider themselves to be American."[8] The implication was that Puerto Rican patriotism must be virtually non-existent. There is a far simpler explanation of poll numbers like this, assuming they are accurate, and that is that Puerto Rico has not been integrated into the American system. In any event, its implication is belied by the level of military service the island has rendered America. If the numbers on the Pledge and the Star-Spangled Banner have any meaning, they must be compared to figures for the mainland, where it is a commonplace that the majority of high school students cannot name the decade in which the Civil War occurred.

Certainly, there is a hint of racial prejudice, or at least favoritism, in the English-language amendments. The English-first legislation that Solomon had supported two years before the H.R. 856 debate recognized the importance of preserving Native American tongues. In the convoluted world of ethnic-tinged politics, this exception has a historical basis and the Spanish heritage of Puerto Rico, brought into the U.S. orbit at Washington's behest as well, does not. The Spanish that is widely spoken in Puerto Rico is actually a hallmark of its cosmopolitan character, not its insular nature. English, rightly understood, is also such a hallmark. It is the dominant language of world politics, and nothing that happens in

Puerto Rico is likely to retard the further expansion of that dominance. There may even be some envy at work in the American conservatives' treatment of the entire language issue. There is a profound lack of understanding of the American past. As Democratic Rep. Sam Farr of California said in an unusually eloquent speech on March 4 against the Solomon amendment:

> *Mr. Chairman, I was sitting in my office listening to this debate, and really the question is what does the 105th Congress have to fear? It really sounds like two things. First of all, we are fearful of Puerto Rico having an election, which is essentially a public opinion election. Since when did Congress fear elections?*
>
> *The other thing we have is we are fearing people who speak other languages. Why? One hundred four sessions that went before us did not fear that. In fact, our forebears who admitted Louisiana, New Mexico, Oklahoma and Hawaii allowed those states to come in and protected the rights of those people to speak French, Spanish, Native American, and Hawaiian, Aloha, a language that everybody uses in business.*
>
> *What about our forefathers who rebuilt this room we are all sitting in, in 1949 and 1950? If you look around, there are 23 lawgivers that we respect* [with friezes on the wall of the House chamber]. *These are the people who historically gave us the under-law for American law. These were the lawmakers, lawgivers, as we call them. There are 23 of them. Only three of them spoke English, and one of them, Thomas Jefferson, also spoke French. Mr. Chairman, who are we afraid of?*

Determined to defeat the bill, Solomon had chosen his amendment wisely. In an attempt to palliate the English-language concerns, Rep. Burton offered an amendment of his own. He pointed out that, no matter what the current status of English and

Spanish on the island, an expressed preference for statehood would take some 10 years for the Congress and subsequent votes on the island to implement. He offered wording to recognize that the ability to speak English was in the best interest of Puerto Ricans, to promote the teaching of English-language proficiency, and to achieve this goal for young people before they reach the age of 10. This "English language empowerment" amendment was a last effort to restore reason and balance to the debate Solomon was determined to provoke. Burton was also able to show his pro-English credentials: he had sponsored and voted for previous English-First legislation and supported a constitutional amendment to achieve the same result.

When the votes came, Burton and his arguments won, but the bill had been wounded. Gutierrez's radical amendment was radically rejected, by vote of 406-15. Then came the crucial vote on Burton's language, which actually was designed as an amendment to Solomon's "English-first" proposal. The tally was 238-182, a comfortable margin in many circumstances, but not with a bill on a subject that had long found its burial ground in the U.S. Senate. Other votes occurred on amendments to the bill, most of them offered by Gutierrez and Velazquez. These amendments stressed the "nationhood" and independent culture of Puerto Rico; just like the independence concept on the island, they received little support. Congressman Serrano offered an amendment, endorsed by Chairman Young, which would have allowed any person born in Puerto Rico, whether living there presently or not, to vote in the 1998 status referendum. This amendment was strongly defeated, 356-57.

One final amendment is worth mentioning because it garnered a fair amount of support. Rep. Barr, now retired, proposed to allow statehood to proceed only if approved by 75 percent of voting Puerto Ricans. This amendment failed, 282-131. Taken together, the amendments aimed at the Young bill from the right and the left were designed to reduce the palatability of one or more of its options to Puerto Rican voters. If adopted, many of the amendments would have increased the level of interference by Washington in Puerto Rican politics. The amendments' defeat produced a bill that was not diluted, but that was nonetheless weakened. When the final

The Young Bill: The Roar of the Coqui

vote came, a jubilant but exhausted pro-referendum coalition had achieved a one-vote victory, 209-208.

It was a stunning result, one more proof of just how important every election is, and there were plenty of smaller surprises wrapped up inside the big surprise of this narrow outcome. That evening, as the vote on final passage was going forward, I was on another nationally broadcast radio show, squaring off for a one-hour debate with Rep. Dana Rohrabacher, a conservative Republican from southern California. What I had always liked most about Dana Rohrabacher is that he will not pull his punches. He will look you straight in the eye and tell you what he thinks. Most members of Congress, I found, when it came to policy, will be pretty straight with you, but Mr. Rohrabacher is that way in spades.

I decided to do the interview in my hotel room while I had the TV on mute and watched the results of the vote. So my attention was split. Mr. Rohrabacher took the interviewer's call at a pay phone in the lobby outside the House chamber where the vote was going forward. Rohrabacher gave all the usual reasons why H.R. 856 was a closet statehood bill and why Puerto Rico should not be a state. I gave all the standard reasons why this was a self-determination bill and explained how it was time that 4 million U.S. citizens were no longer disenfranchised. Neither one of us kidded ourselves that we could convince the other of our viewpoint, but the debate was lively and spirited. I have always enjoyed these kinds of exchanges.

While we were debating, Mr. Rohrabacher kept saying that this bill was not a good thing and that it didn't have a chance. In the meantime, I was sure that the vote would be overwhelmingly in our favor, because our counts showed that we had most of the Democrats and about 120 Republicans solidly in favor of the bill. I kept one eye on the television screen as Rohrabacher and I made our arguments. The House debate drew to a close and the voting began on final passage. I couldn't believe my eyes as one Republican after another voted against the bill.

My biggest surprise came when Chris Cox, another Southern California Republican, was called individually to vote. He voted against it. I couldn't believe it! I had been in close contact with Mr. Cox right up to the last days before floor action and he had constantly assured me, right up to the final minute, that he was with us and that his vote, because he was part of his party's leadership, would bring along other Republicans who were on the fence. When he voted "nay," I yelled out "sonovabitch," forgetting that I was on national radio. Fortunately, at that precise moment the studio had cut away for an ad break and only the moderator heard my expletive.

Now that I have been through many debates in Congress, I know more about the little surprises elected officials spring on their constituents. It only makes me appreciate the Rohrabachers more. Oppose you or support you, at least you know where they stand. I also know now that a member's vote isn't secure until he has put his voting card into the slot and pushed the yea or nay button *and* the end of the vote has been called and that vote cannot be changed. Then you start all over again before the next vote, even if it is on the same issue. Still, actions like Cox's are deeply disappointing and the sting goes on. What makes our system of government so strong is that we have 535 lawmakers in two houses, and the majority rules. It would be nice if it were otherwise, but we do not need to have all 535 members to be truthful about their intentions.

CHAPTER 10

Eulogies for the Young Bill

Much of what you have read thus far is a public record of the debate and its outcome. It is what readers of *The Congressional Record* would make of the House battle over the Young bill. In fact, there are a handful of transparent actors in most Washington dramas, people whose words and deeds mean exactly what they appear to mean and are motivated by exactly what they say their motivations are. The same is true of many news articles on political topics that appear in the national media, especially papers like *The New York Times* and *The Washington Post*. True professionals out to balance every story they write are rare. Most of those who ply the trade are reliant on sources and are aware of, and perhaps party to, the worldview of their publications. When reading their public accounts, it's essential to ask some fundamental questions. Who was the likely source for this story? If it relied on inside information, who provided that information and what did they hope to gain from providing it? This is the real story behind every printed story.

A former deputy at a Cabinet-level agency in Washington offers this example. The agency secretary wanted a certain report's findings to be told but did not believe in leaks and manipulating the press. He did, however, have a healthy distrust of the media that he used to advantage. He agreed to a meeting with a prominent reporter. The agency secretary placed a copy of the report on the corner of his desk, and he had arranged prior to the meeting to be called out of the room by his deputy to resolve an urgent personnel question. When he returned, as he had expected, the report was gone from the desk. The reporter finished his interview, on an unrelated topic, and, in due course, a story on the report appeared in the newsman's paper.

What *really* went on behind the high-minded rhetoric on the House floor on March 4, 1998, tells a great deal about the dynamics that continue to confound the self-determination rights of the Puerto Rican people and the best interests of mainland Americans. Despite its bipartisan underpinnings, the Young bill was undone by a politically polarizing challenge from conservative Republicans, many of whom had been persuaded by Solomon and others that control of the House of Representatives was at stake in the Puerto Rican status debate. Then-House Majority Leader Dick Armey of Texas agreed with Solomon and stood in the well after the final vote, chastising the Republican minority behind Young that had backed the bill. "I hope you are happy," he said, "We let them divide us and pass their bill with more Democrats than Republicans in the majority. We're not supposed to do that, people, but that is what we just did."

One of those "happy" people to whom Armey was apparently referring was his fellow GOP leader and Texas conservative, Tom DeLay. Speaker Newt Gingrich was another. A third, had he been present in Washington and involved in the proceedings, was Ronald Reagan. DeLay is one of the capital's most discussed and most-often misportrayed figures. He is a strong conservative and as focused as any GOP leader is on raising funds and building his party. He has been nicknamed "The Hammer" because of the avidity with which he rounded up votes as his party's Whip, and the media love to caricature him as a six-shooting Texan with a blunt style and raw partisan instincts. There is another aspect of DeLay, however, and it was on display in the debate over Puerto Rico. As events unfolded, DeLay, as a party leader, did not take to the floor and make ringing speeches for the Young bill. Even so, DeLay worked the issue aggressively, meeting with members in his office and urging them to hold for H.R. 856.

DeLay, like Gingrich and Reagan, believed strongly in the right of self-determination for the Puerto Rican people. He viewed this as a fundamental moral principle of politics. This was consistent with his ideas for growing the Republican Party by increasing its long-term attractiveness to Hispanic voters, but, criticism to the contrary, it has been his consistent philosophy vis-à-vis other international issues where the political yield for his party seems slim. The most notable examples are Taiwan and Israel, where DeLay has staunchly advocated friendly U.S. policies toward governments that live in a sea of hostility. DeLay's hard fight for H.R. 856 reflects his biography as well. He was born in Laredo, Texas, and spent his early years in the rural interior of Venezuela, where his father was an oil and gas executive. The congressman's web site says that his "years in Venezuela were a formative political experience. His family lived through the turbulence and uncertainty of three revolutions. Two of these events were violent and neighboring townspeople died at the hands of marauding revolutionaries." He credits this "early exposure to political violence" as the origin of his life-long "passion for freedom."[1] My similar history has imbued me with the same passion.

Gingrich's commitment to Puerto Rico was based on an intellectual consistency, but it was no less passionate than Delay's or my own. I had first met Congressman Gingrich a couple of weeks before the 1994 election, the watershed that carried him into the Speakership of the House. Up to that point my impression of him, fueled by what I had seen of him on national TV, was of a mean-spirited and hardheaded ideologue, who seemed to epitomize the expression, "It's my way or the highway." I even objected to making the trip to Atlanta to meet him to solicit his support for action of Puerto Rican self-determination. I felt that we were wasting our time. Fortunately, one of the members of our group, Dr. de Ferrer, convinced me that I should go anyway.

Never had I been so wrong about a public figure. Anyone who has met Gingrich personally walks away with a completely different impression. He listened intently to what we had to say, asked some very pointed questions, and came up with some extremely insightful responses during our conversation. In person, I saw a completely different individual from what I was used to seeing projected on TV.

Gingrich came across as a true intellectual with the uncanniest sensitivity to humanitarian issues of any politician that I had ever met. Many members of Congress will "yes" you to death while they are trying to figure out how they can use you to accomplish what they want for themselves. Gingrich seemed to detach himself completely from his own agenda (which must have been weighing on him very heavily at that time in 1994 considering that he was not just running for re-election, but for Republican control of the House and the Speaker's position) just to listen to a small group of people on an issue that was not on the front burner in Congress. Moreover, we weren't backed by the billions that the pharmaceutical companies had at their disposal or the voting clout to give him and his party any aid in the 1994 elections.

The ideas at stake in the debate fascinated Gingrich. He was fully engaged in the arguments we put on the table. Here, we said, the United States was celebrating the collapse of the Soviet Union and the loss of its colonies, and now we were hanging on to a colony of our own, just to gratify a handful of companies that were milking the Treasury out of billions of dollars in tax credits. Gingrich saw the historical impact of this image of America as an imperialist state, and he understood immediately how that image would be exploited in the eyes of the world and make it more difficult to achieve our goals in the United Nations. He was able to rise above the petty political spats and see Puerto Rico's territorial status as one of the stumbling blocks to America's worldwide effectiveness.

As a matter of fact, many of the observations that Gingrich made during our brief conversation in 1994 became centerpieces of the arguments I and others used to promote the Young bill in the months and years that followed. Gingrich became a supporter and cosponsor of the Young bill not because he was showered with campaign money or because he was promised a key voting bloc, but because he felt it was the right stance, not just for Puerto Rico but for the United States. This was the most incredible display of integrity I had ever seen in any elected official. When I learned in 1998, just after the mid-term elections, that Gingrich had decided to leave Congress, I felt that we had lost a great visionary. I continue to believe that his leadership could have earned us the backing we need from the rest of the world to fight the threat of terrorism to our country today.

Other legislators on both sides rose above the political gamesmanship as well. This is, naturally enough, nearly impossible for political figures to do. They can't succeed at any of their ideas if they can't win elections and help their fellow party members do the same in increasing numbers. Nevertheless, there are legislators in both major political parties who almost always weigh the issues on the merits. One of those who impressed the most this way was then-Congressman Bill Richardson of New Mexico.

Shortly after the Young bill passed the House by one vote and before it died in the Senate, I was at a party in Washington and ran into Richardson, a person for whom I had much personal regard and respect. What was interesting was that whenever we spoke to one another about personal things, we spoke in Spanish, and whenever we talked shop about the status bill, we spoke in English. Richardson was a big supporter of the Young bill and a very active cosponsor.

He saw me and called me over. He said to me in English, "Well, what a surprise, you guys did it." My reply was, "Well, we all worked very hard for it and thanks for your help and support." He just shook his head, declining the compliment, and said, "No one expected it, but you did it and I congratulate you!"

By contrast, the most passionate opposition to H.R. 856 was focused on short-term partisanship. An editorial that appeared in a *National Review Online Special* in September 1998 pulled no punches in pursuing this theme. "Anybody who thinks that Puerto Rico, whose people have roughly half the per capita income of those in Mississippi, would elect conservative Republicans is deluding himself," the unsigned editorial read (conveniently failing to explain why this comparison was apt, given the two Republican senators Mississippi routinely sent to the U.S. Senate). "Then there's the added challenge of admitting a state whose people don't even speak English."[2]

By taking this approach, the House GOP, which delivered 177 of the 208 votes against the Young bill, explicitly abandoned the legacy of its most popular 20th century president, Ronald Reagan. From the beginning of his quest for the White House in 1980, Reagan made it clear that he advocated statehood for Puerto Rico as an ultimate goal, but self-determination as the first priority so that the people of the island could decide for themselves their future relationship with the United States. During the House floor debate, advocates of the Young bill circulated a flier with Reagan's picture and a sampling of his quotations over the years, which consistently betrayed openness to the island's joining the Union of the 50 states. The flier noted that Reagan had said in his first term, "In statehood, the language and culture of the island – rich in history and tradition – would be respected, for in the United States the cultures of the world live together with pride."

It was not an out-of-the-ordinary statement for Reagan, a Californian, to make. Most people above the age of 30 remember the extraordinary scene at the start of the Los Angeles Summer Olympics in 1984. At the opening ceremony of the Games, a parade of people from almost every nation on Earth, well over 100 countries, marched into the Los Angeles Coliseum to express the international variety and depth of the event. These were not the athletes from the competing countries, but American citizens who had emigrated from those countries and come to live, not in the United States as a whole, but in the Los Angeles area alone! "Dutch" had not been the governor of a state filled with Western Europeans, and he knew that a populace united by something besides ethnicity and national origin had elected him. His campaign identified those unifying factors, as "work, family, neighborhood, peace and freedom." At least a handful of House Republicans in 1998 were willing to echo the big-hearted optimism and good nature of the man who re-founded their party.

The invocation of this modern Republican heritage (it is also the older Republican heritage of Lincoln) on the House floor sent opponents of H.R. 856 into a tizzy, especially Solomon. He could be seen and heard from the House gallery literally grabbing members who were wavering upon learning that the Gipper thought Puerto Ricans were worthy of equal rights. With a dose of expletives Solomon reportedly threatened several of his GOP colleagues that he would use his powers as Rules Committee chairman to block legislation important to their districts.

When Solomon found out that the flier had been prepared by the Puerto Rico chapter of the National Federation of Republican Women (NFRW), he called the national headquarters of the NFRW and threatened to have the Republican National Committee cut off their funding. He also demanded a letter from the Reagan Library in Simi Valley, California, stating that it had not authorized use of the GOP icon's photograph. When the letter arrived he took to the floor to denounce the handout, seeming to place more value on who controlled the rights to Reagan's picture than on what the former president believed about the issue at hand. Solomon was not the GOP Whip, and the leadership endorsements of the bill ensured that it was not subject to a whip call, but the congressman from Saratoga Springs, the site of a pivotal victory in the American fight for independence, used a whip hand that would have made even LBJ proud.

The work done by the beneficiaries of special tax policies for Puerto Rico was the least visible of all, but among the most vital in pushing H.R. 856 to the brink of defeat. Naturally, this issue did not come up in debate; stressing the evenhandedness of the proposed referendum, advocates of H.R. 856 did not point fingers at defenders of the status quo who wished to benefit from continued tax breaks in Puerto Rico or from the political contributions generated by these benefits. The closest the topic came to discussion was an amendment by Gutierrez, rejected on a voice vote, that would have retained corporate tax breaks for Puerto Rico for 20 years after statehood and exempted Puerto Ricans from having to pay federal income taxes until the island's per capita income equaled that of the lowest existing state.

The day after the narrow victory on the House floor, Charlie Black asked for meetings with Senate GOP leaders Trent Lott of Mississippi and Don Nickles of Oklahoma. That same day, March 5, the bill was referred to the Senate Committee on Energy and Natural Resources, chaired by Sen. Frank Murkowski of Alaska. It immediately became clear that the bill faced insurmountable obstacles. Soon after Black's contact with Lott, the Mississippi senator (who, one would think, might have wished to relinquish Mississippi's status as the poorest state in the Union!) sent a letter to a member of the Puerto Rican House of Representatives laying out his concerns about H.R. 856. That letter was seized upon by commonwealth advocates as summarizing their objections to a congressionally designed referendum on Puerto Rico's future.

Lott wrote, "I'm concerned that the language of H.R. 856 does not clearly provide a workable option for the citizens of Puerto

The definition of commonwealth in the bill will conceivably take away existing rights of Puerto Ricans, including the guarantee of American citizenship. Further, the commonwealth definition will in effect return Puerto Rico to the status of a territory without many of the self-governing rights clearly afforded Puerto Ricans. Given a choice between that definition of commonwealth and statehood, Puerto Ricans would have no real option and the choice will be more one of statehood versus independence."[3] This paragraph from Lott's letter was quoted in full, and approvingly, on April 2, 1998, by the president of the Popular Democratic Party in "testimony" he gave before Murkowski's Senate committee.

The letter was disingenuous at best, even if one accepts the idea that Puerto Rico's commonwealth status rests on a stronger legal basis than the description provided in H.R. 856. None of the options in the bill was self-implementing, in the sense that any change in law or the status of Puerto Rico would flow immediately and inevitably from its being selected by a majority. As the sponsors stressed time and again, the referendum was advisory; what distinguished it from the votes initiated on the island in 1967 and 1993 was the effort it represented to have Congress identify the options and describe them accurately. Here, Lott's letter was even more misleading. He spoke of a guarantee of citizenship being weakened, as if anyone in Congress intended that result to occur. The idea of a weakened guarantee, which is no more (and no less) than a political process, was on no one's agenda.

If Puerto Rico voted to keep the *reality* of its commonwealth status (putting aside for a moment the differences in how each side described that reality), the citizenship of Puerto Ricans, established under the Jones Act and reinforced by eight decades of experience, would have remained exactly the same. If the island's voters had chosen independence, it could only be with the knowledge and the result that citizenship would not be available to the next generation of Puerto Ricans. This is what independence would be all about. If Puerto Ricans chose statehood, as opponents of H.R. 856 constantly stated was the intended result of the bill, the citizenship of Puerto Ricans would be as "guaranteed" as it is to any resident of the 50 states. If so, advocates of H.R. 856 had a hidden agenda to *strengthen* the guarantees of citizenship, not to weaken them. If

Lott wished to argue that the Congress did not have any power to alter the Jones Act of 1917, or that the Puerto Rican Constitution trumped U.S. law in this area, he could have made such an argument more explicit. It is the kind of argument that tempted the South in the 1960s but was proved unavailing by subsequent events.

The word "testimony" above is in quotation marks because the hearing at which the PPD president spoke was not actually a hearing on the legislation, but an unusual proceeding that the Committee labeled a "workshop." Representatives of all the major Puerto Rican parties appeared and spoke at this fascinating event. The witnesses included PPD President Anibal Acevedo Vila; PNP Chairman Luis Ferre (then 94 years old); Independence Party president Ruben Berrios Martinez; and the sitting governor of Puerto Rico, statehood advocate Pedro Rossello. Chairman Murkowski made it clear in his opening remarks that this was an unusual meeting, that he was disturbed by what he called the "inconsistencies" in the U.S. relationship with Puerto Rico, and that the workshop's purpose was only to "familiarize members of the Senate with this particular issue and the prevailing attitudes of the people of Puerto Rico." To say the least, this was a modest ambition for the centennial year of Puerto Rico's acquisition by the United States.[4]

Murkowski's real views on the matter were made more explicit in reports the next day. He was not interested in fostering a Congressionally supported and determined referendum in the island. According to the League of United Latin American Citizens (LULAC), Murkowski's view was that Puerto Rico should "hold its own referendum on whether to become the 51st state before Congress takes any action on the issue." That Puerto Rico had already held such inconclusive referenda and its major parties unanimously petitioned Congress for its views on the matter did not impress Murkowski. LULAC also reported that Senator Lott had met with Governor Rossello that week and had told him that he did not believe there was enough time in 1998 for the Congress to consider S. 472 and adopt a bill to authorize a referendum that year. A strategy of workshops, endless deliberation, and substantial delay was in full gear.

Several months later, in July, Murkowski's Committee held two days of hearings. It had become obvious that S. 472 was not likely to win approval. The number of Senate cosponsors had peaked at 17, and one of them, Craig Thomas of Wyoming, had dropped off the bill, increasingly frustrated with the pressure on Congress to advance a consensus that seemed lacking in Puerto Rico. The partisan interests of members of Congress had a new dimension, as Democrats, who had overwhelmingly supported H.R. 856 in the House, saw a chance both to be the party of statesmanship on Puerto Rico and the champion of Hispanic Americans. For them, there was a silver lining in every step by the Republican leadership to defeat or defer S. 472.

Finally, in September, Senator Robert Torricelli of New Jersey introduced a compromise measure that was designed merely to put the Senate on the record as favoring Puerto Rican self-determination in the centenary year. The resolution had a bipartisan list of cosponsors, including the Minority Leader Tom Daschle but not including Lott. Desirous as he was of a full bill setting forth the criteria for a referendum, Senator Craig endorsed the bill. So, too, did Murkowski. The resolution had a modest list of preambles followed by a short paragraph that said little more than the obvious: "[T]he Senate supports and recognizes the right of United States citizens residing in Puerto Rico to express democratically their views regarding their future political status through a referendum or other public forum, and to communicate those views to the President and Congress; and the Federal Government should review any such communication."[5]

That was it. Congress had labored for the better part of four years to respond to the Puerto Rican people after their 1993 vote and two petitions for guidance and reaction. The greatest deliberative body on the planet had deliberated and delivered – a cryptic nod of the head. The measure was so general it had no difficulty passing with unanimous consent. Craig took to the Senate floor on September 17 and expressed his regret that the Senate could not do more, acknowledging (as Lott had predicted many months earlier) that too little time remained for action on his bill. Sen. Torricelli, who would withdraw from his re-election bid two years later under a persistent ethics cloud, nonetheless gave one of the more eloquent statements about the meaning of the failure of Congress in 1998 to offer Puerto Rico a more significant statement of the alternatives:

> *It is a peculiar and tragic irony of history that the first republic to be created out of colonialism might now enter the 21st century in a neocolonialist position.*
>
> *No American should be content with this contradiction of our own history, and some might claim—some might even accuse—that this U.S. Government is in a position with the people of Puerto Rico that is anything less than full, free, fair, and democratic. Yet, by the definition we have applied for ourselves, it would be difficult to defend against the charge. Written on the walls of this Capitol from the inaugural address of President Harrison in 1841 is, "The only legitimate right to government is an expressed grant of power from the governed."*

Brave words like these could not mask the fact that, once again, our campaign for congressional guidance on Puerto Rico's options was coming up short. Soon after this reality began to sink in, I was invited to a small dinner sponsored by Harvard University at a Boston hotel. There were perhaps 10 of us present, along with members of the university administration, some professors, and Congressman Patrick Kennedy, a Democrat from Rhode Island. His father, Sen. Edward Kennedy, had also been invited, but at the last minute he could not make it. Congressman Kennedy was a staunch supporter of the Young bill and the energy that he gave to it was absolutely monumental. His disappointment, when the Senate version of the bill was stymied, was very visible and very vocal.

As the evening progressed and the cocktail hour came to an end, everyone was feeling consoled and the waiter began to take our orders for dinner. The main course was served to everyone at the table, but mine did not appear. Then the waiter appeared and said, apologetically, that they had run out of the item I had ordered, but that I could choose anything else on the menu and they would bring it right away. I ordered a steak, thinking it wouldn't take very long to prepare. Everyone at the table was very polite and waited for me to receive my main course, but once again the food failed to arrive. At that point, Patrick Kennedy jumped up from the table, ran into the kitchen, came out with a steak, and served it to me himself. As he did so, he declaimed, "Everyone by now knows that Puerto Ricans are disenfranchised citizens and are always getting the short end of the stick! They have no say in Congress, yet whatever Congress decides to do they have to abide by it. Everyone knows that I am always ready to defend the rights of Puerto Ricans, and I don't miss any opportunity to do it. So here is your steak, Alex!"

The table applauded. This incident was an appropriate symbol for years of effort. Four million people in Puerto Rico are sitting with their hands tied behind their backs while everyone else does whatever they want to them – the pharmaceutical giants, the U.S. Congress, other industries that see in Puerto Rico little more than a legal glitch that can multiply their profits. Puerto Rico can do nothing for itself. It always needs someone off the island to help it get something done.

As the last phase of the discussion of Puerto Rico in the 105th Congress wound down, it was clear that the island would proceed with a plebiscite that year, even without the U.S. authorization it had sought. It was also clear, as some of the senators implied as they voiced through their vague resolution, that this vote would proceed using definitions of the status options that tracked, to some degree, the definitions set forth in H.R. 856.

The vote was set for December 13, 1998. This was late in the calendar year for an election day, but Puerto Rico is little influenced by the time of year, except for the late summer hurricanes. There was another one of these, Hurricane Georges, which struck just four days after the Senate's lackluster vote. It was a devastating Category 3 storm that left 12 people dead, three-fourths of the island without power, and some $2 billion in damage in its wake. The people of Puerto Rico could be forgiven for feeling a little battered by forces beyond their control in 1998. The ballot, however, was once again in their control, not as they had hoped but now as they determined to proceed with not just three, but four status options.

The first three options tracked the concepts that had been framed by the House of Representatives. The first was a straightforward statement, opposed by the Popular Democrats, to the effect that Puerto Rico should continue as an unincorporated territory of the

United States. The second alternative was the idea of sovereignty in Free Association with the United States. The third was to proceed to incorporation and statehood. The fourth was a finesse of the first order, "none of the above," into which a voter could pour any and all manner of protest. It was the fourth option that was seized upon by the Popular Democrats, who, though out of power in the governorship, were nonetheless a potent political force on the island. Once again, the Puerto Rican people showed their accustomed alacrity about voting, sending 71.3 percent of voters to the polls.

Independence, repeating the pattern, drew poorly, garnering fewer than 40,000 votes, or 2.5 percent of the returns. The current "territorial" status fared worse, getting fewer than 1,000 votes, or only one-tenth of 1 percent of the electorate. This means that the remaining two options, statehood and none of the above, captured more than 97 percent of the vote. The margin between these two options was small, with 787,900 (50.3 percent) pulling the lever for "none of the above," and 728,157 voting for the path to statehood. On the surface this tally could be seen as similar to 1993, when "enhanced commonwealth" eked out a small victory over statehood. The Popular Democrats jumped to claim this very thing, insisting that voters had responded to their call to protest the "territorial" definition of commonwealth and had endorsed the PPD's version of commonwealth as the way forward.

There were a significant number of problems with this assertion. The attractiveness of "enhanced commonwealth" status to many people lay in the very fact that it was a template into which they could inject all sorts of understandings of the desired form of the relationship between Puerto Rico and the United States. Because that was the case, and because the territorial definition, unappealingly worded as it was, nonetheless was the legally correct term for the island's status, it can be concluded that overwhelming majorities of Puerto Ricans voted for a changed relationship with the neocolonialists in Washington. In the five years since the 1998 vote, the truth of that fact has been demonstrated time and again as the PPD has looked to its allies and lobbyists in Washington for new political formulas that combine special economic benefits from the United States with recognition, in various forums, both public and private, of its putative status as a nation.

This was not lost on the Congress, which heard from Puerto Rican leaders in 1999 about the meaning of the vote the previous December. In some ways, the process of 1993-94 was being repeated, with the Puerto Rican parties appealing to Washington for an interpretation of what they had just voted to do. This time around, however, the number of congressmen and senators who were frustrated with and exhausted by the political maneuverings around the issue had grown, and the statesmanlike comments that were common in 1998 became less frequent. After 1998, moreover, and the failure of H.R. 856 or another clarifying measure to pass, Puerto Rico was passing into the second century of its unusual "compact" with the United States with no roadmap at all and no timetable for another vote. Not only was the ultimate resolution unclear, the path to achieving resolution was unmarked.

The tone on all sides was angry. Gov. Rossello, in his second term, told a crowded hearing of the Senate Energy Committee that Congress had failed in its responsibility to define the choices. He castigated the Popular Democrats for presenting voters with a "false, unattainable and unconstitutional choice, a mix of the benefits of statehood and independence." "After 100 years of waiting, we would expect Congress to act on its responsibilities," Rossello told the senators.6 The rebuke was justified, given the caliber of the partisan and profit-motivated resistance to the Young bill, but one senator, Craig Thomas, fumed to Rossello, "[Y]ou constantly come here and shift the blame to the Congress." Thomas's rebuke also had justification, as other senators were quick to point out. Congress had not clarified the ballot, but it had truly been muddled by the commonwealth advocates. They were looking for a "free lunch," complained Sen. Mary Landrieu, a Louisiana Democrat. Jeff Bingaman, Democrat of New Mexico, chimed in, borrowing Republican Billy Tauzin's caustic phrase for commonwealth, calling it the "beer and barbecue option."

A Zogby poll taken in Puerto Rico after the vote showed that the vote for "none of the above" was actually composed of many factions, as one would expect. Visions of a future Puerto Rico endowed with U.S. citizenship and subsidies no doubt motivated tens of thousands of "none of the above" voters. The poll was sponsored by the *Puerto Rico Herald*, an online publication that maintains an extremely well organized archive of documents and reports on Puerto Rican self-determination. Zogby found that 37.3 percent of the "none of the above" voters favored a definition of commonwealth that was not on the ballot, arguably the enhanced commonwealth idea advanced by the Popular Democrats. At the same time, 44.8 percent of the "none of the above" category cited some other protest idea as the basis for their vote.

So the centenary of Puerto Rico's sale to the United States had come and gone without the defined and Congressionally authorized plebiscite the island's parties had all desired. To this date, Congress has not set forth the alternatives it would be willing to accept using definitions precise enough to allow an informed vote and accurate enough to be achievable under U.S. law. In the five years since the 1998 plebiscite, the debate over status has remained intense, and economic conditions on the island, paralleling those in the United States after the burst of the dot.com bubble, remain poor and a spur to change. The mid-term after-effect of the Congressional failure was to shift the management of the issue back to the Executive branch of the federal government. Republicans were deeply divided and Democrats welcomed the possibility that a Democratic President might handle it well.

The course of action the White House chose was a special appropriation in a fiscal year 2001 spending bill that authorized $2.5 million for Puerto Rican election activities. The money was appropriated to a unique White House fund called the "unanticipated needs" account. These funds could be released on the President's approval and sent to the Elections Commission of Puerto Rico after March 31, 2001. Clinton signed the bill on October 24, 2000, before he or anyone else in the country knew who would occupy the White House the following year. Politically, the funds allowed Congress to "punt" on the issue of Puerto Rican status. The Elections Commission in San Juan was to use the money for educational activities about status and to pay for a future referendum, provided that the White House had satisfied itself that the prospective referendum offered "realistic" versions of each of the status options.

Advocates of a Congressionally defined set of options, like Sen. Craig, supported the funds, stressing their symbolic importance.

Craig endorsed the spending provision on the Senate floor on October 12, saying, "This is historic because it represents the first authorization from Congress for the United States citizens of Puerto Rico to choose the ultimate political status for their island. Presidents since Truman have been seeking such an authorization and each house has passed similar language in the past, but the same language has never passed both houses and been enacted into law." Congress, of course, could not take itself completely out of the process and the fact remained that, if the authorized spending eventually went to underwrite a referendum, Congress would have to initiate steps to interpret and implement the results if they signified a change in the relationship.

Once again, the irony and the truth of Puerto Rico's unique situation were on display in this legislative and executive branch maneuver. The idea of a nation underwriting the electoral education and voting of another entity that is "sovereign" in its affairs was an absurdity. The very mechanism of this appropriation to a discretionary presidential account only underscored the lack of full liberty in Puerto Rico's current status. Two weeks after Clinton signed the bill, the American people went to the polls. Once again, Puerto Ricans on the island did not vote for president, only this time the office they were unable to vote for was the office that would administer the funds to decide their future. In December 2000, President Clinton turned one last bit of attention to Puerto Rico and established another Presidential Task Force on the island's future. It was two days before Christmas and just weeks before Clinton's exit from the White House.

The Executive Order was treading water, postponing action as power passed to a Republican president, but its virtue was that it focused the issue on the legal heart of the matter, defining status options for Puerto Rico in a neutral way and appointing the federal government's chief legal officer, the Attorney General, as chairman of the task force. By delegation the Task Force would have the responsibility to recommend to the president when and if the funds appropriated by Congress to the special White House account could be released. Presumably, the Executive Order was worked out with the incoming Bush Administration as part of the transition process. With the Republicans in Congress largely opposed to status definition legislation, the arrival of George W. Bush was viewed with optimism by many Puerto Rican political observers.

Among Republicans, Bush was a proven vote getter with Hispanic Americans. He had labeled himself a compassionate conservative, and his politics of the heart had appeal to Hispanic voters in Texas, as did his facility with Spanish. He was an unlikely individual to want to repeat Gerry Solomon's gear-clogging debate over the English language. He had run on a platform of self-determination for Puerto Rico, as both parties had done for many election cycles, and that GOP platform made no mention of the English language issue in its paragraph on the island. There was ample reason to believe that Bush was a Republican in DeLay's mold, a relentless party-builder but not an ethnically driven politician unable to see beyond the next two or four years.

Texas was 25 percent Hispanic when, as governor, Bush sought re-election in 1998. He described himself as Mexico's "best friend" north of the border. In a triumphal march back to Austin for a second term, Bush won 49 percent of the Hispanic vote, not to mention 27 percent of the state's African-Americans, 27 percent of its Democrats, and 65 percent of women. These were almost unheard-of numbers for a statewide Republican candidate in the modern era. Bush became the first Republican candidate for governor of Texas to win the heavily Hispanic and Democratic border counties of El Paso, Cameron and Hidalgo.

Duplicating this feat in a national election in 2000 turned out to be quite difficult. Democratic candidate Al Gore beat Bush by a 2-1 margin nationally. Bush managed 43 percent of the Hispanic vote in Texas, but only 32 percent nationally. Most analysts viewed this as significant progress for the GOP, as Bush received 1,000,000 more Hispanic votes than did the hapless Bob Dole. Even so, Ronald Reagan received a higher percentage of the Hispanic vote (37 percent) in his second run for the White House, prompting Andy Hernandez of the U.S. Hispanic Leadership Institute to describe Bush's performance among Hispanics as "about average."[7] As would be expected, Hispanics vote differently based on their country of origin as well as their place of residence in the United States. Cuban-Americans in Florida backed Bush nearly four-to-one. Puerto Ricans overall went for Gore by 71 percent to 19 percent, and the Hispanic margin for Gore and Hillary Clinton in New York was even larger.

With such numbers, it might be expected that Bush would devote more of his policy initiatives and outreach to Cuban-Americans than to the concerns of other Hispanics. The GOP majority in Congress had held up the 1998 status bill, and memory of that was fresh. The picture was complicated further by the generally tough position, unpopular with Hispanics, the Republicans perennially took on immigration issues. Clearly, Gingrich and DeLay's endorsement of H.R. 856 was not enough to overcome the reluctance of U.S. Hispanics to put aside their favorable view of government spending and affirmative action and to embrace a party that was much closer to their own views on family issues like marriage and abortion. In some respects, the position of U.S. Hispanics on government activism was similar in spirit to the Popular Democrats reliance on U.S. subsidies of Puerto Rico, both through tax breaks and transfer payments.

Adding to the potential tension between Bush and Hispanics was the narrow victory of the Popular Democratic nominee for governor of Puerto Rico, Sila M. Calderon. She defeated Carlos Pasquera, the NPP nominee and a man who would prove to have a flair for the dramatic. The first female governor of the island, Calderon won a hotly contested race that was the weakest link in what was, overall, a sweeping victory for the PPD over the pro-statehood party of Pasquera and former governor Pedro Rossello. The PPD won majorities in both chambers of the Puerto Rican legislature and in the election for the non-voting delegate to the U.S. Congress. Taking office nearly three weeks before Bush, Gov. Calderon issued a strong call in her inaugural address for the immediate departure of the U.S. Navy from Vieques. This was not a partisan issue on the island, as all three major parties favored the Navy's departure, but the insistence on immediate action was strongly resisted in Washington.

Bush, nonetheless, did more in his first year to alienate his conservative, non-Hispanic base than he did to upset the Hispanic majority that had rejected him. Through the "no child left behind" legislation, he made an expansion of federal education funding a cornerstone of his 2001 domestic program. The White House even put a fact sheet on its official web site that displayed the Puerto Rican flag and noted some of the truly mammoth increases in federal education payments the bill would bring to Puerto Rico. The site claimed that the new bill would benefit an estimated 613,000 students attending more than 1,500 Puerto Rican schools. It increased total federal education funding for the island to more than $1.2 billion, an increase of 30.6 percent over fiscal year 2000 levels. Title I funding for disadvantaged children was increased by an even larger amount over the year 2000, some 32.9 percent. Pell grants — need-based, college-level cash grants that need not be repaid — rose by a similar amount.8

Still, the debate over Puerto Rican status was politically draining as an internal matter for the Republican Party. The pitch made on the White House web site to Puerto Rico probably had less to do with courting the island than with the general aims of the new Administration to narrow the GOP's electoral gap in the United States over which party was more "pro-education." Evidence began to accumulate that the Bush White House would not engage in a rapid, high-priority effort to placate Calderon or reignite the status debate. Bush's first public action on the issue was to amend the Clinton Executive Order to give the President's Task Force on Puerto Rico three more months, until August 1, 2001, to complete its initial report.

Just before that date, a Bush White House aide who would soon be named the co-chair of the Task Force, Ruben Barrelas, stirred controversy. Attending a celebration in San Juan, he suggested that the only route forward for resolution of status would be for Puerto Rico to face a forced choice between independence or statehood – no more commonwealth option, enhanced or not. The aide's remarks brought an instant rebuke from Gov. Calderon's chief of staff, who denounced the statement as implying an "absolutely undemocratic" resolution. Shortly after that, silence flowed over the topic again like the sea closing over the treasure dropped by Joseph Conrad's Nostromo in the great book of that name. It was left to the aging Gov. Ferre, operating as a kind of de facto spokesman for the White House in Puerto Rico, to announce that the Task Force had been renewed, with Barrelas and Attorney General Ashcroft as its co-chairs. Then, the topic indeed was swallowed up in the "immense indifference of things" in official Washington.

In April 2002, a White House spokeswoman answered a reporter's inquiry about Puerto Rican status by acknowledging that the Task Force re-established in August 2001 had met only once – in August – by conference call. Of course, a major distraction for the United States and for the Attorney General had happened soon after that conference call: the attack on the World Trade Center and the Pentagon by radical Islamists under the leadership of Osama bin Laden. As had happened so many times before, the mind of the Administration and the Congress went elsewhere. In addition, the economic factors that shook the American economy as the Clinton Administration wound down, and that accelerated after September 11, 2001, hit Puerto Rico with hurricane force. An economy that had depended on a distorting and expensive tax break for more than a generation had little room for error.

The Clinton-Gore campaigns for the White House took as their theme a popular song by the rock group Fleetwood Mac called "Don't Stop Thinking About Tomorrow." With the new factors at play in the Bush-Cheney era, the theme song, as applied to Puerto Rico, might have more fittingly been another Fleetwood Mac song, the one with the refrain, "You Can Go Your Own Way." With the PPD blocking the 1998 legislation that had offered the best opportunity in years for a Congressionally defined vote, with the eyes of the President and the Congress fixed on other overseas targets, with an economy dragging its feet like a lame mule team, the party leaders and other major figures in Puerto Rico each pulled in a different direction, experimenting with new ideas, castigating one another for their unwillingness to cooperate, and seeking advantage for their party in the next election.

It was a sorry, and angry, state of affairs. Resentment continued to pile up over the Vieques bombing range. Sensitivities in the United States about the value of the training programs there was heightened by America's perception of the danger it faced, and yet the pressure on the island to close the base continued. It did not add much charm for many in the U.S. Congress that Lolita LeBron, who, as a young woman, had fired the first shots inside the House chamber on that unforgettable day in 1954, joined the Vieques protestors. The clashes among Puerto Rican politicians, and between a kind of environmental nationalism and U.S. security needs, fomented a level of rancor and recrimination that had not been seen in the island's political temperament in many years. The tragedy of the last American colony seemed to be deepening, even as the United States embarked on missions to promote democracy and freedom in the Middle East. Could it be that, after so many decades of expanding self-rule and admiration for the United States, the island was moving now into a position of confrontation?

The impact of all these dissonant forces has made, for the short run at least, the future of self-determination in Puerto Rico a deeply uncertain prospect. As noted at the beginning of this chapter, the process is intensifying. On the whole, and with respect to other contentious additions to the Union and completed independence movements, new intensity has signaled progress toward resolution. That may well be the case now, as there have been some signs among the leaders of the various parties, at least those who have held office in the past and are not seeking it in the future, of a willingness to compromise on their own definitions of the future in order to stage a new referendum. It is also possible that progress will not come, and one of history's more unfortunate ironies – the failure of amicable disputants to reach reasonable results while amicability still reigned – will play itself out in Puerto Rico.

To coin a phrase, the array of disarray in Puerto Rico today is truly impressive. The PPD leadership in the Puerto Rican legislature has broached ideas for a constitutional assembly, its participants determined by election, to propose status alternatives. In April 2002 the PPD majority in the Puerto Rican Senate was able to eke through a bill calling for just such an assembly. The Puerto Rican Independence Party joined in support of the assembly idea, continuing the island's pattern of alliances shifting like sand in the Caribbean tides. The PNP's senators opposed the assembly, calling it an "elite" rather than populist solution to the status question. As the debate ended and the measure was approved, even its advocates stressed that it was but one more option, not a mandate, for progress on status.

Former Governor Rossello, who has indicated his planned candidacy for governor on the New Progressive Party ticket in 2004, now says that he favors a lawsuit against the United States that will petition the Supreme Court to resolve the status question and provide "guarantees" of U.S. citizenship for residents of the island. Talk of appealing to U.S. obligations under international treaties and United Nations standards is rampant, just as the U.S. Administration's attitude toward the UN has reached perhaps an all-time low. It appears highly unlikely that the Supreme Court would decide such a fundamentally political question, thrusting Puerto Rico out from under the territorial clause of the Constitution, but the level of animus is clear when even a mainstream party leader in San Juan thinks this scenario is plausible. Rossello says that he will pursue this course in 2005 if he wins the governorship.

Pasquera, meanwhile, has found ways to keep himself in the public eye. In June 2002 he led a group of NPP activists into the lobby of a government building in San Juan to forcibly raise the U.S. flag. The head of the government office, Maria Dolores Fernos, an independence advocate, had refused to display the American flag. Earlier in the week of Pasquera's dramatic gesture, Fernos had been ordered by Gov. Calderon to display the American flag, but two days later she still had not done so. Pasquera then led his contingent of some 100 U.S. flag-waving Puerto Ricans to Fernos's office. Pasquera's actions followed a series of debates over display of the American and Puerto Rican flags that had led the NPP leadership to charge that the Puerto Rican government was deliberately pushing the United States away from Puerto Rico. The flag fracas left dented cars, smashed windows, and bruised egos in its wake.9

Calderon attempted to quell some of the disturbance by inviting Pasquera to take part in yet another initiative in Puerto Rico to promote status resolution. Her idea had the appealing Puerto Rican acronym CUPCO, which referred to a Committee for Unity and Consensus (Spanish and English are related enough that, aside from word order, acronyms tend to hold up in both languages). Pasquera responded harshly, scoring Calderon for her poor relationship with the Bush Administration and her failure to negotiate successfully on such issues as Vieques and new Section 956 tax breaks. "Calderon's efforts have been fruitless," he said, "even on issues she considers to be a priority. The committee [CUPCO] is just a strategy to divert attention from what it is, without any doubt, an administration that has failed to have any accomplishments." Once again, the fractured nature of Puerto Rican politics, where status overshadows and cuts across other policy principles, was in evidence.

The current status of Puerto Rico operates in this climate – especially in an economically challenging climate – like a heroin addiction. It is both self-reinforcing and damaging, and even the realization by the addicts that the drug is having devastating effects seems to do little to break the impasse. With increasing boldness and recklessness, Gov. Calderon and the PPD are testing the waters of U.S. patience with a raft of actions designed to show Puerto Rico as an independent actor in foreign affairs, particularly in Latin American affairs. Few steps are more certain to garner an unfavorable response in Washington, where the rock refrain for the relationship is more likely to be U-2's "I can't live/With or without you."

During her term in office, Calderon and her Secretary of State, Ferdinand Mercado, extended a practice of enrolling Puerto Rico in various international organizations. Acting as a kind of quasi-independent state, Puerto Rico sought and was granted membership in 28 international groups (eight of these at Calderon-Mercado's initiative) and had applied, by August 2003, for membership in 17 more. Mercado described the practice as a first-time effort by Puerto Rico to have "a clear policy to promote cultural and commercial relationships with other countries."[10] As an example of the latter, Puerto Rico, he said, had signed cooperation agreements with other Latin American countries, including Panama, Chile, the Dominican Republic and Costa Rica. As such these expanded contacts would seem to clearly be in Puerto Rico's interest. Restraints on its trade and economic relations were a chronic burr under the island's saddle for centuries under Spanish rule. Some officials on the island have a dream of establishing a mammoth port on the southern side of the island to facilitate increased trade with South American countries on both the Atlantic and Pacific sides of the continent.

While these ideas seem reasonable, Gov. Calderon's steps toward a more political international role have been adding volatile fuel to U.S.-Puerto Rican tensions. In November 2002 Gov. Calderon attempted to win a seat as a "special participant" at the 12th IberoAmerican Summit held at Santo Domingo, the Dominican Republic. The rub was that the summit was intended for Heads of State. "principals only" to use the corporate phrase, and Calderon was secretly trying to be included in their number. Her administration also reportedly lobbied Dominican officials to meet her entourage at the airport with head-of-state protocol. Learning of this just before the event, the U.S. State Department notified Dominican officials that the United States would be very upset if Calderon was accorded the same treatment as governor of a territory that would be due to the President of the United States.[11]

Calderon spent most of her time at the summit, according to the *Puerto Rico Herald*, "fuming in her hotel room." The *Herald* also reported results of an online poll that showed that Puerto Ricans rejected Calderon's attempt at "enhanced" nationalism by a margin of 3-to-1. On her return to San Juan, a U.S. State Department spokesman interviewed by the *Herald* told the publication that the United States would repudiate any effort by Calderon to portray herself as the leader of a nation or to assume any other role that would portray Puerto Rico as sovereign. Calderon has been nothing if not persistent. She has also sought membership for Puerto Rico in the Association of Caribbean States and in United Nations-sponsored entities such as the International Labor Organization and the World Food and Agricultural Organization.

Undaunted, she has reportedly contacted Nicaragua secretly in a further attempt to have Puerto Rico admitted as a special participant in the 2003 IberoAmerican Summit scheduled for November 2003. This gambit prompted U.S. Secretary of State Colin Powell to send a personal letter to U.S. ambassadors to Latin American countries urging them to remind their host governments that they, and not Calderon, represent the government of the United States, of which Puerto Rico is a part. Calderon reacted to news of the letter by first expressing doubt that it existed and claiming that her relationship with the Bush Administration was excellent. Both the PIP and the NPP lambasted Calderon for embarrassing the island, reinforcing the unequal status it possesses, and antagonizing the U.S. government on which it depends for many billions of dollars annually.

In May 2003 Calderon announced her decision not to seek a second term in 2004. The island's non-voting delegate in the U.S. Congress, PPD member Anibal Acevedo-Vila, became the PPD's sole candidate in the 2004 gubernatorial election. He has made it clear that he plans to continue Calderon's policy of pursuing independent international links, if he is elected, and that he regards those links as consistent with the idea of Puerto Rican autonomy under commonwealth status. The year 2004 promises to be another part-comic and part-cosmic chapter in Puerto Rico's tangled history as an unincorporated, territorial, federally subsidized, increasingly autonomous, and ultimately Congressionally controlled possession of the United States. Even so, it is clear that, over the past 25 years, sentiment on the island for changing the current status has grown. Statehood advocates have gained some ground and now contest for island-wide office in every election. Restlessness is the rule, and the growing Hispanic population in the United States ensures that the interests and needs of this subpopulation will continue to enthrall ambitious politicians.

At least one prospect for the leadership of the PPD a few years down the road deserves some mention here. Jose Hernandez Mayoral, the son of the former Governor Rafael Hernandez Colon, who was himself a protégé of Muñoz Marin, is one of the most impressive, up-and-coming political leaders on the island. I first met Jose through a good friend whom I have known for more than 30 years, Luis Irrizarri. Luis is a brilliant estate planning and tax attorney and one of the most vocal and committed *independentistas* I have ever met. He and I have had many prolonged philosophical discussions regarding Puerto Rico's political status, and he, along with Manuel Rodriguez Orellana, had done a great deal to help me see that the island's current status is colonial and territorial at its core.

Both Irrizarri and Orellana were coming from the viewpoint of deep feelings of nationalism as native Puerto Ricans. Since I could not relate to that emotion – or to any nationalistic emotion, for that matter, having been ejected from the country where I had been born – I saw the Puerto Rico status issue as an intellectual exercise. From that perspective, I was finally able to muster enough emotion to get my heart into the issue as well as my head. The difference was that my love for America's freedoms and the democratic system of government that we enjoy in the United States made my status preference different from theirs. My goal became to get rid of this destructive and disabling colonial/territorial status, which exploits both the U.S. taxpayer and the Puerto Rican resident. The answer was clearly to achieve sovereignty, whether through independence or statehood. Although I favor statehood, either option for me would be much better than the current colonial status.

One day Luis arranged for me to have lunch with Jose. It was the most revealing experience. Besides being very impressed with this young man's intellect and quiet self-assurance, I saw and heard a person who was genuinely on a mission to make Puerto Rico a better place in which to live. That afternoon I had an opportunity to catch a glimpse of Muñoz Marin's dream of Puerto Rico's ultimate status through the eyes of a new member of the PPD leadership.

During that first conversation with Jose, I realized that the ultimate goal of the PPD had not changed. In its own way, the party was still trying to gain sovereignty for Puerto Rico. It sought to do this by gaining the two additional elements of sovereignty that had eluded it within the current status. Putting legal and constitutional considerations aside for the moment, the goal was to make Puerto Rico an independent nation, yet one with very close ties to the United States, similar to those enjoyed by the Northern Marianas under their "compact." These two elements of sovereignty were, specifically:

- The right to accept or reject the laws passed in the U.S. Congress, and
- The right to enter into trade and tax treaties with other countries without the approval of the U.S. Congress

These two elements would give Puerto Rico status as a nation within the United Nations' definition, but the price would be the loss of U.S. citizenship, at least for the next generation of Puerto Rican children born in the island's hospitals and homes. As constitutional scholars, including former U.S. Attorney General Richard Thornburgh, have previously proclaimed, "A nation of U.S. citizens that would vote in the United Nations could not be put in a position to oppose other U.S. citizens on the mainland." In short, U.S. citizenship for residents (at least those who were not "grandfathered" in) of another sovereign nation would be unconstitutional.

Nonetheless, it was this type of sovereignty that Muñoz Marin was shooting for back in 1950 when P.L. 81-600 was passed by

Congress and approved by President Truman.

When Muñoz Marin did not get this result, he got up in front of the U.S. Congress and told them he had won nothing more than the same territorial status along with the ability to write a constitution that, in the end, was subject to the approval of the Congress. In other words, "the same old colony." He told Congress that he would present this option to the people of Puerto Rico and that, in his own words, "if they went crazy and rejected it," he would be back. In the meantime, when Muñoz Marin went back to Puerto Rico, he sold P.L. 81-600 as a "bilateral compact between two nations" that could only be broken with the consent of both parties. He translated the term "commonwealth" as "Estado Libre Asociado," or "Associated Free State."

This was a complete lie. There is *nothing* "free" or "associated" under the Territorial Clause that defines Puerto Rico's status as a U.S. possession. The statement in Article IV, Section III, Clause 2 is simple and straightforward and it links the words territory and property: "The Congress shall have Power to dispose of and make all needful Rules and Regulations respecting the Territory or other Property belonging to the United States."

Puerto Rico is war booty that can be sold or traded off at will by the U.S. Congress, something like a professional baseball player who is not a "free agent."

Muñoz Marin had faith that, sooner rather than later, the two elements of sovereignty would be granted to Puerto Rico and that this wishful thinking – the lie, really, that he sold to the people of Puerto Rico – would someday become a reality. When John F. Kennedy was elected president, Muñoz Marin thought that he now had the opportunity, because of his close ties with the Kennedys, to turn his little lie into a living truth. The Kennedy administration turned its back on him and didn't give him the time of day. In his frustration and disappointment, Muñoz Marin turned over the helm of the PPD to Roberto Sanchez Vilella and retired from politics, brokenhearted.

Personally, I think that the lie Muñoz Marin told the Puerto Rican people was a brilliant move at the time. He faced great pressure from the independence party and its sympathizers to gain sovereignty. He himself had started out as an *independentista*, like his father. He was anxious to implement his industrial development program, along with FDR and Rex Tugwell's New Deal social programs, to boost the economy of Puerto Rico and erase its stigma as the "Poorhouse of the Caribbean." Muñoz Marin's decisions and actions lifted Puerto Rico out of the deepest part of the poverty hole and sped its economic development in the 1950s and '60s. On the other hand, this lie left millions of Puerto Ricans with a misconception about the legal regime under which they were living. Outside interests used this misconception in a Machiavellian way to deny Puerto Ricans self-determination while using the people's fears of economic stagnation against their long-term self-interest.

During our lunch, Jose did not have to recount any of this history to me, because it is available in many historical publications, with analysis from any and every point of view. What Jose did confess to me is the dilemma that the PPD is facing as an enduring advocate of enhanced commonwealth. The majority of Puerto Rico voters, well over 90 percent, want to keep their U.S. citizenship at all costs. If the PPD begins to move its position closer toward sovereignty through more independence, it will lose the thin margin by which it wins elections from time to time. By hanging onto the myth that there is some kind of "Associated Free State" arrangement with the United States, the PPD can continue as a viable party until either the U.S. taxpayers get tired of subsidizing Puerto Rico with billions of dollars in social benefits and cut the island loose, or a more favorable climate emerges for Puerto Ricans to accept the eventual loss of citizenship that inevitably comes with sovereignty.

Jose made it plain that he understands this reality. He was willing to be candid about it with me, knowing where I stood on the question of making the status options clear and available for an effective plebiscite now. I believe that the kind of honesty Jose displayed is to be commended and encouraged. It rises above mere politics to true statesmanship. I also believe that if this point were made public by the PPD, they would gain a more solid ground on which to stand. Many Puerto Ricans would accept independence if it were thrust upon them. If, in the end, statehood proves not to be an option that Congress is willing to accept, then independence will be a quick and indeed the only viable solution to the dilemma. All of the consequences of independence might not be foreseeable, but this status would be much better than today's arrangement, which exploits Puerto Rican and American families alike.

Jose Hernandez Mayoral has already tried once for island-wide public office. Jose squared off against Acevedo-Vila in the primary to determine who would be the PPD candidate for Resident Commissioner. Governor Calderon knew that Jose would be the stronger candidate. Just before the primary vote, however, she declared her preference for Acevedo-Vila. This was unprecedented in Puerto Rico because the gubernatorial candidate traditionally does not intervene in a contested primary election in her own party. The contending candidates are given a chance to promote themselves and prove their popularity. With Calderon's boost, Acevedo-Vila won by a thin margin. As a result of this step up the ladder, Acevedo-Vila was one rung from the top and is, as I said above, the PPD candidate for governor in 2004.

Political winds can shift on a dime, making predictions hazardous, but, as it stands now, the former governor, Pedro Rossello, will once again be our governor after November 2004. This won't necessarily occur because Rossello would be a better governor than Acevedo-Vila, but because the people of Puerto Rico are upset, as the polls have shown, with Gov. Calderon's handling of the economy and feuding with the United States over international affairs. Acevedo-Vila may be caught in the backlash against her administration. What this means is that Jose Hernandez Mayoral could well become the PPD candidate for governor in 2008.

If so, I personally think he will be a tough candidate to beat, and I would wish him the best of luck. He would make a fine governor, and, I hope, he could bring honesty and candor into the PPD message. Once the people of Puerto Rico recognize that, in the final analysis, they have only two status options, statehood or independence in close association with the United States, the first real step toward self-determination will have been achieved. Moreover, these options exist for only so long as Congress is willing to listen to us, and not just get fed up with the annual $22 billion financial drain and kick us out the back door as it did with the Philippines in 1947. With the U.S. Navy on the verge of making an unhappy exit, the United States has one less reason to value what Puerto Rico provides. A window of opportunity may be about to close.

There is at least one wild card that could be played and affect the course of this drama, that is, of course, Cuba. The United States is absorbed in late 2003 with the need to defend itself from a wave of international terror that is targeted at innocent people. In its glaring ferocity, this terrorism may continue for some time to blot out any attention that might be given to Puerto Rico and its generally genteel demands for action on its concerns. Terrorism hit closer to home than did Pasquera's gesture and the shards of broken glass that accompanied it. More and more, it seems that 1998 was a precious opportunity missed, and Puerto Rico's best hope for clear status and a brighter economic future will depend on a new period of statesmanship in San Juan and Washington.

In the meantime, Cuba is "closer to home" for the United States as well. Any events that put Cuba's political situation in play and portend a significant change in Castroite communism could occupy America's attention in the Caribbean for many years. The political and geographical calculations would be clear. Puerto Rico is a fractious place, America's last colony, but it is also relatively docile and urbane. Its poverty is persistent and appalling by U.S. standards, but faith and a positive outlook buoy its people, and they have seldom been tempted by radicalism. Cuba, on the other hand, has sparked the frequent outrage of the United States. It has been the last bastion of communist dictatorship, a fomenter of revolution and challenges to American well being, from the Cuban Missile Crisis to Angola and Grenada.

Cuba is also a mere 90 miles from the United States. The word "Havana" has an allure in the States that has dulled the political senses of many liberals, who have given Castro a free pass, and sharpened the senses of many conservatives, who love the cigars and bravado, and still think of Havana as an emblem of the tempting Caribbean culture that attracted Hemingway and others earlier in the century. The United States Navy is leaving Vieques, but there is no talk of changing the U.S. presence at Guantanamo Bay, another vestige of the Spanish-American contretemps. Politically, if the Republicans continue to dominate in Washington and in Florida, the strong support of Cuban Americans for the GOP and for Cuban freedom could be rewarded, post-Castro, with a new diplomatic and economic focus for the United States, much closer to its shores than is Puerto Rico, 10 times further away to the east.

In August 2003, Fidel Castro turned 77 years of age, and two months earlier his revolution reached the 50-year mark. A crackdown on dissidents in early 2003 provoked near-universal condemnation of Castro and strained severely Cuba's relations with the European Union, which had been sending some 850,000 tourists to the island each year and had granted Cuba an additional $16 million in annual aid. The Bush Administration has tightened the Cuban embargo and in June 2003 Secretary of State Powell pressured the Organization of American States and its members to join the United States in a letter complaining about the crackdown. Only half of the 34 OAS members signed aboard, but there was no doubt in 2003 that Cuba's economic and political isolation was increasing.

A new leader without Castro's charisma and historic symbolism could, unwittingly or not, introduce a period of rapid change, which a shrewd Washington could speed to a more democratic conclusion.

All of this illustrates merely that forces are not always in the control of even the most alert political actors. Cuba has always seen a significant part of its population "vote with their feet," in actuality, with their paddles and petrol tins. Rafts and ferries and makeshift boats are always leaving the island. Indeed, a hijacked ferry was the incident that led to the most recent crackdown and the executions of the hijackers that sparked the most international criticism. In early 2003 12 Cuban refugees were picked up, no less, as they attempted to float away from Cuba in, astonishingly, a 1951 Chevy pick-up truck. As 2003 steams toward its conclusion, Puerto Rico's status, and its contending parties, seem similarly adrift. A time may soon come when they realize the opportunity they missed to flee the no-man's-land of commonwealth dependency and find a shore of true freedom.

Since the final failure of the Young bill in 1998, I have had many opportunities to reflect on the many ironies that affected the debate. The GOP, the party that usually does everything in its power to counter the effects of welfare dependency, largely voted against eliminating the incentives for Puerto Rican dependency. The Democrats, who are often happy to gain a constituency by promising it more and more "free" government services, took a stand in favor of a genuine plebiscite that might have resulted in a significant economic shake-up among Hispanic Americans, a group their party has successfully courted in election after election.

There were ironies on the island as well. One of the most frequent comments that I routinely received from members of Congress relating to Puerto Rico was," You guys (Puerto Rican residents) should decide what it is you really want and stop talking out of both sides of your mouth." I had always thought this was a jab at the inconclusive way that we seem to vote on our local referendums. Perhaps there is another explanation for that comment.

El Nuevo Dia is the leading Spanish-language newspaper in Puerto Rico with a circulation of some 300,000 readers, and it is considered the political voice of Puerto Rico. It was founded by the Ferres, the family of the former governor. Luis A. Ferre was the founder of Puerto Rico Cement in Ponce and, more precisely, the founder of the United Statehooders organization in the late 1960s. Don Luis's son, Luis Antonio Ferre, was for a long while the principal driving force behind the newspaper and, right now, his son and daughter are pretty much running the paper.

Even though newspapers go out of their way to insist that they are objective and apolitical, it is pretty well known that most newspapers have a political ideology. For many years, El Nuevo Dia appeared to be leaning toward Republican/statehood thinking. However, in the last few years the paper appears to have switched its leanings and to be supporting commonwealth issues. Strange, how a newspaper founded by the number one Republican/statehooder in Puerto Rico is now boosting Commonwealth. Children have traditionally shown a tendency to rebel against their parents, so it could be very understandable behavior now that Mr. Ferre's grandchildren are running the newspaper.

Now, here is a theory that has no basis in fact, but does challenge the intellect.

When Mr. Hernandez Colon was Governor of Puerto Rico, he decided to abolish estate taxes on any properties that are held by Puerto Rico residents and that are located on the island. On the other hand, properties held on the mainland United States by Puerto Rico residents are subject to substantial death taxation on the island.

If you have a substantial estate and Puerto Rico were to become a state, you would now be subject to estate taxes on all your Puerto

Rico properties, island and mainland alike. What compounds the problem is that Puerto Rico has forced heirship laws similar to, but much more restrictive than, those of Louisiana. This means that you cannot do any effective estate planning in order to minimize Federal estate taxes. So, if you have a substantial estate or if you are going to inherit a substantial estate, if Puerto Rico becomes a state, half of the estate's value will go to the Federal government.

This creates an interesting mix of emotions. "Yes, I want statehood (philosophically), but, practically, I would rather wait a while until the estate tax issues are settled."

This is pure speculation on my part, but the behavior of the tax-sheltered manufacturers in this drama is not. Since the end of 1998, the pharmaceutical industry has been busier than ever, trying to allow controlled foreign corporations (CFCs) based in Puerto Rico to repatriate their profits back to their parent companies tax-free. They want to do this by adding an amendment to Section 956 of the tax code that will allow this repatriation to happen immediately, rather than merely later on when the corporation is dissolved. This would essentially resurrect the income side of Section 936. How long will U.S. taxpayers continue to be asked to shell out more than $20 billion a year just to backwash $4 billion in profits into the pharmaceutical giants' coffers? How long will we carry, in Alejandro O'Reilly's memorable phrase from another era, this "perpetual and heavy burden"?

CHAPTER 11

The Cries of Patriots

On April 2, 1998, the former Governor of Puerto Rico, Luis Ferre, testified before a special meeting of the Senate Energy and Natural Resources Committee in support of S.472, the companion bill to H.R. 856. Ferre, who was 94 years old at the time of his testimony, is ailing at the time this manuscript was prepared in 2003. As he notes in his testimony, he was born in 1904, within hailing distance of the beginning of Puerto Rico's relationship with the United States. In his remarks, he makes the case, with all the vigor that characterized his many decades in public life, for self-determination and, ultimately, statehood for Puerto Rico.

This statement, as delivered, is presented here not because the authors agree with Ferre's final recommendation, but because his words underscore key truths about U.S.-Puerto Rican history and the nature of the present, unworkable status. The remarks have been slightly edited for grammatical consistency. The "chairman" referred to in the text is the Energy and Natural Resources Committee Chairman Frank Murkowski, Republican of Alaska.

> **Governor Ferre:** My name is Luis A. Ferre. I am a former Republican governor of Puerto Rico, as well as the current state chairman of the Republican Party, as well as the founding chairman of the New Progressive Party, a coalition created in 1967 for the

purpose of seeking statehood for Puerto Rico. I am, of course, a very young man, burdened with 94 years of experience.

The Chairman: 94? I should have Senator Strom Thurmond to introduce you.

Governor Ferre: I have to compete with him.

The Chairman: It would have been our only senior colleague that could have properly done that. Please proceed, Governor.

Governor Ferre: Thank you. It is in this last capacity and by delegation of our party chairman, Governor Rossello, that I have the privilege of appearing before you today. I wish to congratulate and thank Chairman Murkowski for so expeditiously scheduling this first workshop. Puerto Rico's self-determination is a subject of paramount importance to our great nation. How we handle it can burnish or soil our luster as the greatest democracy in history. I address you today as an American, as a Republican, and as a Puerto Rican.

I was born in Ponce, Puerto Rico in 1904. My life has spanned the 20th century and virtually the entire history of Puerto Rico and its relationship to the United States.

Americans have a great deal to be proud of. In this century, we have perfected the fairest, most stable and most prosperous democracy in history. We have the right to approach very carefully any process, which might result in the incorporation of another four million citizens as full partners. Legitimate questions have been raised regarding the process of self-determination for Puerto Rico. I have the answers.

Are we rushing into the process? This hardly is the case. Puerto Rico has been a part of this country for a hundred years. Furthermore, the House of Representatives has held extensive hearings in Washington and in Puerto Rico since 1995, and the Senate also has done so. Is this a statehood bill? Not at all. This bill initiates a process of self-determination and does nothing more. If the commonwealth option wins this referendum, nothing changes. If either statehood or independence wins, a lengthy process is triggered; only Congress decides it. And under such circumstances, a change of status will take place.

Moreover, the legislation does not favor statehood. On the contrary, if any option is favored, it is commonwealth, since that is the status that prevails if no option wins a majority in the referendum. There is a clear need for Congress to act. A referendum was held in Puerto Rico in 1993 — in which each party was allowed to define its own option. Even under these circumstances, which gave an unfair advantage to commonwealth, less than 50 percent of the voters supported the status quo. We have, therefore, a constitutional crisis in Puerto Rico that can be summarized as follows.

Fully 100 percent of the voters demand changes. Over 95 percent of the voters, those favoring statehood or commonwealth, favor permanent union with United States, but do not support the current system. Clearly, Puerto Rico is no longer being governed with the consent of the governed. As a territory, Puerto Rico does not have the authority to fix this problem on its own. For that reason, our legislature has petitioned Congress to set in motion the self-determination process that we are discussing here today.

What about language in Puerto Rico? Contrary to a campaign of misinformation that is underway, the majority of Puerto Ricans are proficient in English. It is our policy on the island to ensure that everyone speaks English. In fact, English has been the official language of Puerto Rico since 1902, longer than any other jurisdiction under the United States.

We developed our own educational system, and our political institutions gear those in cooperation into the mainstream of America, retaining those unique qualities of our cultural identity that would enrich the quality of life in our nation. As a result, the present generations of Puerto Ricans are comfortably engaged in athletic, professional, educational, artistic and political activity in the 50 states. Some have achieved distinction as public servants, such as Admiral Horacio Rivero, former commander in chief of Naval Forces in Southern Europe, and ambassador to Spain; Dr. Antonia Novello, former Surgeon General of the United States; and Judge Juan Torruellas, chief judge of the 1st U.S. Circuit Court of Appeals.

And all the while, Puerto Ricans have treasured their association with the United States, cherished their American citizenship, and loyally done their duty. A duty which in Puerto Rico meant the highest rates of volunteer enlistment in our armed forces, the service of more than 200,000 Puerto Ricans in wars during this century, over 2,000 of our soldiers killed in action, and the award to four of them of the Congressional Medal of Honor. And I had the honor of having my grandson participate in the Gulf War.

Puerto Ricans are and always will be Americans. What will statehood cost? Of all the status options that are before this committee, commonwealth has proven over a 40-60 year period, that it will be never be self-sufficient. In fact, over the last ten years the cost of commonwealth exceeds $64 billion, while new economic studies which have been submitted to the committee show that statehood would save the taxpayer between $2.1 and $2.7 billion a year, and more as the Puerto Rican economy reaches its full growth, which is expected to be $29 billion by 2025.

The real question before the American people, therefore, is whether we as a nation should support the expensive status quo or let the people of Puerto Rico have the opportunity to consider a new status that ends this subsidy. What about apportionment? Some have voiced a concern about which state might lose seats in the House [of Representatives] if Puerto Rico became a state. The answer is, none will. Nothing in the Constitution prevents the House from increasing its size to accommodate new members from Puerto Rico.

Allow me now to speak briefly as a Republican. I know many in my party are apprehensive about a process that might result in two Democratic Senators and six representatives. At the risk of upsetting my Democratic friends, let me say Republicans have nothing to fear. Puerto Rico has had an active Republican party since 1902. The birthday of the party's founder, Dr. Jose Celso Barbosa, is an official holiday on the island. Currently, Republicans hold the balance of power in our legislature, and among our Mayors and we have come a long way to implement a Republican agenda, as the governor has explained to you. In the government we have today, out of the legislature there are 29 members of the House that are Republican, and 23 Democrats. In the Senate, there are 14 members who are Republicans and 13 Democrats. And the mayors, there are

46 municipalities that are Republican and 32 Democrats. So you see that in Puerto Rico, the Republican party controls the elected members of the government, and therefore there's no way to think that there's going to be Democratic control, like some people think, of our delegation in Congress. It will be, I imagine, divided between two parties.

Puerto Rico has always been fertile ground for the Republican Party. In Puerto Rico we Republicans have made historic changes.

In conclusion, let me speak as a Puerto Rican. As an American. What we want is simply to enjoy all of the rights and privileges of American citizens while, at the same time, to assume all of the inherent duties and responsibilities. We just want to be equal under the law, and we are ready, able and eager to assume those responsibilities. It is impossible, Mr. Chairman, to expect this change to come from Puerto Rico. Congress, and only Congress, can properly define the options available to Puerto Rico and put into place a process of full implementation.

And it is time to act, Mr. Chairman. We hope 4 million Puerto Rican Americans and the attention of our nation are now focused on the historic process that is underway here in Congress. The eyes of the world will soon follow, as America debates extending the right of self-determination to 4 million of our citizens after such a long wait. Congress has steered this republic to extraordinary accomplishments during our 222 years of increasing greatness. I have no doubt that it will do the right thing here once again.

And let me tell you. For a hundred years we've been under the American flag. We were brought in under the American flag by American troops that landed in Puerto Rico. We were very friendly to those troops. We received them with our open arms. There was no shot fired by a Puerto Rican against an American when they came into Puerto Rico in 1898. I know this because having lived so long I remember exactly stories of all the people who lived through all this period. So Puerto Ricans were completely decided to be free of Spain, but they didn't want to be a colony of any other country. And we accepted the Americans to come to Puerto Rico with open arms because they promised us at that time that we were going to be equal to them in the enjoyment of the rights of a republic and in equality, and we expected to become a state of the union from the very beginning. That is why the Puerto Ricans have always wanted American citizenship and have all the time fought to maintain our line of union with the United States.

In 1917, we were given the U.S. citizenship. Since then, we've been U.S. citizens, but U.S. citizens without the full rights. And that is all we are now fighting for. Puerto Ricans are U.S. citizens, but we want them to have all the rights of all the other citizens. There is no more room in this world for second-class citizens. There's no more room in this world for people who are subject to the authority of one body in which there is no representation from them. We feel that Congress should now respond to this question and give Puerto Rico the chance to say which way it wants to have its authority, its sovereignty. Sovereignty as a state of the union, or sovereignty as a republic.

Any other intermediate case, you will have to decide upon. But we cannot go on fooling the people of Puerto Rico. I have been fighting the party that has been now calling for commonwealth for 60 years. Since I became a Republican, in '38, I came to Washington to testify before the Senate, against the Tydings Bill for independence of Puerto Rico, and since then I've been coming back and back and back to assure that Puerto Rico becomes a state of the Union. That is what we have been looking for, that is what the people of Puerto Rico and the majority want to have, and that is why they want to have American citizenship and there is no reason why we should try to evade the issue and let the commonwealth group dominate the election by having — by promising something that they cannot deliver.

Puerto Rico wants equality. There are 2 million Puerto Ricans in the mainland who are doing a very fine job in many ways. We have to have that equality in order to be able to enjoy our citizenship and to do our country the best, as we want to do. We have fine people today. When you compare Puerto Rico in 1898 and Cuba, we were the same. We started out the same. But we said no, we want to pick our American citizenship association; the Cubans wanted independence and they got independence. A hundred years later, the experiment has shown who were the wise ones; our grandparents were the wise ones.

Puerto Rico Historical Timeline

AD 600	The Taino Indians become the first notable indigenous people to settle on the island. They call it Boriken, which means "the great land of the valiant and noble lord."
1493	The Spanish, led by Christopher Columbus, invade the island and claim it for the king of Spain. They name the island San Juan Bautista (St. John the Baptist) and they call its largest city Puerto Rico (Rich Port).
1508	Juan Ponce de Leon is named the first governor of the island.
1511	The Taino Indians unite with the Carib indigenous peoples in revolt against the Spanish colonists. Disease and war soon devastate the Taino population, which dwindles from an estimated 70,000 people to near extinction.
1518	African slaves are brought to the island to make up for the depleted workforce caused by the decreasing Taino population.
1521	Ponce de Leon switches the name of the island, San Juan Baptista, with the name of the largest city, Puerto Rico.
1626-1759	As a reaction to the harshness of life as a colony under military dictatorship with no representation or rights, Puerto Ricans begin to incorporate smuggling as a way to circumvent high Spanish taxes and the resulting poverty.
1765	Alejandro O'Reilly is sent by the Spanish crown to maintain order on Puerto Rico. At this time, a substantial majority of the island's 45,000 residents have become *contrabandistas* (smugglers).
1800	Population rises to 155,000 from 45,000 largely as a result of O'Reilly's reforms, which include a dropping of trade restrictions, lower tax rates, and an increase in Puerto Rican national identity.

1808	Puerto Rico gains its first representative in the Spanish government.
1810-22	Puerto Rico becomes a refuge for Spanish loyalists seeking to escape revolutions occurring in Spain's other American colonies.
1868	Revolutionaries in the town of Lares revolt and proclaim Puerto Rico an independent nation. Spanish forces quickly quell the attempt.
1873	Spain abolishes slavery in Puerto Rico.
1897	Spain declares Puerto Rico to be an autonomous state.
1898	The Spanish-American war comes to an end after the United States lands in Puerto Rico. This results in the ceding of Puerto Rico to the United States.
1899	More than 62 percent of Puerto Rico's exports are to the United States.
1900	The Foraker Act incorporates Puerto Rico as a United States territory, with a civil government headed by an American governor.
1917	The Jones Act grants U.S. citizenship to Puerto Rican residents, who now number over one million.
1930	U.S. corporations control 45 percent of the land in Puerto Rico, pushing many small, land-owning farmers out of business and into poverty.
1935	Five people are killed when police officers clash with Puerto Rican nationalists at the University of Puerto Rico.
1937	Violence erupts at a nationalist parade in the southern coastal town of Ponce when police open fire on marchers. Nineteen people are killed and over one hundred are injured. This becomes known as the "Masacre de Ponce."
1938	Nationalists attempt to assassinate Governor Winship, the man whom they consider responsible for the Masacre de Ponce.
1946	Jesus T. Pinero becomes the first Puerto Rican to govern the territory, under appointment from President Harry S. Truman.

1947	Congress passes the Crawford-Butler Act. The Act allows Puerto Rico to elect its own governor.
1950	Public Law 81-600, signed by President Truman, allows Puerto Rico to draft its own constitution.
1950	Two Puerto Rican nationalists, living in New York, make an assassination attempt on President Truman to dramatize Puerto Rico's desire for independence. Many nationalists, including leader Albizo Campos, are jailed for complicity.
1952	The Puerto Rican constitution is approved by vote and Puerto Rico becomes an official Commonwealth of the United States. The Popular Democratic Party (PPD) wins the subsequent election. The Independence Party (PIP) comes in second with 125,000 votes compared to the *populares'* 429,000.
1954	Four members of the Puerto Rican Nationalist Party open fire in the United States House of Representatives. Five congressmen are injured.
1959	The Fernos-Murray Bill, which would have expanded Puerto Rico's autonomy, fails to pass the U.S. Congress.
1959	Alaska and Hawaii gain statehood.
1967	A referendum discovers that 60.5 percent of Puerto Ricans are pro-Commonwealth, 38.9 percent are pro-Statehood, and only 0.6 percent are pro-independence.
1968	Luis A. Ferre, member of the pro-statehood New Progressive Party (NPP), is elected governor of Puerto Rico, narrowly beating the Popular Party candidate. Ferre's win ends 28 years of Popular Party control.
1970	The Puerto Rican pro-independence group, MIRA, claims responsibility for 19 terrorist acts and pledges to continue the violence.
1981	U.S. Customs launches Operation Greenback in an attempt to battle the chronic drug money laundering in Puerto Rico and other Caribbean islands.

1993	The U.S. Congress authorizes a referendum on Puerto Rican statehood. Forty-nine percent of Puerto Ricans vote for a commonwealth status based on an unrealistic wish list, 46 percent vote for statehood and four percent for independence (one percent of the votes were declared null).
1994	The U.S. Office of National Drug Control Policy proclaims Puerto Rico to be a High Intensity Drug Trafficking Area (HIDTA). The goal of the designation is to highlight drug trafficking in the area and to reduce the use of the islands as a means of getting drugs into the Continental United States.
1996	U.S. Congress votes not only to end tax breaks and incentives for companies looking to establish themselves in Puerto Rico but also to phase out benefits over a ten-year period for companies already established there.
1998	Puerto Rican governor Pedro Rossello calls for another referendum on statehood. The final tally shows little or no support for either independence or continuation of the Commonwealth status quo. Instead, 46 percent of the voters choose statehood and 51 percent select "none of the above," indicating a desire for the "free beer and barbecue" option (as characterized by Rep. Billy Tauzin) which represents, full U.S. citizenship, autonomy, no federal taxes, and full federal benefits.
1998	The Drug Enforcement Administration, U.S. Customs, and the Joint Interagency Task Force initiate Operation Journey, which results in the seizure of more than 16 tons of cocaine that were being sent through the Caribbean.
1999	A stray U.S. Navy bomb kills a Puerto Rican civilian, David Sanes Rodriguez, and results in increased demands for the Navy to cease occupation of the offshore island of Vieques, where the Navy performed mock invasions and live-fire exercises.
2001	Under pressure from notable Puerto Ricans, such as

The Cries of Patriots

2001 — Ricky Martin, and Americans, such as Jesse Jackson, the U.S. Navy pulls out of the western third of Vieques. U.S. President George Bush pledges to have the Navy completely depart by 2003.

President Bush forms the President's Task Force on Puerto Rico's Status with the expressed goal of enabling Puerto Rican citizens to choose the territory's future.

NUMBER OF YEARS UNDER US GOVERNMENTCONTROL TO REACH FULL SELF GOVERNMENT		
NAME OF AREA	YEARS	FINAL FORM OF SELF GOVERNMENT
Cuba	3	Independent
Marshall Islands	39	Free Associated State
Federated States of Micronesia	39	Free Associated State
Palau	47	Free Associated State
Philippines	47	Independent
Hawaii	61	State
New Mexico	64	State
Arizona	64	State
Alaska	92	State
Oklahoma	104	State
Puerto Rico	106	???

CHAPTER 12

The Eternal Territory

How much can happen in a little more than a century? Between 605 and 710 A.D., very little that most of us could describe happened. In a more recent time frame, the length of this span is more obvious. In 1860, the Civil War had not yet occurred. In 1965 two years had passed since Martin Luther King, Jr.'s "I Have a Dream" speech. In 1879, Thomas Edison invented the first practical incandescent light bulb using a piece of sewing thread for the filament. In 1984, the United States consumed 74.1 quadrillion BTU's of energy to maintain its electrical power needs. In 1900, the first telegraphic connection between London and the source of the Nile was established when the Uganda Railway completed a connection across that mysterious river. In 2003, a Russian state company signed a contract with the British satellite company SSTL to launch eight micro satellites, with an African nation among the partners in the venture.

In 1900 a map of Europe showed Austria-Hungary and the Kingdom of Serbia, the Ottoman Empire and the Empire of All Russias. A map of Africa showed French Equitorial Africa and French West Africa, Nyasaland, Zanzibar, and Rhodesia. A map of Southeast Asia included French Indochina and the Netherlands East Indies. In the year 2000 the maps of these regions showed that they had lost many of their kingdoms, most of their empires, and a great number of their foreign colonial adjectives. Between 1900 and

2000, of course, Soviet communism came and went, with another radical redrawing of the map of Eastern Europe and the creation of new republics from China in the east to Poland in the west to Iran in the south. Tides of immense and irresistible change flowed over the planet, leaving scarcely a single country untouched.

In 1900 the landmass of the United States of America, all 45 states of it, minus the territories of Hawaii, Arizona and New Mexico and the unorganized territories of Oklahoma and Alaska, was approximately 2.56 million square miles. A little more than a century later, the United States had grown by five states with a land area of nearly 1,000,000 square miles, an increase of some 38 percent. It might have grown even more had President Ford taken the advice of his enterprising and plutocratic Vice President, Nelson Rockefeller, who urged him to propose the purchase of Greenland from Denmark.

As it turns out, 105 years, the time, at this writing, that has elapsed since Puerto Rico came into the direct orbit of the United States, is time enough to exceed the transitions of every other major piece of American territory that moved into a new status since the mid-1800s. It adds nothing to the reputation of the United States that only one of its significant territories has endured such a span of uncertainty. It only adds to the luster of Puerto Rico's patience (that patience may be part of the explanation) that it has endured this state of affairs with its pro-American posture largely intact and without the bloody rebelliousness that has characterized the colonies of other powers over the past century. It only detracts from the compelling character of the U.S. engagement in Iraq when we speak of self-government in Baghdad and have failed to deliver it for ancient Boriquen.

Consider the chart on page 302. It lays out, in capsule form, the names and fates of 11 territories that have entered into some original relationship with the United States since 1848. Two of them, of course, were colonies in open rebellion against a European power, that is, Cuba and the Philippines against Spain. The United States declared war against Spain, fulfilling a desire in Washington to expel European power from the Caribbean, after the explosion and sinking of the battleship *Maine* in Havana harbor in February 1898. One of the mainmasts of the *Maine* stands as a memorial in

Arlington Cemetery across the Potomac River from the U.S. capital, in memory of the 266 American lives lost that day. The U.S. declaration of war, backdated to April 21, 1898, was preceded by the adoption of the Teller Amendment, in which the United States declared its intention not to assume sovereignty over Cuba.

The United States quickly defeated the overextended Spanish, and by 1902 Cuba had formal, not quite in name only, independence. The Teller Amendment was replaced by the Platt Amendment, which reserved to the United States certain rights to intervene in Cuba to preserve its citizens the guarantees of life, liberty and property. This reservation was exercised on several occasions over the next 30 years as U.S. military forces arrived under its provisions to restore order or protect U.S. interests. This Amendment was finally abrogated in 1934. Seventeen years later, Fidel Castro Ruz would ensure that Cuba became a thorn in the American foot, but, nonetheless, Cuba had attained its freedom from Spain and from the United States in less than 40 years.

For the Philippines, the process of achieving independence from the United States consumed almost half a century. President McKinley had not wanted a long-term relationship with the island, but he bowed to domestic U.S. pressure and military leaders' desire for a naval base in the Far East and reacted to the competition from European powers, particularly Germany, which had sent warships to Manila to underscore their own interest. The sum of $20 million was paid to the Spanish Crown to indemnify Madrid for its captured possessions in the Philippines, as well as for Puerto Rico and Guam. In contrast to Cuba, the U.S. involvement in the Philippines was initially bloody. The nationalist General Emilio Aguinaldo, at first an ally of the Americans in their war against Spain, unilaterally declared independence for the Philippines in June 1898.

When Washington reached its separate peace with Madrid in the Treaty of Paris in December 1898 and the Philippines was sold to the United States, the nationalists were incensed. Aguinaldo declared a Philippine Republic in January 1899 and launched a guerrilla war against the American occupation. It took 126,000 U.S. troops to quell the uprising. The resulting conflict inflicted military deaths of more than 20,000 (four fifths of them Aguinaldo's men) and civilian losses of as many as 200,000 lives, possibly from disease and famine. U.S. military rule was ended in June 1901 and eventually the guerrilla campaign was suppressed by local Philippine forces.

For the next 30 years, government in the Philippines developed along some of the same lines as Puerto Rico's. A federal law, the Philippine Organic Act, was enacted in 1902. It extended the protection of the U.S. Bill of Rights to Filipinos and created a bicameral legislature, with the lower house popularly elected and the upper house directly named by the President of the United States. The Jones Act of 1916 replaced the appointed upper house with a locally elected Senate. Another act of Congress, this one in 1934 (the same year that the Platt Amendment affecting Cuba was finally terminated), created the Commonwealth of the Philippines. On July 4, 1946, as Americans celebrated their first independence day after the surrender of Japan, the Philippines celebrated its first independence day as a new nation. Forty-eight years had passed since Aguinaldo's declaration, and he would live to be honored at ceremonies of the Republic into the 1960s.

Guam followed its own political course after the U.S. purchase. In some respects, it resembled Puerto Rico, in that it had belonged to another colonial power, was a relatively small island, had an excellent harbor with real military significance in a strategic part of the world, and was largely homogeneous religiously (i.e., Roman Catholic). Like Puerto Rico, it is an unincorporated territory of the United States, with aspirations for something more. If the 1,000 miles that separate Puerto Rico from the mainland seem significant, the 6,000-mile stretch of Pacific Ocean that separates Guam from the continental United States seems imponderable. Most of all, perhaps, Guam is not populous. Even today it has only 154,000 people (more than 10 percent of whom are U.S. military personnel), compared to the teeming population of Puerto Rico. Were it represented in the U.S. Congress by an actual voting member, as opposed to the non-voting delegate that represents it today, its size would earn it only ¼ of a congressman.

The preferred status of most Guamanians today is commonwealth. The U.S. Navy managed Guam until 1950, when the U.S. Government transferred that responsibility to the Department of the Interior (the federal government owns one-third of the island's approximately 540 square miles). Beginning that year, when Guam was first permitted to elect a local legislative body, it has steadily acquired additional hallmarks of home rule, including, in 1970, the right to elect its own governor and lieutenant governor and, in 1973, the right to choose its own non-voting delegate to the U.S. Congress, who sits in the House of Representatives. A status plebiscite in 1982 endorsed a continued relationship with the United States.

This relationship is a financial lifeline to the island. Although the United Nations has criticized the military presence of the United States in Guam as inhibiting the island's self-determination, its economic dependency on Washington is not likely to change. In fiscal 1997 alone, according to the Central Intelligence Agency's *World Factbook*, Guam received $147 million in U.S. transfer payments. Like Puerto Rico, its inhabitants are U.S. citizens who pay no federal income tax; the transfer payments represent a complete net gain to the Guamanian economy that would be hard to replace. Moreover, even the federal income taxes paid by U.S. civilian and military employees on Guam are deposited into the Guam Treasury, instead of the U.S. Treasury. Altogether, these are arrangements that produce little pressure for change, and the U.S. military forces relied on Guam's strategic importance as recently as the 2003 Iraq War. When all is said and done, Guam is simply not beset with the historical and demographic pressures and internal dissensions that have made the status issue such a pressing matter for Puerto Rico.

For the other jurisdictions included in the chart on page 302, the most obvious observation is that all were able to complete the process of reaching a final status in less time, usually much less time, than Puerto Rico. With each passing day, of course, the gap widens. Puerto Rico has now doubled the average time to transition to permanent status (56 years) achieved by the typical territory. Moreover, it is clearly not the case that there has been any kind of uniformity about these transitions, either in the size or geography contiguousness of the territories, in the presence or absence of "native populations," in previous colonial heritage, in initial acquisition by force of arms, or in any other major factor. The preponderance of a foreign language, particularly one that has its origin in a highly developed European nation, is perhaps one distinguishing characteristic, and the role that language played in blocking the

1998 status legislation pays tribute to the importance of that fact.

However you look at it, Puerto Rico is a territorial sore thumb for the United States. The longer the dispute has gone on, the messier the politics of the situation have become. This does not mean, however, that a solution has become more remote. Chaotic and controversial entries into the Union have been common enough, and transitions to independence have not always been smooth. The experience of Alaska offers a wide array of parallels with the experience of Puerto Rico today. Along with Oklahoma, Alaska endured the longest period of transition in the past century and a half, some 92 years, from the 1867 to 1959. Like the island of Manhattan and the Territory of Louisiana, Alaska was purchased in one of the greatest bargains in the history of the planet: $7.2 million. The sale, as every student of history knows, was lambasted as a waste of good cash on a trackless wilderness.

Secretary of State Seward, whose name will forever be associated with the ironic phrase "Seward's Folly," envisioned Alaska's perhaps becoming "many states." In its early years as a U.S. colony, the Congress did little more than think of it as a source of certain natural resources: fish, hides, and timber. As has happened with other territories, Alaska, with its predominantly coastal population in the southeast panhandle, was governed by the U.S. Navy for a time. In 1884 Congress got around to passing the First Organic Act, providing Alaska with a civil and judicial infrastructure of judges and marshals. At this time the population of the territory was just 32,000, only 430 of whom were white settlers. Tension and violent confrontation with the majority native population were common.

The First Organic Act made no provision for Alaskan representation in Washington. The territory drifted on the periphery of national interest. Not only was Alaska geographically remote from the United States, but it was outside the continuous border of the country, out of sight, out of mind. This changed to a significant degree at the beginning of the 20th century when the Klondike Gold Rush brought 30,000 new settlers into the region. President McKinley, already absorbed with the challenges of the new U.S. possessions obtained from Spain, also turned his attention to Alaska. He called on Congress to give Alaska's civil administration more form and order, and Congress passed a comprehensive code and a system of taxation for the territory in 1900.

Further progress toward Alaskan self-rule and representation was blocked during the next period in its history by the actions of what was called the Alaska Syndicate, a group of wealthy "captains of industry," including J. P. Morgan, who controlled much of the transportation industry and a major copper mine and were able to profit handsomely from the territory similar to Puerto Rico's pharmaceuticals. As historian Eric Gislason has put it, in words that should resonate with any observer of Puerto Rico's enthrallment to vested interests today, critics of the Alaska Syndicate "argued that Alaska's resources should be used for the good of the entire country rather than exploited [by] a select group of large, absentee-controlled interests."[1]

The Syndicate managed to halt reform until a scandal involving the illegal insider distribution of Alaskan coal claims in 1910 split the Republicans and prompted President Taft, in 1912, to support legislation to weaken the Syndicate's grip on Alaskan resources.

Congress adopted this legislation, the Second Organic Act in April 1912. It made Alaska officially a U.S. territory and bound it more closely to the lower 48. Under the act, the governor remained an appointed official, but Alaskans with voting rights were permitted to elect their own territorial House and Senate. The acts of this legislature were subject, however, to the approval of Congress. The federal government also retained regulatory control over the state's primary natural resources, its fish and game and fur trade, an exercise of authority that rubbed the Alaskans the wrong way. Despite the influx of settlers, the territory remained thinly populated and the attitudes of its Aleuts, Indians, and Eskimos toward a distant government also complicated the process of change.

By 1916 the far-sighted James Wickersham, a McKinley appointee to the Alaskan bench and by that time the territory's non-voting delegate to Congress, introduced the first statehood bill. It sparked little interest in the free-spirited territory or in Washington, where businessmen were still using the peculiarities of Alaska's status to reap financial rewards through shipping regulations that forced Alaskans to use Seattle ports. Local government in Alaska began to pull in different directions, and federal relations became more and more complicated (shades of modern Puerto Rico, indeed) as some 52 federal agencies had various ranges of responsibility for the territory's affairs. The situation prompted Wickersham to remark that "there actually exists today a congressional government in Alaska more offensively bureaucratic in its basic principles and practices than that which existed here during the seventy years of Russian rule under the Czar."[2]

Little progress in improving Alaska's administration occurred in the 1920s, and the Depression hit the territory hard, as it did Puerto Rico. As dependent as Puerto Rico was on its monocrop, sugar, Alaska was even more dependent on its natural resource exports and the regulatory whims of the federal agencies and the neighboring states. The New Deal ideas of the Roosevelt Administration were no more successful, and certainly, some of them at least, much more bizarre than the land reforms that were experimented with in Puerto Rico. FDR proposed that displaced farmers from poorer northern states, like Minnesota, Wisconsin, and Michigan, could be induced to colonize the Matanuska-Sisitka region of Alaska. Another, related idea was a similar failure. It involved a proposal by a group called the United Congo Improvement Association to move 400 African-American farmers to Alaska. Racial prejudice and the general impracticality of the proposal spelled its doom.

Just as with Puerto Rico, World War II brought an end to the New Deal experiments in the territory, and security concerns, involving Japan rather than Germany, impelled the U.S. government to "notice" Alaska and invest heavily there. Funds poured into the territory to secure America's northwest frontier, the Alaska Highway was built, military bases were erected, and the Aleutians were fortified. Alaskan was approaching a turning point. In 1940 there were only 1,000 U.S. military personnel in a territory with a total of 75,000 residents. Three years later there were 233,000 people in Alaska, 152,000 of whom were military. This military concentration dropped sharply immediately after the war, but rose again with the onset of the Cold War. The continuing strategic interest of Alaska, and its modest population, turned the jurisdiction into something more akin to Guam than to Puerto Rico in the post-war period. Puerto Rico was already home to 2.2 million people in 1950.

The following decade featured a crush of events in Alaska that moved the territory into statehood. On the record, by voting percentages and the like, statehood had popular support. The reality, as always, was far more complicated, and statehood did not come before some local political figures in the 1950s demonstrated dramatic leadership and others, already known for their national leadership, demonstrated their partisan weaknesses. The former included the future senator from Alaska, Ernest Gruening, and the latter included the former Supreme Allied Commander, President of the United States from 1952 to 1960, Dwight D. Eisenhower.

The war years had put Alaska on the national news map. *Newsweek* published a report on the state and its writer, Richard L. Neuberger, referred to the territory as a "feudal barony" and a "looted land." This kind of vivid language was new for the national media; the conflicted consciences that often troubled U.S. officials about places like Puerto Rico and the Philippines had not been deployed on behalf of Alaska's plight, but the plight was real, and the situation was exploitative. In a maritime version of King Sugar and the Section 936 largesse, as Gislason writes, "keeping territorial government and tax structures to a minimum benefited Seattle-area interests such as the Alaska Steamship Company and the Northland Transportation Company, who enjoyed an effective monopoly on steamship travel and shipping and charged unusually high rates." Outside companies simply profited too handsomely from Alaska's status to encourage change.[3]

Gruening, whom FDR has appointed governor of Alaska in 1939, joined forces with Edward Lewis "Bob" Bartlett, who had been a staff assistant to a previous Alaskan delegate to Congress. FDR made Bartlett Secretary of Alaska in 1939 and in 1944 Bartlett ran for and won the delegate position in his own right. From 1945 on, Bartlett was Alaska's only official representative in Congress. The vested financial interests opposed to statehood have finally met their match. From 1943 to 1953 Gruening and Bartlett organized leading Alaskans, including its many frustrated local business people, into a force for economic development and self-rule, leading to statehood. The first vote in this direction came in a territory-wide referendum in 1946, and pro-statehood forces prevailed with a 60 percent majority.

In 1948 Bartlett introduced another statehood bill in the House of

Representatives. In another interesting parallel, this time with the fate of H.R. 856 for Puerto Rico 50 years later, the Bartlett bill was tied up by opposition from the chairman of the House Rules Committee. The Alaska Statehood Committee was formed the next year, and Gruening set about courting supporters in the lower 48, including the establishment of a "Committee of 100" notables that included Pearl Buck, Arthur Schlesinger, and other prominent Americans from various walks of life. The following year this pressure resulted in a pro-statehood vote in the House of Representatives, but the bill was killed in the Senate. Interestingly again, the opposition to the bill in the Senate had partisan political overtones. Senate Republicans joined with the Dixiecrats to derail the Alaskan statehood measure.

Concern about a shaky GOP majority in 1998, as discussed in the previous chapter, was a hidden motivation in the defeat of the Young bill. The sense of déjà vu here should prompt some reflections about the irony of events in 1950. The GOP had been all but wiped out in Congress with the onset of the Depression and the election of FDR. Their narrow 218-216 majority in 1932 turned overnight into a 313-117 minority, and they were headed to double digits (just 89 seats) in the House by the end of the decade. The situation in the Senate was just as dire in 1939; Democrats dominated the GOP by a count of 76 to 16. A decade later the Republicans had recovered and captured both Houses of Congress, but their margin in the Senate was narrow (51 to 45) and it was precarious in both Houses.

The Republicans, including Eisenhower, who won the presidency in 1952 and retained the GOP's suspicion of statehood, were persuaded that Alaska would surely send Democrats to Congress, making their resurrection more difficult. In 1954 Ike included language in his State of the Union message calling for the admission of Hawaii into the Union, making no mention of Alaska. The Republicans evidently believed Hawaii would send Republican reinforcements when they were needed most. A sharply divided Senate (only one vote separated the two parties) ultimately put together a bill to admit Hawaii and then Alaska, putatively maintaining the parties' delicate balance. As history would have it, of course, and typically history has it its own way, the balance was maintained by Hawaii favoring Democrats and Alaska favoring

Republicans over the years. In any event, Alaskan groups, including Operation Statehood, flooded the Congress with messages demanding "statehood now."

Other proposals were floated in Washington, including one endorsed by the famed commentator Walter Lippmann, to make Alaska and Hawaii commonwealths with elected governors, as had been done for Puerto Rico. This idea had no traction. Alaska was in the opposite position of Puerto Rico in a vital respect: it paid federal taxes, but had no representation. In 1955 the rambunctious Alaskans staged a constitutional convention without Washington's permission. On this occasion Gruening delivered a stirring speech titled "Let Us End American Colonialism." The emotional sequence of events led up to the territory's approval of the constitution in 1956. The end game was at hand.

Alaskan statehood advocates' next move was to adapt what was called the "Tennessee Plan" to their own circumstances. This maneuver had been followed successfully by Tennessee, Michigan, California, Oregon, Kansas, and Iowa. Under the plan Alaska elected a Congressional delegation without waiting for Congress to authorize an election. The election took place in the spring of 1956 and Gruening was one of the "senators" thus elected. Though Congress refused to seat him and his colleagues, their persistence began to wear down even the redoubtable Speaker Sam Rayburn, who changed his position and endorsed statehood in 1957.

In early 1958 Eisenhower made public his endorsement of statehood. By this time the House of Representatives was in Democratic hands, where it would stay for nearly 40 years. Once again, a powerful Rules Committee Chairman, Howard Smith of Virginia, obstructed the statehood bill. Advocates bypassed the committee, brought the bill up on a privileged motion and prevailed by nearly 40 votes. The Senate, which had been considering its own bill, took up the House version and passed it 64-20. Non-voting delegate Bob Bartlett was still in the mix, and his many friendships in the House and Senate helped steer the measure to final passage in July.

Finally, in August 1958, Alaskans went to the polls to approve statehood. The voters had to vote yea or nay on all three statements regarding statehood that appeared on the ballot. Unlike the most recent Puerto Rican plebiscite, "none of the above" was not an option. The state had many dissidents, settlers who had come a long way, as well as native peoples, who wanted nothing to do with the remote and interfering government in Washington. They stayed away from the polls, and of the 46,000 who went to vote (many thousands more than the previous high-water mark in status elections in the territory), six of every seven voted to join the Union. The die was cast, and the following January Eisenhower declared the vast terrain of Alaska the 49th state. Later that year, Hawaii was admitted as the 50th state.

It should be noted that despite the high percentage vote (nearly 90 percent) for Alaskan statehood, many people stayed away from the polls. The centrifugal spirit of the Alaskan pioneer was strong, and resentment of statehood was no small matter in the early years after Alaska's admission. I was stationed in Alaska in 1961 after entering the service. The military brass there warned all the new servicemen not to wear the U.S. uniform in public, as it could provoke physical assault from locals who resisted the American military presence. It was advice worth taking.

Today, some proponents of the status quo in Puerto Rico try to scare those who favor statehood by predicting violence if Puerto Rico were to become a state. They base these predictions on cultural issues. Where were the cultural issues in Alaska? Yet when Alaska became a state, unlike Puerto Rico, the majority of its residents favored independence and stayed away from the polls because that option was not offered in their referendum.

As this sequence of events illustrates, the road to status resolution has hardly been smooth, even in a case like Alaska, where the additions in resources, including incredible natural beauty, make us wonder today how there could have been any hesitation or debate. Nonetheless, Alaska's entry involved partisan political intrigue, insider deals that allowed outsiders with major economic interests to lobby successfully for the status quo, a recalcitrant Rules Committee, and a Senate willing to bury a bill that had significant popular support. In this sense, the recent challenges facing Puerto Rico are nothing new. The preservation of *perceived partisan advantages* (because subsequent history has so often proved them untrue) and of entrenched financial interests that are actually inhibiting local growth operated in the same way to deter Alaska from achieving its real potential. Against that partisanship and entrenchment, only persistence, ingenuity, and, with Bartlett, the cultivation of extensive friendships worked to effect change. It is likely to be the same with Puerto Rico.

That change obviously need not be to statehood; for three of the U.S. possessions depicted in the chart on page 302, the free associated state was the outcome. The Marshall Islands, Micronesia, and Palau all achieved this status of independence and true sovereignty in the period 1983-86 (Palau's was not fully implemented until 1994), under a conservative administration working with a Democratic Congress. The process took 47 years for Palau and 39 for the other two territories. Like Guam, these Western Pacific Islands have had a keen interest for the United States because of their military value in a region where air and ocean distances represent major obstacles to strategic operations. The region was a battleground in World War II, with the Japanese either occupying these islands or struggling with the United States for control.

After the armistice the United States exercised military authority until 1947 when the area became the Trust Territory of the Pacific Islands, a designation created by the United Nations with the United States as Trustee. This status lasted for nearly four decades, with the United Nations and its decolonization committee, in cooperation with the territories themselves and a cooperative United States, constantly looking toward self-determination for these territories. Finally, in the 1980s, the Reagan Administration worked out the terms of a compact of free association. The Republic of the Marshall Islands voted for the compact in 1983 and the Congress approved it in 1986. The same bill also provided for free association status for the Federated States of Micronesia.

These were true compacts (not the false compact that political partisans in Puerto Rico have ascribed to its continuing territorial status) between sovereign nations. Each of the island governments is sovereign and their citizens are not U.S. citizens. The compact, indeed the entire relationship, can be cancelled at the instigation of either party. The FAS (Freely Associated States), as they are often called, are nations and recognized as such in the United Nations, where they cast their own votes on their own initiative (though these votes are typically supportive of their continued financial partner, the United States). In fact, the compact between the FAS and the United States in existence at this writing has formally expired and is awaiting a likely new 15-year extension. It is likely to be extended, but Congress could clearly elect not to do so.

Certainly, the compact just expiring contains important bilateral terms that both the FAS and the United States value. Most important, it mandates consultation on military and strategic affairs and prohibits, as under a treaty arrangement, the FAS from concluding military agreements with any other foreign power. In exchange for this privilege, the United States provides economic assistance to these states. Moreover, although they are not U.S. citizens, FAS citizens can, under the compact, volunteer for U.S. military service and many are in such units as the 101st Airborne. Like Puerto Ricans, they serve in Iraq and other hot spots. Still, as Congressman John Duncan has noted, the overall arrangements represented by FAS status are "not some screwy scheme of co-mingled nationality or neo-colonial entanglements. Indeed, the whole point of free association is that it continues as long as it serves the mutual interest of the parties."4

This does not mean that some version of the screwy scheme cannot surface in the context of the free associated state. Theoretically, this kind of screwy scheme should be called "foreign aid." One wrinkle of FAS status is that residents of these countries are permitted under the compact to migrate freely to the United States. As individuals living on fairly remote islands, the idea of living in a state (including one in which, under another wrinkle, they must register for the draft) where there are more economic options is appealing. Thus, many have migrated to Hawaii and to Guam. When the compact of free association with the Republic of the Marshall Islands and the Federated States of Micronesia came up in August 2003, Senator Daniel Akaka of Hawaii indicated he planned to offer an amendment to make these FAS migrants eligible for food stamps, Medicaid, and welfare!

However this issue of benefits is worked out, and whether it is described as welfare, or foreign aid, or immigration policy, at the end of the day the *contents* of the U.S. relationship with the FAS approach a normalcy and predictability that serve, as Rep. Duncan said, the parties' "mutual interests." Puerto Rico is in no such shape. *Per capita*, its citizens derive five times as much in federal benefits from Washington as the residents of the FAS do through their compact. Like FAS residents, they pay no federal income taxes, but unlike them, they yearn for equality and respect in the international arena, and this eludes them. Would FAS status work for Puerto Rico? Obviously, its terms – what amounts to mutual interest – would have to be worked out. Certainly, federal subsidies would be reduced and Puerto Rican pride would be honored. Under the FAS precedents, U.S. military service need not be ruled out. The United States could maintain bases in Puerto Rico, but it would do so under a treaty, which would be negotiated, subject to change, and, if you will, "market-priced" in strategic terms.

FAS status is not much favored in Puerto Rico. It received a few tenths of one percent of the vote in the nonbonding plebiscite of 1998. Given the diminished benefit levels to which it might lead and the loss of guaranteed citizenship to Puerto Rican newborns to which it would certainly lead, this is perfectly understandable. But it is, after all, an honorable option that would leave the island free to join the United Nations, the OAS and other international bodies, and free to attend as many IberoAmerican summits as its elected leaders chose to attend, without embarrassing cables from the U.S. State Department accompanying their arrival. *Washington Post* reporter Bob Woodward reports in his book on Bill Clinton, *The Agenda*, how the late-Sen. Pat Moynihan went to the White House and explained to the Administration how the Puerto Rico's tax gimmickry was a trade-off for its continued acceptance of second-class citizenship and a denial of quality.

That is a heavy price to pay for any benefit. It was a not a price even the residents of the Marshall Islands, survivors of U.S. nuclear weapons testing on their territory, were willing to pay. Why should Puerto Ricans tolerate such a price, 105 years after they first began to pay it, heirs of a new century of dependency, the longest in the history of American freedom?

Section III

Character

[The vignette that follows is a work of fiction. It does not depict real events or persons, living or dead. The characters and events are purely imaginary, and no resemblance to real persons or events is intended.]

VIGNETTE 1

Moncho's Other Family Business

―――⋙◆⋘―――

The small boat rocked gently against the dock under the warehouse roof. Moncho and his brother Juanito and their cousin Augustin climbed aboard, pulling the drawstrings of their windbreakers tightly around their waists.

* * * *

Moncho was born and raised in the same town where he lives now, as were his father, his mother, his grandparents and great grandparents, as far back as he can trace his bloodline. He is a respected businessman, a local seafood restaurant owner and fish wholesaler/retailer in a small town on the south coast of Puerto Rico. He lives on the water with his wife and three children, just outside of town, about 500 yards down the road from his restaurant and warehouse. Moncho is successful in his trade, a member of the local Lions Club and also of the local Masonic Temple. He owns a very fast 42-foot sport fishing boat, which he can anchor outside his house or moor inside the warehouse.

Moncho has another trade as well. He uses his boat to pick up bales of cocaine and heroin that have been dropped off some 15 to 20 miles off the southern coast of Puerto Rico by either larger vessels or airplanes from Colombia, Venezuela and Panama.

The boat and a satellite homing device were the key tools of that trade. Moncho would set out in the night with his brother and cousin and they would locate the floating contraband. They would haul it aboard swiftly, rev the engine full, and return home at high speed, with Juanito at the helm and he and Augustin busy on the narrow deck, transferring the bales into suitcases. Once they were home, the suitcases would be packed into boxes and crates, just like the ones he used for supplies and even fish in his restaurant and wholesaling business.

On a typical night, he and his relatives would bring back a load of 500 kilos, more than 1,000 pounds, of cocaine and heroin. The round-trip took little more than four hours, beginning at midnight. By the time they were within the walls of the warehouse and easing up to the dock, the drugs would have been broken down into about 25 suitcases or other travel bags, ready for sealing up. Moncho and Juanito would lift the bags onto the warehouse concrete, next to the restaurant, while Augustin would "take a look around" to make sure no one was taking any special interest in their night fishing trip.

Two hours later, the small vans and private cars would begin to pull up to the warehouse. They would pick the boxes, to all appearances the usual product of Moncho's trade. These vehicles did not attract the attention of the police. They looked like all the other trucks and cars that rolled up to Moncho's every morning to pick up the previous day's catch. Each vehicle would take two or three boxes, with one or two suitcases inside. Loading itself did not take long, but the vehicles did not arrive together. That would not look right. They came at intervals, and by noontime all the boxes would be loaded in the six or so vehicles needed for this transaction. Once they were gone, so was the evidence, save perhaps a large quantity of cash that would have to be hidden among Moncho's legitimate profits.

Moncho and company did not have to do very much night fishing like this. Two or three times a year were enough to yield him and his family a cool $700,000 plus per year. Non-taxable, too. His regular business was profitable and he paid taxes on it. He did not have to worry about the Internal Revenue Service. This was a local business and there would no IRS scrutiny.

Moncho's Other Family Business

Moncho knew that his take was small change in the big picture. He was passing along drugs that were worth a minimum of $30 to $40 million, and perhaps as much as $150 million when it was cut up, diluted, and sold on street corners and in parks. His own portion would go for spending money, or real estate, or some speculation in the stock market. With Merrill Lynch, Paine Webber, and Charles Schwab, Moncho keeps more than $6 million in stocks, bonds, and GNMAE's

It was good business, a lot less work than the warehouse and the restaurant. It was worth the risk, Moncho thought. A trip every four months. Lots of others do it, too, spreading the risk around. Once in awhile, someone got caught. He, Juanito, and Augustin had been at it several years. It had all started with a seemingly casual question from a visitor to the restaurant, a political discussion about drugs and the government's many crackdowns. It turned out to be a proposition, not politics. Moncho was surprised at how readily he agreed. But someone was going to go to the bank and it might as well be him...

* * * *

It was hot in the tropics, even at night, but soon the speed of the boat and the spray from the ocean would pelt and chill them. The wind would push up from the south, soft and insistent, hinting of the Venezuelan jungles hundreds of miles away. They were used to this trip and its discomforts.

Moncho and his companions worked quietly and quickly, Juanito storing a few items for the trip — food packets wrapped in canvas, the squat barrels of gasoline, a small radio, the fishing tackle they would not use — and Augustin tending to the massive outboard engine that kept the nose of the boat high in the water as it skimmed across the surface.

The trip was not long, but there was time to think. Moncho was not an unreflective man. As a youth, he had dreamed of the green diamonds of America, of playing baseball under the bright lights before big crowds. He could handle a bat and play the game. He loved the legendary "Baby Bull" and read about his father, but there were others, even in his neighborhood, who could play the game better, and only the best – the heroes – went north in the spring. Now here he was, under the dim lights of the Caribbean stars, a few twinkling signs of human habitation on the distant horizon behind him. He and the others were surrounded by silence, except for the purring of the motors.

Hernando, another cousin, was in the marijuana trade. He sold the stuff on the island. Sampled some for himself, Moncho thought. It was grown the old way. He wanted no part of that action. The product was bulky, and selling it directly to the users brought one into contact with all sorts of unsavory characters. It did not seem like business. The coca plant and the poppy were different. A small amount went a long way. The profits were excellent. He and Juanito and Augustin were middlemen. They spent most of their time at their legal labors. They did not deal with the users. For them what they hauled out of the water may as well have been flour or sugar except for the payoff that they banked for every trip.

"I would never do that," Moncho said to himself. He let out the throttle a little on the go-fast boat. Like Orion striding down the night sky above him, Moncho knew his place in his small universe. He was a middleman, yes, but trafficking in this part of the world meant fewer middlemen than there were along the land routes from Colombia, through Guatemala and Mexico, to the States. It was essential to buy one's passage from the people in power, if you went by land. "And they do nothing," he thought to himself, "but hold out their palms as the drugs pass. I am fortunate, there are no palms to cross out here. What is mine, I keep."

The speedboat was now five miles from shore. Juanito and Augustin had finished their minimal duties and lay stretched out across the watertight boxes that lined one wall of the boat, ready to receive their "catch." Moncho spied the dark form of Caja de Muertos ahead and to his right. The intermittent gleam of its lighthouse flickered across his line of sight. Caja de Muertos. "Coffin Island," they also called it. He had steered around its scrubby edges many times, but it was without interest.

The night was predicted to remain clear ("no weather" was good weather), and there would be no moon for another four hours. By then he and his companions would be at the drop site. No need for speed now. The water was smooth. Moncho mused that he could practically sleep at the helm and arrive safely, so straight was his direction.

Across open sea the speedboat could do 40 knots. "A to' meter," as Moncho would call it in his Boriqua jargon. It could be exhilarating. Moncho glanced at his instruments from time to time. It was uneventful and he had made this trip too many times for excitement, but there was a thrill to this thing, an adventure, money to be made, and, almost more exciting, a chance something could go wrong.

Now as the foam of the northern Caribbean flew past the boat's flanks, time sped up as well. They should pick up the signal from the bales soon. He turned to Augustin and nodded. Augustin adjusted the headset.

Moncho first confirmed the drop. He selected the frequency, pulled the microphone to his lips, and spoke three words that would be cryptic to anyone but the intended recipient. "Vamos mete mano." The reply was two words. "Pa'lante." Fifteen more minutes and they were within range of the floating bales. The signal in Augustin's ears was strong now. Five minutes more and they were alongside the bales, bobbing in the moonlight.

The three men hauled their catch aboard. It was best to get it done and not to linger. Juanito lifted the false bottom from the interior of the watertight containers. From Moncho to Augustin, five hundred kilos of sealed packets passed, then quickly to Julio, who thrust them into the containers, a second layer of plastic shielding the precious powder from the elements. A few more moments and the fishing trip had accomplished its purpose. The catch was aboard. Juanito had brought along a crate full of yesterday's real catch, which he spread over the packets.

Moncho grinned and said nothing. He stood once more at the helm and turned his boat back to the north. No other boats were in sight. Not this night. Perhaps they had come earlier and picked up other bales from the same freighter. The drops were probably miles apart and the couriers were likely from other southern ports. Moncho and his partners did not view themselves as in league with them. In truth, they scarcely knew who they were. Some might even wear badges or sit at government desks in their regular jobs. Moncho had no desire to know them. He was paid well. And it was not graft. He worked hard for his money, took the risk, and he was proud of this.

Now the difficult part of the trip began. Already in the east the sky was lightening a little. Distant clouds sent their gray fingers into the sky. It was an active sky, but not threatening. A shower, perhaps. But they would reach the warehouse before it hit. He was confident of his craft's abilities. No, what nervousness he had was from the nature of his cargo, and one half-decayed load of fish was not going to disguise that. Concealment on the boat was only useful for casual inspections. It would not fool the police. No, to be stopped was to be caught. There was no point in carrying firearms. He was in this trade for a better life, not an early death. The speedboats almost always got through. If they did not, surrender was the only option.

In his heart, Moncho envied the land-based couriers who would take the cocaine by road up to San Juan. They could be more creative and less conspicuous. Sometimes he and Juanito did this themselves. "One less mouth to feed," he thought. The ship's officers in the Port of San Juan who helped them, for a fee, had it even better. They had thousands of containers in their control to choose from for hiding places. They operated from one of the busiest ports in the world. The drug police had many investigators but few interceptors. Interdiction was dangerous work, and those who did it often came to see it as futile. Still, Moncho was worried. Word on the street was that more pressure was coming. More Americans. They missed most of the drugs coming through, but they liked their shows of strength.

The speedboat made its way north across the sea. They wanted to be inside the warehouse before 4:00 a.m. The return trip to Puerto Rico always seemed slower. It was the clock wound by anxiety's hand. He knew that they could outrun anything U.S. Customs or the Coast Guard had. The Puerto Rican patrol boats were no match for them, either. Moncho pressed down on the throttle for the last push.

That was when he saw it. "Y se quedó pasmao!" He froze! Actually, Juanito and Augustin saw it first, streaking across the water toward them. It made no spray. It was a helicopter, 200 feet above the water, approaching from their right. Moncho turned. His companions' eyes told him it was true. It was too early for a recre-

ational flight. Businessmen did not fly this low or this fast. Forty knots would not be of much use if they turned and ran, that was clear. Moncho nodded. Julio turned and pulled up the container lids. He struggled with the false bottoms. Their precious cargo was about to make a visit to the deep. The macabi looked very forlorn as an alibi. Was it a crime to be a poor fisherman?

The helicopter was fast, too fast, but it was not as fast as the bullets that raked over the heads of the three men. Reflexively, Moncho eased up on the throttle, guiding the boat in a circle. His turn brought him parallel to the helicopter's course. In an instant, the Blackhawk was upon them, and the restaurateur-drug runners could see its markings clearly, lit by the chopper's running lights. They could also see the marksman poised in its doorway, the .50-caliber automatic rifle trained on the boat, their speeds now matched.

"Puñeta," Moncho muttered under his breath. They were like a dog on a leash now, being taken for a walk. Soon the dogcatchers would be here, too, the cutter or the local patrol boat, maybe both. Juanito slammed down the container lids. He shook his fist in the air. Ricardo cursed again. Of all the dumb luck. He had heard about the Blackhawks and the MH90s. And maybe this gunman was El Diablo, the sharpshooter they had been told about. But there were hundreds of go-fast boats and thousands of square miles of ocean. What were the chances?

Moncho cut the engine. His wife and children would be surprised, he mused. They thought these rare fishing trips were a remnant of his bachelorhood, a night out with his brother and cousin, a harmless if annoying pastime. Now they would find out it was something else. And he would get the questions. It was a good thing he knew so little. So little about the visitor, the freighters and their origins, the trucks and their owners. He and Juanito and Augustin were small pieces of the puzzle. The Americans wanted the big fish. They were going to be disappointed, he thought.

CHAPTER 13

Mainlining Our Kids

A remarkable shift has occurred in the drug trade over the past few decades in the Americas. The origins and the destinations have not changed. The producers are still the rich and jealous drug lords presiding over their kingdoms in the Colombian jungle. The consumers are still largely from the United States and Canada, mostly urban but increasingly small-town, often young, sometimes affluent, sometimes poor, often soon-to-be-poor, sometimes violent. But the products are different, more potent, and the smuggling routes are more varied than ever.

Call it diversification. The drug lords of South America and the amphetamine entrepreneurs of Western Europe, out of ingenuity born of necessity, have found new avenues to the American mainland that are evermore difficult to police. Some of those avenues are broad, none more so than the boulevard that runs through and around the gateway island of Puerto Rico. The trend is dramatic: in the early 1990s, the Caribbean was the way station for less than 30 percent of the cocaine bound for our shores. By 2000 this region was the source of 47 percent of the coke reaching the mainland, eclipsing Mexico's role as the busiest route northward. Puerto Rico's annual flow of cocaine and heroin is huge, some 110 to 150 metric tons.

The attractions of the island chains to our south are many for the drug cartels.

First, drugs that pass through this region touch fewer hands.

More hands means more risk of infiltration and detection, more bribes to be paid. As one analysis of the Caribbean drug trade puts it, drug gangs are powerful in some countries because "they have better access to a valuable national resource – corruption."[1] That resource has its price. Land-based movement of Colombian drugs to the United States involves "tariffs" paid to corrupt officials all along the smuggling routes. As the Drug Enforcement Administration has testified, "Criminal organizations have utilized their financial capabilities to corrupt mechanics, longshoremen, airline employees, and ticket counter agents, as well as government officials and others, whose corrupt practices broaden the scope of trafficking."[1]

The open seas of the Caribbean and the Eastern Pacific mean, in turn, that handoffs are limited. Small freighters, fishing boats, the "go-fast" craft, cruise ships, and a few airplanes can transport the contraband a long way.

The Caribbean routes take advantage of economic conditions that help to convert large numbers of young people, mostly men, into potential drug couriers and, in turn, potential drug dealers. They offer a multitude of options for transshipment points: Haiti, the Dominican Republic, Jamaica, the Virgin Islands, Cuba to a lesser degree and, most important of all, Puerto Rico. The ancient island of Puerto Rico, site of the oldest continuously used dwelling in the New World, a gateway for explorers and exploiters for centuries, offers smugglers something that no other pathway through the Caribbean affords. When they get there, their precious cargo will already have entered the United States.

This advantage is unique. To enter Puerto Rico does not solve all of the drug smugglers' challenges, but it does overcome the obstacles of customs inspection. Puerto Rico offers the Coast Guard and island border patrols a major challenge. The island is roughly rectangular, 40 miles by 90 miles. It is 50 times the size of the District of Columbia and one-third the size of Connecticut. It has one densely populated metropolitan area on its north coast, San Juan, and a sparsely populated south coast with numerous cays and coves. Overall, government agents, including Customs, the Coast Guard and Puerto Rican police, must monitor, 24 hours a day, 363 miles of Puerto Rican coastline and another 105 miles of coast in the U.S. Virgin Islands to the east.

Unwind that 363 miles of Puerto Rican vulnerability and you span the distance between the island and the coastline of South America, Colombia and Venezuela. Colombia remains the house of origin for the largest portion of the drugs that transit the Caribbean headed not only for the United States, but also for Canada, Europe, and the Caribbean countries themselves. Venezuela shares a long north-south border with Colombia and offers its own array of shipping options. The transit from South America to Puerto Rico is a matter of hours in the low-profile "go-fast boats" that now account for an estimated 50 to 85 percent of the drug traffic flowing north, toward the pastimes, addictions, and disposable incomes of continental North America. Flight time can be a matter of a hundred minutes or less.

On most occasions, the go-fast boats need not traverse this full distance: small freighters, fishing boats, and planes meet them part way, often dumping their load of contraband into open ocean. The smugglers use Global Positioning Satellite systems to dump their drugs and the go-fast boats locate them, making their pick-ups and returning to their places of origin before daylight.

Responding to this shift in smuggling tactics, the U.S. Office of National Drug Control Policy has designated Puerto Rico and the U.S. Virgin Islands one of the nation's five High-Intensity Drug Trafficking Areas (HIDTA). The shipments involved are large. Cocaine is the most popular item for the smugglers. All told, the Caribbean HIDTA sees the transit of some 110 to 150 metric tons of Colombian cocaine a year. This accounts for 30 percent of the cocaine consumed, aspirated really, on the U.S. mainland. Enterprises of this magnitude do not get by on a handful of participants and resources. The U.S. government estimates that there are some 100,000 to 125,000 people employed directly in the Caribbean drug trade, and maybe five times that many engaged in the collateral businesses that sustain the trade. If so, one of every 20 people in the region is dependent to some degree on drug running.

These are deep roots for an industry that produces plentiful cash in neighborhoods where per capita income is only a fraction of Mississippi's, the lowest on the U. S. mainland. Uprooting such an in-grown economy is an extreme challenge. But drug smuggling has roots of another kind, historical and habitual, because the

Puerto Rican economy has never been permitted to follow a normal path of development. Under the Spanish Crown, Puerto Rican trade was tightly controlled. In true colonial fashion the island and its slave population were operated like a private preserve for the benefit of Spain: gold until the last mine petered out officially in 1570; coffee, sugar and tobacco for the comfort of Iberia's leisure class. Exploration of the New World was a mercantile enterprise, and its sponsors expected, and typically experienced, profit.

Puerto Rican goods in the 17th century included sugar and leather, and these raw products were shipped to Seville under the auspices of the Campania de las Indias, Spain's version of the Dutch East India Company. Accountants in Spain set the market prices in the motherland for the sale of these goods. In return, the residents of Puerto Rico received an occasional galleon full of clothing and furniture. These goods carried a high tariff, and they were out of the reach of typical islanders, ensuring the perpetuation of their poverty. This state of affairs drove many Puerto Ricans off the island. Some went to seek their El Dorado in the continent to the south. Others coped by engaging in smuggling, not of contraband per se but of licit goods that were prized in other ports besides Seville.

What the Crown defined and punished as smuggling, ordinary Puerto Ricans conceived of as private free trade. For a century and a half, from 1626 to the mid-1700s, illegal trade constituted a significant part of the Puerto Rican economy. By 1765 a substantial portion of Puerto Rico's population could be described as *contrabandistas*. Reform of this self-defeating economic system was inevitable, but that is not to say it was swift in coming. During this period one of the more colorful figures in the history of the Caribbean, Lieutenant-General Alejandro "Bloody" O'Reilly, an Irish-born soldier-adventurer, traveled through Puerto Rico and conducted a survey for the Spanish Crown. Existing policies, he found, had stifled the island's growth.

O'Reilly earned his sobriquet for the swift trial and execution of rebel leaders in Louisiana in 1769. He earned a just reputation as a reformer as well. In December 1769 he declared it to be contrary to Spanish law to enslave and hold Indians captive. With regard to Puerto Rico, he recommended liberalization of the trade laws, lower taxes, and an enhancement of Puerto Rico's national identity.

He might be said to have been one of the Americas' first supply-siders. These long-overdue measures contributed to a doubling of the island's population between 1775 and 1800. In 1778, the Crown was compelled to recognize the right of private ownership of land. A century later Puerto Rico's population would near 1,000,000.

Caribbean smuggling in the 20th century turned to products that were, temporarily at least, illegal. But the first shipments of contraband through the region were not the illegal narcotics, but rather alcohol. The 18th amendment to the U.S. Constitution, or Prohibition, was ratified by the states in 1919 and became part of the Constitution one year later in January 1920. Compliance with the amendment lasted a few months, but the simmering opposition, especially in urban centers and port cities, to a dry nation soon spawned a widespread and inventive resistance. Illegal breweries and moonshines appeared domestically. Importation of illegal spirits also sprang up, two thirds of it coming across the Canadian border into the United States and the other third making its way here via the waterways.

The Roaring 20s roared nowhere more fiercely than on what came to be called Rum Row, a string of freighters, tugs and other maritime vessels that carried illegal cargoes of whisky and rum and perched just outside the U.S. territorial limit. From the mainland, especially cities like New York and Boston, the '20s version of the go-fast boats would zip out to the "mother ships" (they sailed under foreign flags to avoid being subject to U.S. jurisdiction and prosecution) in the middle of the night and pick up their bootlegged "hooch." As a plenteous source of rum, Puerto Rico played a role in this illegal trade that lasted until the repeal of Prohibition in 1933.

The short-lived nature of Prohibition lends portrayals of the era's conflicts an air of rebellious insouciance. Some of J. Edgar Hoover's *Untouchables* in the Brian de Palma film pine for a stiff drink even as they zealously pursue Capone, Nitti and other hoodlums. Ernest Hemingway's *To Have and Have Not*, published in 1937, depicts the uncouth and murderous Capt. Harry Morgan adapting to the political turmoil of the era as if it were mere shifts in the trade winds, hauling Chinese illegals, running liquor from Cuba to Key West during Prohibition and after, and chartering the occasional legitimate fishing trip. The atmosphere of amorality that permeates Hemingway's novel seems familiar as one reads the reports and testimony of DEA officials from the past decade of the drug wars in the Caribbean.

Occasionally the drug couriers are even escorted and protected by Puerto Rican police. The case of the Alejo Maldonado gang is well known. Maldonado and several fellow gang members were convicted of kidnapping in 1983. It was but one of the crimes these members of Puerto Rico's elite police force, the Criminal Investigations Corps, committed in a wave of drug-related terror in the 1970s. Maldonado himself was reportedly involved in at least eight murders. Echoes of that case reverberated across the island in 2001, thanks to the aptly named "Operation Lost Honor." Twenty-nine members of the 19,000-strong police force of Puerto Rico, including several from the top narcotics control branch, were arrested and charged with transporting and protecting cocaine shipments.

Smuggling habits and corruption are entrenched problems in Latin America, and, as it did in 1925, the United States government has responded with sharp increases in resources for enforcement and interdiction. Again, as in 1925, the resources involve improvements in seagoing vessels, increases in personnel, adaptation of airborne surveillance, and new communications technology and techniques. These personnel face formidable foes who have collected billions of dollars in annual profits, fleets of boats, freighters, trucks, and airplanes, sophisticated communications technology, and armor and armaments. These foes have also cultivated refined methods for gathering and laundering their profits.

The coastal rum runners of the 1920s set a precedent late in that decade by building or adapting vessels that were better suited to elude capture. As historian Donald L. Canney writes, these "contact boats" coursing beyond the U.S. territorial limit to the mother ships were constructed with "virtually bare hulls," were 30 to 40 feet in length, and were strapped to as much horsepower as they needed to rush a good load of contraband back to shore.[3] The Office of National Drug Control Policy estimates today that some 500 metric tons of cocaine flow through the entire Transit Zone in the Gulf of Mexico, the Caribbean, and the Eastern Pacific. In dollar terms, this cocaine accounts for 85 percent of the narcotics traffic in the region. Private boats and ships carry 80 percent of this tonnage, and the most popular form of transportation is the "go-fast boat." These boats, latter-day "contact boats," are low, speedy, practically invisible to radar, and hard to visually spot in daylight. The ONDCP estimates that some 90 percent of these craft successfully deliver their cargo.[4]

The response of the United States and more than two dozen other governments in the region has been to devise an array of new programs, initiatives, and structures designed to move against the drug cartels in every phase of their operations. In the Puerto-Rico-Virgin Islands HIDTA, the effort is overseen by a 20-member task force, 16 of whose members are based in Puerto Rico. Anti-drug personnel in the area now total some 1,450 men and women who work for federal, state, and local agencies.

Interagency and intergovernmental task and strike forces abound. For almost every U.S. government agency there is a corresponding Puerto Rican bureau. U.S. efforts to counter the drug trade involve the Customs Service, the Coast Guard (formerly in the Department of Transportation, now part of the Department of Homeland Security), the DEA, the Bureau of Alcohol, Tobacco and Firearms, the U.S. Navy, the Internal Revenue Service, the Immigration and Naturalization Service, the Federal Bureau of Investigation and others. In Puerto Rico there is the island's own Treasury Department, the Office of Drug Control, the National Guard, the Police Department, the Special Investigations Bureau and more.

The Customs Service and the Coast Guard are particularly proud of their own "go-fast boats," which occasionally patrol alongside attack helicopters, with sometimes-spectacular results. In August 1999 then U.S. drug czar, Gen. Barry McCaffrey, revealed that the Coast Guard had made arrests of cocaine smugglers by firing at their engines from helicopters. He made the announcement at a Transportation Department press conference as he stood beside an MH90 Enforcer chopper of the type used in the new operations. "We have made the drug smugglers afraid," McCaffrey said. "We will now make them disappear."[5] It was the first time since Prohibition that the Coast Guard had fired on smugglers from the air.

These and other operations, each involving a different matrix of agencies, have begun to make a dent in a flourishing business. Since

1990, Operation HALCON, a joint Mexico-U.S. initiative, has picked up nearly three tons of cocaine, more than nine tons of marijuana, and 27 aircraft. The pace of these and similar efforts is accelerating. In fiscal year 1997, Caribbean counter-narcotics efforts disrupted only 12 drug trafficking organizations. By calendar year 2001, the number of drug trafficking and money laundering operations disrupted had risen to 250.

DEA, Customs and the Joint Interagency Task Force-East (JIATF-East), a U.S. military contingent, combined energies in Operation Journey and targeted the Colombian networks, arresting 40 people, including the maritime mastermind Ivan De La Vega. In 2000 the Coast Guard conducted Campaign Steel Web, seizing 23,000 pounds (about 12 metric tons) of cocaine. That same year the Coast Guard cooperated with the Mexican Navy in the capture of some 30,000 pounds (or 16.5 metric tons) of cocaine. Spring 2000 also saw the DEA's Operation Conquistador. This 26-country initiative (it's not clear how popular its title was in some quarters) resulted in the arrest of 2,331 individuals and the confiscation of 55 kilos of heroin, almost 5,000 kilos of cocaine, 13 boats and 172 land vehicles.

Action has become brisk around Puerto Rico as well. In September 2000 the U.S. Customs Service's Caribbean Air and Marine Branch investigated a suspicious ship near Luquillo, on the northeast coast of Puerto Rico. It was a 22-foot *yola*, a small, fast vessel popular with the drug couriers. Customs hit pay dirt, as the *yola* turned out to be hauling 1,375 pounds of cocaine. Two men were arrested. Two other men were not so fortunate during another Customs bust in Luquillo in May 2001. Customs and the Puerto Rican Police Department were called to the scene of an apparent gun battle and found the body of a Mexican national sitting in a pick-up truck containing 16 bales of cocaine. Two suspects were detained afterward, one of whom had also sustained a gunshot wound in the incident.

All told, renewed U.S. and regional government efforts in the Caribbean have increased drug intercepts to the point where some 63 metric tons of cocaine with more than $4 billion in street value was seized in 2001, a record year for drug seizures. Keep in mind, however, that official estimates of the volume of cocaine moving through the entire area are some eight times this figure. The agility of the traffickers in redirecting their product and finding new avenues of delivery has taxed law enforcement's ability to respond. The White House Office of National Drug Control Policy has reported cocaine seizures in Puerto Rico for 2002 were less than half what was seized in 2000 (a record year) and a 25 percent decrease from 2001. A few large busts can disguise underlying trends that are actually adverse.

None of this should obscure just what it is that makes Puerto Rico so attractive for the drug and money laundering organizations. It is Puerto Rico's unique accessibility and unique legal status. When South Florida became a hot bed of drug money laundering more than a decade ago, Congress could and did respond with new banking legislation and stepped-up investigations. Puerto Rico provides an opportunity for the cartels to get drugs inside U.S. territory that is more than 1,000 miles from South Florida, but every inch of which is American soil. Once over this hurdle, the avenues into the continental United States multiply and the Customs Service and, to a certain degree, the Coast Guard, are no longer in the picture. Peculiarities in U.S. law owing to Puerto Rico's status make the money laundering options there all-too-fruitful.

From its earliest years as a Spanish colony, as described above, Puerto Rico has relied on trade. Until that trade was generalized beyond Spain, the country's growth was stifled and its ability to exchange cash crops for needed goods was limited. "Puerto Rico," or rich port, was not the original name of the island, but of the beautiful natural harbor of San Juan. With good reason. Today, given Puerto Rico's position as a gateway island between the Caribbean, the Gulf, and the Atlantic for ship traffic coming to and from the Panama Canal, Europe, the United States, and Africa, San Juan has become one of the biggest and busiest seaports in the world. It is, in fact, the largest port south of the United States, the fourth largest port in the Western Hemisphere, and the 14th largest in the world.

The cocaine and heroin that reach Puerto Rico's beaches are moved by car or truck to the Port of San Juan, Ponce, Aguadilla, or others. There they are smuggled onto freighters or onto one of the hundreds of cruise ships headed for the U.S. mainland. The drugs are often hidden in massive freight containers holding other cargo.

One recent drug bust, for example, found a large cache of drugs stowed away in a crate of auto parts. Since Puerto Rico is part of the United States, there are no further customs inspections for cargo leaving San Juan and other ports bound for the mainland U.S., just as there are no customs inspections for cargo leaving Hawaii for shipment to the rest of America.

The tonnage that passes through San Juan alone is impressive. The Puerto Rico Ports Authority has said that San Juan transshipped some 1.8 million containers of cargo in the fiscal year that ended June 30, 2001. Outside authorities believe the actual number is significantly lower, some 1.1 to 1.2 million containers. Let us say that the real figure is somewhere in-between, 1.5 million containers.[6] This is the equivalent of a fleet of 1.5 million tractor-trailers. With such a large volume of freight coming in and out of San Juan harbor, law enforcement agents just can't monitor it all. As the DEA has testified to Congress, "The sheer volume of commercial activity is the traffickers' greatest asset."

Another popular route for transshipment is the individual courier. The former Major Leaguer and future Hall of Famer Orlando Cepeda fit this profile. Couriers can board planes in San Juan or elsewhere in Puerto Rico and be anywhere in the mainland U.S. within hours. Air traffic to the island brings in some 8,500,000 travelers a year. Any one of them can be a drug "container" on return to their point of origin. Again, since Puerto Rico is U.S. territory, there is no customs inspection of passengers taking flights from the island to the mainland. Security has been tightened since September 11, 2001, of course, but these inspections are seeking weapons and are not invasive. Stowed luggage is only spot-checked. A flight from San Juan to New York is no different, therefore, from a flight between Miami and New York under U.S. law. With 75 daily commercial flights between Puerto Rico and the U.S. mainland, and other less frequently scheduled flights, the opportunity for mischief is immense.

The smugglers are ingenious at avoiding routine drug law enforcement. Couriers can hide small amounts of drugs in body cavities or specially designed clothing. They can use checked or carry-on luggage with false bottoms, stitched-in panels, or hollow tubing. Some particularly hardy — or foolhardy given the occasional breakage — couriers have been known to ingest vials or packages filled with drugs, ultimately passing them upon arrival on the mainland. Disgusting and dangerous, but effective and remunerative.

Another smuggling option is the U.S. mail system, which is now a robust mix of the government-subsidized U.S. Postal Service and various private carriers like Federal Express and UPS. For many years, the U.S. Postal Service was notoriously wide open for smugglers of all types, not only for drug runners. The Postal Service took the position that it is a quasi-government agency not subject to the authority of other government bureaus like Customs or the DEA. It purported to conduct its own inspections, but these were widely known to be haphazard and unsophisticated. Shipments done this way could be designed to reveal very little information about the sender and the recipient in the unlikely event discovery occurred. Even so, after the anthrax incidents of 2001, the mail is now under much greater surveillance by many different agencies. Drug flows through regular mail are believed to be way down. Needless to say, packages from foreign nations shipped by private carriers like FedEx would be subject to full customs inspection, but Customs has no jurisdiction over such packages originating in Puerto Rico.

The utility of Puerto Rico for the drug trade is enhanced by the social conditions in other nations of the region that feed into the business in various ways. Poverty in the Dominican Republican and Haiti helps to furnish a significant supply of young men willing to take significant risks for huge gains. The Dominican Republic is some 70 miles west of Puerto Rico. It shares the island of Hispaniola with the desperately poor and politically unstable Haiti. Law enforcement in the Dominican Republic is not particularly sharp, but the DEA says about Haiti, "There is no effective law enforcement or judicial system . . . so there are few legal impediments to drug trafficking."[7] In addition, "there is effectively no border patrol between the countries [Haiti and the Dominican Republic], allowing essentially unimpeded traffic back and forth."[8]

As a result, getting drugs to Haiti from South America offers little challenge. Once there, the drugs are easily moved into the Dominican Republic. Dominican ports offer their own opportunities for direct shipment to the United States, not to mention transfer to Puerto Rico, less than two hours away by the go-fast method. There is also nearby St. Martin, or St. Maarten to use its Dutch spelling, which is an international free port. No import or export restrictions, no tariff or import fees, apply there. Nothing has to be declared and nothing is inspected. Freighters can consequently bring drugs into St. Martin with little trouble, offering an approach to Puerto Rico from the east.

Indeed, this traffic is not limited to young renegades. A doctor from Puerto Rico was recently discovered taking his yacht to St. Martin, loading drugs on board in various nooks and crannies, and returning to Puerto Rico. A wealthy American living on St. Martin who owned his own helicopter would stow drugs on board and fly to Puerto Rico for visits. Since he was an American citizen and not apparently importing anything, he received no customs scrutiny upon arrival. Drug agents finally uncovered the scam.

Passenger cruise ships that stop in St. Martin and then move on to Puerto Rico and back to the U.S. offer still another option. While ashore in St. Martin, couriers pick up drugs and scurry back on board with them. The aforementioned means of concealment are then used to move the contraband along. A cruise ship that is just stopping off in Puerto Rico on its way to other Caribbean ports is generally not subject to any serious customs inspection. These are often U.S.-flag vessels, and American passengers on them are returning to American soil. They are neither importers nor immigrants and intrusive inspections are not common or, for commercial reasons, very welcome. These vessels are generally allowed to go on their way.

The essential point here is that Puerto Rico's unique status, which elevates its desirability while lowering its defenses, is a keystone of the Caribbean drug trade. As the DEA has also told Congress:

> More than ever, international drug trafficking organizations utilize Puerto Rico as a major point of entry for the transshipment of multi-ton quantities of cocaine being smuggled into the United States. Puerto Rico has become known as a gateway for drugs destined for cities on the East Coast of the

United States. Puerto Rico's 300-mile coastline, the vast number of isolated cays, and six million square miles of open water between the U.S. and Columbia, make the region difficult to patrol and ideal for a variety of smuggling methods.9

What began as an accident of time and nature has become embedded in a culture. Illegal drugs flow out of the Andes Mountains of Colombia, Peru, and Bolivia, South America, like a mighty river. History, geography and politics combine like a gravitational force to make this happen. The Andes, high, relatively unpopulated, covered with jungles and with mist, have proved to be an excellent region for growing the coca plant, from which cocaine and its low-cost crystal form, crack, are derived. For many years the drug lords found ways to move their product overland to the United States, to the point where the idea of a Puerto Rican drug culture was confined to urban America. A portrait of New York's Puerto Rican neighborhoods from 1972 quotes a young woman named Maria who was born on the island:

> My mother and I stayed in Puerto Rico for many years and I went to a Catholic school. It was run by nuns. I like Puerto Rico much better than New York. In Puerto Rico you've got no problem with colors. It doesn't matter what color a person is. You don't have problems with street gangs and fights like you do here, and I never saw anyone take drugs in Puerto Rico. There was no problem there about walking in the street late at night[.]10

Something, of course, has changed in the past 30 years and the drug problems that once by-passed the Caribbean islands and penetrated the ethnic islands in America have permeated their cities as well. Narcotics are not just shipped through these nations, but they are consumed there as well and they bring with them the same kinds of personal and family destruction. The transshipment agents often take their payment in cocaine rather than cash. They turn and make their own sales on the street. Puerto Rican police estimate that there is one drug distribution point for every three square miles on the island, roughly 1,200 such "points" in all. The going rate for a rock of crack cocaine in Puerto Rico is approximately $5, according to the ONDCP.[11] Jamaica, in turn, to the west of Hispaniola, has proved to be fertile ground for growing marijuana.

Moreover, a major heroin connection has also been established through Puerto Rico. The primary source for heroin coming into the U.S. has long been Southeast Asia, where the poppy plant flourishes. South American drug lords began moving into this market aggressively in the early 1990s. They started growing their own very high quality crop in remote South American fields. They were so successful in increasing the heroin supply on the street that the price was cut almost in half.

The proven effectiveness of the Puerto Rican drug smuggling route is also enticing European producers of the party drug Ecstasy. Chemically known as methamphetamines, or MDMA, Ecstasy is popular at wild youth dances in the U.S. known as raves. It is a synthetic drug, originally concocted in the underground laboratories of Europe. European Ecstasy smugglers easily travel to St. Martin by plane or cruise ship. Once they reach that free port uninspected, they take go-fast boats to Puerto Rico. They can send the drug to St. Martin or Haiti by freighter as well, and use go-fast boats to finish the trip to Puerto Rico. From there they travel the well-worn routes to the mainland U.S.

The human cost of the illegal drug trade is expressed in different ways. Close to 20,000 Americans die each year due directly to their own drug abuse, according to the Federal Centers for Disease Control. Many innocent people also die as a result of drug-related accidents, particularly with cars. The international drug cartels prey on the financial lifeblood of America's poorest communities. Americans spend close to $70 billion each year on illegal drugs, draining quantities of the financial capital that inner-city neighborhoods desperately need to have any hope of climbing up into mainstream America. In Puerto Rico, the toll from the drug trade is extreme. Michael S. Vigil, special agent in charge of the San Juan Field Division of the DEA, has told Congress of estimates "that about 80 percent of all documented homicides in Puerto Rico are drug related."[11]

Drug abuse is also associated with the spread of lethal diseases like the human immuno-deficiency virus (HIV) and hepatitis B and C. Compared to the continental United States, Puerto Ricans have a higher rate of injection-caused HIV infection.[12] Clearly, this highway of drug death and disability must be shut down. It is poorly understood how much Puerto Rico's semi-colonial status has to do with keeping this highway open and running freely. Without its unfettered access by sea and air to the vast U.S. drug market, Puerto Rico would be a minor player in the international drug wars.

The modest progress that has been made in achieving the goal of interdiction in recent years has been extremely expensive. Armed interventions have been used under both the Clinton and Bush administrations to underscore a new seriousness of purpose. The U.S. government has been sharply increasing the resources devoted to anti-drug law enforcement in Puerto Rico. From 1990 to 2000, expenditures by the U.S. Justice Department in Puerto Rico increased by 350 percent.[13] Over the same period, expenditures on the island by the U.S. Treasury Department, which ran the Customs Service until March 2003, increased by 250 percent.[14] After that date, Customs joined other, smaller border control agencies in the new Directorate of Border and Transportation Security in the Department of Homeland Security. This name change will not trim the cost.

The possibility is real that the Federal Government is now losing ground in the drug battle in Puerto Rico. For years, U.S. Navy aircraft carrier battle groups making routine cruises through the Gulf of Mexico set their sophisticated surveillance equipment to monitor small planes taking off from Colombia and heading to Puerto Rico. The Navy would notify Customs in Puerto Rico, and often they would be on site to greet the go-fast boats trying to pick up and return to shore with bales of drugs dropped from these planes.

This coordinated action produced a sharp decline in the use of this avenue of smuggling. After 9/11 and, most recently, the war in Iraq, the U.S. military has acquired new responsibilities, and the routine military presence in the Gulf of Mexico has wound down. The Vieques standoff, which we describe elsewhere in this book, will only compound this problem. Concerns about terrorism, at least that substantial part of terrorism that is not narco-terrorism, will put new stress on already-stretched anti-narcotics initiatives.

Moreover, there are fundamental challenges in maintaining a full contingent of Federal drug enforcement agents in Puerto Rico. Assignment to Puerto Rico is not widely viewed as a plum. The standard of living in Puerto Rico is substantially lower than on the mainland, with fewer amenities than most government employees are used to enjoying. The heavily Hispanic influence on the culture and extensive use of the Spanish language can leave agents from the mainland and their families feeling out of place. Spouses of the agents with professional careers of their own find the economic opportunities in Puerto Rico quite limited. It is an expensive place to live. Most locals do not pay any federal income taxes, but employees of the U.S. government do not share in this perk.

The DEA and other agencies are fighting back with special bonuses and benefits for Federal agents and their families willing to transfer to Puerto Rico. The DEA has summed up the lack of attraction to Puerto Rico rather bluntly:

> [W]e have had continuing difficulties retaining federal law enforcement personnel in the Commonwealth of Puerto Rico. Few personnel from the Continental United States are willing to accept a transfer to Puerto Rico, and those who do often want to leave soon after arrival. Such quality of life issues as inadequate public services, unreliable utilities, limited accessibility of medical care, the high cost of living, an exclusionary social structure, limited availability of appropriate schools for dependent children, and the high incidence of crime have contributed to early turnover and family separations.15

This statement is a little like saying, "Other than the explosion, my vacation on Bikini Atoll was very pleasant." The DEA has begun an effort – expensive, of course – to enhance its recruiting for the island. Special agents, diversion investigators, and intelligence analysts are offered such items as relocation expenses up to a maximum of $15,000 tied directly to remaining in Puerto Rico; a foreign language bonus program of 5 percent of base pay; a chance to choose their next tour of duty on a preferential basis; five-year, government-funded access (another item that may falter with the U.S. Navy's retreat from Vieques and Roosevelt Roads) to Department of Defense Schools on the island; Defense Department commissary privileges; a 10 percent cost-of-living adjustment; and several other unique benefits. Altogether, it is a formidable package.

So far, however, these incentives are not working. The government is still having a hard time filling out its already inadequate quota of agents and law enforcement personnel in Puerto Rico. The average tour of duty on the island has not been extended beyond the typical two years. Most important among the effects of this situation is the lack of experience and cumulative judgment among antidrug officers in Puerto Rico. New personnel are constantly matching wits with sophisticated criminals who know the island and its environs inside out. The situation is not much better for young men considering a career in the Puerto Rican police forces. As Robert Becker, a columnist for the *Puerto Rico Herald*, points out, the starting salary for most Puerto Rican police is $18,900. "The public assumes most cops . . . are corrupt," he writes, with the result that public trust in and respect for the profession are low.[16]

The drug gangs, on the other hand, are culturally ingrown and benefit from unusual cohesion. The island's heritage as a haven of smugglers has already been described. The gangs themselves are often based on long family traditions. The participants are literally blood brothers or lifelong friends. This virtually eliminates the opportunity to infiltrate such gangs, or turn one of their members against the other. Just gathering evidence on such a drug operation can be very difficult. It is also dangerous: police personnel earn blue-collar wages for whitewater work.

Victims of the drug trade abound, but they are not typically along the smuggler's route. Movement of contraband relies on quiet and stealth. It is usually far removed from the conflicts in the jungle where the drugs are produced or on the streets of America where sellers clash over territory and price. Law enforcement chases an elusive foe anxious to leave no evidence of his passing. In a murder case, the body and the crime scene offer a trove of clues. In drug transactions, everyone involved is in on the scam and sharing the profits. That only changes when a dispute leads to other, violent crimes, an outcome longtime family ties can minimize.

If this portrayal suggests something of a Wild West atmosphere in the seas to our south, keep in mind that because Puerto Rico is part of the U.S. the full panoply of constitutional protections applies to law enforcement efforts there. This means that in order to tap a phone line, for example, drug agents need a sponsoring U.S. attorney and an approving judge. First, they must produce an affidavit of 70 to 100 pages to show, among other things, that they have exhausted all other means of investigation. Then, using the affidavit, they must get approval from Justice Department headquarters in Washington to seek a warrant from a judge.

Meanwhile, the drug smugglers use temporary, disposable phones, each with a new phone number. By the time a warrant is issued, the phone it is aimed at is usually used up and thrown away. The wheels of justice can grind exceeding slow, while the roaring engines of the *yolas* and the speeding wheels of the hijacked cars race exceeding fast. In sports, the offensive player has the basic advantage of knowing where he wants to go while the defender must prepare for all the routes his opponent has to choose from. So it is in our Western Hemisphere's own South Seas. Defenders of our borders must guard an area of millions of square miles, equal to the area of the continental landmass.

Clearly, the effort is not futile, and just as clearly interdiction is but a small part (two of the 16 multi-agency anti-drug initiatives in the Caribbean HIDTA are focused on stopping shipments and the rest are investigative and intelligence-oriented) of the national drug control strategy. Just as clearly, however, seemingly small advantages on either side of the drug wars leverage enormous amounts of activity, whether that advantage is in the speed of watercraft, the corruption of a few key officials, weaponry, or a handful of unregulated banks. Status matters and, in the case of Puerto Rico, status means a drug war tilted heavily to the purveyors of addiction and their customers,

How would a change in status, or more precisely, a permanent status, affect Puerto Rico's role in the drug war in the Caribbean? If Puerto Rico were a state, then the full panoply of law enforcement resources that the mainland U.S. uses to control drugs would be available on the island. Operating with standard constitutional restraints would be more manageable because staff, information resources, and investigative techniques would be more plentiful and better integrated. The local Puerto Rican police would likely be more professional and more successfully networked into the national law enforcement matrix. More resources would be devoted to local law enforcement, and more police agents would be hired. They would be better paid, attracting a higher quality and greater longevity of personnel. They would also be better trained and consequently able to cooperate more effectively with federal drug agents.

Indeed, because the status of Puerto Rico is unresolved, current cooperation is limited and evolving. Moreover, since Puerto Rico does not have the resources to devote to building a complete first-rate police force, efficient coordination is limited in any event. The new economic prosperity that would result from statehood, which we discussed in previous chapters, would help produce the resources needed to establish a state-of-the-art local law enforcement apparatus similar to those in many mainland communities.

Moreover, if Puerto Rico became the 51st state, more Federal law enforcement resources would be devoted to it as well. The current Justice Department budget for Puerto Rico is about $82 million per year, about the price of a baseball cap per person per year. The entire Federal drug enforcement work force in Puerto Rico and the surrounding area amounts to a couple of hundred agents at most. This is no match for the drug nation and its tens of thousands of allies throughout South America.

With statehood, Puerto Rican living standards would converge more with the rest of the country and Federal agents from elsewhere would be more willing to take an extended tour of duty or relocate there. More local Puerto Ricans would be recruited for Federal service as well. A state of Puerto Rico would undoubtedly draw more attention in Washington. Having a state overrun by drug smugglers unleashing a flood of drugs into America would be seen as the intolerable invasion it really is. Indeed, as a state, Puerto Rico would draw more national media attention, and the problem would be much more widely appreciated. Puerto Rico's voting representatives in Congress would also be able to generate more attention to the problem. Their votes on spending bills and other close issues would matter, and they could use that fact to leverage more funds and more resources. The arguments they raised would not seem like special pleading, but rather like the common concerns of U.S. citizens they really are.

Alternatively, if Puerto Rico were to become an independent nation, its problems, and ours, would be much more manageable as well. Drug smugglers would no longer be on U.S. soil once they got into Puerto Rico. There would be full Customs inspection of everything coming into the States from Puerto Rico. Freighters from the busy port of San Juan would be fully examined upon arriving in the U.S.; indeed they would likely be especially targeted for drug investigation. All of this would make an economically edgy Puerto Rico and its government more vigilant about the security of vessels leaving its ports.

Flights from Puerto Rico would no longer constitute U.S. domestic air travel. They would be subject to the same inspection and scrutiny as other international air travel. The closeness of the free port of St. Martin to Puerto Rico would no longer be relevant. Such close proximity would provide no special leg up for drug smugglers to insinuate their wares into the U.S., for Puerto Rico would be a different country. Our two nations would, in keeping with our intersecting heritages, desire friendly relations. Failure to act against the drug problem would be seen in the United States, a treaty partner and source of aid, as a matter of unacceptable hostility or indifference right on our back door-step.

Neither of these options, statehood or independence, would fully solve the problem, of course. As long as selling drugs is a lucrative enterprise and as long as people are willing to trade their well being for instant gratification, the drug wars will go on. But either way, with statehood or independence, drug law enforcement in regard to Puerto Rico would be much more effective. The drug supply would be reduced and drug use and all the devastation that results from it would decline. America would no longer have an unguarded back door.

Just ask Orlando Cepeda, the Baby Bull, born in Ponce, Puerto Rico, the only Major Leaguer ever to win unanimous votes for both Rookie of the Year and MVP honors. A towering first baseman who wielded a 40-inch bat and slammed 379 home runs, Cepeda went, as he titled his biography, from "hardball to hard time." He began smoking marijuana, he wrote, to relieve pain and depression induced by knee injuries. Ultimately, his involvement in drugs led to his arrest at the San Juan airport for attempting to smuggle marijuana back to the United States.

Cepeda was arrested on "Three Kings Day" in Puerto Rico, the religious holiday known in the United States as the Epiphany. This occasioned a widely circulated joke. In Puerto Rico Three Kings Day is a feast for gift giving nearly as important as Christmas. Children go to sleep on the eve of the feast and place grass clippings under their beds. In the morning they awake and find the grass replaced by the presents their parents have put there for them. Cepeda, Puerto Ricans jested, must have been looking for lots of presents under his bed.

Today, Cepeda has turned his life around and won election to Cooperstown. He spends much of his time speaking to Puerto Rican audiences in Manhattan and the Bronx, urging young people to stay in school and stay away from drugs. He represents the San Francisco Giants as a goodwill ambassador and as a member of Athletes Against AIDS. Cepeda was a pioneer for Latino, and certainly for Puerto Rican, ballplayers entering the major leagues. His story represents the heights and depths that can befall any person. In both his falling short of his potential and his ultimate heroism, he epitomizes the balance of aspiration and danger that is Puerto Rico.

[The vignette that follows is a work of fiction. It does not depict real events or persons, living or dead. The characters and events are purely imaginary, and no resemblance to real persons or events is intended.]

VIGNETTE 2

A New Friend of Commonwealth

⇒✧⇐

Jose Fernandez Antonsanti is a Puerto Rican entrepreneur. He comes from one of the oldest and best-known families in Puerto Rico, a family that can trace its roots to the 18th century and, before that, to Spain and Corsica. His early education was from one of the best private schools in San Juan. Later, he received an engineering degree from MIT and an MBA from Harvard.

Although the family was prominent in Puerto Rico, agricultural products have not been a hot property for the making or keeping of fortunes for almost a century. The Antonsantis have survived by living off the real estate investments their ancestors made with their long-gone plantation profits. As a matter of fact, there was barely enough cash flow to keep Jose in college. But Jose was a bright and imaginative young man and, with the help of scholarships and federal assistance (he was considered a "minority," though he was anything but that on the island), he managed to keep his financial head above water and graduate with honors.

His lucky stroke was to have as his roommate at MIT one Juan Luis Cabral, a young man from a wealthy family in Cali, Colombia. Juan's family had properties and businesses all over the world and especially in their home country, in Medellin.

Juan introduced his new friend Jose to his family in Colombia and he became like another son to the Cabrals.

When Jose graduated from Harvard he took his newfound engineering and business skills and went to work for the largest building contractor in Puerto Rico. After a few years there, he tried his luck as a developer, but lacking strong financial backing made the going very tough. Although the Antonsantis still had a significant net worth, all of Jose's aunts and uncles were so dependent on the rental cash flow from the crumbling buildings they owned in San Juan that it was impossible for Jose to tap that equity for new ventures.

One day Juan invited a frustrated Jose to his family home in Cali and made him an offer he could not refuse. Jose was tendered full financial backing for major real estate developments in Puerto Rico. Jose was enthralled. This was the fulfillment of Jose's dream, the focus of all his schooling.

There was a catch. Even though on the surface Jose would appear to be the sole owner of a real estate development company, he would have no say in the disposition of the resulting cash flow. Nor would he be privy to all the financial transactions related to those projects. Yet he would have to sign-off as the chief executive officer of the corporation on all its tax returns. Jose would run the business, but Juan's family would run the money.

Jose recognized immediately that it was not his nickel that was on the line. He had everything to gain and nothing to lose. He said "yes" immediately.

The biggest challenge for any successful drug production and smuggling operation is that its proceeds are in cash and most of its expenses are also in cash. The profits that accrue to the higher-level drug producers and importers have to be converted into legitimate investments. Otherwise, this perishable paper would rot in their suitcases. Most small-time dealers find ways to dissipate their income. It's not that difficult to process into legitimate businesses hundreds of thousands or even one or two million a year in cash. When you are talking about tens and hundreds of millions of dollars a year, you now have a serious problem.

To launder money in these amounts and bring it into the mainstream of business activity in the industrialized world, a cooperative bank willing to accept suitcases full of cash is needed. This bank will be of little use if it is within a jurisdiction where banks must report and bank regulators routinely scrutinize unusually large cash transactions. Moreover, tax agencies can make matters truly difficult for businesses with cash flows out of all proportion to other size or their character.

In Puerto Rico, money launderers have a good half of what they desire. Even though the Puerto Rican banking system is part of the U.S. system and is subject to comparable regulatory oversight, there is no equivalent of the Internal Revenue Service to monitor the income of local businesses with local income. The result is that the island is a magnet for Caribbean Basin drug profits, a funnel that, properly managed by its manipulators, can disperse drug proceeds into sheltered accounts all over the world.

If you are one of big drug dealers, you can always pull up a boatload of cash to a sandy beach in the Cayman Islands, the Bahamas, or any other remote jurisdiction that specializes in bank secrecy and has not signed a U.S. cooperation agreement. You can easily dispose of this cash by depositing a few dozen suitcases of the stuff into a local bank, using a numbered account issued to a shell corporation, which you control. You can now shuffle this money all over the world via wire transfer from one shell corporation to another. Eventually, tracing the money becomes all-but-impossible.

Now suppose you want to invest part of this money in the United States. Your primary business is risky enough; you don't want to have comparably risky investments so you want the safest financial markets on the globe. The moment your money hits a corporate or individual account in the United States, you have a law enforcement periscope fastened on your stern. You ponder your options.

Someone tells you about Internal Revenue Code Section 933. Under this provision, all income generated in Puerto Rico by U.S. citizens living on the island, or by corporations domiciled in Puerto Rico, is not reportable to the Internal Revenue Services for U.S. income tax purposes.

Bingo! A license to launder.

So long as Puerto Rico remains a territory of the United States, whatever name is assigned to that territorial status, this condition will apply.

Jose now learns the lessons of his new financial partnership. If he wants to build a $100 million shopping center in San Juan, he has access to all the capital he wants. He can have a Swiss shell corporation, as an investor, guarantee a loan through his local bank. Thus, a Puerto Rican bank provides the cash for a mammoth business development backed by deposits in another part of the world. The best part is that the Internal Revenue Service will never ask where the money came from and why a Swiss has so much confidence in a novice developer in Puerto Rico. It's a financial global village, no? As long as Section 933 is in force, the IRS has no interest in the income generated on the ground in Puerto Rico.

For local people, Jose's success, sudden as it may be, isn't newsworthy. They will say, "Ah, it's young Fernandez Antonsanti. He's from a leading family and I knew his grandfather personally. How hard they worked!" So no questions asked.

Once a business is opened on U.S. soil, the Commonwealth of Puerto Rico included, millions of dollars can be poured into it, expanding property, building hotels, shopping centers and office buildings, without the Internal Revenue Service making a single inquiry. Territorial income is isolated income, and practices that would subject your business in Seattle or Peoria to intense examination trigger nothing when your business is in San Juan or Ponce.

Consider the impact of this windfall on Jose Fernandez Antonsanti's politics. Suddenly he is a champion of territorial status. He will support a local political party that advocates maintaining the status quo, and he will make contributions from his windfall to U.S. politicians (he can do so because, though he does not vote for president or a voting member of the Congress, he is still a U.S. citizen) who will work to resist Puerto Rico's transition to statehood or independence. He may even become a local civic leader for the cause, rallying his fellow Puerto Ricans for a cause that serves his pocketbook in the short term and compromises theirs forever.

All of this he will do, not with his own money, but with the cash supplied by the Cabral family of Cali. If Jose were ever to take a close look at the books of the company he heads, he would see income that he is unable to explain and expenses and loans that are a complete mystery. It is better for him if he does not look, even though the Internal Revenue Service will never ask about lapses in the conduct of a prosperous CEO.

CHAPTER 14

Welcome to the *Laundromat a la Boriqua*

―――≫◆≪―――

Stopping the drug trade in the Caribbean is a near-impossible task, regardless of the legal status of the territories and nations involved. The drug trade permeates the region, like inflamed veins running under the scalp, likewise afflicting sovereign countries (Colombia, Guatemala, Mexico, the Dominican Republic), territories (the U.S. Virgin Islands), and a commonwealth (Puerto Rico) with the scourges of smuggling and corruption.

While debates over such issues as legalization, partial decriminalization, mandatory minimums and interdiction proceed in the United States, all sides agree that the challenge to law enforcement in the region is daunting. Any beneficial impact of Puerto Rican statehood on the drug trafficking problem would be long-term in most respects, as a rising economy would reduce the temptations, for some at least, of quick riches from illicit activity. The most important impact of the statehood option would be on the cash-processing end of the drug trade: money laundering.

Puerto Rico's peculiar status and relationship to the United States and, especially, its banking and tax anomalies make it an ideal place for conversion of drug cash into "legitimate" revenue. Just how anomalous an anomaly can be was driven home to me through my experience with an entity called Girod Bank and Trust back in the late 1970s. I had just returned to Puerto Rico from a disastrous detour in the insurance business in Florida and Texas. One day I ran into a man I will call Juan. He used to work for a big insurance operator, Manuel San Juan. I knew him from my days at the Banker's Club, a social watering hole in San Juan where business, alcohol, and song mixed in a heady cocktail that lubricated many a friendship and lucrative deal. When I asked Juan what he was doing now, he said that he was recovering from alcoholism. He also said that he was involved in operating the insurance division of a local bank whose president, curiously enough, was a young man in his late twenties.

The young man's name was Alberic Girod. Alberic was an absolute genius. When I asked Juan how he could be running an insurance operation from a bank, when the Commissioner of Financial Institutions rules strictly forbade such affiliations, Juan replied that Alberic knew how to get around such issues and that he was going ahead full steam. He invited me to meet Mr. Girod, and that meeting took the form of a tour of the bank. I had no idea that I was about to step into an operation of unusual character, an institution of almost Wild-West proportions.

The bank building was located at 355 Tetuan Street in Old San Juan. It was a five-story structure built in the mid-1800s that reflected the architecture of that era. It stood defiantly facing the San Juan Harbor, with a view of all the ships going in and out in the centuries-old rituals of commerce and adventure. Right around the corner was the Tapia Theater, where, it was said, Caruso himself had performed and where Pablo Casals gave his thronged concerts every year. The building stood out among its older companions, built a couple of centuries previously and only two or three stories high. As I walked through the grand entrance, I saw a fabulous marble circular staircase that led to the mezzanine, with a classic antique elevator stuck in the middle. From the windows, one could see not only the maritime traffic in the harbor but also the profile of Hato Rey, the new business section of San Juan. The effect was one of timeworn elegance and of seriousness of purpose.

Juan told me that Alberic had just bought the building and was in the process of renovating it. Alberic Girod was seated behind a huge antique desk in his office, which partook of the magnificent view of the water. The desk looked even bigger than it actually was

Welcome to the Laundromat a la Boriqua

because Alberic was five-foot-six. His feet were dangling above the floor of the office as he sat suspended in the massive black leather captain's chair that seemed to swallow him whole, like a fearsome sea creature. Seeing me, he leapt from the whale's mouth, ran around the desk, and immediately began to ply me with his plans for the future of his bank.

The vision of the Girod Trust was to capture the "Al Portador" market in Puerto Rico. "Al Portador" is Spanish for "bearer." Puerto Rican banks would issue "bearer" certificates of deposit to people who brought in cash without filling out an Internal Revenue Service Currency Transaction Report. The CTR, as government shorthand calls it, must be filled out and forwarded for entry into a massive federal database maintained in Detroit. U.S. banking law requires cash deposits and other transactions of more than $10,000 to be registered in this way to aid in the detection of criminal activity. In the late 1970s, estimates of the total value of bearer CD's issued in Puerto Rico ranged as high as $4 billion.

Alberic frankly acknowledged that Puerto Rican banks were subject to federal rules that mandated use of these reporting forms. Nonetheless, it was his view as the bank president that nobody was complying with the rules and that such U.S. laws should not apply to Puerto Rico anyway. He told me of his plans to open a subsidiary in Panama, which could be used to wire such deposits anywhere in the world without leaving a trace. He noted that he was making money not just on the interest spread on these deposits but on the fee he charged his customers for taking in the cash. This made his bank a very profitable enterprise.

The guided tour Alberic offered next showed just how profitable. Besides the insurance department Juan managed, Girod Trust had a loftily named "commodities department." Alberic was particularly proud of this section. A walk through the department's waiting room brought one past an array of characters who looked like refugees from the bar scene in *Star Wars*. Their unsavory appearance was aided not one bit by the way they clutched little brown bags filled with something that was obviously very important to them.

Alberic introduced me into the next room where some 20 tellers were busy attending to these customers. Each customer would pour out the contents of his little brown bag, spilling gold chains and trinkets onto a table. The scene was more bazaar than bank. The teller would take each piece and rub it with a clear liquid that would reveal whether it was 14-carat or 18-carat. When all the pieces were assayed and separated by quality, the teller would weigh each pile and then pay the customer in cash based on the market price of gold.

Alberic introduced me to Alvarez Lau, a Cuban Oriental who had the glorious title of Vice President for Commodities at Girod Trust. He was just the man to oversee this busy department. When he first came to Puerto Rico as a Cuban refugee, Alvarez, it was said, shined shoes at the El San Juan Hotel in Isla Verde. He was good at the art of the deal, however, and he managed to get rich. Alvarez explained his system to me: "I fly to New York three times a week, just for the day, with a couple of suitcases of this stuff, and I sell it there because that's where you get the best price." The bottom line, according to Alberic: "We average $300,000 profit a month in this commodities operation."

The Girod Trust had no reputation for asking its brown-bag customers where they had gotten their troves. Any tourist who had a gold chain snatched from her neck in Puerto Rico during this period now has a good explanation for what likely happened to it. Alberic went on about the possibilities in Panama. "We'll be able to give our customers real privacy and confidentiality then, and we won't have the FDIC breathing down our necks," added the young chairman of the board of the fastest growing bank in Puerto Rico. "You should come to Panama for the opening. We'll have a great party. You'll have a blast." Alberic also had a business proposition for me. Some of the cash that came in could be placed in Aetna annuities. We would make a fortune, Alberic assured me.

I told Juan as we departed after our personal tour that I had other plans for resuscitating my insurance operation in Puerto Rico. I saw Alberic again some time later, at a financial planning convention. Alberic had a booth and by then he was pushing his up-and-running Panamanian bank. He told me about the various options he had developed for hiding money. I politely told him I would get back to him. Even in Puerto Rico in that era, such open discussion of suspicious activity was a dangerous business. Alberic may have had a genius for hiding money, but he had little genius for hiding the fact that he hid money. A few years later, I read about Alberic in the newspaper. He was in federal prison. Apparently, U.S. officials took a different and somewhat dimmer view of his brown-paper-bag "commodities trading" and his "al portador" activity.

Unfortunately, the problem of money laundering often seems to require such blatant activity in order to be detected and prosecuted. The situation is a result of a combination of factors. The amount of money that enters the international system in this way is large and there are great profits to be made by banks and other financial institutions willing to handle some of this "risky capital," so to speak. Different laws apply in different international settings, and the option to attract funds by establishing a loose regulatory or oversight regime has attracted a number of countries around the world, including, of course, the Cayman Islands and Puerto Rico. Third, the number of transactions that take place each day in the banking world is enormous – the Treasury received some 12.8 million Currency Transactions Reports in 1996. The number must be even larger now. Investigators have huge quantities of information to sort through.

Fourth, money-laundering techniques display a bewildering array of sophistication and variety. Criminal enterprises have gained vast experience in outwitting public officials by employing novel methods of breaking up large deposits, using legal businesses to conceal transactions, and creating shell corporations around the world to process and shuttle funds. Fifth, the number of people involved in tracing and investigating dubious transactions is quite small relative to the size of the problem. For example, FinCEN, the U.S. Treasury Department's agency for monitoring suspicious banking activity, employs only 200 people. Talented as these officials are and as useful as computer databases have become in spotting unusual patterns, investigators are drawn to cases where anomalies are more obvious and investigative trails have not grown cold.

Finally, the reach of investigative agencies is a major issue, and it is here that Puerto Rico presents its own unique challenges. While FDIC rules apply to Puerto Rican financial institutions, the Internal Revenue Service has limited authority on the island. Individuals and businesses in Puerto Rico pay federal income taxes only on earnings from federal employment or from enterprises or employment on the mainland. As long as income is attributed to a Puerto

Rican source, it need not be reported to the IRS and the IRS will not audit it. It does not matter if the business or income is generated solely by activity directed toward the United States, as most of the Caribbean drug trade could be said to be. Puerto Rico has its own banking and tax laws, of course, and these can sometimes bite a malefactor, but operating without fear of an IRS review can be a liberating experience that U.S. citizens on the mainland can scarcely imagine.

While drug money is not the only source of excess cash that figures in these transactions, it is certainly the largest portion, and the history of drug money laundering in the United States illustrates just why Puerto Rico is such a Godsend for the drug cartels.

At about the same time that Alberic Girod was developing his novel banking practices, a major shift in the drug trade was occurring. This shift can be described as an opportunistic infection. A virus finds an entry point that facilitates its attack on the body. In the case of South Florida, the entry point was the turmoil that hit the fishing industry when the government of the Bahamas closed its territorial waters to Cuban-born fishermen operating out of the Miami area. Some of these idled boats were converted to illegal uses. Throughout the 1960s and 1970s in the United States, the demand for marijuana had grown. U.S. and Mexican anti-drug authorities had devastated the Mexican growing fields by spraying paraquat. That closed door led to a resurgence of Colombian-grown marijuana, and agents of the cartels came to South Florida and offered boat captains a tempting way to "stay afloat."

Once the marijuana hook was embedded, it was not long before the less bulky, more easily concealed, and more profitable cocaine smuggling trade was attached to it. The cartel representatives did not stop at establishing South Florida as the point of ingress for illegal drugs into the United States. If the U.S. distributors owed them large sums of money, they told them to bring the cash to Miami. Virtually overnight in the late 1970s and early 1980s, the flow of laundered funds into Miami-area banks and financial institutions became, in the words of Mike McDonald, a 27-year veteran of the Internal Revenue Service's criminal division, "enormous" and "unconscionable."[1]

Just how bad was it? Bad enough that depositors began to show up in Miami bank lobbies pushing dollies loaded with cash. Bad enough that in 1978 and 1979 the entire currency surplus in the Federal Reserve System was attributable to South Florida. According to McDonald, the IRS became aware of 12 individuals alone who were depositing $250 million *annually* in non-interest bearing checking accounts. This was before many if not most banks were aware of their responsibility to file Currency Transaction Reports. Banks were breaking the law, as McDonald explains it, but this time everybody really was doing it. In 1979, five years after the U.S. Supreme Court upheld the law at issue, the Bank Secrecy Act of 1970, only 129,000 CTRs were actually filed. This disjunction sparked the IRS in the early 1980s to launch a massive counter-attack on money-laundering in Florida called "Operation Greenback."

Operation Greenback brought together the resources of the FBI, the Drug Enforcement Administration, U.S. Customs, the IRS, U.S. Attorneys and other law enforcement offices. Federal officials came to believe that the currency and suspicious activity reporting laws were even more important to their efforts to defeat the drug cartels than were standard tax reporting and compliance laws. The goal for the Colombian traffickers was to get their money into the international banking system where it could be moved around the world and ultimately made available for the purchasing side of their operations. The cartels developed incredible resiliency in moving money around the world; if one of their depositors were caught, he would be replaced by five others whose total transactions would replace what had been lost with the first man's capture.

Civil libertarians of various stripes complained (and still complain) about the Bank Secrecy Act as a violation of financial privacy and property rights. (One member of Congress referred to the Act in October 2000 as a "stealth war against wealth."[2]) The law does not require notification of the depositor or account holder about the reports that are filed under its provisions, but the existence of the reports quickly became common knowledge. In Miami, one bank simply posted a notice, in English and Spanish, advising depositors and potential depositors of the existence of the law and the bank's policy of fully complying with it. The bank's security cameras soon after picked up cash customers entering, reading the notice, and swiftly exiting.

The reaction of the cartels to these enforcement actions reaffirmed the belief of IRS agents that they were on to very effective tools. Soon after U.S. officials seized an airplane ferrying $1.2 million in cash Colombian, one family member of each pilot was reportedly killed by the cartel. Drugs were fungible and so too were couriers. Losing cash was a complete loss for these enterprises. As the IRS became more effective in South Florida, the cartels reacted in other ways. They had developed relationships with "money managers" who fit the fictional description of Jose Antonsanti at the beginning of this chapter. These individuals were intelligent, had family connections, were often multi-lingual, and had European financial contacts. In short, these were people who would be very attractive for normal and legal business relationships as well, people likely to value discretion and caution.

The cartels also have traditionally found new laundering avenues in the authoritarian governments that have long dominated the Caribbean Rim. Panama in particular was a tempting alternative because of its close proximity to Colombia. Panama's General Manuel Noriega, deposed and captured by the Bush Administration in 1990, became a money-laundering power in the late 1970s and 1980s, and therefore a target of Operation Greenback. Agents stopped a plane departing for Panama that had not filed any type of Customs form and found that it was carrying $5.4 million in currency. The pilot acknowledged ferrying about a billion dollars to Panama over a seven-year period. He was operating his own personal "FedEx service" for illegal money laundering.

It is vital to note that one aspect of Panama's appeal, in addition to the presence of a strongman who could make and enforce deals with the cartels, was the fact that its banking system accepted U.S. dollars. Drug deals in the United States were consummated in cash, but pesos, not dollars, were the preferred currency for the Colombian drug lords. The peso was the currency for purchases in Colombia for items the drug lords want, whether luxuries or necessities. It was also the currency of corruption, for deal-making with government officials who wanted the dominant currency as well. Even so, dollars could be spent in a variety of ways for certain goods, and a black market developed for private conversion of dollars to pesos.

This black market was not created by the drug trade, but it turned out to be tailor-made for it. As McDonald puts it, the drug lords want to "get paid in pesos, because they want to party in pesos."[3] The black market peso dealers include both small-time and big-time operators. They or their agents in New York accept the cash due from the drug distributor and they pay out pesos to the drug lords. The brokers then turn around and sell the dollars around the world to individuals who need dollar-denominated currency and can pay in pesos at a higher rate than the broker just parted with for the dollars he is laundering. These transactions happen outside the normal exchange system and there are discounts and diversions along the chain, but the system brings more people into the money-washing enterprise and helps to distribute the risk. It can also add a layer between the drug lord in Colombia and the distributor in the United States.

The IRS notes that nearly every American business that carries on trade in Latin America is potentially facilitating the black market in pesos, which may account for as much as $5 billion in laundered funds each year. In a normal south-north business transaction, a Latin American businessman would convert his pesos to dollars through his bank and order the materials or products he wants from the U.S. supplier. If that businessman wishes to pay less for his dollars to conduct this purchase, to avoid import duty taxes in his own country, or just to avoid disclosing information about his net worth, he can go to the broker instead and convert his pesos to dollars. That the dollars originated in the drug trade may be outside his knowledge, as it may also be outside the knowledge of the U.S. company processing an order this way. In recent years, however, the Treasury Department and the IRS are taking new steps to deter U.S. companies from taking part in this black market. They have pursued a legal theory of "willful blindness" under which a company that ignored all the hallmarks of an illegal transaction would be adjudged to have participated knowingly in illegal activity. Stupidity about the law should be no excuse.

Operation Greenback achieved some notable successes, as outlined above, but in Puerto Rico it yielded as its biggest prize Alberic Girod and his fencing operation.

Girod, despite his flourishes, was more perch than big fish. His commodities department was just a conduit for small-time street thieves, a lucrative sideline for one bank owner but not a linchpin of the drug trade. Despite its good intentions and novel techniques, Operation Greenback left the internationally drug money laundering operation that runs through Puerto Rico virtually unscathed.

When we interviewed FBI officials in Puerto Rico, they told us that the island is more than a center for money laundering for the South American drug cartels. Organized crime all up and down the east coast of the United States from New York to Miami sends money to Puerto Rico to be scrubbed clean. The dons of the drug cartels and other organized crime kingpins have a much bigger problem than the street pickpockets served by Alberic Girod. They reap billions of dollars in cash each year, far more than they can spend, try as they might, even on black market weaponry. Options are few. They can't just show up at their local bank to open a savings account with a billion or two in cash. In that case, they might just as well save everyone the time and phone ahead to the FBI to meet them at the bank.

The big-time crooks need to make their massive cash deposits look like legitimate funds when they enter the banking system. How do they do it? The crime syndicates use legitimate small businesses all over Puerto Rico that operate on a cash basis, primarily those serving lower-income communities. These businesses include liquor stores, gas stations, auto repair shops, bakeries, jewelry stores, grocery stores, fish processors, and bars and restaurants. These operations deposit part of the illegal drug money in their business accounts, claiming that it comes from their routine operations.

The business may be owned directly by a front for the drug syndicate. Or the syndicate may pay off the small business owner to cooperate. The owner can transfer the legitimized drug money back to the crime syndicate by setting up a sham purchase of more goods to sell. It can later claim to have sold these phantom goods and then deposit even more drug money in the bank, asserting that it is the proceeds from those sales.

Another popular mechanism for money laundering in Puerto Rico is the *cambio de exchange*. Local guest workers from the Dominican Republic use these storefronts to cash their paychecks and send money back to their families. More and more of these bureaus have cropped up in recent years in the United States for Mexican immigrants who are sending funds back home. Agents for the drug dealers show up at these *cambios* in Puerto Rico and send money to the bank accounts of collaborators in the Dominican Republic, making them appear to be repatriated wages.

Then there are the officially designated "offshore banks" in Puerto Rico. A recent published estimate put the number of such banks at 40, and Puerto Rican officials are talking about expanding this activity. An offshore banking law was adopted in Puerto Rico in 1980 to encourage development of international banking on the island. The goal was to take advantage, yet again, of Puerto Rico's low-cost environment and geographical proximity to the major markets of North and South America. Offshore banks are not insured by the FDIC and are outside federal banking regulation. They are subject to the oversight by local officials, but these officials, public avowals to the contrary, are notorious for less than aggressive pursuit of money laundering leads.

The offshore banks now hold some $52 billion in funds. No one has ever proved that they are involved in money laundering, but given the history of regulated institutions in falling for these practices, it is not difficult to imagine that the offshore banks have succumbed to them as well. The cartels are increasingly sophisticated in their financial dealings. They have business fronts throughout the Caribbean that can deposit drug proceeds in these institutions while identifying them as legitimate profits. From there it is a relatively simple task to get their money into the U.S. banking system with the minimum possible oversight. Various federal anti-laundering task forces chase these laundered funds, with particular focus in the New York area, but the amounts are staggering. The official website of FinCEN demurely declines to say how much money flows into the world's banks from the drug trade. "Many believe that it is impossible to pinpoint the amount," FinCEN said in the summer of 2003.[4] One widely quoted estimate in 1999 put the figure at $57 billion per year in laundered sums from criminal activity.[5]

The black market peso exchange (BMPE to the federal agents involved in rooting out the practice) operates in Puerto Rico as well, though sometimes it is the reverse of the usual pattern whereby drug-originated dollars make their way back into the U.S.

economy. In the Puerto Rican variants, fronts for the drug syndicate buy goods in Columbia and other Latin American countries with pesos and other non-American currencies they have accumulated. They then export these goods to the United States through the massive San Juan seaport, selling them to legitimate American importers for dollars, which are then perhaps deposited in one of the offshore banks. These banks can wire these funds around the world, and even into regulated U.S. banking institutions, which are known as "correspondent banks" when used in this manner. These correspondent banks are located in major financial centers like New York and London.

After all these transaction, the actual source of the funds that bought the original commodities exported via San Juan is extremely difficult to trace. The drug money has entered the U.S. banking system disguised as the legitimate earnings of international trade. Once in regulated banks, it is handled consistent with the law, but its way stations in the offshore and unregulated system allow its source to be obscured and elude the grasp of law enforcement. There are many ways to accomplish this goal of "distancing" the source from the funds, and regulators have developed their own language for some of the options. Breaking up a deposit or other regulated transaction so that normal rules do not apply to it is known as "smurfing."

As a result of the prevalence of these mechanisms, Puerto Rico has been identified by the FBI as one of the five High Intensity Financial Crime Areas (HIFCA) in the nation. This distinction, if it can be called that, goes hand in hand with the area's designation as a HIDTA. As one agent told us, this simply means that Puerto Rico is one of the money laundering capitals of the world. Current estimates are that tens of billions of dollars in drug and organized crime profits are laundered through Puerto Rico each year. Federal officials charged with addressing this challenge devote much of their energy to increasing intelligence and data sharing among international banking institutions, but the process can be as difficult as chasing international criminals who use the Internet to hide behind international borders and create jurisdictional hurdles. Cooperation is sometimes lacking.

Operation Greenback was followed by other initiatives and

investigations designed to carve out a deeper chunk of the illicit money caches. One of the most significant of the latter involved a banking affair with national security implications, the notorious case of the Bank of Credit and Commerce International (BCCI). In the memory of official Washington, the BCCI Affair will forever be linked with a series of efforts by Middle Eastern sheiks and shady arms dealers to gain control of American banks in contravention of U.S. law. The scandal did severe damage to the reputation of well-known Washington figures, including Clark Clifford, Robert Altman and Bert Lance, and prompted the Senate Foreign Affairs Committee to issue a detailed report and recommendations for reform of U.S. international financial data collection and information-sharing practices among key agencies of our government.

The scope of BCCI's fraud and other criminal activity was immense, and it relied, in part, on the offshore banking opportunities provided to it in the Grand Caymans and Panama. This activity, according to the Foreign Affairs Committee, included:

> fraud by BCCI and BCCI customers involving billions of dollars; money laundering in Europe, Africa, Asia, and the America; BCCI's bribery of officials in most of those locations; its support of terrorism, arms trafficking, and the sale of nuclear technologies; its management of prostitution; its commission and facilitation of income tax evasion, smuggling, and illegal immigration; its illicit purchases of banks and real estate; and a panoply of financial crimes limited only by the imagination of its officers and customers.[6]

Former Senate investigator Jack Blum complained that the scope of BCCI's malefaction was so great that no media enterprise could cover it. "The problem that we are all having," he said, "in dealing with this bank is that . . . it had 3,000 criminal customers and every one of those 3,000 criminal customers is a page 1 story."[7] The page 1 drug story came to a head in October 1988 when BCCI officials were indicted in Tampa, Florida, for engaging in laundering of drug money. BCCI handled these dollars through its affiliates in Panama, Luxembourg, and Switzerland. Noriega, naturally, was one of the primary customers for these transactions. According to the Senate committee, BCCI "managed some $23 million of criminal proceeds out of its London branches"8 for Noriega and also laundered drug proceeds from U.S. sales for Pablo Escobar of the Medellin cartel, Rodriguez Gacha of the Medellin cartel, and members of the Ochoa family.

The Tampa case was one of the first bricks pulled from the wall that eventually led to the collapse and forced closure of BCCI in 1991. The full extent of the bank's crimes may never be known as the Bank of England permitted voluminous records of the bank's transactions to be repatriated to Abu Dhabi, where foreign investigators have been denied access to them. Other records were shredded and lost forever. Had BCCI officials been vigilant, the international scope and chosen locales of the bank would have rendered it vulnerable to drug traffickers' laundering in any case. The culture of secrecy at the bank, its determination to accumulate deposits and other assets to hide its losses, and the character of its leadership made it a flagship financial institution for the traffickers and their political cronies. A BCCI official who cooperated with the U.S. investigation testified that the bank's welcoming of drug money became obvious to him when it decided to purchase a Colombian bank in 1983.

BCCI also provided an early object lesson in the collocation of criminalities. BCCI was not fastidious about serving the drug cartels while steering clear of other evils, such as illegal immigration, smuggling, arms dealing, and terrorism. It became instead a one-stop shop. It was able and apparently willing to deal with anyone who could help the company bolster its cash inflows. In the 1990s, U.S. anti-money laundering activities were stepped up (FinCEN was established by the Treasury Department in 1990). The largest was Operation Casablanca, which targeted money laundering for Colombian and Mexican drug cartels via Mexican and Venezuelan banks. The operation resulted in nearly 200 arrests and the seizure of some $100 million held in laundered funds and six tons of narcotics.9 An additional $9.5 million in drug proceeds was seized in connection with the Venezuelan laundering activities.10

Remember, however, that these seizures and arrests, important as they are, represent a tiny fraction of the dollars in circulation as a result of narcotics trafficking. Then-Treasury Secretary Robert Rubin noted in late 1995 that worldwide money laundering was estimated to be a $300-$600 billion annual enterprise, with some $100 billion of that sum attributed to drug trafficking proceeds in the United States. Government officials were taking a ladle to a raging stream in many cases, even if one accepts the lower figures for the laundering take ($57 billion annually) cited above.

Consider for a moment why Puerto Rico provides such an attractive option for a sizable share of this illegal activity. Several factors related, once again, to Puerto Rico's status and location have converged to make this happen. First, because Puerto Rico is not a state and the federal income tax does not apply there, the IRS has no real presence or authority on the island. Customs officials are on the front lines against money laundering, but the IRS plays a crucial role because it has the authority to investigate and monitor transactions to determine whether income is being properly reported. When South Florida became a free-flowing cash washing zone in the late 1970s, IRS agents swarmed all over the area and were able to stem the tide through Operation Greenback. The money laundering went elsewhere, and naturally it tended to go to places the IRS had difficult in reaching.

As long as a taxpayer on the island claims that all his income is from Puerto Rican sources, the IRS has no jurisdiction to investigate him. That is why the cartels focus so intently on small neighborhood businesses, where income is expected to be 100% from Puerto Rican locals and the possibility of the IRS becoming involved is very remote. These businesses are economically vulnerable as well, because even a modest role in the drug trade can provide them with cash equivalents of months of operation of their legitimate businesses.

On top of this, Puerto Rico has no local sales tax. With a sales tax of, say, 5 percent of the purchase price, the amount of sales tax paid to the government implies that a certain amount of legitimate sales were made. If a business deposits much larger amounts into its accounts on a regular basis than could be expected from the nature of its products or services in a given area, mixing illegal drug money with its sales proceeds, then the sales tax enforcers monitoring transactions would be tipped off that illegal activity is taking place. Some restaurants are more popular than others, of course, but a restaurant that was 20 times busier than the similarly sized eatery a few blocks away would raise an eyebrow or two. Indeed, even if the drug networks using local businesses to launder the funds were willing to pay the tax on the drug money deposited as legitimate sales income by the business, the large tax take would translate into an unbelievable sales volume for the small businesses, alerting investigators that something nefarious is going on.

Without the sales tax, there is no routine mechanism to monitor the daily transactions of the thousands and thousands of small businesses across Puerto Rico. They don't report their transactions, and there is no body of enforcers to investigate them. If they did, it would take a while for benchmarks to be developed that would give investigators cause to look into a particular business's books more deeply. This leaves the opportunity for a loose network of liquor stores, gas stations, bakeries, pizza parlors, and so on to create one of the most effective money laundering systems in the world. The small number of successful enforcement actions against Puerto Rican money laundering underscores this point.

Columbians and other South Americans linked up with the drug syndicates easily fit into the Latin population and culture of Puerto Rico. They can operate without being conspicuous. When Puerto Rico added the offshore banks in 1980, the perfect combination of factors had come together to create, as the FBI says, one of the money laundering capitals of the world. If Puerto Rico were a state, however, financial regulators and law enforcement would gain new leverage on the money laundering networks on the island. All federal laws, including federal tax laws, would apply there. The IRS would have full authority to monitor and investigate transactions, along with the FBI. Investigative resources could be committed to a State of Puerto Rico commensurate with the size of the problem there.

Perhaps Puerto Rico would still not have a state sales tax if it were admitted into the Union (as of January 2003, only five of the current 50 states did not have a sales tax of some kind on consumer goods, excluding, in most states, food and prescription drugs), but it would certainly have a fully professional police force more integrated into national law enforcement efforts. Officers would be paid wages more closely reflecting the value and the danger of their work, which would attract more top-notch, competent personnel. The Puerto Rican police force would consequently reach their full potential as a powerful ally in detecting and shutting down money laundering. In addition, the offshore banks would be fully subject to federal regulations, including those aimed at detecting money laundering. Put another way, they would cease to be offshore banks. The FBI would also target illicit activity at the "cambios de exchange."

Alternatively, if Puerto Rico became an independent country, ease of travel from the U.S. mainland with loads of dollars intended for its banking system would be at least somewhat more difficult. In the heyday of Caribbean money laundering (that day is scarcely over even if some of the racier techniques used by U.S. operators are better understood), pilots would conduct same-day excursions to tax haven islands like Anguilla, bringing along a passenger list composed of drug traffickers with their bags of cash. As one such launderer turned informant told the IRS, these flights had the atmosphere of a short and pleasant vacation. The traffickers would make their deposits in the local banks on the island, using shell corporations set up by handsomely paid local lawyers. When their bank business was done, the traffickers would repair to a favorite restaurant and enjoy a succulent meal before their flight home.

The informant, a Miami lawyer named Kenneth Rijock, noted for authorities how frivolous this illegal activity had become. The traffickers were so confident and comfortable in their impunity that they would endorse their deposit slips with prefabricated stamps from toy stores bearing the images of Minnie Mouse and Goofy.[11] For this serious exercise in banking, they would receive in return their certificates of deposit. Within hours, however, Rijock would have arranged for the transfer of these laundered dollars to correspondent banks in New York, London, Asia and other parts of Latin America. Rijock spent two years in jail after his role in moving funds this way was uncovered. These traveling parties often made use of rented jets and remote airfields in the host countries.

As an independent country that would be seeking to maintain as friendly as possible a relationship with the United States, Puerto Rico might well make new efforts to avoid welcoming such visitors from the north. The island would still be a tempting target for the traffickers, and the movement of funds in and out of Puerto Rican banks would still present regulatory and enforcement hurdles, particularly with regard to what independence would mean to the future of suspicious activity and currency transaction reporting on the island. In any event, with diminished responsibility for Puerto Rico's citizens and institutions, the U.S. Government might, ironically, exert even more pressure on the government there to mind its own house. The longtime tradition of U.S. attention to Puerto Rico for national security and strategic reasons, rather than those rooted in social responsibilities, might induce a high level of cooperation in San Juan.

Obtaining stronger cooperation among international banking institutions had become a high national security priority more than two decades ago when, as in the case of BCCI, law enforcement officials realized that money laundering was more than a Mafioso enterprise. Banks that allowed their facilities to be used to process cocaine dollars back into the global economy were likely to be the same ones processing funds from the sale of illegal weapons and nuclear materials as well as transactions between terror cells and their handlers. New efforts to detect and curb these practices attracted the attention of entities from the U.S. Congress, to the G-7 financial powers, to the United Nations, to the European Commission. All of this activity was sharpened diamond-hard by the acts of terrorism on September 11, 2001 that struck at the very heart of the American financial system in the World Trade Center towers.

Today the U.S. Customs Service is part of a new Department of Homeland Security, underscoring this shift in and ratcheting up of U.S. interest in money movement around the globe. The United States is deeply antagonistic to the drug lords and their minions; it is determined to capture and kill the agents of global terror. That is no small difference. In June 2003 Robert C. Bonner, Commissioner of the U.S. Customs Service, briefed the elite Egmont Group, an association of financial crimes intelligence units from around the globe, on the new Operation Greenquest. This effort is aimed at ferreting out terrorist networks that funnel money to perpetrators in countries as far-flung as Kenya, Bali, Iraq, and Northern Ireland. This goal has been promoted by new legislation that elevates the penalties for violations of what heretofore had been perceived more as banking rules than criminal statutes.

The new currency smuggling law was incorporated in the USA Patriot Act when it was adopted in 2001 and signed into law by President Bush just seven weeks after airliners struck the WTC and the Pentagon. While the Patriot Act has received intense public attention and scrutiny because of its provisions related to communications intercepts and other civil liberties issues, more than a third of the bill's text deals with the threat of money laundering activities in furthering terrorists and those who support them. The law establishes bulk currency smuggling into or out of the United States as a federal felony, when it is knowingly done with the purpose of evading reporting laws. The law also sharply increased the penalties for money laundering, allowing confiscation not only of the laundered funds but imposing minimum penalties and new maximums. Previously, the maximum civil penalty for laundering was $10,000, a tax a large-volume launderer would find little difficulty in paying. The new maximum is $1,000,000 per violation.

There may be a lot of things wrong with the New Patriot Act in terms of robbing Americans of their basic rights previously guaranteed under the constitution. The Patriot Act goes further, however, and attempts to deal with the underlying problem of international cooperation in banking. As long as offshore banks and tax haven economies exist, drug traffickers and terrorists will find ways to access them and use them for nefarious purposes. Countries, or individuals, anxious to attract capital without curiosity about its origin will be all-too-ready to open new banks that service this sector. The Patriot Act attempts to get at this challenge in a number of ways. It outlaws the use of correspondent accounts on the mainland when the overseas bank is merely a shell, little more than a postal address with wire transfer capabilities. It amends the Bank Holding Company Act of 1956 to make a bank's failure to address money laundering effectively a consideration in whether it will be allowed to take part in mergers and acquisitions. It extends the reach of U.S. law to transactions that occur in foreign banks if any portion of the funds used in the transaction or derived from the transaction is held in the United States.

The Patriot Act requires the Secretary of the Treasury to take other actions to "encourage" foreign governments, for example, to require that the name of the originator of wire transfers in a foreign country accompany the transfer at every point from its origination to the point of disbursement. How useful this provision proves to be is highly dependent on the cooperation of those foreign governments, but it is instructive that no such international requirement exists and the Secretary of the Treasury only has authority to encourage other countries to adopt such practices and enforce them. The ability to move money around the globe through these vehicles, without identification of the sender, is a crucial asset to money launderers. As already noted, the volume of these transactions, creating a haystack over the needles, is also crucial. For that reason, the Patriot Act directs the Treasury Secretary to report on ways to reduce the glut of unnecessary reports that can bedevil investigators looking for illegal activity.

Which brings us back to the anomaly that is Puerto Rico. Back in 2001, just one day before Congress passed the Patriot Act and two days before President Bush promptly signed it into law, a senior Puerto Rican banking official announced that the government there and the Puerto Rican Office of the Commission for Financial Institutions (OCIF) were combining to turn the island into what a reporter termed a "reputable low cost international financial center." Translated, this means more offshore banks. The Puerto Rican official, deputy commissioner Luis Oscar Berrios, told Tax-News.com that he was seeking to persuade international and Latin American financiers to increase the number of offshore banks on the island by "as many as possible in the shortest time possible."[12] He counted 40 such banks and noted that there were already six more applications, including one Spanish and one Swiss, in the pipeline.

Certainly, the Puerto Rican government does not envision promoting money laundering by drug traffickers or terrorists, but the possibility of terrorists moving operating funds via offshore banks in U.S. territory to individuals operating on an island where everyone is a U.S. citizen, is, to say the least, not remote. Puerto Rico has an additional item on its sales prospectus, as already discussed. Senor Berrios said it well when he told Tax-News.Com that Puerto Rico was appealing because "In other financial centers, you usually end up paying some kind of tax, but here you don't have to pay anything – absolutely nothing." For drug traffickers, the minimal tax imposed by occasional detection of a courier and confiscation of funds is likely more than offset by the lack of oversight and taxation directed at his funds that evade identification.

Puerto Rican officials are not blind to the changed environment in the world of international finance post September 11, 2001. Even so, the intensity of law enforcement is not a given anywhere. The BCCI debacle once more alerted governments everywhere to the manifold holes in the Swiss cheese of international financial processes, but that alert was not sufficient to permit U.S. federal officials to identify the Al-Qaeda network poised to strike on our shores in 2001. Terrorist incidents in the United States have been deterred as of this writing, but more incidents overseas remind us that there is no lull in these crimes when they are totaled on a global scale. Puerto Rico's best intention to provide a "clean banking alternative" to blemished tax havens may be overcome by the reality of the evil genius of the perpetrators of terror.

In July 2002, an elated U.S. Attorney for the District of Puerto Rico, H.S. Garcia, announced the dismantling of a drug dealing and money laundering plot involving some 2,500 pounds of marijuana. Garcia and a team of federal and local officers from the U.S. Customs Service, the IRS, the office of the Puerto Rican Secretary of Justice, and the Puerto Rican Police celebrated the success of Operation High Wire. Their haul was 19 indictments and 15 arrests of individuals involved in all the classic phases of the illegal drug distribution and cash laundering business. The official release from the Customs Service dryly noted that the defendants had borne and brandished firearms to protect themselves from "rival drug trafficking organizations and rival members of the same organization."[13]

Ironically, it was one of Puerto Rico's regulated banks, not an offshore entity, that earned headlines recently for its involvement in some very transparent money laundering activity. The incident involved the Banco Popular, august, respected, more than a century old and the largest financial institution on the island. Even more ironically, the kinds of activity that led to the scandal and public humiliation of Banco Popular was not subtle and difficult to detect, but rank and open in the style of the cash bazaars of South Florida from the late 1970s. Banco Popular is more or less the Chase Manhattan of Puerto Rico, holding some $33 billion dollars in assets at the time of the $21.6 million fine levied against it by federal and local bank regulators in January 2003.

This fine represented the near-equivalent of the $20 million in drug money that made its way into Banco Popular's coffers in the second half of the 1990s. The money was carted into Banco Popular branches in paper sacks and gym bags. Moreover, the cash was in small denominations, the kind of deposit that should attract the attention of any banking official with a few minutes' experience in the business. Authorities reported that procedures had become so lax at Banco Popular that on one day work at the Old San Juan Branch all but halted when tellers were herded together to count some $1 million in small bills. Banco Popular avoided criminal prosecution in the case by agreeing to pay the fine, and it was probably fortunate to get off so easily, inasmuch as bank officials had failed to file a Suspicious Activity Report or had submitted misleading Currency Transaction Reports.

A writer for *The Orlando Sentinel*, Ivan Roman, observed correctly that the scandal showed "just how deep and brazen the island's drug industry ha[d] grown."[14] One of the launderers convicted as a result of the investigation was Roberto Ferrario Pozzi, who operated a shop in Old San Juan called Gilligan's. The bank freely acknowledged that its employees failed to file the required reports, or filed incomplete reports, knowing that the deposits they were getting were anything but ordinary. Bank employees often walked by Gilligan's, a short distance from the bank branch, and commented on how so much cash seemed out of keeping with a shop that attracted very little business. Pozzi originally defended his deposits on the grounds that they were proceeds from other small businesses and the result of wire transfers. Just how wire transfers ended up in bags of small bills he had some difficulty in explaining.

In many ways, the story of Banco Popular is a cautionary tale indeed. The president of the bank, Richard Carrion, is well-known both on the island and in the United States, where he was a Governor of the Federal Reserve Bank in New York. From the standpoint of the drug traffickers, Banco Popular would seem to have been a most unlikely target for adventurous banking. Perhaps the traffickers thought the bank's size would obscure a million-dollar transaction here and there, and modest effort was made to break up some of the deposits so as to evade the $10,000 CTR threshold. In the final analysis, Banco Popular paid a fine that was little different in size from the illegal deposits it received and none of its personnel faced criminal sanctions. Overall, the message to drug traffickers might be that even in egregious circumstances of laundering it will take bank regulators a while to catch up with you. To the rest of us the message is equally clear: if this can happen at Banco Popular, what is going on in the offshore banks and tax havens probably boggles the mind.

The challenge is a crisis of world politics and criminality. It involves much more than status issues, but those issues cannot be avoided. In Puerto Rico, the United States has an Achilles Heel whose status is an invitation to some of the worst malefactors in either hemisphere. Could the island become a transit point for either terrorists or their financial maneuvers? Historically, Puerto Ricans have been proud of their unique ties to the United States, and nothing in the character of the people makes them any more prone to involvement in violent activity than any other sector of American society. The violent actions that characterized the island's pro-independence Party were short-lived and never enjoyed broad popular sympathy, even with a person of the charisma of Albizu at the party's head. The shots that rang out in the U.S. House of Representatives in 1954 were fired by U.S.-based sympathizers with Puerto Rico's plight, before the era of modernization and growth took hold in the island.

It would be grossly wrong to characterize Puerto Rico as a hotbed of radicalism or a place likely to spawn or nurture individuals or groups hostile to American values. Even so, the island's peculiar history makes it a place that terrorists could quickly discover and exploit. It is little-known in the North that Puerto Rico is home to a sizable, longstanding Arab enclave. That community has always been quiet, moderate, and law-abiding. But terrorists from the Middle East could easily settle there and provide havens for others to follow. Unregulated banks could be used to finance their presence and help them create personal histories that, with patience, could become platforms for future acts of violence. From the island, with fake IDs, they could fly anywhere in America to carry out a terrorist attack.

The same challenge exists for the far broader problem of illegal immigration. Puerto Rico is economically weak relative to the United States, economically strong relative to many of its neighbors, including the Dominican Republic and Haiti. In many of the years where Puerto Ricans migrated to the mainland, the island had net increases in immigration due to arrivals from those two locations as well as from Cuba. The boat ride across the Mona Passage to Puerto Rico is short and impoverished people are willing to risk its perils in hope of a better life. As the *Miami Herald* put it in an 1998 editorial, "Most of the Cuban [illegal immigrants] later try to join the huge flow of Dominicans smuggled by boat each year to Puerto Rico to the east. From San Juan, it's a no-passport flight to Florida, New York, or New Jersey."[15] Our immigration laws have been lax everywhere; in the midst of great controversy over that subject, Puerto Rico is barely an afterthought. That must change.

Section IV

Identity

CHAPTER 15

Mejorando la Raza
(Improving the Race)

Who is a Puerto Rican? If you asked a Puerto Rican the timeless question, "Quo vadis?" – where are you going – what would he or she say?

The American people have always seemed to have a sense of themselves, however carefully they advance and then retreat in some aspect of that self-awareness. They come to history with a penchant for terms like Manifest Destiny, for the settling of the West; the New Frontier, for JFK's forward-looking administration; the Caribbean Basin Initiative, for a project to bring economic prosperity to that region. In these terms are found most of the answer to the question of American self-identity. When Lincoln called the United States the "last, best hope of earth," commentators detected his melancholic tone but did not dispute his characterization.

Many Americans may have little sense of who a Puerto Rican is. The generation of Bernstein's West Side Story had a portrait with very little to recommend it. The Puerto Ricans were the Sharks, street-toughs with a hatred for Italians and a willingness to display that hatred with knives and fists. Even the young Puerto Rican women had little good to say, or sing, about their homeland:

> Rosalia: Puerto Rico... You lovely island ...
> Island of tropical breezes
> Always the pineapples growing,

> Always the coffee blossoms blowing...
>
> Anita (mockingly): Puerto Rico ... You ugly island...
> Island of tropic diseases
> Always the hurricanes blowing,
> Always the population growing...
> And the money owing,
> And the babies crying,
> And the bullets flying.

A walk in Puerto Rican neighborhoods in that era or this, whether in New York or Chicago, might only reinforce this characterization.

Fame, instantaneous but evanescent, does little to answer the question, "Who is a Puerto Rican?" Is a Puerto Rican Roberto Clemente, the beloved Pittsburgh Pirate Hall of Famer, the right fielder with a gold bat and a golden arm, who died young in a plane crash while transporting relief supplies? Is a Puerto Rican Jennifer Lopez, singer and actress bringing down-to-earth charm to a film role as a maid-turned-mistress of a luxurious Manhattan high-rise? Is a Puerto Rican Denise Quinones, the fourth Puerto Rican woman to win the Miss Universe contest, a remarkable feat for an island no more populous than Tennessee?

Is a Puerto Rican a comic like Sammy Davis, Jr., a boxing champion like Hector "Macho" Camacho, a Latin heart-throb like Ricky Martin, an award-winning actor like Jose Ferrer or Benicio del Toro, a ubiquitous news reporter like the New-York born Geraldo Rivera? Is a Puerto Rican Sosthenes Behn, or his brother Hernand, the founders of a telephone and telegraph company in Puerto Rico in 1920 that blossomed into the International Telephone and Telegraph Company?

Chances are if you spend any time at all in front of cable television or reading People magazine, you recognize most of these names. Chances also are that you will have been, until now, unaware of most of these persons' Puerto Rico nativity or connections. That is in part the answer to who, or perhaps better, "what" is a Puerto Rican. Americans have a better idea of the generality of being Puerto Rican than of the specifics of who is Puerto Rican. In truth, both ideas are far from the reality.

About five years ago I had an incident that illustrated perfectly for me how mistaken perceptions can be. I had a meeting with Rep. Joe Kennedy, Democrat from Massachusetts, who, I might add, has been a good friend of Puerto Rican causes, especially as they relate to human rights issues. With me at the time was a member of the Puerto Rican Senate, Charlie Rodriguez, who later became the senate president.

We were discussing the merits of H. R. 856, "the Young bill," so named for Alaska's only member of the U.S. House of Representatives, Republican Don Young. This legislation was pending for a vote in the House. It would have allowed the voters of Puerto Rico, for the first time in the hundred years since the Spanish-American War, to express themselves on their political future in a referendum sponsored by the U.S. Congress.

At that moment, Charlie and I were intensely pitching why the bill was a good piece of legislation, when I noticed that Rep. Kennedy wasn't really listening to me but was instead looking me over very carefully. I paused for a moment to get some feedback, when Rep. Kennedy leaned forward and asked me point-blank, "Are you Puerto Rican?"

I answered by saying that after living in Puerto Rico for close to 30 years, I was as close to being a Puerto Rican as a Russian could possibly get. I guess Rep. Kennedy still didn't quite understand what I said because he came back to me very quickly, saying, "But you don't look Puerto Rican!"

I was shocked by his response, but after thinking about it, I realized that this was the problem with Puerto Rico's racial and cultural identity. Only a stereotype was accepted – not in 1860s or 1920s America but right now in 1990s and 2000s America – as "The Real Puerto Rican."

If you are a typical mainland American, you may still not fully appreciate the humor of this incident. Let me illustrate it another way.

Do you remember when the Rev. Jesse Jackson went to Belgrade to ask President Slobodan Milosevic of Yugoslavia to free his American prisoners? Well, what if Mr. Milosevic had looked at Rev. Jackson and said matter-of-factly, "Are you an American?" And after the good reverend nodded in the affirmative, what if Milosevic had then said to him, "But you don't look like an American!"

Now, imagine that it was Madeleine Albright, then U.S. Secretary of State, who was sitting in front of Milosevic asking for the release of our prisoners. Would Milosevic ask that same question, even if he knew that Ms. Albright was born right there in Belgrade (as the daughter of the Czech ambassador to Yugoslavia) and came to the United States as an immigrant?

The point here, I think, is clear. To have a stereotype of someone of Puerto Rican origin as a dark-skinned person of African descent is as erroneous as having a stereotype of an American as a person of white European origin, or at least as someone who could pass as a white European.

Having lived in Puerto Rico for 30 years, I don't see much difference between racial cross-sections of Atlanta, Georgia; New York, New York; Los Angeles, California; and San Juan, Puerto Rico. There are as many "European-looking" people and "African-looking" people in Puerto Rico as you would find in any other major American city. When you add to this scenario in our officially race neutral but truly race-conscious society the fact that many Puerto Ricans speak Spanish as their first language, then you have an incubator for some deep-rooted prejudices to mature and burst forth.

Sammy Davis, Jr. used to complain that he had it twice as tough because people would dump on him not just because he was African-American, but also because he was also Jewish. Can you imagine how difficult society would have made it for him if it had realized that he traced his ancestry through Puerto Rico?

Teodoro Moscoso, a famous local intellectual and political leader who orchestrated the successful industrial development program of Puerto Rico in the 1950s and early '60s, liked to tell stories. He shared this one at the San Juan Rotary Club. This club is one of the oldest Rotary groups in the world; it has more than 250 members and is the only English-speaking club among the 63 leading business clubs on the island. The meeting took place in the early '70s, when I first came to Puerto Rico. Moscoso said:

> When I first left Puerto Rico to go to college, my parents sent me to Georgia State University. My

classmates noticed that I spoke Spanish and, not having met many Puerto Ricans before, they labeled me as "the Latin Lover." Later, I did my graduate studies at NYU and there they called me that "f—— Puerto Rican." I'm not sure they meant the same thing.

Of course, America does not own the intellectual property rights on prejudice. Being from Europe, I can write without fear of being accused of jingoism that Europe is a prime example of prejudice gone wild. The Europeans have been so busy managing their historical ethnic and religious prejudices that they are only now discovering their racial biases. Century after century there brought the Inquisition, religious persecutions, anti-Jewish pogroms, and, most recently, the clashes in Bosnia and Kosovo. France, the Netherlands and Austria in particular have seen the resurgence of xenophobic parties and leaders, and continent-wide collapses in birth rates are inflicting fresh tensions.

None of this is to say that Puerto Rico is an ethnic paradise, though it is in fact a place where, on a day-to-day basis, the color of one's skin matters not a whit. Here, however, is the way prejudice seeps even into Puerto Rico's tolerant mores.

When I first arrived in Puerto Rico, I immediately fell in love with the island. Besides the natural beauty and the lack of crime (at the time), what impressed me most was the way the people seemed to be of various skin colors and diverse hair texture and oblivious to the very thought of it. It appeared on the surface that Puerto Rico had achieved a degree of racial mixture and toleration that the States, in 1970, had just begun to discover. Initially I believed that I had come to a place in the world that was on the cutting edge of complete racial equality. This was wonderful. It was the way I thought the entire world ought to be and I wanted to be part of it!

I lived in this state of color-blind bliss for many years, through my arrival in New York, my meeting Julie, our marriage in Alaska and the birth of our children, our move to Puerto Rico, and ultimately our divorce. Soon I would be moving in a somewhat different circle. I began dating a young woman who came from one of the upper-class families of Puerto Rico.

When talking about certain people, she would habitually rub the tips of her fingers over her cheek. I was supposed to figure out what that meant. She told me about a certain, very prominent and wealthy family that was refused admission to an exclusive private social club called AFDTA. The reason they were barred from joining the club was explained by that motion of the tips of her fingers over her cheek.

There was another social club that only the "best" Puerto Rican families were invited to join. It was called the Casino de Puerto Rico. The young woman told me a story about a friend of hers who was among a group of debutantes set to have their coming-out party at age 16. This friend had a darker skin tone than her brothers and sisters. There were rumors that . . . she waved her fingers over her cheek . . . you know what. She told me that this girl's mother did not allow her daughter to go to the beach for six months before the debutante party because she didn't want her to add a tan to her troubles. The girl's mother was reportedly worried that the family would be asked to resign from the club "in shame."

It took me a long time to figure out what this was all about. I had not encountered these attitudes among everyday Puerto Ricans. Eventually I was fully exposed to the well-hidden Puerto Rican concept of "Mejorando la Raza" that ruled society ever since the first African slave was traduced there in the early 16th century.

Here is some background as to how it worked.

Over the last few hundred years, Puerto Rico was populated by people from various parts of the world. Specifically, the countries of origin for most of the immigrants were Germany, France, Spain, Corsica, China, and, of course, beginning in 1518, African slaves imported to work the coffee and sugar plantations.

Some immigrants landed by accident. For example, in the mid-1700s, during the Spanish Inquisition, a group of Sephardic Jews made a deal with the King of Portugal to acquire some land in Brazil. The Jews bought a ship and hired a crew from the Balkans, the future Yugoslavia specifically, and set sail for Brazil.

Their voyage took them through the Mona Passage between Puerto Rico and Hispaniola, where they were shipwrecked during a storm. They made it to the western shore of Puerto Rico, settled there, and founded a town called Boqueron. Even today many of the town's businesses carry Jewish names: Colmado Ruicof, Panderia Colberg, Gasolinera Frank (all common last names in Puerto Rico. There is even a Farmacia Wiscovic, a very Yugoslavian last name.

The joke the descendants of these survivors tell now is that, in the end, the Inquisitors won. They are all Catholics now.

Right from the beginning, the racial and ethnic composition of Puerto Rico has not been much different from that of America. For many European immigrants, as a visit to Old San Juan will affirm, Puerto Rico offered a small taste of their own world back home.

It struck me early in my time on the island how similar the local attitudes and customs were to those I experienced growing up on the Adriatic coast. I remember every Christmas when my uncle would butcher a pig and make roast pig and blood sausage. Puerto Rico's traditional food during Christmastime is "lechon y morcilla," which, translated, means roast pig and blood sausage.

By 1873, a decade after Abraham Lincoln's Emancipation Proclamation, when Spain declared the slaves free after surrendering the authority of its monarchy, many biracial children had already been born to slaves and freedmen. They were sired not only by their masters, but also by the condemned prisoners who were sent to Puerto Rico from Spain to earn their freedom through hard labor, and by indentured servants who came to Puerto Rico to escape some form of persecution in their own countries.

These former slaves and their children represented the artisan class of Puerto Rico. They were the carpenters, the cobblers, the silversmiths, the tailors, and the masons. From this class came some very famous Puerto Rican intellectuals and artists - for example, Campeche, a world-renowned painter, whose works are sold regularly at Christie's and Sotheby's. Composers like Tavares and Campos also hail from this class, along with Rafael Cordero, a famous teacher-professor at the local university. The artisans also include a locally renowned labor leader, Iglesias, who became an intimate of a prominent U.S. Senator, Dale Bumpers of Arkansas. Political leaders like Betances and Barbosa were also descendants of this class.

The term used to describe this racial mixture that characterized the artisan class was "Prietusco," which was an endearing way of saying mulatto. As always, manual dexterity, leadership qualities, and high intellect did not necessarily translate into wealth and social position. It wasn't long before the former slaves and their children noticed that it was the white people who had all the money and the dark people who were begging for scraps from the banquet table. Subconsciously, perhaps, or less so for some, the idea of becoming "more white" over a few generations had an irresistible economic appeal.

A good friend of mine, Ruben Gomez, told me this story from his youth. Gomez was a pitcher for the old N.Y. Giants who helped lead the team to many World Series victories. He holds the record for the longest career as a professional baseball player, because after his stint with the majors, he pitched for many years in Puerto Rico. Naturally, he is a Puerto Rican.

When Ruben was little, he noticed that the white kids had all the good food and nice clothes and toys, and he had nothing. One day he decided to douse himself with flour. When his parents came home, they asked him why he had done this. He told them that since his white friends had everything while he suffered with nothing, he wanted to be white, too. His parents proceeded to give him a nice, understanding whipping. He protested and asked them why he was being punished. They replied, "We just wanted to give you a taste of what happens when someone who looks like you suddenly decides he wants to become white."

Ruben Gomez never again wanted to be a different color. After he retired from baseball, he became a professional golfer. The rumor is that he is the only person whom Chi-Chi Rodriguez won't play for money. Ruben tells this story often, with relish, and if you ever happen to be hanging around the Dorado Beach Hotel in Puerto Rico you might run into him and hear this story firsthand.

Returning to the former slaves of Puerto Rico, the rumor is that it was they who devised the concept of "Mejorando la Raza," or "Improving the Race." It was simple. If you were dark, the name of the game was to marry someone lighter. Then your children would marry someone even lighter and so on. Pretty soon, when your family tree began sprouting white offspring, you will have arrived and now be ready to assume a higher place in society with all the financial benefits that could bring. Or so the myth went.

One preferred way of "Improving the Race" was for attractive young women of the artisan class to marry white men who came from formerly rich families that had fallen on hard times. This way, their children had better access to investment capital from their paternal cousins, who were white and who had not lost their wealth. Even today, if you refer to a young lady, regardless of her races, as "mi negrita" you are complementing her on her beauty and her charms. This is not a phrase you would want to use in English to a young woman in Atlanta, Georgia, or any other American city, for that matter.

Ultimately, racial self-definitions prove to be inhibiting factors. It would be difficult to prove that resistance to Puerto Rican status change rests on any racial (the island is predominantly Hispanic) or religious (it is no longer majority Catholic) prejudice, but it is virtually certain that whatever part such prejudice plays in the debate is averse to American and Puerto Rican interests. One hundred and forty years after the Emancipation Proclamation the United States is still debating in its courts and colleges such issues as affirmative action. The U.S. Supreme Court issued another ruling on the subject, affirming diversity but rejecting a quota system, in the summer of 2003.

Nearly 200 years after the death of Thomas Jefferson, the question as to whether or not he fathered a child by a family slave, Sally Hemmings, still occasions vigorous controversy. When descendants of Ms. Hemmings decided to attend a Jefferson family reunion a few years ago, they were welcomed by some and rejected by others. For some, the dispute was all about DNA and circumstantial evidence; in truth, the dispute is about a much deeper drama, one that is slowly playing out against a background of increasingly mixed racial heritages.

In this respect, Puerto Rico and the rest of the United States have a great deal in common. Isn't racial prejudice, whether in Puerto Rico or on the American mainland, nothing more than denial, what the psychologists call "reaction formation"? Prejudice is tragic, and efforts to overcome it through "marrying white," as an end in itself, have a tragicomic aspect. When someone from the "Prietusco" class, through intermarriage, did reach a new level of racial "purity" and gained fresh economic status, they would invent new family trees that led to Spain or Corsica or some other

European fountainhead. To create a new future they would invent a new past. The aim was to become one of the undoubted and unquestioned whites, the blanquitos.

Sometimes, when such people would make claims too bold to withstand scrutiny, their bluff would be called by someone asking, "Y tu abuela, donde esta?" "Where is your grandmother?" The implication was that she was hiding in the kitchen because her visage would show your true racial origin. Before long, there was an entire crop of Puerto Ricans who were hiding their grandmothers.

Rather than let the cause of racial convergence take its course, there were elements of Puerto Rican society that were enlisted in the drive to retain racial purity. The Catholic Church on the island was solicited for help in preserving the blanquito class, particularly the parish priest. It was he who kept all the birth and baptismal records in the town and, as a result, it was a reliable way to trace someone's ethnic heritage.

The mothers of eligible-for-marriage youngsters were usually in charge of this qualification process. Whenever one of the young people would express a desire to marry someone whose parents, grandparents, and great-grandparents were not readily known, the Catholic priests were asked to check the prospective bride or groom's family tree. If the search uncovered any "shady" background, the marriage would be denied to the young couple. When the broken-hearted young person would ask why, the mother would wave her fingertips over her cheek. Nothing more need be said. The romance was over.

It wasn't long before the darker-skinned population of Puerto Rico began to catch on as to which side the Catholic priests were assisting through this process. Little by little, they began to shift to various Protestant denominations. The Protestant leaders were not as loyal as the Catholic majority to Puerto Rico's white aristocracy and did not open their registries as readily. There are many Baptists today on the island, as well as Pentecostals, Jehovah's Witnesses, and Seventh-Day Adventists. In fact, the most recent statistics show that Puerto Rico is now some 50 percent Catholic, with an equal part distributed among other faith groups.

This does not mean that the law of inertia in the redistribution of wealth has changed. From a practical standpoint, wealth in Puerto

Rico today is still concentrated in the hands of the island's white and very light-skinned population. Puerto Ricans of darker countenance sit at a much lower rung on the social and economic scale. The temptation of "Mejorando la Raza" still beckons. Perhaps, for the rest of the United States, the idea of Puerto Rico as a poor neighbor whose status need not concern us beckons in the other direction.

Some evidence exists that these age-old tensions and fears hold sway regardless of the political circumstances. A visitor to Communist Cuba today would witness a similar pattern. Most of the people who represented the plutocracy in Cuba fled when Castro and his Marxist cohorts came to power in the early 1960s. The ones who stayed were either the dark-skinned Cubans or the whites who ran the revolution. Today, four decades later, the people who run the country are white while the rest of the nation is dark. The contrast is obvious, even stark, in some settings. When the Cuban national baseball team played games against the Baltimore Orioles, photographs of the pre-game ceremonies showed dark-skinned players and a light-skinned Cuban diplomatic corps.

Who is stronger even than Castro? Mejorando la Raza!

These influences continue to feed into the political system in Puerto Rico and its interactions with the mainland. One of the most prominent Puerto Rican leaders at the turn of the 20th century was Jose Celso Barbosa. He was a doctor and a graduate of the University of Michigan. Barbosa came from Puerto Rico's artisan/Prietusco class; his father was mason bricklayer and his brother a tailor. When he returned to Puerto Rico after graduation, he was not allowed to practice medicine. Some say that this was because U.S. medical degrees, unlike European degrees, were not acceptable. Others say it was because he was black.

Unable to find work in his chosen profession, Barbosa turned to politics. He began the Republican Party in Puerto Rico and became a powerful advocate of statehood. As in the United States at the time of the founding of the party of the same name, the "Republicans" in Puerto Rico were those who represented the rights of the black population.

Barbosa's struggles in the early 1900s to make Puerto Rico a full and equal state in the U.S. federal system are legendary. The significant point here is that even at the dawn of the modern era, with intermarriage and the "Mejorando la Raza" that had been going on for centuries, the dividing line between white and non-white citizens in Puerto Rico was so sharp that a political movement had to be formed to advance the interests of the darker-skinned. Was this not a precursor to the story of Martin Luther King, Jr. in 1950s and '60s America?

If this is not the typical mainlander's view of Puerto Rican history, it is partly because of the consequences of that history. As soon as the U.S. Congress granted citizenship to the Puerto Rican people in 1917, a wave of immigration brought people north to New York and other cities that have long spoken to the globe of a better life. Those who left Puerto Rico, those for whom it was not a rich port but rather a cul-de-sac, were predominantly dark-skinned islanders. In the words of "America":

> I like the shores of America!
> Comfort is yours in America!
> Knobs on the doors in America,
> Wall-to-wall floors in America

In those days and right up until the '50s, Puerto Rico was called, with justice, "The Poorhouse of the Caribbean." It had the lowest per capita income of any Caribbean island, even Haiti and the Dominican Republic. The unemployment rate in those days ranged to 50 percent. Well-to-do whites and those who managed to achieve, without detection, "Mejorando la Raza" stayed, and the unemployed blacks left.

These men and women emigrated in droves, imitating, in fact, the migration of southern U.S. blacks to America's urban north. Some replaced the departing American blacks and many more merely joined them in the cities. They picked corn and plucked tobacco leaves, dug potatoes, became maids, and hopped aboard as garbage collectors and dishwashers, searching for an economic seam that would give them and their families an opportunity. Wave after wave came north, after the First World War, during the Great Depression, and again after the Second World War and right into the 1950s.

Today, when someone tells me that I "don't look like a Puerto

Rican," I can see that this person has never spent any time in Puerto Rico or even with a volume of Puerto Rican history in his lap. His frame of reference is from those Puerto Ricans who migrated to the United States in search of a better life, many of whom found bitterness and welfare and drugs instead. These were poorer people with the urban afflictions that tended to greet new arrivals from any shore (with some noteworthy exceptions, of course). They gravitated to areas where their neighbors, Puerto Rican or not, had countenances like their own. They clustered in upper Manhattan, Brooklyn, and the South Bronx. Like me. they were fleeing limits on their opportunities. They assimilated to the new culture that existed in these neighborhoods, losing, many of them, the distinct Spanish language and customs whose vestiges were drawing me in.

In the 1950s, as these Americans were "going north," I found myself going south and learning ever more about the disjunctions, the complexity, of Puerto Rican society. Prejudice and class are always subtle warriors against freedom. The real differences among people do not involve these superficial matters. This point was driven home to me once again when President Bill Clinton pardoned the FALN terrorists from Chicago. The Washington pundits were up in arms about what they regarded as a political act designed to aid the fortunes of Clinton's wife Hillary, then running for the U.S. Senate. The truth was that most people in Puerto Rico were as upset as any other Americans over the freeing of these criminals.

People on the island did not even consider these terrorists to be Puerto Ricans. They were all born on the U.S. mainland, many of them spoke little or no Spanish, and they did not represent the political views of 98 percent of Puerto Ricans. Moreover, most of the two percent of Puerto Ricans who believe in Puerto Rican independence also believe in achieving that goal through democratic means. Jose Fuentes, then-Attorney General of Puerto Rico affirmed those feelings in an editorial printed in the Wall Street Journal in October 1999, not long after President Clinton's decision. He wrote:

> I fear President Clinton may only have succeeded in igniting resentment and suspicion against the Puerto Rican people – by fueling the assumption that we all

supported the clemency decision. Most of us did not. And we do not want to give our fellow Americans the mistaken impression that our sympathies lie with terrorism. Mr. Clinton needs to know that Puerto Rico stands with the U.S. against terrorism – and we emphatically reject any insinuation to the contrary.

Nonetheless, differences in cultural and political orientation between people of Puerto Rican extraction who were born and raised on the mainland and those who were born and raised on the island had become very evident in the early 1970s. When the federal food stamp program took effect in that decade, Puerto Rico's economy had begun growing for reasons described in previous chapters. Compared to the United States, then as now, Puerto Rico was economically to the rear; compared to the rest of Latin America, an economic miracle had begun. As a consequence, many Puerto Ricans who had immigrated to the States, or whose parents or grandparents had emigrated, saw opportunities to return to the land of their origin, either to engage in new businesses or to claim new benefits.

In a case of reverse injustice, the local Puerto Ricans did not take kindly to these "rearrivals." They coined a term for them – the Neoricans – because they regarded them as representing the New York City slum culture and not the traditional cultural hierarchy of the island. The Neoricans were the last in line to get jobs and they found it difficult to enter the mainstream of Puerto Rican society.

Thus they settled in their own neighborhoods and co-existed with their new neighbors as best they could. Most of them still had family links to the island. It did not take long for the Neorican label to fade away as reassimilation continued. But something did happen in the early 1970s that has had a profound and lasting effect on the island. Puerto Rico, which had known very little criminal activity prior to the '70s, suddenly became a crime haven. Opportunities for new prejudices rose from this fact. The reputation of the Puerto Rican communities of New York in the 1960s became the reputation of the island in the 1990s.

At the end of the day, the final prejudice about Puerto Rico is the one in which Americans fail to fully realize that in the island are found their countrymen. Puerto Rico is different, a land in limbo, a crowded place struggling with crime but full of good people as well, who are part of the United States and Americans citizens through and through. As Anita and the full chorus in West Side Story tell it:

> ALL: Immigrant goes to America,
> Many hellos in America,
> Nobody knows in America,
> Puerto Rico's in America!

The biggest mistake that most Americans make is assume that Puerto Ricans are "Latinos". Following this assumption, they subsequently assume that all "Latinos" are Democrats and like welfare. These assumption could not be further from the truth and reflect many assumptions that could place the "assumer" in the category of the first three letters of the word "ASSume".

I always try to remember this analogy when I start "assuming".

So let me try to dispel this misconception.

Just because Puerto Ricans happen to share a common language with Latinos, it does not mean that their attitudes and values are the same. To illustrate this point let me ask the question: "How many Cubans are Democrats?"

But the key difference between those who are perceived as Latinos and Puerto Ricans is in the way they had come to America and the motives for them doing so and their perception of their place of birth.

Most "Latinos" landed in America because they were escaping poverty or political oppression or both. Most have come from countries like Mexico, Colombia, Guatemala, Dominican Republic, Venezuela etc. Some came illegally and had to struggle to get their American citizenship.

For Puerto Ricans, U.S. citizenship was not an issue. They have been U.S. citizens since 1917 and they could come to the mainland U.S. anytime they wanted to. Those who were poorer, came to the U.S. during the 30's, the 40's and the 50's to seek job opportunities and continued to go back and forth. The 80's and 90's saw a migration of professionals and business people, a "brain drain" if you will.

The "Latinos" who left their countries of birth, left real countries. And after they left them, even though they became American citizens, they could still keep their national ethnic pride so to them, the status of their countries was not an issue. Puerto Ricans, on the other hand have never had a country. They have been a colony since 1492 when Columbus claimed Puerto Rico for Spain and after 1898 when the U.S. took over that claim.

The contrast, then, between "Latinos" and Puerto Ricans are issues of citizenship and national identity.

For "Latinos" immigration is a big issue. So are issues dealing with legal and illegal aliens. For Puerto Ricans, these issues have no value. To them, the political status of Puerto Rico is the big issue.

Mainland Puerto Ricans have been here for two or three generations, and many of them do not speak Spanish. However, their ancestors settled in the urban areas of New York and Chicago and other areas in the northeast. As a result, they have felt the full brunt of racial prejudice and relate more to urban/black Americans than they do to other segments of the population.

But since other Latin ethnic groups do have a strong sense of National origin, mainland Puerto Ricans were never allowed that luxury. As a result, perhaps one third of Puerto Rico origin Americans have a strong feeling for Puerto Rico's independence.

Since Puerto Rico parties are not divided based on ideological lines but on political status lines, which represent, Statehood, Independence and "Commonwealth," the majority of U.S. Puerto Ricans are in favor of the current status for Puerto Rico (because they believe in the Muñoz Marin lie of "Estado Libre Asociado") or full independence.

It is understandable that they don't care what is really the best economic status solution for Puerto Rico because they have their Statehood by living in New York or Chicago. Theirs is strictly an emotional decision based on never having had the sense of "country" (as opposed to Latino's) because of the 500+ year old colonial status.

On the other hand, Puerto Rico, Puerto Ricans, are overwhelmingly in favor of keeping their U.S. citizenship and approximately 50%, who would prefer to keep the status quo (the PDP party) are really doing it just so they can get all the Federal benefits without paying Federal Taxes.

The independence party only draws approximately 2% of the vote.

In summary, a referendum vote, given a two way choice, Statehood or Independence, would result in 85%+ for Statehood. On the other hand, if a similar referendum were held in New York, you would probably see perhaps 30% to 50% voting for independence.

This diversity of emotion creates friction between Puerto Rico, Puerto Ricans and Neoricans.

But most importantly, this conflict isolates Puerto Rico issues from those associated with typical "Latino" issues.

In summary, if you want to capture the hearts and minds of U.S. "Latinos" you talk about immigration, citizenship and the rights of aliens, legal or illegal. If you want to capture the hearts and minds of Puerto Ricans, either U.S. mainland or island residents, you talk about Puerto Rico's political status.

CHAPTER 16

The Last, Full Measure

On July 6, 2003 *The Washington Post* published a gallery of photographs and brief biographies of the American servicemen killed in Iraq in the previous few months. The roster of names in the article read, as all such articles now do, like a smorgasbord of the American experience. There were Hispanic names, African-American names, Irish names, Italians, Poles, East Europeans, Scottish and English. The eye could travel down each row of nine images and find someone whose name, biography or residence brought him "close to home" for the reader.

Of all the names and photographs, however, there was one, and only one, man who would have been immediately identifiable for other reasons. About him one would immediately know at least one fact beyond his having given his life in his country's service: he was the one unable to vote for or against the Commander-in-Chief who sent him into a war zone. This man was not ineligible because he was too young, or because he had been convicted of a felony, or because he was a foreign citizen. This man was of age, of spotless enough record to be a military policeman, and very much an American citizen. His name was Specialist Richard P. Orengo. Specialist Orengo was unable to vote for or against his Commander-in-Chief because he had the accident of being born and living in America's semi-colony, Puerto Rico. Nonetheless, like his brothers-in-arms, he gave the last, full measure of devotion for the country he loved.

Richard Orengo hailed from Toa Alta, Puerto Rico., a town on the Rio de la Plata southwest of San Juan. He was a member of the 755th Military Police Company based in Arecibo, Puerto Rico. He was only 32 years old when he was shot and killed in Najaf, Iraq, while investigating a car theft. It may have been routine police work, or it may have been something more. Cars used in bomb attacks against military targets in Iraq are often stolen vehicles. By appearance and personal history, it would be hard to distinguish Specialist Orengo from the other 44 men depicted in the *Post*'s gallery of heroes. Perhaps he was a little older than most of these young soldiers. That was all.

Soldiers like Richard Orengo have served bravely in the armed forces of the United States for a century. They have given their lives and shed blood as red any that flows through American veins. Their names are inscribed on our monuments and memorials. They are honored by their fellow citizens in parades and their graves are adorned with flowers and flags – never enough for any who made such sacrifices – in our national cemeteries. They have served willingly and with great love of country. This does not mean, however, that they are unaware of the peculiarity of their status, and that they do not wish to see it changed.

Just before the 2000 U.S. presidential election, Air Force veteran Jose Lausel and several other Puerto Rican citizens filed suit in federal district court in San Juan seeking the right to vote for president. They were residents of the island and they wanted the November 7 ballots printed there to contain the names of George W. Bush, Al Gore and the minor party candidates for the White House. "Anyplace in the world, I'm an American and I can vote, but not here," Lausel said. His point was simple: he is a U.S. citizen. If he moved to the Bronx or Orlando, Florida, he could vote for president. If he were on active duty in Kosovo, he could vote for president. Because, however, his address at the time of the suit was on the island, he could not vote. Puerto Rico's unique status does not just mean that a territory is treated differently; it means that the same person is treated differently solely on the basis of his address.

Lausel's suit was only the latest effort to gain through the courts what has been denied to Puerto Rico through the political process.

It is no way to do business. Excitement was briefly raised on the island in 2000 when federal district judge Jaime Pieras, Jr. ruled in San Juan on August 29 that Puerto Ricans must be permitted to vote for president as a matter of fundamental right for U.S. citizens. He noted how the current situation operates in reverse for Puerto Ricans. Other U.S. citizens are permitted to be out of the United States and vote by absentee ballots. Puerto Ricans, on the other hand, are denied the vote only when they are home on the island. Judge Pieras, in an act of undoubted political popularity and judicial nullity, ordered Puerto Rican governmental officials to print ballots with the presidential options included.

The decision, of course, was immediately appealed, and U.S. and island legal experts were quick to say that the judge's ruling would be promptly reversed by the U.S. Court of Appeals for the First Circuit in Boston. The Clinton Justice Department acted with dispatch to argue the appeal on straightforward Constitutional grounds. The election of the president of the United States is actually carried out through the Electoral College. Only those jurisdictions that have membership in the Electoral College participate meaningfully in presidential elections, and those jurisdictions are explicitly recognized in the U.S. Constitution as the 50 states and, after the adoption of the 23rd amendment in 1961, the District of Columbia.

Puerto Rico's voting advocates could be forgiven for concluding that U.S. courts don't always abide by the spirit or even the letter of the Constitution. Nonetheless, a three-judge panel for the Court of Appeals overturned Pieras's ruling just a month before the election. Undaunted, the Puerto Rican legislature continued with its instruction that ballots be printed on the island with the U.S. presidential candidates listed (U.S. ballots, of course, actually contain the name of Electors for each of the presidential candidates, and it is for these Electors that voters actually cast their ballots). The Puerto Rican vote would thus have had the status and effect of a non-binding referendum, and mainland media would be left with the option of giving the outcome much or little attention. It may have fueled a footnote or driven an aside in someone's commentary.

As it turned out, even this symbolic vote was barred when the Puerto Rican Supreme Court, acting much like a state supreme court, ruled that the ballots could not be printed with the presidential candidates' names on them. The reason: because the votes would not be part of any official tally, printing and counting them would be the expenditure of public funds for a non-public purpose. Ironically, as everyone knows, the disparity between Al Gore's popular vote victory and George W. Bush's Electoral College triumph dominated the news after the election. If ever the meaning of a symbolic presidential vote in Puerto Rico were going to get national attention, focusing the public mind on the island's status as "Senor In-Between," this would have been the time.

The emotional appeal of this latest lawsuit is strong, and the choice of military veterans to be among the litigants has a powerful appeal. There is nothing "in-between" about military service, and there has been nothing in-between about the level of Puerto Rican commitment to the U.S. Armed Forces. Authorities report slightly different numbers for U.S. citizens from Puerto Rico who have joined or been drafted (the draft laws apply in Puerto Rico, even if the federal tax laws do not) into uniform, but the estimates all hover in the 200,000 range.[1] With this level of service in international conflicts, which dates to the First World War, there has come a high level of sacrifice. The Americans Veterans Committee for Puerto Rico Self-Determination reports that 6,220 Puerto Rican members of the Armed Forces have been wounded and 1,225 have been killed in our nation's service.

It could be argued that citizens of other nations have died fighting on our behalf, and every American schoolboy and schoolgirl has heard the names of the Marquis de Lafayette and Thaddeus Kosciusko. If nothing else, however, these individuals volunteered for service and the Continental Congress had no claim on their persons. Puerto Ricans are subject to the military draft and today every young male on the island who reaches his 18th birthday must register by law. Moreover, these individuals can vote if they happen to leave the island and establish residence in one of the states or in the District of Columbia. True, if they happen to choose the nation's capital, they are not represented in the House or Senate, and their lot has not improved vis-à-vis Congressional representation. This only proves that if the District of Columbia has half a loaf, Puerto Rico has less than a quarter.

The status of the District of Columbia is an issue all its own, and it is unreasonable to compare its history to that of Puerto Rico. The District of Columbia is a federal enclave under the Constitution, the seat of the national government, an area defined under law from the country's founding. Apart from that fact, it is also but one piece, and a diminishing one at that, of an urban area, a geographical entity much smaller and less economically and topographically diverse than even the smallest of the 50 states, Rhode Island or Delaware. Puerto Rico on the other hand has all the classic hallmarks of a political jurisdiction that "works" either as an independent nation or as the 51st American state.

Puerto Rico, as noted earlier, is some 50 times the size of the District of Columbia. It has natural geographic definition, like Hawaii. It has a major city and one of the world's busiest ports, a collection of smaller cities, hamlets and backwater towns. It has rivers and mountains, a rain forest and beaches. It has its own economy, struggling though it may be, and it produces items for export, sugar and coffee and rum. It supports a bustling tourist industry, an array of manufacturing concerns, and a growing population. It is nearly 4 million people strong, and, were it a state, it would have at least seven members of the U.S. House of Representatives.

One needn't, however, even consider the justice of permanent new status for Puerto Rico by comparing it to other entities. The truth is that whatever justice one chooses, be it statehood or independence, Puerto Rico's claim to that justice is compelling on its own merits. Through the 23rd amendment, Congress heard the pleas of residents of the District of Columbia and gave the city's residents the opportunity to vote for the new president who, every four or eight years, rides down the main street of the city, Pennsylvania Avenue, to take the Oath of Office. Puerto Rico has not been extended even this privilege, and, in so doing, the United States has deprived some 2.4 million citizens, registered voters, of their right to vote for those who represent their nation in the White House and in Congress. Rich and poor alike, Puerto Ricans do vote. Mindful of their full colonial past and chafing under their semi-colonial present, some 2,000,000 Puerto Ricans voted in the local elections of 2000. That figure represents voter turnout in excess of 80 percent, numbers now unheard of on the mainland.

Puerto Rico is indeed fit for self-determination; its people practice the most basic art of democratic self-rule, voting, to the maximum degree.

Proposals have indeed been raised for a new U.S. Constitutional amendment for Puerto Rico along the lines of the 23rd amendment. Writing just a month after the Bush-Gore 2000 election, with the chads still hanging in the balance in Florida, Edda Ponsa-Flores, a San Juan attorney, wrote a column in *The New York Times* expounding on the failed Lausel litigation and asking, "Why not pass a new constitutional amendment guaranteeing the vote to United States citizens of Puerto Rico and, perhaps, other territories?" She noted that this action need in no way be linked to the statehood question, just as it was not so linked for the District of Columbia.[2]

It is not difficult to imagine that this proposal provokes a variety of responses in the sea of opinion that surrounds not only Puerto Rico's status in particular, but the whole question of territorial possessions and special enclaves. On the one hand, it is hard to believe that the dynamics of creative democratic reform and the doctrine of expanding human rights could falter on the rocks of places like Puerto Rico and Guam. On the other, there are surely advocates of permanent status for Puerto Rico who believe that half-measures like expanded voting rights would only sap energy from a broader campaign for Puerto Rico's future. Moreover, granting Puerto Ricans voting rights in Congress and for the presidency would push a separate injustice further in the wrong direction. Isn't there more to citizenship than military service, as vital and heroic as that is? After all, only a minority of men and women serve and only a small percentage of those who serve actually suffer injury or death. Does it make sense for Puerto Ricans to have elected representatives in Washington if, for example, they pay no federal taxes and those elected officials may only assist in preserving that unfairness? The United States was founded on rebellion against taxation without representation. Could Puerto Ricans sensibly be given representation without taxation?

Clearly, the only sane route to a just and permanent resolution of Puerto Rico's status is one that leads to full citizenship or to full independence. The longer these alternatives are postponed, the longer illusions about the identity of Puerto Ricans will be extended, the deeper will become the blemish on American history from the failure to resolve a political anomaly that mocks our nation's principles. No, the situation is not as extreme as the most left-wing critics of the United States (many of them homegrown) would have it, but it is a situation that offers many openings to the long-term detriment of both the island and the mainland. Consider the example of the debate over Vieques. Every aspect of the complex U.S.-Commonwealth of Puerto Rico relationship has been on display in this seeming dispute over a bombing range, which has been, in reality, a shadow drama about the heart of the American proposition itself.

The U.S. military presence in Puerto Rico dates, of course, to the Spanish-American War and the arrival of Rear Admiral William T. Sampson and seven warships, which exchanged fire with Spanish shore batteries in Old San Juan Harbor in May 1898. This inconclusive battle was followed by a military force that landed in the southern coastal city of Guanica in July, with a complement of some 3,400 men. Shortly thereafter, in a militarily and politically well-chosen move, a fleet led by General Nelson A. Miles landed at Ponce, Puerto Rico's main southern city. Removed from the capital and imbued, as the historian Arturo Morales Carrion observed, with a "strong nativist spirit," the residents of Ponce greeted the Americans as liberators.

The U.S. military role worldwide played an interesting role in accelerating the process by which Puerto Rico moved away from the pure colonial status of its first two decades of association with the United States and became something much more. On the eve of the U.S. entry into World War I, President Woodrow Wilson became concerned about the "uneasiness" of the Puerto Rican people under American domination. If the world was to be made safe for democracy, in Wilson's famous phrase, it made no sense for the archangel of that safety to maintain a Caribbean colony that did not enjoy self-determination. Wilson made the then-pending Jones Bill one of his three top priorities in his 1916 message to Congress. As a result of that pressure, a curious mix of domestic politics and international public relations, the legislation passed and the Puerto Rican people were made citizens of the United States. This step instantly made adult males on the island eligible for military service. A full Puerto Rican Regiment was formed and readied for deployment to Panama.

Thus began the history of military service that has seen so many thousands of Puerto Ricans serve in the U.S. Armed Forces over the past eight decades. In World War II, the U.S. military role in Puerto Rico was dramatically expanded. This time around, it was strategic military considerations, rather than diplomatic and image-driven concerns, that prompted the build-up of naval assets on the island. The reason was the same one that had figured so prominently in Puerto Rico's history since the raids of the Caribs and the arrival of Columbus. The island simply sits in a gatekeeper's role in the South Atlantic, of strategic importance to European and other powers (China seems to be the most interested power today) seeking access to the Caribbean, the Panama Canal and the Pacific. U.S. commanders feared the free operation of German submarines in the South Atlantic would pose a major threat to America and they moved to boost the U.S. presence on the island.

The result was the building of the 8,600-acre Roosevelt Roads Naval Station almost an hour east of San Juan, on the eastern tip of the island. President Roosevelt ordered the establishment of the base in 1940 and the Naval Station (it was renamed Roosevelt Roads in 1957) was completed in 1943. The Navy's vision for the area included training and maneuvers in a warm-water environment, and in 1941 the Navy began to acquire land on the neighboring island of Vieques. Use of Vieques for this purpose began in 1947. Vieques' elongated landmass totals a little more than 100 square miles. It is located across a narrow strait just east-southeast of Puerto Rico. Off-and-on over a 60-year period the more remote parts of Vieques were used by the Navy for bombing exercises. Roosevelt Roads itself saw more or less activity, depending on budgets and the world situation, and the base was even closed down on seven occasions after World War II. That changed during the Cold War. In 1955 the Navy opened its Atlantic Fleet weapons training center there, bringing new activity to Vieques.[3]

Roosevelt Roads developed as a massive and influential presence in Puerto Rico from that time onward. The airstrip on the base is more than two miles long. Although the base has not been the homeport of any U.S. military vessels, some 300 Navy, NATO and foreign military ships pay calls there every year. The local economic impact of this presence, as with any military base, is huge. The base directly supports an estimated 13,000 people, including some 4,300 active duty military and family members, more than 2,000 civilian employees, and nearly 8,000 retired military. This leaves out all of the private employers and business people, and their families, who derive income from the operation of Roosevelt Roads. The U.S. Government's official estimate of the infusion Puerto Rico receives from the base is $300 million per year. Other estimates run much higher, and one private assessment of the total value to the Puerto Rican economy of Roosevelt Roads-related activity runs as high as $2.2 billion annually.

Opponents of the Vieques range have existed for a long time, but they gained no traction until a stray projectile killed a Puerto Rican security guard in April 1999. It was the first fatality in the more than 50-year operation of the range, a remarkable safety record by most measurements. Ending the U.S. bombing exercise became a *cause celebre* for pro-independence forces on the island and a parade of liberal icons on the mainland, from the new Catholic Archbishop of San Juan, Roberto O. Gonzalez, to left-wing perennials like the Revs. Jesse Jackson and Al Sharpton. For all the attention Vieques ultimately received from activists pursuing their various agendas, one would have thought that the island had had a long love-hate relationship with U.S. military forces. Instead, if the whole of Puerto Rican society is considered, the opposite was true.

The Clinton Administration responded to the Vieques death by reaching an agreement with the then Governor Pedro Rossello, under which a referendum would be held in Puerto Rico to decide whether the Navy should remain there. Most important, that agreement was basically written into law in the final defense authorization bill President Clinton signed into law during his last year in office. President Clinton also issued a directive transferring the western part of the range to the government of Puerto Rico. With blood in the water, Jackson, Sharpton and their allies seized the opportunity to lambaste the U.S. military as insensitive to the wishes of Puerto Ricans on the island and in the United States. Sharpton became one of the Vieques 4 (the other three were Bronx politicians) after his arrest over involvement in an anti-U.S. Navy protest. During a visit to New York in the early summer of 2001, Archbishop Gonzalez campaigned for the Navy's removal from

Vieques. During a sermon delivered in Spanish at St. Patrick's Cathedral in Manhattan, the Archbishop conjoined his celebration of the beatification of the first Puerto Rican with a call for revision in the expected referendum on Vieques' future. The sermon was a tour de force, linking a religious theme, the beatification of a man who died a generation earlier, with a purely political aim, the Archbishop's desire to champion "peace" by expelling an American peacekeeping force.

The Archbishop told the Catholic congregation, some of whom were displaying Puerto Rican flags in the cathedral's vast nave, that he intended to urge the New York general assembly to add an option to the referendum. The planned alternatives for the referendum were two. Under one scenario, the Navy would continue its exercises using dummy bombs for three years and the United States would provide a $40 million economic development package. The other proposal would have allowed the Navy to continue bombing indefinitely with live munitions, while paying an additional $50 million a year for the privilege. Archbishop Gonzalez pledged to pursue a third option, the immediate cessation of all Navy bombing exercises on Vieques. He reportedly told the congregants that he recognized Sharpton was a controversial figure, but that "the solidarity of the [Vieques] four [had] made a strong statement to the cause of peace in Vieques."[4]

Shortly after (but not because of) the Archbishop's visit, the Secretary of the Navy, Gordon England, announced that the Navy would cease training and bombing exercises on Vieques by May 2003. In testimony a few days later to the House Armed Services Committee, Deputy Secretary of Defense Paul Wolfowitz indicated that the Secretary of Defense supported the decision to close down the Vieques training, acknowledging that the vast majority of the 9,600 residents of the island were strongly opposed to it and would almost certainly vote that November to eject the Navy. He made it clear that defense officials were deeply concerned about the adverse precedent that would be set by allowing a popular vote on the question. "[D]ictating national security decisions by local referendum is fundamentally flawed public policy," Wolfowitz told the committee. "Win or lose on the Vieques referendum, it is a mistake to allow local elections to dictate essential matters of national security."[5]

To avoid that precedent, which would have had peculiar force because of the status issue in Puerto Rico, President Bush asked the Congress to cancel the Vieques referendum. This decision occasioned howls of cynical protest from some of the mainland activists who had campaigned most loudly for the Navy's removal. One of them, James E. Garcia, the editor of politicomagazine.com, wrote an editorial for the *San Francisco Chronicle*, "Bush v. Vieques," in which he personalized the debate and dramatized the issue as a kind of "peasants' revolt" against the imperial power of the Bush Administration. "The truth is," Garcia wrote, "that the president's team of political advisers has decided to wage war against the Vieques activists. Not with bombs and bullets, but with the flak of politics and public pressure." He went on, apparently without intentional hyperbole, to describe the Vieques "movement" as the "first time since Puerto Rico's colonization by the United States" that the island's residents were exercising "real power."

First time or not, national security issue or environmental dust-up, the Vieques debate was and is an "only in Puerto Rico" phenomenon. The bad precedent of the Navy's retreat from Vieques and search for a new bombing range and training center in Florida or North Carolina may turn out not to be a bad precedent, because it is virtually inconceivable that the attributes of this drama could exist anywhere else. Anywhere else on the globe the U.S. military presence is secured either by the fact that the land at issue belongs to the federal government and is protected by legal sovereignty, or is granted for use by the United States and is subject to treaties and other agreements that make the process of its continued use an orderly matter. In most places that presence is further secured because the local population desires it, the land at issue has little or no other value or use, and the economic benefits of the military establishment are critical to the local economy.

These factors worked no magic in Vieques, but the same cannot be said for Roosevelt Roads, and it is here that the real powerlessness of Puerto Rico under its current status is on full display. The spasm of protest over Vieques, fueled by partisan political interests on the mainland seeking to embarrass the Bush Administration on an environmental/war-and-peace issue, followed, as always, the law of unintended consequences. Defense officials and members of

Congress on the House and Senate armed services committees reasoned that if the United States Navy and Marine Corps could no longer train at Vieques, even with dummy munitions, then the entire Roosevelt Roads naval presence was unnecessary and should be closed. The decision was logical, but it was not taken without emotion, the kind that has been triggered on both sides in the past precisely because the underlying status of Puerto Rico is a nagging bone of contention. Rep. Randy "Duke" Cunningham, a 20-year Navy veteran and a member of the House Appropriations Defense Subcommittee, spoke for many in Congress when he said on July 20, 2003, "If you take the [bombing] mission away from Vieques, you don't need that base anymore. Sometimes you get what you wish for."[6]

Soon after Cunningham's statement the House of Representatives voted unanimously to close Roosevelt Roads six months after the enactment of the 2004 defense spending bill. The action was castigated by some Puerto Rican officials and members of the U.S. Congress who claimed it was punitive, but the Department of Defense had been warning for months that the closure was the natural corollary of the end of training programs in Vieques. Rep. Jose Serrano, a liberal Democrat from New York, said, "I think it's punishment" for the protests. "We are being punished," he told *The Washington Times*, "for winning an issue against the federal government. The Navy said, 'Oh yeah. We're going to fix you. We're going to close the base.'"[7] Atlantic Fleet Commander Robert Natter had said months earlier that, without the Vieques training site, "[T]here is no way I need the Navy facilities at Roosevelt Roads. It's a drain on Defense Department and taxpayers' dollars."[8]

Commentators in Puerto Rico, as well as in Congress, noted that Gov. Sila Calderon would be blamed for exacerbating tensions over the issue and failing to appreciate that the fate of Roosevelt Roads hung in the balance. John Marino, the city editor for *The San Juan Star,* wrote that Calderon would be vulnerable to charges by the New Progressive Party that Calderon, who launched a federal lawsuit meant to accelerate the end of training on Vieques, had instituted policies that would mean "the Americans are lowering their flag from Puerto Rico." As this is written the immediate political fallout of the Battle of Vieques, as it has been dubbed, is uncertain. Prior to word of the base closing, when the economic implications were more hypothetical than real, the political leadership in San Juan, conservative and liberal, disagreed on tone but not on substance.

Now it is obvious that the economic implications, in the short- to mid-term, are major, and that there is more to the economic implications even than mere economics. Towns nearby the base, including Ceiba, Fajardo and Naguabo, would be especially hard-hit, including landlords who rent to military families and civilian employees at the base, restaurants, car repair shops, chain stores like Wal-Mart, K-Mart and Sears, and hundreds of smaller enterprises that depend on income generated by the wages, paid at federal standards, to base employees. Home values could drop by as much as one third. These facts created a counter-movement to the Vieques protestors, but it was a movement that was not well-organized and that did not have the New York publicity resources available to the celebrities who took up for the Navy's evacuation. As Maria Padilla wrote for *The Orlando Sentinel*,

> This [the region around the base] is the part of Puerto Rico where the contrarian point of view on the much-publicized Vieques movement is found. Here, direct and daily interaction with Navy personnel – and direct and indirect benefits to local economies – mean Vieques is not an issue of stark contrasts, but one with blurred edges. The Navy is a friend here, not an enemy. And everyone knows someone who either works for or benefits from Roosevelt Roads.[10]

The town of Ceiba in particular enjoys a per-household income of $31,000, the highest in the region. Residents of the town say they worry about becoming another Naguabo, where the average household earns something like $10,000 less per year. Unemployment in scattered rural Puerto Rican towns already stands at a stunning 50 percent. Padilla reported that some Ceiban locals believe the base closure will lead to the demise of the town's last manufacturing plant. Talk of ghost towns has been heard. A local reporter described a visit to Ceiba in stark terms. "During a tour around the town's surroundings, WOW News observed many abandoned properties, streets are in bad condition, and buildings like the City Hall and the public library showed poor maintenance. More than a dozen signs of properties for sale or rent were seen."11

The Puerto Rican government continues to yearn for restoration of the special tax breaks that Congress repealed in the mid-1990s. Once again, however, deficits are the order of the day in Washington and the Bush Administration is under fire from Democrats over tax policies they say favor Republican special interests. Placating Puerto Rico through new tax relief does not seem like a likely prospect for an Administration that says candidly it felt trapped by a Clinton Administration decision to allow a Vieques plebiscite on American security policy. The events of September 11, 2001 did nothing to ease this feeling. In the meantime, consider this irony: Puerto Rican officials are scrambling to renew the drug companies' tax gimmick in a desperate effort they claim is needed to preserve 20,000 jobs, the same number their rash actions on Roosevelt Roads will cost the Puerto Rico economy in short order!

The non-economic implications of the Roosevelt Roads base closing may be the most profound in the long-term. The base has also been used by the U.S. Drug Enforcement Administration. Military assets maintained and operated in Puerto Rico by the Navy include a massive over-the-horizon radar system that has been deployed to detect and give advance warning of unidentified aircraft and shipping approaching Puerto Rico from the south, the origin of much of the area's illicit drug trade. The radar system, called ROTHR, for relocatable over-the-horizon radar, was installed on Vieques and at Fort Allen in the late 1990s over the opposition of Puerto Rican and international green and socialist groups. The same array of anti-colonial and environmental arguments was used, combined with the usual dose of suspicion about U.S. intentions, some of it, naturally, hysterical. Monica Somocurcio of the Workers World Service deplored the "militarisation" of Puerto Rico and approvingly quoted the Cuban ambassador Rafael Dausa that Puerto Rico's "political prisoners" must be freed before Puerto Rican "independence" could be achieved.12

Such views have always characterized only a tiny minority of the Puerto Rican population, as is also true on the mainland United

States. The impact of Vieques-rooted militancy on the potential or likely removal of the radar system will affect every Puerto Rican and more than a few mainlanders. The reason is simple: the radar performs a unique task and performs it well. Writer Guillermo Moscoso noted in *The San Juan Star* in 1997 that the previously existing anti-drug radar system, based in Chesapeake, Virginia, and northeast Texas had been successful in helping to interdict large quantities of cocaine being moved by air. Adding ROTHR to the system gave U.S. and Puerto Rican anti-drug forces a third leg that would make "the movement of drugs by air to Puerto Rico and through Puerto Rico to the United States . . . exponentially more difficult for the narcotraffickers."[13]

The other two legs of the system had been redeployed for anti-drug trafficking purposes after the end of the Cold War. They had originally been developed to allow the United States to pick up air traffic, such as Soviet Backfire bombers, departing from Siberia for the United States. The ROTHR system can read air traffic as far south as Bolivia. Once again, Puerto Rico's strategic position afforded a strategic opportunity, this time the chance to detect and observe and track the round trips of craft departing the home stations of the drug lords. Moscoso described the way in which information from the radar was processed and how it has been used to serve not just U.S. and Puerto Rican law enforcement, but the national police of the trafficking countries, the men and women on the front lines of the fight. "Suspect tracks," he wrote, "are sent to the Joint Inter-agency Task Force East (JIATF East) in Key West, where intelligence from all the participating agencies, such as the FBI, Customs, etc., is introduced and appropriate law enforcement agencies are notified."

Puerto Rican law enforcement officials fear, justifiably, that the loss of the radar, if it occurs, will diminish their ability to apprehend drug transshipments through the region just at the time they have been able to improve coordination and interdiction. It was reported by U.S. officials in February 2003 that ROTHR had been responsible, just since December 2002, for the seizure of "more than 9,000 kilos of cocaine and more than 1,000 pounds of marihuana, as well as 27 airplanes, 14 boats, and 97 AK-47 rifles[.]"[14] A Ceiba policeman identified in a press report only as Officer Delgado lamented the potential loss of the radar and noted that friends of his at the base had already lost their jobs. "When [radar operators] see a suspect vessel, they notify local authorities, and we do the job. It seems that we are going to have more work to do in that aspect if the base closes," Delgado said.[15]

In short, it is an atrocious time for the island and the mainland to go separate ways on a subject that is in the interest of public safety not only in these two locales but also throughout the Hemisphere. Such is the dynamic of Puerto Rico's uncertain status, however, because an outcome like this is inconceivable except under today's extraordinary circumstances of quasi-territorial status. The left-wing, *independentista* forces at work on the Vieques issue had outsized influence in these debates, but performed at least one public service, that is, they freshly underscored the unsustainability (and exploitability) of Puerto Rico's commonwealth form of dependence. As Moscoso wryly observed, impotent as they generally have been, the "separatist sectors . . . oppose anything American (except dollars from Washington)[.]" Thus, in the face of an angry Congress and Administration, Puerto Rican officials are left to float ideas about development funds and resuscitation of repealed tax breaks that will only turn a fundamental debate into a funding debate.

Clearly, Vieques should not be viewed as just one more skirmish between the anti-war American left and a conservative Administration devoted to prosecuting a war against America's enemies overseas. The dramaturgy over the bombing range and defense installation would simply not have occurred if Puerto Rico were fish or fowl, that is, a state or independent nation. If Puerto Rico were a state, the idea of the U.S. presence as a military imposition in the area (an idea that makes little sense given the fact that the Puerto Rican people are U.S. citizens) would have no more relevance than it does in Newport News, or Newport, Rhode Island. Over the past 15 years, as base closings have occurred around the United States, there have been plenty of local debates, jockeying and horse-trading among members of Congress, and lobbying campaigns to avert or postpone particular recommendations of the base closing commission established by Congress.

This process has become routine, but that is just the point. Base closings are not easy matters, and easing the economic dislocations they can cause is a matter of national as well as local concern. In Puerto Rico, however, this process was freighted with various kinds of distractions owing to the overall state of the U.S.-Puerto Rican relationship. As a consequence, the closure of the largest (in terms of physical size) U.S. military installation outside the 50 states was accomplished in a disorderly, partisan and politically charged manner that has maximized the collateral political damage. The process has left a bitter taste between the island and the mainland, and may ultimately do severe damage to U.S. and island neighborhoods where the flow of drugs may increase even as the economic stresses are acutely felt among small businesses, landlords, and home owners.

With regard to military decisions on the mainland, the Department of Defense most assuredly does not have a free hand. Relationships with surrounding communities at defense installations are subject to many influences, and the behavior of soldiers from particular bases (Camp LeJeune, North Carolina, has in the not-so-distant past offered up more than its apparent share of incidents involving conflicts between Marine recruits and the owners of local establishments) is sometimes a severe public relations test for the department. Acts of civil disobedience are a staple of the American political scene as well, and, while they experienced their heyday in the age of the Berrigan brothers and Vietnam protests, clergymen and nuns with hammers are arrested with some regularity as they seek to enter secure U.S. missile sites. Again, however, these incidents are routine in a sense, and they have done little to dampen the overall endorsement of the American populace for defense readiness and the facilities needed to guarantee this result.

Politically, this situation represents the normal operation of our democracy, and this operation occurs with a regularity that masks the truth that it has been earned only by long and deep experience. Even in the case of Vieques, the practitioners of protests followed a well-rehearsed formula of protest, arrest, publicity and speechmaking that is by now quite familiar. Most civil protests fail, of course, and those that succeed typically do so only because they are the tip of an iceberg of social feeling or of a cause that is simultaneously moving a phlegmatic public from passivity to conviction for change. The civil rights movement of the 1960s comes to mind as the premier example of a protest movement that succeeded because it was much more than a protest and because it eventually tapped a deep reservoir of belief in the majority of citizens.

The Vieques protest was wrapped up in larger issues, including environmental contamination and, for some, the idea that this Caribbean island close to Puerto Rico could yet become a flourishing destination in its own right. Closure of the bombing range became the position of the major political parties on the island, but a Pyrrhic victory ensued because Puerto Rico's political powers are not captains of their own fate, but crew members aboard a ship steered by a curious compact. Affection for the United States, a feeling of shared faith and a shared future, is dominant in Puerto Rico, but there are times and places, and Vieques is one of them, when the streak of emotion in every citizen there that the country occupies a place of indentured service surges to the fore.

Suppose, in turn, what might have happened if Puerto Rico were an independent nation. Entertaining this option in the context of Vieques is a highly speculative proposition, of course. *As San Juan Star* columnist John Marino pointed out, however, it is not as if Roosevelt Roads had no other use for the American Navy than the nearby training and bombing range. He points out that Puerto Rico is the near-neighbor of an "outer range consisting of 200,000 square miles of open ocean," an area "that has been used for weapons testing, fleet maneuvers and submarine training."[16] In addition to the DEA, the base has also been used by Army Special Operations units and the U.S. Coast Guard. While Navy officials, under force of necessity, have taken steps to relocate the functions carried out at Roosevelt Roads, former Chief of Naval Operations Jay Johnson was unstinting in calling the base the "crown jewel" and the "world standard" of military training areas. It was, according to Heritage Foundation analyst Jack Spencer, "the only training area in the entire Atlantic Ocean where the Navy and Marines can engage in land, air and sea exercises that closely simulate combat."[17]

A quick glance at a map shows that Puerto Rico is hundreds of miles closer to Liberia than the continental United States, to name just one current hot spot. Only a more detailed map shows how close the island is (only 75 miles) to the deepest waters of the Atlantic. Only a specialized FAA map would show that Vieques is not located on any routes used by commercial air traffic. All of these factors combined to make Roosevelt Roads the logical choice for location of the U.S. Navy's South Atlantic Command. Were Puerto Rico independent, and issues of sovereignty no longer a burr under its saddle, the strategic value of the island and the U.S. presence there would be determined, as it were, in the marketplace. The United States operates bases around the world that have been established by the confluences of modern history, including warfare, but are now operated on the basis of treaty agreements and defense pacts that are subject to renewal and negotiation. In the context of Europe, the United States operates our air and sea bases at Rota, Spain, and Verona and Naples, Italy, and the principle of consensus applies. The United States pays the bulk of the freight for these sites, and particular uses of them (overflight, for example) are subject to review by each nation in the alliance in particular settings.

An independent Puerto Rico would be free to negotiate with the United States on the use of its territory for mutual and hemispheric defense purposes. Its hand would be significantly strengthened in such a circumstance, and while there are always advantages to being a superpower in any bargaining context, Puerto Rican officials would have the maximum opportunity both to lead their nation responsibly on this subject and to obtain the "consent of the governed" on any arrangements they reached with the United States. Perhaps more important, the tangle of international and domestic politics that Puerto Rico represents would be simplified, and the notion of partnership, which has served the mainland and the island well in many contexts, might actually drive a new era of economic and strategic cooperation in the Caribbean. Puerto Ricans of all political persuasions have never felt fully respected by their European colonists and their American semi-colonists. Nonetheless, they have seen the potential of freedom and close cooperation with the United States. Advancing as equals, with common opponents like communism and the cartels, could usher her in a healthier relationship that would radiate throughout Latin America to the benefit of all concerned.

This truth should not be obscured just because such a relationship has not always been the goal of independence advocates on the island. In this regard, a few comments on the role of the Catholic

Church are in order. One of the common perceptions of Puerto Rico, of who is a Puerto Rican, is a belief that the island is predominantly Catholic, and conservative Catholic, owing to its Spanish heritage. At one time, and for many decades, this perception would have been true. It is only nominally true today. Christopher Columbus's experience with Puerto Rico was glancing, but to touch was to possess in the New World, and the reach of the Spanish monarchy was reinforced by ecclesiastical power. In May 1493 Pope Alexander VI granted exclusive authority over the discovered lands to the Catholic kings of Spain, a position that rankled England and France and did nothing to deter ferocious competition among the European powers. That competition spawned sporadic attempted invasions of Puerto Rico by, in turn, France, England, and the Netherlands, but none of these incursions succeeded and the island remained in Spain's hands as an outpost of colonialism for more than four centuries.

Puerto Rico was, in fact, the first Catholic see, or diocese, in the New World. It also had a papally appointed role in the protection of Catholic orthodoxy, as Bishop Alonso Manso was made Inquisitor of the Indies in 1519, a role the diocese maintained until the function was transferred to Cartagena in the early 1590s. The dedication of the island, and ultimately, in an inversion of names, its capital city to John the Baptist epitomized the determination of the Spanish to evangelize as they explored, to impart spiritual riches as they sought material riches. The building of churches, which would eventually dominate town squares throughout the island, was begun when Ponce de Leon erected a wooden chapel at Caparra and King Ferdinand provided for the establishment of a monastery and chapel in 1511. The Catholic Church in Puerto Rico coexisted with the subjugation of the island's Indian and Negro population, ensuring that they received Christian instruction and accepted Christian rites. A first convent for women was opened much later, in 1651.[18]

The Church reinforced social bonds with the people, even though it did not disturb the institutions of slavery throughout its early history in Puerto Rico. Two hospitals for the indigent were built in the 16th century, the Hospital de San Alfonso in San Juan and the Hospitales de la Concepcion in San German. Bishop Manso also believed in education and opened the first grammar school on the island. In the late 1600s Bishop Francisco Padilla established an elementary school in San Juan. He believed so strongly in the importance of literacy that he even considered penalties for parents who did not send their children to receive this free education, and he petitioned the crown to fund clothing for the children to allow them to attend. The Dominican Order, which was founded in the island in 1521, established a house of study and a library that served both laymen and potential clergy and that historical sources praise for their academic quality.

Throughout the Spanish colonial era, Madrid and Rome were mutually reinforcing epicenters in the life of Puerto Rico. In the late 1890s, before the Spanish American War, Puerto Rico managed to achieve a real measure of autonomy. The renowned political figure and journalist Luis Muñoz Rivera led Puerto Rico's Partido Autonomista (autonomist party) in its drive to convince Spain to grant the populace new political rights and local control. The aims of the autonomists were largely achieved in November 1897 with the establishment of a charter that created a bicameral legislature for the island. While the king would continue to appoint a governor general as chief executive with various appointive powers of his own, the elected legislature had new power to devise laws for Puerto Rico in many areas. This experiment was abruptly halted by the war between the United States and Spain. The autonomist legislature convened on July 17, 1898. Seven days later American forces landed on the island.

The new territorial status for Puerto Rico signaled a new era in relations between the government and the Catholic Church. Separation of church and state along the lines of the U.S. model became the norm, and while the Church retained a powerful role among the people and their leaders, it typically played no direct role in government. Given its presence among the people, however, the impact of the Church on Puerto Rican laws and mores was considerable, and this included economic issues. From the time of the papal encyclical *Rerum Novarum* (Leo XIII, 1891), which set forth a vision of the appropriate roles of capital and labor, rejecting atheistic Marxism and worker exploitation alike, the Catholic Church elaborated a theology of economics that had worldwide impact. In Puerto Rico, that impact was felt most strongly through the beliefs of Luis Muñoz Marin, who steered his middle course of commonwealth and economic development with the support of the New Dealer Rex Tugwell and, two decades later, John F. Kennedy's Alliance for Progress.

Muñoz Marin rendered the influence of Catholic social teaching on his political philosophy in very clear terms in his final State of the Commonwealth message in 1964. Here Muñoz Marin drew directly upon Pope John the XXIII's encyclical *Mater et Magistra*, setting forth a definition of social progress that encompassed not only economic growth, education and personal health, but also a vision of neighborliness and community harmony rooted in religious values. Muñoz Marin specifically endorsed the notion of a "family salary," a concept that Catholic thought had advanced as a means to ensure the protection of mothers and the education of children. The idea of the family salary was to secure the family's income through the employment of a head of household, typically the father, with wages sufficient to support the entire family.

Had the role of the Catholic Church in Puerto Rican political affairs continued to manifest itself through the ebb and tide of ideas, and not the ad hoc forays of individual bishops pursuing their preferences, negative effects all around might have been avoided. One particularly consequential series of events occurred in 1960. After the Spanish-American War, despite the strength of the Church in Puerto Rico, no native clergyman had attained the rank of bishop. The bishops were exclusively North Americans. Then-Bishops James McManus of Ponce and James P. Davis of San Juan made an unusual foray into political life with at least two goals. One was to introduce religious instruction into island schools, and the second was to resist the dissemination of birth control and sterilization information and practices. Bishop McManus had one other motivation: he was a strong opponent of commonwealth status and believed that Puerto Rico should seek statehood.

At a rally held in May 1960, Bishop Davis went further, criticizing the Popular Democrats (PPD) under Muñoz Marin and calling for the formation of the Christian Action Party (PAC). The initiative backfired. In November 1960 the PAC achieved only 52,096 votes, less than one-eighth of the PPD's tally. Only the *independentistas*, accustomed cellar-dwellers, finished behind the bishops' handmade party. The result was a bitter lesson for McManus and Davis. PPD representatives quietly complained to Pope John XXIII at the Vatican and, shortly thereafter, both clerics were reassigned away from the island. From that time forward, local dioceses have been led by men of Puerto Rican heritage.

While this abortive political gambit occurred on behalf of statehood, the Church has occasionally lent tacit support, as it did on the Vieques matter, to forces whose focus is criticism of the United States and achievement of independence. As poll after poll, and multiple plebiscites, have shown, opposition to the United States and desire for independence are not the view of most Puerto Ricans. Affection for and identification with the mainland, despite the tensions of status, whatever term is applied to it, be it territory or tutelage, compact or commonwealth, cannot be interpreted as anti-Americanism. Some critics point to the elevation of the Puerto Rican flag and its display in competitions with the United States (indeed it is notable that Puerto Rico even fields teams in competition with the United States in events like the recent Pan American Games, where Puerto Rico beat a U.S. college team in Santo Domingo in what Michigan State Coach Tom Izzo called a "hostile environment") as signs that the island's loyalty is questionable. A yearning for recognition and appreciation, however, should never be mistaken for disloyalty; otherwise, Texans' and other state residents' devotion to their state flag should be taken as subversive.

Misreading the public mind has certainly begun to impact the Catholic Church in Puerto Rico. Having a wrongheaded idea of the nature of the Puerto Rican is not confined to secular institutions and leaders. While the moral conservatism of the Church stills tracks strongly with the values of the people, the Church has seen its sway on the island weaken over time. Some of this is due to the same forces of consumerism and secularization seen throughout the developed countries. Some is due to the influence of the growth of other religions, particularly Protestant denominations that have steadily evangelized the island for their own creeds over a century of religious freedom in Puerto Rico. Some of it is also likely due to perceptions of the Church's role in certain social questions, including its cooperation in *mejorando la raza* and the flirtations with anti-American figures.

Most mainland sources, including the *CIA Factbook 2002* and *The Catholic Almanac*, published by Our Sunday Visitor, continue to describe Puerto Rico as predominantly Catholic, with the percentage of the population listing an affiliation with the Church in the range of 80 to 85 percent. As on the mainland, this affiliation for many is like listing ethnic extraction, suggestive of influences but not determinative of behavior. Sharp distinctions exist in worldview between those who attend church on a regular basis and those who do not. Polls put the Catholic population at roughly 50 percent. Other religions, Pentecostals, Lutherans, Jehovah's Witnesses, and smaller populations of Jews and Mormons exist on the island and some are growing rapidly.

It would be a mistake, however, to conclude that these changes signal a wholesale liberalization of Puerto Rico, at least on social questions. On economic issues, the island has relied in no small measure on activist government, both on the spending and tax side of the equation. As noted above, Catholic ideas of social welfare, the dignity of the worker, and community have influenced the politics of the people and ensured that mistrust of government as a populist theme never took hold on the island. Puerto Rico's political disposition is thus more northern than southern in terms of comparison to U.S. states; it could be said that, despite its relative poverty, it is more Minnesota than Mississippi. Culturally, however, it is more Mississippi than Manhattan.

This truth can be seen in the results of a poll conducted by Wirthlin Worldwide in May 1998 for the Citizens Educational Foundation. The poll found that 64 percent of Puerto Ricans consider themselves to be conservative on social issues. Electorally, voters said they support "moderate to conservative" candidates and that they vote for the candidate and not the party. Some 80 percent of registered voters said they planned to go to the polls, a participation rate unheard-of on the mainland and typical of Puerto Rican elections.

The socially conservative disposition underscored in the poll was reflected in the numbers on particular questions. Fully 82 percent of the respondents said they support policies to protect the life of the unborn (anti-abortion). Three of four voters support mandatory sentences for serious crimes. As on the mainland, 77 percent support policies to reform the welfare system (this was subsequent, of course, to the dramatic welfare reform bill enacted by a conservative Congress and signed into law by President Clinton in 1996). The supportive numbers on other social questions are also impressively high: for school prayer, 91 percent; for school vouchers, 83 percent; favoring right-to-work laws, 82 percent; for a strong national defense, 78 percent. These are numbers characteristic only of religiously conservative states on the mainland – of Idaho, Louisiana, and Arkansas. Catholicism, despite its demographic weakening, plays an historical role here. As Maria Teresa Babin wrote even of those who have left the island, "[F]or every Puerto Rican and his or her descendants, Catholicism is the spiritual and moral guide that shapes their understanding of evil and goodness and all the actions and reactions of human beings." [19]

Who would the Puerto Rican be politically if the illusion of commonwealth dissolved and a new course were chosen? Speculation about the implication freezes many politicians and inspires a few. Most political leaders want sure things. They devise congressional districts to maximize the number of secure seats for their party. They do this whether they are Republican and Democrat, and they operate with a relatively free hand within the constraints of the Voting Rights Act and U.S. Supreme Court decisions that condemn race-conscious districting and promote the principle of one-man/one-vote. Politicians also resist sure things that cut against their interest. A logical case can be made against statehood for the District of Columbia, for example, but a conclusive political argument is made for Republicans by the mere fact that full voting rights for the District would mean two new Democratic senators and one new House Democrat, all three likely very liberal for as far as the eye can see.

Historically, the more conservative, or Republican, party in Puerto Rico has supported statehood. The late Luis Ferre, who died at age 99 captured the governorship of Puerto Rico in 1968, two years after his longtime friend and ally, Ronald Reagan, won his first election for governor of California. Ferre ran as the candidate of the newly christened New Progressive Party (PNP, following the acronym in Spanish), the successor to the Republican Statehood Party Ferre and his brother-in-law, Miguel A. Garcia Mendez founded in 1952. The Popular Democrats (PPD) have a longer heritage and are equally intense in their support for retention and elaboration of commonwealth status. Since 1963, when the visionary Muñoz Marin left the governorship, the PNP has occupied the governorship of Puerto Rico for 20 years and the PPD for 18. This 50-50 division of rule tracks closely the most recent divisions in the 1998 plebiscite on Puerto Rico's future.

Over-simplification of Puerto Rican politics is always a mistake. Ferre's years in office coincided with the term of Lyndon B. Johnson, and the statehooders sought to increase the flow of federal funds to the island under the Great Society. They saw this as equal treatment for Puerto Rico as it moved from dependent status to statehood, where access to federal programs would be as comprehensive as any other state's. When President Ford was in office and promoting statehood, the island was electing Hernandez-Colon, who resisted Ford's policies and followed the PPD's platform of building upon and improving commonwealth status. The PNP and PPD split the governorship during President Reagan's term, and Pedro Rosello, pro-statehood and the leader of the PNP, was governor during the entirety of Bill Clinton's two terms in office. To make matters more confusing, Rossello who was perceived as a republican, "caucused" with the Democratic Governors' Association, was close to Vice President Al Gore, and endorsed Hillary Clinton for Senator from New York.

The current governor, Sila Calderon, the island's first woman governor, hails from the PPD. She has been outspoken on ending the U.S. presence in Vieques, a champion of commonwealth like her political forebears, but she has also consistently and steadfastly proclaimed her independence from both the national Democratic and Republican Parties. In July 2002 she announced her intention to help register some 700,000 Puerto Rican voters who live in the United States but do not vote, even though they can vote for every elective office in the jurisdictions where they live. She told *The Orlando Sentinel* that her goal was to encourage Puerto Ricans to exercise their political clout in a nonpartisan way. "For good reason," *The Sentinel* commented, "she has enough on her hands with island politics."[20] Even so, it is common knowledge that non-Cuban Hispanics in the States tend to vote for Democrats, who may differ with them on religious and family values but support them on labor issues and government services.

The major party platforms in the United States have, for Democrats and Republicans alike, broadly endorsed "self-determination," but there are significant differences between the tenors of the party's positions. In 2000 the Democratic platform adopted in Los Angeles once again affirmed that Puerto Ricans "are entitled to the permanent and fully democratic status of their choice."[21] In a sense, after three island-wide votes over a 30-year period, this statement seems self-evident. The platform goes on to say, in similarly elliptical language, "Democrats will continue to work in the White House and Congress to clarify the options and enable them to choose and to obtain such a status from among all realistic options." The problem with this assertion is that there are varying levels of realism, including constitutional realism and economic reality. As continued commonwealth status has moved below majority sentiment, the recognition seems to be dawning that what the Constitution may allow is economically unrealistic for a populous island struggling to define its future.

The Republican Platform, like the Democrats' since the Truman presidency, also endorses self-determination for Puerto Rico. However, the text adopted in Philadelphia in August 2000 nods twice in the direction of Puerto Rico's admission to the Union, if that is the choice of the people. Procedurally minded as always, the GOP affirms that the ultimate fate of Puerto Rico rests with the U.S. Congress, which "has the final authority to define the constitutionally valid options for Puerto Rico to achieve a permanent status with government by consent and full enfranchisement."[22] Indirectly, the Republican platform is highlighting that Congress in the exercise of its full authority now permits Commonwealth status at its discretion. Every measure of self-rule that Puerto Rico has elaborated, from having its own legislature, to the election of its governor, to the appointment of nonfederal judges, could be rescinded by an act of Congress. Every idea to "clarify" and extend commonwealth status is an idea to limit the role of Washington without limiting the discretion of Washington, because Congress cannot abdicate such ultimate authority without amendment of the Constitution's territorial clause.

The key word that both platform planks use is "permanent." It can be argued that no legal arrangement in this world is permanent. Nations and borders come and go, as the shifting cast of characters at the United Nations during its brief existence attests. Nonetheless, the only reasonable meaning of "permanent" in the constellation of options for Puerto Rico is the choice between statehood and independence. On the one hand, statehood would offer Puerto Rico the chance to interact with the national government along the same lines of federalism traversed by 50 other entities, each with long experience in nurturing and developing state prerogatives vis-à-vis the national government. As an independent nation, Puerto Rico would very likely behave like the best of neighbors, friendlier even than Canada and certainly no outpost of revolution like Cuba. The point is, however, that it would be sovereign to determine its path, and the change would be, in all normative international usages, permanent.

The stance of commonwealth advocates is often phrased in terms of seeking a different kind of permanence, a continuity of culture that, they argue, would be destroyed if the United States were to "absorb" Puerto Rico. "Absorption" conjures up images of macrophages overwhelming unwelcome bacteria. In the context of Puerto Rico's future, it is hard to see how this term has any real meaning. To begin with, it is ironic that the political left, with all its rhetoric (in certain contexts only) about the irrelevance of differences among human beings, would advance the idea that ethnic and cultural distinctives must be preserved at all costs. Either such differences matter, or they do not. The truly aggressive left seeks a "diverse" condition in which each person is a citizen of the world with precisely the same personal value of never imposing a value on others. In this the left is insincere, because, of course, it is anxious to impose all kinds of values in the economic and personal sphere.

Second, it is highly dubious that, of all the options available to it, Puerto Rico will find its cultural distinctives best preserved by commonwealth status. Independence would clearly seem to offer the most secure course for ensuring that political, social and artistic traditions develop on the island according to internally generated standards and influences. Commonwealth can be and is a kind of one-way financial street, in which Puerto Rico draws net benefits from the mainland it does not repay in federal income taxes, and a handful of mainlanders, primarily drug companies, draw benefits to themselves that outstrip what the island receives. Whatever the merits of this economic arrangement may be, they are not in the area of cultural preservation. Culture, especially popular culture, cannot be a one-way street, and the coming and going on the island by its U.S. citizen population ensures that the emanations of popular culture will flow both ways, north and south.

Finally, it can be argued that Puerto Rican culture is not the Spanish monolith some would depict it to be, that the island already is a kettle of influences from many nations, a modern locus with all the demographic variety of the states, at least of certain states that are often heralded as exemplars of the polyglot American future. I may write with some prejudice on this matter because I am a Yugoslavian-born ethnic Russian, but this point of view is not unique to this work. Most other Spanish colonies in the New World had a higher proportion of Spanish inhabitants than Puerto Rico. Columbus did not make much of his visit to San Juan Batiste and devoted much more time and attention to other places, like Hispaniola. Madrid's other small colonies, Cuba and the Dominican Republic, for example, were blessed with more plentiful resources than Puerto Rico. The latter had arable land to go with favorable climate, allowing them to establish plantations and to grow sugar, coffee, bananas, and coconuts. Puerto Rico, in contrast, was very mountainous in its interior with a limited amount of tillable land.

As a result, though some of the early land grants, the *mercedes de tierra*, were for plots as large as 200 acres, Puerto Rican farms were generally small and widely dispersed and the farmers could afford only a small number of slaves who, with time, integrated into the farmers' families. Puerto Rico lingered through the years as a shabbier place than most other Spanish colonies, earning well its sobriquet of the "poorhouse of the Caribbean." Marshal Alejandro O'Reilly, a favorite of the Spanish King Charles III, was dispatched to Puerto Rico in 1765 to examine conditions there, including its economy and fortifications. His report to the crown that year fully analyzed the colonial failure that Puerto Rico had become. In Puerto Rico O'Reilly found a population of nearly 45,000, only one of every nine of whom remained slaves. The island was characterized by laziness, a cadre of sailors who had fled their ships and were using the island's mountains as hideaways, and smuggling enterprises that O'Reilly could not help but admire for being "punctual" in their dealings with overseas English and Dutch markets.

O'Reilly recommended a number of reforms designed to increase legitimate trade. He also recommended that uncultivated land be returned to the crown, where it could be reissued to investors who were to be enticed from overseas to establish plantations. O'Reilly recognized that the success of slavery depended upon demographics; in order to have a significant number of slaves to work farms during their productive years, it was necessary for the slave owners to support a much larger population of children and elderly unable to work (an interesting parallel to our own social security problem). Thus, as he did in Louisiana, O'Reilly promoted large land grants to individuals who would come to the territory and bring African slaves with them (enslavement of the Indian population was barred by law). O'Reilly offered 1,000 acres to any immigrant to Puerto Rico who brought with him 125 slaves. An additional 10 acres was awarded for each additional slave.

This policy resulted in a huge influx of foreign slave owners to Puerto Rico from countries like France, Corsica, Italy, Germany and other European countries, as well as from the United States. This changed the demographic face of Puerto Rico and differentiated it from other Spanish colonies. The island acquired a cosmopolitan flavor that other Spanish colonies did not possess, and its ethnic composition became closer to that of America than to that of other colonies. O'Reilly's policy failed to transform Puerto Rico economically, but its cultural impact was extensive. This is not to say that Puerto Rico's Spanish heritage is not a point of great pride and a focus of the arts and political activism. The history of English language usage on the island underscores this; as late as 1991 the Popular Democratic government attempted to remove English as an official language. There is more to culture, however, than language, as emotional an emblem as it may be.

Meanwhile, the demographic forces driving the Western Hemisphere's populations closer together, where they inhabit the same territories, cross-pollinate daily habits and tastes, discuss and share similar notions of human rights and political freedom – these forces are far more powerful than the mini-powder keg issues that drive these related peoples apart. The century that Puerto Rico has occupied a place of colonial subservience to the United States has seen more positive than negative changes in these areas on both sides of the relationship. Prosperity is part of the reason. Tensions have always existed in the Americas between established groups and new arrivals, whether Irish or Jewish, Russian or Puerto Rican. The ability to take advantage of opportunity, to found businesses and build neighborhoods, to raise children who love their country and salute a common flag has been the gateway to the relaxation of prejudices against wave after wave of newcomers.

The verses from *West Side Story* quoted at the beginning of this chapter epitomize the prejudice, rooted in the island's crowds and poverty and their migration to New York, that characterized an earlier era. In its own way, an over-emphasis on Puerto Rico "culture," a culture that is far more diverse and "American" than some political forces care to admit, is an anachronism, a way to hold onto a past that had more than its share of sorrow and failure. The romantic figure of the *jibaro*, the man of the soil, should never disappear from Puerto Rican consciousness, anymore than that the ideal of the sturdy yeomanry should disappear from Americans' consciousness of their earliest conceptions of democracy and independence. It would be wrong, foolish, and impossible for these conceptions to dominate a future that looks to affluence, urbanization, and modernization as the touchstones of the human future.

In this regard, an element of common culture that has united Puerto Ricans, indeed all of the Caribbean and the United States, is worthy of special mention: that is, baseball. A whole new chapter in the history of Puerto Rico, which already has a rich story to tell about its role in the American pastime, seemed to open when Major League Baseball announced that the troubled Montreal Expos would play quite a few home games in San Juan in 2003. In Puerto Rico, the "Boys of Summer," as Roger Kahn deemed them in his renowned book, are also the boys of winter. The game goes on year-round on the island, as it does in the Dominican Republic, Cuba, Mexico, Panama, and Venezuela. The promise of a warm day and the hope of a hot career have driven thousands upon thousands of young Latinos to the sandlots and clearings in neighborhood after neighborhood. In the 1980s and 1990s, when baseball was losing ground in the U.S. inner city to the asphalt rectangles of basketball, the lure of the Big Leagues lost next-to-none of its strength across Latin America.

The informative and adulatory Latino Legends of Sports web site lists some of the many major baseball figures who have made their marks in the United States after paying their dues in the Caribbean. The names are known to every American schoolchild who follows the game: Juan Marichal, Luis Aparicio, Rod Carew, Roberto Clemente, Tony Perez, Luis Tiant, Orlando Cepeda, Lefty Gomez, Livan Hernandez, Benito Santiago, Albert Pujols, Robbie Alomar, Juan Gonzalez, Rafael Palmeiro. It was only fitting, therefore, that Alomar became the all-time runs-scored leader among Puerto Rican players when he passed Clemente on April 12, 2003, in an Expos victory over Alomar's New York Mets — in San Juan. The summer leagues had come to the Caribbean, with the promise of more Expos' home games in 2003 and the tantalizing prospect of an Expos move to San Juan for 2004.

Whether or not that happens, the Expos' visit crossed a threshold, or, to put it more precisely, turned a threshold into a two-way passage. It does not take a detailed examination of biographies for any baseball fan to know that the Latin presence in baseball, begun with the career of Hiram Bithorn in the 1940s, has now become permeation. Latin players represent roughly a third of all major league rosters, up from just 13 percent as recently as 1990. These players occupy the pinnacles of the game. Many now consider Alex Rodriguez, New York born of Dominican heritage, the game's top player today. In the summer of 2003, the Latin Legends site could compile wire service reports that highlighted the facts that Hernandez was the National League hurler of the month for July, Pujols was in the midst of a season's best 30-game hitting streak, and Rodriguez was the American League Player of the Month for August.

In coming to Puerto Rico, Major League Baseball was coming home in two ways: to a place that is the origin of 33 current major league players, but also to an island that is U.S. territory, something Montreal is certainly not. Does there not seem to be a natural progression at work here? The number of Latin players in the majors now exceeds by far the number of African-American players. This was not so before 1997, and, in truth, the entry of Latin players (many of whom are of African heritage, of course) into the game's upper ranks has some of the same hallmarks as the entry of African Americans. Every schoolchild knows the name of Jackie Robinson, but prejudice against Latin players has a similar patrimony and similar effects and is not as well understood.

Ozzie Gonzalez has written of the case of Vic Power, a power-hitting first baseman in the Yankee farm system in the 1950s who hailed from Arecibo, Puerto Rico. Gonzalez writes that the Yankees, who considered Power a top prospect, nonetheless gave up on him because of his dark complexion and reports that he dated white women. He was traded in 1954 to the Philadelphia Athletics, without taking a single at-bat in a Yankee uniform. Power went on to become a regular all-star and a fan favorite.

Latin players have also faced the same challenges as African American players when it comes to winning front-office and managerial jobs. This situation persists to the present day. The popular Tony Perez, the great Cuban slugger for the Big Red Machine, survived only a short stint as the club's manager. In 2003 Felipe Alou is the manager of the division leading San Francisco Giants, a team that benefited early on from Latin players like Cepeda and Marichal, but that nonetheless spawned one of the most notorious statements by a manager about his minority players. In 1964, the Giants' manager Alvin Dark created a storm of controversy when he said, "We have trouble because we have too many Negro and Spanish speaking players on this team, they're just not able to perform up to the white players when it comes to mental alertness."[23] This, about a team that depended on performers like Mays, McCovey, Cepeda and Marichal.

Alou, who was born in the Dominican Republic, is pessimistic about the front-office situation changing anytime soon, although it is hard to believe that any sport with designs on a wider audience could afford to shut out leaders from among one third of its players and a substantial part of its fan base. Alou has said, "The numbers of Latino players will continue to mount, but I don't believe that managers will."[24] If he is correct, it won't be because Major League Baseball has not raised expectations. The Expos' homestand in San Juan is the prime example of this. In the summer of 2003, as a decision about the future of the Expos loomed, it was a subtle comment on the changed state of the sport that two of the prime competitors for the team were San Juan and the Washington, D.C. area. If baseball means ultimately to put the Expos in the nation's capital, why the tantalizing games staged on the island? If the waters of San Juan were only being tested, or a hint of the old barnstorming style resurrected, the game risked raising hard feelings.

Most of the players and managers, American or Caribbean-born, involved in the games at *Estadio Hiram Bithorn* were happy to be there and enjoyed their part in a new chapter of baseball history. Hall of Famer Frank Robinson, the Expos' manager, commented in November 2002, "It will be great to play in front of the people down there. They're great fans. I spent nine years down there managing in winter ball."[25] If baseball was looking for more than a chance to pay its respects, or say thanks, if it was hoping for swarms of fans who would demonstrate that a San Juan team would thrive, the 2003 games do not seem to have supplied such a conclusive answer to its Canadian quandary. After two homestands in Puerto Rico, Montreal remained dead last in the Major Leagues for attendance. The club averaged 11,133 fans per game in Montreal, but only 14,216 in San Juan, far below the stadium's capacity.[26]

Bob DuPuy, chief operating officer for Major League Baseball, was at the sport's cryptic best when he said on the eve of the 2003 All-Star game, "Puerto Rico has made a proposal to play all 81 home games in Puerto Rico, and it has not been rejected."[27] To give the baseball owners their due, any decision they make in the areas of expansion and relocation invariably hurts the feelings of several communities that have made intense investments in public relations to attract a franchise. Whether or not San Juan emerges as the first offshore home for Major League Baseball, the events of 2003, and the run-up to them in previous year's exhibition games, are a watershed of sorts. They underscore that in matters near the heart of the American experience, Puerto Rico and the mainland are closer than 1,000 miles of open ocean would suggest. If Puerto Rico ends up waiting for a place in the summer league, it will almost certainly wait a shorter time than the island has waited for a political place in the sun.

Even in baseball, appeals to simple humanity often are the most compelling. The great Puerto Rican-born Hall of Famer, Roberto Clemente, illustrates this truth. The name of the Hall of Fame right fielder for the Pittsburgh Pirates has come, literally, to symbolize the humanitarian character of the sportsman, and it did so in a decidedly international context. Clemente, born in Carolina, Puerto Rico, never forgot his origins and used his prestige to establish a sports center for youth on the island designed to impart sportsmanship and to keep boys and girls away from the temptations of drugs. When an earthquake devastated the Nicaraguan capital in December 1972, Clemente organized relief efforts and personally assisted in carrying them out. A plane carrying him and four others with relief supplies crashed near Puerto Rico, killing all aboard. He had done perhaps all he could do in a baseball career, batting .317 lifetime, winning 12 Gold Gloves and playing in the same number of All-Star games, hitting .310 and .414 in two World Series triumphs for the Pirates.

It will never be known how much more he might have done for the cause of goodwill and closer fraternity between Puerto Rico and the United States. On July 23, 2003, President Bush honored Clemente with the Medal of Freedom, presenting it to his widow Vera at the White House. Bush said simply, "[T]he true worth of this man, seen in how he lived his life, and how he lost his life, cannot be measured in money. And all these years later, his family can know that America cherishes the memory of Roberto Clemente."[28] Indeed, it was three decades after Clemente, the first Hispanic entrant to the Hall of Fame, a man one year away from being named MVP of the World Series, gave his life in service to others. Today Major League Baseball honors its athlete-humanitarian of the year with an award named in Clemente's honor. Even his name means "merciful."

If Roberto Clemente can be a hero to all Americans, honored on the same day with the same medal granted to John Wooden and the late Dave Thomas, founder of the Wendy's chain of fast-food restaurants and a champion of adoption, then "culture" cannot be the boundary that some advocates of commonwealth status say it is. Between the chalk lines of the baseball diamond, in the trenches where freedom is safeguarded, in the aspirations for a better life on well-lit streets and in secure homes, U.S. citizens around the world, in Frankfurt and Frankfort, Peoria and Ponce, pay homage to a common diagram of liberty. It is a liberty that must inevitably lead away from ambiguity toward clarity, away from inequality toward equity, from dependency to self-determination, from artifices of human history to the graces of human dignity. These are the reasons why the bonds between Puerto Rico and the United States must be tied more firmly, held horizontally and steadily, whether through statehood or true Puerto Rican sovereignty.

Commentators on Puerto Rico's modern political history frequently note how often status issues have been thrust to the background in the debates among the island's shifting parties. Necessity has been the mother of this political invention. Issues of economic well-being and challenges like drugs and crime impose themselves on daily life in poignant ways, while status issues seem abstract and irrelevant. The truth is that status is the heart of the matter. Its shadow is cast across every decision of economics and law the island makes, and that same shadow, less potent for the distance it travels, darkens the character of the mainland, too. The United States is not an empire and it ought not to own any territory or people. We have no right to tire of this question, anymore than we have the right to tire of questions about our national security. Patience can be a virtue, a conservatizing influence, but too much patience can be the enemy of progress.

The U.S. government has repeatedly asserted its intention to honor the wishes of the Puerto Rican people, regardless of the status they choose, provided such status is consistent with "the Constitution and basic laws and polices of the United States." This phrase is a contingency that swallows the intent of many Puerto Ricans to this day, the "have your cake and eat it, too" policy of continued commonwealth. Commonwealth is enormously costly to the American people; over the past 20 years alone it has been a $200 billion drain on the American taxpayer. But it has been equally if not more costly for the Puerto Rican people, who are taxed in ways they cannot see, by growth that has not occurred and sound policies that cannot develop and flourish in dependency.

The time for action on Puerto Rico is always now, especially now. The golden apple of freedom will never hang higher than it does today. It would be a great irony if the possibilities of a permanent relationship with the United States should effect Puerto Rico by climactic change in another former Spanish colony, Cuba. While

Castro lives and continues to rule with an iron hand, while Congress upholds the U.S. embargo that has reinforced Cuba's isolation, there is restiveness on both sides of the 90-mile strait between the two countries. It does not take a leap of fantasy to see that modest and perhaps inevitable events, including the aging Castro's demise, could shift mainland attention to an island that has long captured the American imagination. For now, Puerto Rico is the epicenter of U.S. interest in the Caribbean.

It may not forever be so.

CHAPTER 17

More Than a Hero, Less Than a Citizen

Euripides Rubio was born on March 1, 1938 in Ponce, Puerto Rico. Were he alive in the year 2003, he would be reaching retirement age. He might be looking forward to spending more time with his wife or his grandchildren. Captain Rubio died at age 28 in Tay Ninh Province, the Republic of Vietnam.

Capt. Rubio was attached to the 1st Battalion, 28th Infantry of the U.S. Army. He had entered service at Fort Buchanan in Puerto Rico. He was serving as his unit's communications officer when it came under fire from the Viet Cong. Capt. Rubio and his comrades were badly outnumbered. The communist forces raked the American position with machine gun fire and launched mortar rounds and rifle grenades into the midst of the Americans.

Had he remained where he was, Capt. Rubio might have been safe. Instead, he left his position and moved to the area where the firing was the most intense, distributing ammunition, tending to the wounded, and helping re-position the Army defenders. By exposing himself this way, he was wounded twice, but he kept on. When one of the battalion's rifle company commanders was wounded and evacuated, Capt. Rubio quickly took command. Moving among his men to rally their spirits in the face of the devastating Viet Cong fusillade, he was wounded a third time.

When more men were wounded, Capt. Rubio attended to them

when he noticed something that put the company in danger of drawing friendly fire. A smoke grenade that had been dropped to mark the position of the Viet Cong for U.S. air strikes had fallen dangerously close to the American and Republic of Viet Nam lines. Rubio rushed to grab the smoke grenade and reposition it to safeguard his countrymen and our allies, when enemy fire drove him to his knees. Somehow, undeterred, he scooped up the grenade, "ran through the deadly hail of fire to within 20 meters of the enemy position," as the citation reads, and hurled the smoking grenade into the midst of the Viet Cong before collapsing for the final time.

Using the grenade to target their attacks, allied air strikes were directed to destroy the Viet Cong forces and end their assault. As the citation further reads, "Capt. Rubio's singularly heroic act turned the tide of battle, and his extraordinary leadership and valor were a magnificent inspiration to his men. His remarkable bravery and selfless concern for his men are in keeping with the highest traditions of the military service and reflect great credit on Capt. Rubio and the U.S. Army."[1]

Capt. Euripides Rubio died on November 8, 1966. He is one of four Puerto Ricans who have won the Congressional Medal of Honor. All four were killed in action.

Afterword

The last 13 years that I have been involved in Puerto Rico's self-determination have been the most rewarding ones in my life. I have had the opportunity to contribute to what I believe would be a better life for 4 million U.S. citizens. I own property in and have income from both Puerto Rico and from the United States. My U.S. taxes go to subsidize people in Puerto Rico, who pay no federal taxes yet enjoy all the federal benefits that my tax dollars buy. This is both unfair and irresponsible, and it outrages me. Most of all it outrages me because these billions in tax dollars are spent largely due to the maneuvers of pharmaceutical firms trying to protect their $4 billion annual "cut."

My involvement in this process has helped me gain a better understanding and appreciation of the genius of our founding fathers, who developed the model for our democracy. You will probably not find my definition of our democratic system of government in any political science textbook, but this is what I have learned as I have observed it in action.

Our biggest strength (and perhaps our biggest weakness) is that our elected lawmakers and executives are limited to the amount of integrity they can exercise in our system of government. We usually think of integrity as something good. It typically is, but it can also be very evil. If you look at one definition of the word "integrity," it means commitment to one's values and the guts to stick to them. But who decides which values are good for humanity and which are not? Hitler's values reflected his sordid concept of a master race. With that understanding, his actions had "integrity." Thankfully, under our system of government, that definition of integrity would not fly because it would be filtered through the hearts and minds of America's voters.

False definitions of American values have played a major role in our history. "Manifest Destiny" represented the idea that European Americans were superior to Native Americans and had a natural right to America's resources. The execution of that idea contributed to the relocation and extermination of hundreds of thousands of Native Americans.

Before our constitution was written, the Declaration of Independence proclaimed that "all men are created equal" and that they are entitled to "inalienable rights." As a statement of universal values, this document had tremendous integrity. As applied in real time, however, it was literal, not universal, because in the late 1700s women, indentured servants, Native Americans and slaves were specifically exempt from those "inalienable rights." They were not considered "men."

Eventually, as we all know, the definition of "men" was expanded, sometimes under great pressure, to acquire its universal meaning. All those wrongs that were considered "rights" at an earlier time are now history, and our constitution and its provisions continue to evolve.

For more than two centuries, the two forces that drove our government and reflected our contemporary, collective conscience were votes and capital. Every elected lawmaker and executive had to respond to both or he would be out of business. The capital was needed to promote the election of a candidate, and votes were needed to secure the majority. Election reform has been the buzzword of late and as a result, the influence of capital has been defined as evil and corrupt. But before we start condemning capital, let's not forget that it is capital that provides the jobs that put the bread on the table of those who vote. And it is America's freedoms that allow anyone who so chooses to accumulate as much capital as they please.

A candidate who ignored capital would not have the resources to get his message out to the voters and a candidate who ignored the desires of the people who elected him would be shunned at the polls. No candidate could declare, "My conscience and my values dictate this, regardless of what my voters and my contributors may

Afterword

think." That candidate would not even get out of the starting gate.

In our current effort to promote self-determination for Puerto Rico, we sparked initial interest in our cause by using capital, but we had no votes. The only thing that has driven our idea as far as we have advanced it is the limited integrity that our system allowed those brave lawmakers to exercise who believed they were doing the right thing – Republicans like Tom DeLay, Dan Burton, Don Young and Democrats like Dick Gephardt, Bill Richardson, Patrick Kennedy and others like them.

If slaves could vote, would they have voted themselves out of slavery long before the civil war brought their liberation? Eventually, the "right thing" prevailed. That was only because there were people who dared exercise their integrity and in some instances at a great personal cost.

In the end, the cause of self-determination for Puerto Rico will prevail because the "right thing" always does under our democracy.

But unlike the favorite mantra of congress that chants the lie: "It is up to the people of Puerto Rico to decide their future," it is congress that controls that decision. Just like it has for every territory that ever became a state or was given its independence and it's the American voters and American capital that control congress.

So, when will American taxpaying voters (and American capital) finally get fed up with spending over $20 billion a year to support a welfare territory just to enrich a few select pharmaceuticals?

With the Navy's exodus, America's Department of Defense will not have a significant presence in Puerto Rico. To most of us it signifies that Puerto Rico no longer has strategic value to the U.S. So, will Puerto Rico go the way of the Philippines or, will Puerto Rico be asked to pay its fair share of Federal taxes and the 4 million U.S. Citizens be allowed to participate fully in our democratic process?

Only time will determine the final outcome. But until then, both American tax payers and the 4 million disenfranchised citizens who live in Puerto Rico will continue to be shortchanged.

Alexander Odishelidze
San Juan, Puerto Rico
October 2003

Endnotes

Chapter 2
1. Bob Woodward, *The Agenda: Inside the Clinton White House* (Simon & Schuster: New York, 1994), p. 175-176.
2. Ibid., p. 292-293.
3. *National Geographic*, March 2003, p. 40.
4. Ibid., p. 39.
5. Howard Hills, "The Saga of H.R. 856: The 'United States-Puerto Rico Political Status Act," unpublished paper in the possession of the authors.

Chapter 4
1. Office of National Drug Control Policy (2001), *The Economic Cost of Drug Abuse in the United States, 1992-1998*. Washington, D.C. Executive Office of the President (Publication No. NCJ-190636). Accessible electronically at http://whitehousedrugpolicy.gov.
2. Eldon R. Smith, "The Cost of Illness," *The Canadian Journal of Cardiology*, February 2003, Vol. 19, No. 2, available at http://www.pulsus.com/CARDIOL/19_02/edie_ed.htm, visited June 13, 2003.
3. Lorelei Albanese, "Uncle Sam's Billions," *Caribbean Business*, August 14, 2003, in the *Puerto Rico Herald* at www.puertorico-herald.org/issues/2003/vol7n33/CBUncle_Sam-en.shtml.
4. Bureau of the Census, "Federal Expenditures by State," 1981-1993, 1995-1997, Department of Commerce, Bureau of the Census, "Consolidated Federal Funds Report," 1994, 1998-2001; Joint Committee on Taxation, "Estimates of Federal Tax Expenditures," 1986-2001; Department of the Treasury, "The Operations and Effect of the Possessions Corporation System of Taxation," March 1989; General Accounting Office, "Puerto Rico and Section 936" Report GAO/GGD-93-109; in Robert J. Shapiro et al., "The Costs of Puerto

Rico's Status to American Taxpayers," prepared for the American Alliance for Tax Equity, April 2003., p. 8.

5. The federal government's fiscal year and Puerto Rico's fiscal year do not coincide. The federal fiscal year begins on October 1 of each year and ends on September 30 of the following year. Puerto Rico's fiscal year runs from July 1 of each year through June 30 of the following year. This difference, and the use by Puerto Rico of carry-overs from previous year's grants, accounts for variations in the numbers as reported by the federal Office of Management and Budget and Puerto Rico's Planning Board. Unless otherwise indicated, the numbers in this chapter reflect the federal fiscal year.

6. Lorelei Albanese, *op cit.*

7. John Mueller and Marc Miles, "Section 936: No Loss to Puerto Rico," undated article, for Lehrman, Bell, Mueller and Cannon consulting firm, Arlington, Va., circa August 1998, p. 3.

8. U.S. Census Bureau, *The Statistical Abstract of the United States, 2002 Edition*, Washington, DC 2001, Table 1291, p. 806.

9. Lorelei Albanese, *op. cit.*

10. James Dietz, "The Impact of Commonwealth Status on Puerto Rico's Economic Development," in *The Costs of Puerto Rico's Commonwealth Status to American Taxpayers*, prepared for the American Alliance for Tax Reform, April 2003, p. 40.

11. Statistical Abstract of the United States, 2002 Edition, Table 1297, p. 809; Albanese, *op. cit.*

12. *The Family Portrait*, "A Compilation of Data, Research and Public Opinion on the Family" (Family Research Council, Washington, DC 2002). *See* especially pp. 18-20 and pp. 117-121.

13. Emilio Pantojas-Garcia, "The Social Costs of Puerto Rico's Commonwealth Status," in *The Costs of Puerto Rico's Commonwealth Status to American Taxpayers*, prepared for the American Alliance for Tax Equity, April 2003, p. 56.

14. "Puerto Rico Received More than $54 Million from Justice Department Last Year," press release, Office of Communications, Office of Justice Programs, U.S. Department of Justice, April 22, 2003, p. 1.

15. Joanisabel Gonzalez-Velazquez, "Government Announces New Measures to Halt Crime," WOW News, September 4, 2003, reprinted in the *Puerto Rico Herald*, at www.puertorico-herald.

org/issues/2003/vol7n36/Media1-en.shtml.

16. Idem.

17. Pantojas-Garcia, *op. cit.*, p. 71.

18. Idem.

19. Idem., p.74.

20. J. Tomas Hexner and Glenn Jenkins, "Puerto Rico: The Economic and Fiscal Dimensions," prepared for the Citizens Education Foundation, 1998, p. 13.

21. Idem.

22. John Mueller and Marc Miles, "Unemployment and Government Policy in Puerto Rico," Lehrman, Bell, Mueller and Cannon, Arlington, Va., unpublished paper, July 30, 1998, p. 32.

23. Ibid., p. 35.

24. The major political parties do hold primaries in Puerto Rico and voting delegates attend the national party conventions. Republicans, for example, held their 2000 primary in Puerto Rico on February 27. George W. Bush won the primary with 87,375 votes, 94 percent of the total cast. On an island with more than 3.9 million people and a history of higher than average voter participation, the scant voter turnout reflects the cynicism with which the Puerto Rican people greet the fact that they have no say at the finish line.

Chapter 5

1. *A Joseph Campbell Companion*, Diane K. Osbon, editor (Perennial Books, Reprint Edition, 1995), p. 18.

Chapter 6

1. Emilio Pantojas-Garcia, "The Social Costs of Puerto Rico's Commonwealth Status," in *The Costs of Puerto Rico's Commonwealth Status to American Taxpayers*, prepared for the American Alliance for Tax Equity, April 2003, p. 70.

2 James Dietz, "The Impact of Commonwealth Status on Puerto Rico's Economic Development," in *The Costs of Puerto Rico's Commonwealth Status to American Taxpayers*, p. 22; a footnote appearing with this chart cites "Rivera-Batiz and Santiago, 1996, 45; U.S. Bureau of the Census, International database.

3. Vazquez Calzada, *La poblacion de Puerto Rico,* p. 286;

Whalen, *From Puerto Rico to Philadelphia*, Chap. 3; in Pantojas-Garcia, *op. cit.*, p. 62.

4. Pantojas-Garcia, *op cit.*, p. 62.

5. J. Tomas Hexner and Glenn Jenkins, "Puerto Rico: The Economic and Fiscal Dimensions," prepared for the Citizens Education Foundation, 1998, p. 7. Hexner is the chairman of Hex, Inc. and Jenkins is the Director of the International Tax Program at Harvard Law School and Fellow of the Harvard Institute for International Development.

6. Dr. Joseph Pelzman, "Imported Capital Dependency as an Economic Development Strategy: The Failure of Distortionary Tax Policies in Puerto Rico," Occasional Paper Series No. 50, The European Union Research Center, The George Washington University, Washington, D.C., December 17, 2002, p. vi.

7. John Mueller and Marc Miles, "Section 936: No Loss to Puerto Rico," Lehrman, Bell, Mueller and Cannon, Arlington, Va., undated, circa August 1997.

8. Dietz, op. cit., p. 47.

9. Pantojas-Garcia, *op. cit.*, p. 75.

10. *Ibid.*, p. 77.

11. Shapiro, R., et al., "The Costs of Puerto Rico's Status to American Taxpayers," prepared for the American Alliance for Tax Equity, April 2003. Not to paint too rosy a portrait, real average weekly wages have been on the decline in Puerto Rico since 1986, and this trend has continued its steady stair-step downward.

12. Marialba Martinez, "Manufacturing Industry Hopeful of Economic Recovery in FY 2004," *Caribbean Business*, reprinted in *The Puerto Rico Herald*, September 11, 2003 at www.puertoricoherald.org/issues/2003/vol7n37/CBManufIndus-en.shtml.

13. Mueller, J. and Miles, M., "Unemployment and Government Policy in Puerto Rico," Unpublished paper, July 30, 1998, Arlington, Va., p. 2.

14. Hexner and Jenkins, *op. cit.,* pp. 15-16.

15. Hexner and Jenkins, *op. cit.*, p. 46.

16. Pantojas-Garcia, *op. cit.*, p. 69.

17. Hexner and Jenkins, *op. cit.*, p. 17.

18. Pelzman, *op. cit.*, p. 81.

19. Bryan Hiscox, "Princeton U.: Puerto Rico Governor Speaks

at Princeton on U.S. Relations, History," Copyright 2002 U-Wire, reprinted in the Puerto Rico Herald, at http://www.puertorico-herald.org/issues/2002/vol6n16/CalderonPrinceton-en.shtml.

20. Hexner and Jenkins, *op. cit.*, p. 35.

21. Lawrence A. Hunter, "Leave No State or Territory Behind: Formulating a Pro-Growth Economic Strategy for Puerto Rico," Institute for Policy Innovation, Washington, D.C., July 28, 2003, at www.ipi.org/IPIPublications.nsf/PublicationLookupFullText/0ADAB458A7FFB375.

22. Marialba Martinez, "Local Shipping Industry Moves Into 21st Century," *Caribbean Business*, reprinted in *The Puerto Rico Herald*, November 23, 2000, at www.puertorico-herald.org/issues/2003/vol4n47/CBShipping-en.shtml.

23. *Idem.*

24. Jose Martinez, "Puerto Rico Telephone: A New Way of Doing Business," *Caribbean Business*, July 6, 2000, in the *Puerto Rico Herald*, at www.puertorico-herald.org/issues/2003/vol4n27/CBPRT-en.shtml.

25. *Idem.*

26. Evelyn Guadalupe-Fajardo, "Paying the High Price of Crime," *Caribbean Business*, October 12, 2000, reprinted in *The Puerto Rico Herald*, at www.puertorico-herald.org/issues/2003/vol4n41/CBCrime-en.shtml.

27. Joanisabel Gonzalez-Velazquez, "Calderon Reaffirms Policy Against Privatization," WOW News, August 22, 2003, in the *Puerto Rico Herald*, at www.puertorico-herald.org/issues/2003/vol7n35/Media3-en.shtml.

28 Hunter, *op. cit.*

29. Joanisabel Gonzalez-Velazquez, "Calderon: Slight Improvement in Economic Development," WOW News, June 2, 2003, in the *Puerto Rico Herald*, at www.puertorico-herald.org/issues/2003/vol7n26/Media3-en.shtml.

30. John Mueller, and Marc Miles, "Unemployment and Government Policy in Puerto Rico," p. 21.

31. Ibid., p. 5.

32. Hunter, *op. cit.*

33. Jose L. Carmona, "The Little Engine That Can," *Caribbean Business*, July 13, 2000, in *The Puerto Rico Herald*, at www.puer-

torico-herald.org/issues/vol4n28/CBSmallBus-en.shtml.

34. Hunter, *op. cit.*

35. Jude Wanniski, *The Way the World Works,* Gateway Contemporary, 4th Edition (September 1998), p. 299.

36. Ibid., citing Irene Philippi de Soto, "Is There Life After 936 in Puerto Rico?", *The Wall Street Journal*, April 2, 1993.

37. Hexner and Jenkins, *op. cit.*, p. 47.

Chapter 8

1. This discussion owes a great deal to an unpublished dissertation by Sandra Suarez-Lasa, "The Domestic Political Mobilization by U.S. Multinational Corporations; The Protection of the Possessions Corporations System of Taxation, 1976-1986" (Yale University, 1994), UMI Dissertation Services, Ann Arbor, Michigan. The early activity of U.S. business enterprises in Puerto Rico after the Spanish-American War is described in Gordon K. Lewis, *Puerto Rico: Freedom and Power in the Caribbean* (New York: Monthly Review Press, 1963).

2. Arturo Morales Carrion, *Puerto Rico: A Political and Cultural History* (W. W. Norton & Co, New York: 1983), p. 212.

3. Ibid., p. 162, citing Luis Muñoz Rivera, *Campanias Politicas* (Madrid, 1925) 2:136. Muñoz was a leader of a party that became known as the Federalists. They were pro-American in outlook and favored a system of U.S. citizenship with real local autonomy of government for the island. Many aspects of their worldview continue to characterize mainstream Puerto Rican political thought today, even as the use of the island as a factory has continued.

4. Ibid., p. 226.

5 *Detroit Free Press*, May 10, 1953, p. 7 as quoted in Milton Taylor, "Industrial Tax Exemption of Puerto Rico, *National Tax Journal*, December 1954, p. 163.

6. Suarez-Lasa, *op. cit.*, p. 88.

7. *Congressional Record*, July 21, 1982, p. 17235.

8. Suarez-Lasa, *op. cit.*, p. 167.

9. Ibid., p. 192.

10. Public Law 103-66, signed into law by President Clinton on August 10, 1993.

11. Lawrence A. Hunter, "Leave No State or Territory Behind:

Formulating a Pro-Growth Economic Strategy for Puerto Rico," Institute for Policy Innovation, Washington, D.C., July 28, 2003, at www.ipi.org/IPIPublications.nsf/PublicationLookupFullText/OADAB458A7FFB375

12. Statement of Sen. John Breaux (D-La.), on the introduction of S. 1475, *Congressional Record*, September 26, 2001, S 9882.

13. Robert J. Shapiro, "Federal Spending and Tax Benefits for Puerto Rico Financed by U.S. Taxpayers," in *The Costs of Puerto Rico's Commonwealth Status to America's Taxpayers*, prepared for the American Alliance for Tax Equity, April 2003, p. 9.

14. John Marino, "Section 956: Dead on Arrival," "Puerto Rico Report," *The Puerto Rican Herald*, March 15, 2002, at http://puertorico-herald.org/issues/2002/vol6n11/ PRR0611-en.shtml.

15. Ceci Connolly, "An Unlikely Pair Fights for Cheaper Medications," *The Washington Post*, September 1, 2003, A3.

Chapter 9

1. Arturo Morales Carrion, *Puerto Rico: A Political and Cultural History* (W. W. Norton & Co, New York: 1983), p. 134.

2. Letter of Reps. Don Young, Ben Gilman, Elton Gallegly and Dan Burton to the Speaker of the House and President of the Senate, Commonwealth of Puerto Rico, Committee on Resources, U.S. House of Representatives, 104th Congress, Second Session, February 29, 1996.

3. Ibid.

4. Carrion, *op. cit.*, p. 47.

5. "More Details on Calderon Lobbying Expenses Revealed," *Puerto Rico-Herald*, March 1, 2002.

6. Statement of Rep. Dan Burton, *Congressional Record*, March 4, 1998, 105th Congress, 1st Session, H796.

7. Ibid., H785.

8. Ibid., H800.

Chapter 10

1. Web site of Congressman Tom DeLay at http://tomdelay.house.gov/biography.htm, available August 29, 2003.

2. "Puerto Rico: A GOP Death Wish," NR Online Special, September 17, 1998, at http://www.nationalreview.com/daily/

nr091898.html.

3. Statement of Representative Anibal Acevedo Vila, President, Popular Democratic Party (PPD), Transcript of "Workshop 1, S. 472, Puerto Rico Self-Determination Act," Committee on Energy and Natural Resources, U.S. Senate, April 2, 1998; at http://www.puertorico-herald.org/issues/vol2n07/s472-Workshop-980402.shtml.

4. Introductory statement of Senator Frank Murkowski, Transcript of "Workshop 1, S. 472, Puerto Rico Self-Determination Act," Committee on Energy and Natural Resources, U.S. Senate, April 2, 1998; at http://www.puertorico-herald.org/issues/vol2n07/s472-Workshop-980402.shtml.

5. S. Res. 279, September 17, 1998, 105th Congress, 2nd Session, at www.thomas.loc.gov.

6. Statement of the Hon. Pedro Rossello, Governor of Puerto Rico, Transcript of "Workshop 1, S. 472, Puerto Rico Self-Determination Act," Committee on Energy and Natural Resources, U.S. Senate, April 2, 1998; at http://www.puertorico-herald.org/issues/vol2n07/s472-Workshop-980402.shtml.

7. Eric Green, "Hispanics Vote 2-1 for Gore over Bush in U.S. Presidential Election (But analysts say Bush vote from Hispanics is impressive)", Washington File, November 14, 2000; at http://www.usembassy.it/file2000_11/alia/a011140h.htm

8. Fact Sheet, "*No Child Left Behind Act* is Good News for Children and Families of Puerto Rico," White House web site, at www.whitehouse.gov.

9. Ivan Roman, "Pasquera Raises the Flag," *The Orlando Sentinel*, June 21, 2002, reprinted in *The Puerto Rico Herald*, at http://www.puertorico-herald.org/issues/2002/ vol6n25/PesqRaisesFlag-en.shtml.

10. Joanisabel Gonzalez-Velazquez, "Mercado Advocates for His Public Policy on Foreign Affairs," WOW News, August 27, 2003, at http://www.puertorico-herald.org/issues/2003/vol7n35/Media2-en.shtml.

11. "No Seat at the International Table for Governor Calderon," *The Puerto Rico Herald*, August 29, 2003, at http://www.puertorico-herald.org/issues/2003/ vol7n35/ Poll0735-en.shtml.

Chapter 12

1. Eric Gislason, "A Brief History of Alaska Statehood (1867-1959)," at http://xroads.virginia.edu/~CAP/BARTLETT/49state.html.
2. Ibid.
3. Ibid.
4. Statement of Rep. John Duncan, "Sustaining an American Success," *Congressional Record*, Extensions of Remarks, May 8, 2003, E900.

Chapter 13

1. Michael S. Vigil, Statement before the House Government Reform Committee, January 4, 2000, p. 1. Mr. Vigil is the special agent in charge, San Juan Field Division, Drug Enforcement Administration, U.S. Department of Justice.
2. Vigil, *op. cit.*, p. 2.
3. Material on the role of specially designed watercraft during Prohibition is drawn from Donald L. Canney's informative summary, "Rum War: The U.S. Coast Guard and Prohibition," at http://www.uscg.mil/hq/g-cp/history/h_rumwar.html.
4. "ONDCP Fact Sheet: Interdiction Operations," at http://www.whitehousedrugpolicy.gov/publications/international/factsht/ interdiction.html, June 5, 2003.
5. "U.S. Coast Guard Fires at Drug Boats," http://www.helis.com/news/1999/uscgfire.htm, September 13, 1999.
6. John Collins, "Panama Remains Top Container Port in Region," June 3, 2002; *See* http://www.revistainterforum.com/english/articles/060302 collins panama.html.
7. Statement by Michael S. Vigil, Special Agent in Charge, Caribbean Field Division, Drug Enforcement Administration, Before the Subcommittee on Criminal Justice Oversight, Committee on the Judiciary, May 9, 2000, pp. 4-5.
8. Ibid., p. 4.
9. Ibid., p. 1.
10. *Growing Up Puerto Rican*, edited by Paulette Cooper, Foreword by Jose Torres (Arbor House: New York, 1972), p. 125.
11. Vigil, *op. cit.*, p. 2.
12. United Nations Office on Drugs and Crime, *Heroin in the*

Caribbean Region, 2002, http://www/unodc.org/pdf/barbados/caribbean_factsheet_heroin_2002.pdf.

13. Emilio Pantojas-Garcia, The Social Cost of the Commonwealth of Puerto Rico's Development Model, November 4, 2002, pp 22-23.

14. Ibid., p. 23.

15. Vigil, *op. cit.*, pp. 2-3.

16. Robert Becker, "Corruption Finds Fertile Soil in Police Department," *Puerto Rican Herald*, August 24, 2001.

Chapter 14

1. Interview with Mike McDonald, *PBS Frontline*, at www.pbs.org/wgbh/pages/frontline/shows/drugs/interviews/mcdonald.html.

2. Statement of Rep. Ron Paul, "Threats to Financial Freedom," *Congressional Record*, October 19, 2000, p. 1868-69.

3. McDonald, *PBS Frontline*.

4. Website, FAQs, Financial Crimes Enforcement Network, U.S. Department of the Treasury, http://www.fincen.gov/af_faqs.html.

5. Morey Gordon, "U.S. criminals enjoy fun in sun washing dollars in shadowy banks on Caribbean tax-haven islands," Associated Press, in *The Dallas Morning News*. September 13, 1999.

6. "The BCCI Affair," A Report to the Committee on Foreign Relations, United States Senate, by Senator John Kerry and Senator Hank Brown, December 1992, 102nd Congress, 2nd Session, Senate Print 102-140, Executive Summary. This quotation is taken from the final draft version of the report found at www.fas.org/irp/congress/1992_rpt/bcci/01exec.htm. A note accompanying the draft states that it differs only slightly from the formally printed copy of the report.

7. Ibid., at www.fas.org/irp/congress/1992_rpt/bcci/04crime.htm, citing Blum, S. Hrg. 102-350, Pt. 1, p. 61.

8. Idem.

9. Commissioner Robert G. Bonner, Speech to the Egmont Group of Financial Intelligence Units on Tracking Terrorist

Finances, Washington, D.C., June 4, 2003, at http://www.customs.ustreas.gov/xp/cgov/newsroom/commissioner/speeches_statements/archives/oct312001.xml.

10. "Operation Casablanca Continues Its Sweep," *Treasury News*, Office of Public Affairs, U.S. Treasury Department, May 20, 1998.

11. Gordon, *op. cit.*

12. Mike Godfrey, "Puerto Rico Aims to Become International Finance Centre," Tax-News.Com (New York, October 24, 2001) at http://www.tax-news.com/asp/story/story.asp?storyname=5947.

13. "U.S. Customs Service & San Juan 'HIFCA' Dismantle Major Money Laundering and Drug Trafficking Organization: Operation High Wire Results in 15 Arrests in Puerto Rico and California," U.S. Customs Service release, July 12, 2002.

14. Ivan Roman, "Puerto Rican Bank to Pay $21.6 Million Fine over Drug Money Laundering," *The Orlando Sentinel*, January 18, 2003.

15. Editorial, *The Miami Herald*, March 28, 1998.

Chapter 16

1. "American Veterans Committee for Puerto Rico Self-Determination-Heroes," http://www.veteransforpr.com/heroes.htm; web site of the American Veterans Committee for Puerto Rico Self-Determination.

2. Edda Ponsa-Flores, "Citizens Who Can't Vote for President: The Spectacle in Florida Has an Extra Resonance in Puerto Rico," *The New York Times*, December 8, 2000, at http://www.puertoricoherald.org/issues/vol4n50/CitzCantVote-en.shtml.

3. "Roosevelt Roads History and Facts," http://www.navstarr.navy.mil/Homepage/roosevelt_roads_history_and_fact.htm

4. Max Pizarro, "Powerful: San Juan archbishop urges prayers to beatified Puerto Rican in Vieques strife," Online Archive, *Catholic New York*, http://cny.org/archive/ld/ld060701.htm

5. Testimony of Paul Wolfowitz, Deputy Secretary of Defense, Before the House Armed Service Committee, June 27, 2001, at http://www.defenselink.mil/speeches/2001/s20010627-depsecdef.html

6. James G. Lakely, "End of live bombing at Vieques makes base, jobs expendable," *The Washington Times*, July 20, 2003, at

http://washingtontimes.com/national/20030720-115928-5820r.htm

7. Idem.

8. John Marino, "The Bittersweet Vieques Victory," *The Puerto Rico Herald*, January 17, 2003, at http://www.puertorico-herald.org/issues/2003/vol7n03/PRR 0703-en.shtml

9. Idem.

10. Maria Padilla, "Base Closings Will Hit Many Puerto Ricans in Wallet," *The Orlando Sentinel*, January 13, 2003.

11. Joanisabel Gonzalez-Velazquez, "Ceiba Residents Prefer That Roosevelt Roads Stay," WOW News, July 12, 2003, reprinted in *The Puerto Rican Herald* at http://216.219.216.204/issues/2003/vol7n29/RRClosure-en.shtml

12. Monica Somocurcio, "U.S. militarisation of Puerto Rico increases," abridged from Workers World Service at ww@workers.org, at http://www.greenleft.org.au/back/1998/331/331p19b.htm

13. Guillermo Moscoso, "Anti-Drug Radar Should Get Warm Welcome" *The San Juan Star*, Viewpoint, March 12, 1997, p. 50.

14. Associated Press, "Officials: Relocatable Over-The-Horizon Radar Successful," February 13, 2003, reprinted in *The Puerto Rican Herald* at http://216.219.216.204/issues/2003/vol7n07/Media1-en.shtml

15. Joanisabel Gonzalez-Velazquez, op. cit.

16. Marino, op. cit.

17. Jack Spencer, "Vieques Island: Peace vs. Quiet," Knight-Ridder News Wire, April 27, 2001, at http://www.heritage.org/Research/NationalSecurity/ed042701b.cfm.

18. Arturo Morales Carrion, *Puerto Rico: A Political and Cultural History*, see especially pp. 29-31.

19. Ibid., p. 345.

20. Myriam Marquez "Calderon's Voting Push Is Right on The Money, Drive Targeting Florida," *The Orlando Sentinel*, July 25, 2002, reprinted *The Puerto Rican Herald* at http://www.puertorico-herald.org/issues/2002/vol6n32/CaldVotPush-en.shtml.

21. "America 2000: Democratic National Platform: Prosperity, Progress, and Peace," adopted at Los Angeles, California, August 15, 2000; text at www.democrats.org/about/2000platform.html.

22. "Renewing America's Purpose. Together," Republican Platform 2000, adopted at Philadelphia, Pa., July 31 - August 3, 2000; text at www.c-span.org/campaign2000/gopplatform.org.

23. Ozzie Gonzalez, "Latinos in the Major Leagues: The Breakdown 2000," Latin Legends in Sports, June 2000, at http://www.latinosportslegends.com/ LatinsinMLB_2000.htm.

24. Ibid.

25. "Expos to play 22 home games in Puerto Rico next season," November 21, 2002, at http://www.latinosportslegends.com/2002/expos_to_play_22_games_in_puerto_rico-112102.htm.

26. Ronald Blum, "Montreal Expos could play all home games in Puerto Rico next year," July 16, 2003, at http://ca.sports.yahoo.com/030716/6/twqs.html.

27. Ibid.

28. George W. Bush, "President Honors 2003 Presidential Medal of Freedom Recipients," Remarks by the President in Presentation of the Presidential Medal of Freedom, The East Room, The White House, Washington, D.C., Office of the Press Secretary, July 23, 2003, at http://www.whitehouse.gov/news/releases/2003/07/20030723-9.html

Chapter 17

1. "Full-text Listiings of Official Model of Honor Citations," U.S. Center of Military History, http://www.cimy.mil/cmh-pg/mohl.htm.

Index

A
Abu Dhabi, 368
Acevedo-Vila, Anibal, 47, 210, 265, 280–281, 285
Aetna, 97, 100, 161, 358
AFDTA (social club), 386
AFL-CIO, 176
African Americans, 273, 430–431
The Agenda (Bob Woodward), 43
Aguinaldo, Emilio, 305, 306
AIDS. *See* HIV/AIDS
Akaka, Daniel, 316
Alaska, 154, 220, 299, 308–315, 385
Albizu Campos, Pedro, 186, 377
Albright, Madeleine, 384
Alliance for Progress, 420
Alomar, Robbie, 430
Alou, Felipe, 431
Al-Qaeda, 375
Altman, Robert, 367
American Alliance for Tax Equity, 63, 105
American Conservative Union, 234
Americans Veterans Committee for Puerto Rico Self-Determination, 402
Anderson, John, 229
Anderson, Sherwood, 52
Anguilla, 371
Anti-Americanism, 186
Antonsanti, Jose, 362
Aparicio, Luis, 430

Apparel industry, 120, 189, 190
Archer, Bill, 206
Arkansas, 423
Armey, Dick, 258
ASES. *See* Health Insurance Administration
Ashcroft, John, 275, 276
ASSMCA, 85–86
"Associated Free State." *See Estado Libre Asociado*
Association of Caribbean States, 280
Atlanta, Georgia, 384, 389
Atlantic Fleet, 406
Australia, 185
Austria, 385
Autonomic Charter, 221

B
Babin, Maria Teresa, 423
Bahamas, 360
Baltimore Orioles, 391
Banco Popular, 134, 161, 375–377
Banker's Club, 356
Bank Holding Company Act (1956), 373
Banking industry, 202
Bank Secrecy Act (1970), 361
Baptists, 390
Barcelo, Carlos. *See* Romero-Barcelo, Carlos
Barr, Bob, 252, 254

Barrelas, Ruben, 275
Bartlett, Edward Lewis "Bob," 311–313, 315
Baxter Laboratories, 193
BCCI (Bank of Credit and Commerce International), 367–369, 372, 375
Becker, Robert, 345
Behn, Sosthenes, 382
Bennett, William, 155
Bernstein, Leonard, 381
Berrios Martinez, Ruben, 265
Biden, Joseph, 235–236
Big Red Machine, 431
Bilingualism, 252
Bingaman, Jeff, 270
Birth rates, 76
BKSH, Inc., 243
Black, Charlie, Jr., 237, 243, 263
Black Market Peso Exchange, 365–366
Blair House, 224
Blum, Jack, 367
Bolivia, 413
Bonner, Robert C., 372
Boqueron, Puerto Rico, 386
Boriken, 297
Bosnia, 385
Boys Clubs, 98–99
"Boys of Summer," 429
Brazil, 386
Breaux, John, 180, 209–211
Brokerages, 160, 161
Brooklyn, New York, 393
Buck, Pearl, 312
Budweiser, 140
Bumpers, Dale, 387
Bureau of Alcohol, Tobacco and Firearms, 335
Burton, Dan, 15–17, 231, 237, 239, 250, 253–254, 441
Bush, George W., 22, 71, 73, 218, 273–276, 301, 374, 400, 402, 409, 433
Bush Administration (1989-1993), 362
Bush Administration (2001-), 47, 118, 132, 180, 280, 287, 343, 409, 412
Bush-Gore 2000 election, 404
Bustamante, Cruz, 218
Butler-Crawford bill, 223

C

Cabotage laws, 153–154
Calderon, Sila M., 84, 131, 135, 136, 141–142, 154, 208–210, 243, 275, 278–281, 285, 410, 424
California, 20–21, 47, 218, 262, 313, 384
Camacho, Hector "Macho," 382
Cambio de exhange, 364, 365
Cambodia, 250, 251
Campaign Steel Web, 336
Campania de las Indias, 332
Campbell, Ben Nighthorse, 140
Campbell, Joseph, 97, 234
Camp LeJeune (North Carolina), 415
Campos, Albizo, 299
Canada, 242, 426
Canadian Journal of Cardiology, 62
Canney, Donald L., 334
Carew, Rod, 430
Carib, 297
Caribbean Basin Initiative, 168, 203–204, 381
Caribbean Business, 135
Carrion, Richard, 376
Carter, Jimmy, 196
Carter Administration, 146, 196, 205
Caruso, Enrico, 356
Casals, Pablo, 356
Casellas, Salvador, 194
Casiano, Eddie, 40
Castro Ruz, Fidel, 286, 287, 305, 391, 435
The Catholic Almanac, 422
Catholicism, 387, 389, 390, 408, 417–419, 421–423
Cayman Islands, 359, 367
CBO. *See* Congressional Budget Office
Ceiba, 411–412
Celso Barbosa, Jose, 294, 391
Centro de Investigaciones Sociales, 105
Cepeda, Orlando, 338, 348–349, 430, 431
CFC status. *See* Controlled Foreign Corporation status
Charles III, king of Spain, 427
Chemical Works, 183
Cheney, Richard, 147
Chicago, Illinois, 382, 393, 396
Children, 29, 32–33, 66, 76–80, 90, 102, 112, 162, 275, 282, 288, 344, 349,

Index

387–389, 419, 420, 428, 429
Chile, 279
China, 134, 179, 386, 406
Chirstian Seniors Association, 212
Christian Action Party, 420
Christie's, 387
Citizens Education Foundation, 87, 124, 422
Citizenship, 60, 92, 106–107, 145, 222, 223, 235, 240, 242, 264, 270, 278, 282, 284, 294, 296, 298, 300, 317, 392, 395–397, 404
Clemente, Roberto, 382, 430, 432–433
Clifford, Clark, 367
Clinton, Bill, 43, 178, 229, 271, 272, 275, 276, 317, 393, 394, 407, 423, 424
Clinton, Hillary Rodham, 178–179, 393, 424
Clinton Administration, 84, 204–206, 232, 237–239, 276, 343, 401, 407
Club Caborojeno, 53, 54, 234
Cocaine, 329, 331, 334–337, 341
Coffee, 183, 185
Cold War, 406, 413
Colombia, 330, 331, 336, 355, 362, 363, 366, 368, 395
Columbus, Christopher, 297, 396, 406, 418, 427
Commissioner of Financial Institutions, 356
Committee for Unity and Consensus (CUPCO), 278–279
Commonwealth Party, 251
Commonwealth status, 20–22, 41–42, 45, 47, 60–61, 67, 74, 79, 82, 86–87, 89–91, 104–131, 134, 139, 142, 152, 172, 180, 194, 196, 218–220, 223–224, 226–233, 248–252, 263–264, 269–271, 275, 281, 283, 284, 287, 288, 292–294, 296, 299, 300, 306, 313, 396, 405, 414, 420, 421, 423–426, 433, 434
Community-Based School Program, 138
Computable General Equilibrium model, 87
Congressional Budget Office (CBO), 87, 198, 244, 245
Congressional Medal of Honor, 438

Congressional Record, 209
Connecticut, 125
Conrad, Joseph, 275
Constitution (Puerto Rican), 224–226. *See also* U.S. Constitution
Continental Congress, 402
Contract with America, 206
Controlled Foreign Corporation (CFC) status, 66, 88, 122, 127–130, 171, 179–180, 206, 208, 209, 289
Coolidge, Calvin, 181
Coors, 140
Coqui, 217
Cordero, Rafael, 387
Corporate taxes, 80, 88, 151, 188–189
Corsica, 389, 428
Costa Rica, 279
Cox, Chris, 255–256
Craig, Larry, 234–235, 240, 271–272
Crane, Phil, 209, 210, 211
Crawford-Butler Act (1947), 299
Crime, 84–85, 135, 137
Criminal Investigation Corps, 334
Cuba, 171–172, 221, 222, 242, 250, 286–287, 296, 304, 305, 330, 378, 426, 427, 429, 434–435
Cuban-Americans, 218, 273, 286
Cunningham, Randy "Duke," 410
CUPCO. *See* Committee for Unity and Consensus

D

Dark, Alvin, 431
Daschle, Tom, 266
Dauas, Rafael, 412
Davis, Gray, 218
Davis, James P., 420, 421
Davis, Sammy, Jr., 382, 384
DEA. *See* Drug Enforcement Agency
Declaration of Independence, 440
Deferred compensation concept, 160
De Ferrer, Dr., 259
De La Vega, Ivan, 336
Delaware, 403
DeLay, Tom, 239, 258–259, 273, 441
Delgado, Officer, 413–414
Del Toro, Benicio, 382
Democratic Party, 22, 44, 71, 92, 162, 165,

198, 200, 205, 218, 230, 232, 233,
  239, 251, 255, 258, 266, 271, 273,
  287, 294–295, 298–299, 312, 313,
  315, 395, 410, 412, 423–425, 441
Department of... *See* U.S. Department of...
Dependency, 70, 75, 86, 94
Detroit Free Press, 188
Dietz, James, 74, 115, 123
Disease, 63
Displaced Persons (DP) camps, 35–36
Distilled spirits, 183
Distributions to stockholders, 129
District of Columbia, 401–404, 423
Dole, Robert, 178, 198–200, 273
The Dominican Order, 419
Dominican Republic, 168, 279–280, 330,
  339–340, 355, 364, 365, 378, 392,
  395, 427, 429, 431
Dominion status, 185
Donaldson, William, 148
Dorado Beach Hotel, 388
Drug Enforcement Administration (DEA),
  300, 330, 334–336, 338–343, 361,
  412, 416
Drug firms. *See* Pharmaceutical industry
Drugs and drug trade, 45, 62, 83–85,
  329–331, 334–349
Duncan, John, 316
DuPuy, Bob, 432

E
Earned Income Tax Credit (EITC), 89–91,
  245
Economic Development Administration,
  188
Economic indicators, 64, 75, 121
Economic Recovery Tax Act (ERTA), 177,
  197, 198
Economy, 11, 14, 39, 47, 60, 61, 83, 87,
  91, 102, 104–105, 110, 114–115, 117,
  121–122, 125–127, 130–131, 136,
  138, 142, 146–156, 164, 167–170,
  173, 174, 176, 177, 179, 181,
  183–184, 186, 188, 196–197,
  207–209, 229–238, 244, 276, 284,
  285, 294, 307, 331–332, 355, 366,
  372, 394, 403, 407, 409, 412, 427
Ecstasy, 342

Edison, Thomas, 303
Education, 70–71, 73, 78–82, 94, 132,
  137–138, 155, 188, 218, 222, 275
Egmont Group, 372
Eisenhower, Dwight D., 311–314
EITC. *See* Earned Income Tax Credit
Elections Commission of Puerto Rico, 271
Electoral College, 401, 402
Electronics industry, 120, 189, 202
El Morro fortress, 225
El Nuevo Dia, 288
El Salvador, 218
Emancipation Proclamation, 387, 389
Employment, 43, 88–90, 108, 111, 112,
  134, 142, 143, 151, 192, 207, 359,
  420. *See also* Jobs; Unemployment
Energy costs, 135
Engineering, 81–83
England. *See* United Kingdom
England, Gordon, 408
English language/"English First," 222,
  236–238, 241, 243, 246–248, 250,
  252–254, 293
"Enhanced commonwealth" status,
  228–231, 269
Environmental Advisory Council, 136
Environmental Quality Board, 136
EPSCOR. *See* Experimental Program to
  Stimulate Competitive Research
ERTA. *See* Economic Recovery Tax Act
Escobar, Pablo, 368
ESEA, 78
Estadio Hiram Bithorn, 432
Estadistas Unidos (United Stateholders),
  227, 229, 288
Estado Libre Asociado ("Associated Free
  State"), 224–225, 227, 283, 284
Estate taxes, 145, 146, 288–289
Ethnicity, 46, 95–96
Europe, 385
European Commission, 372
European Union, 110, 153, 287
Excise taxes, 139–142

F
Fair Labor Standards Act, 192
Fajardo, 411
FALN, 393

Index

Family, 76–78, 90
Farr, Sam, 253
FAS. *See* Freely Associated States
FBI. *See* Federal Bureau of Investigation
FDA. *See* Food and Drug Administration
FDIC, 358, 359, 365
Federal Aviation Administration (FAA), 416
Federal Bureau of Investigation (FBI), 335, 361, 364, 366, 370, 371, 413
Federal Emergency Management Agency, 86
Federalism, 228
Federal Relations Act (1950), 224
Federal Reserve Bank of New York, 376
Federal Reserve System, 361
Ferdinand, King, 418
Fernos-Isern, Antonio, 224–226, 278
Ferrario Pozzi, Roberto, 376
Ferre, Luis A., 227, 229, 265, 288, 291–292, 299, 423
Ferre, Luis Antonio (son of Luis Ferre), 288
Ferrer, Jose, 382
Figueroa, Orlando, 157
FinCEN, 359, 365, 368
Flag, Puerto Rican, 225, 278
Florida, 218, 273, 286, 337, 356, 360–362, 369, 375, 378, 404, 409
FOMENTO, 176, 188, 189, 194
Food and Drug Administration (FDA), 112, 120, 166
Food stamp program, 74–75, 87–88, 94, 121, 143, 192
Foraker Act (1900), 183, 222, 297
Ford, Gerald, 195, 304, 424
Ford Administration, 146–147
Fort Allen, 412
Fort Buchanan, 437
France, 385, 386, 418, 428
Freedom House, 46
Freely Associated States (FAS), 315–317
Friedlander, Stanley, 108
Frontline, 84
Fuentes, Jose, 393–394

G
G. D. Searle, 193

Gacha, Rodriguez, 368
GAO. *See* General Accounting Office
Garcia, H. S., 375
Garcia, James E., 409
Garcia Marquez, Gabriel, 95
Garcia Mendez, Miguel A., 423
GDP. *See* Gross Domestic Product
General Accounting Office (GAO), 244
General Agents and Merchants Association, 101
Generation gap, 46–47
Georgia (country), 28–30
Georgia (U.S. state), 384
Gephardt, Dick, 441
Germany, 212, 305, 386, 428
Gift taxes, 145–146
Gingrich, Newt, 206, 239, 258–260
Girod, Alberic, 356–360, 363–364
Girod Bank and Trust, 355, 358
Gislason, Eric, 309, 311
Giuliani, Rudy, 84
Globalization, 153
GNP. *See* Gross National Product
Gomez, Lefty, 430
Gomez, Ruben, 388
Gonzalez, Juan, 430
Gonzalez, Ozzie, 431
Gonzalez, Roberto O., 407–408
GOP. *See* Republican Party
Gordon, Kermit, 148
Gore, Al, 238–239, 273–274, 276, 402, 424
Gore, Robert Hayes, 186
Government Development Bank, 188
Graduated surtax, 145, 146
Great Britain. *See* United Kingdom
Great Society, 424
Greenland, 304
Gross Domestic Product (GDP), 110–114, 121, 133
Gross National Product (GNP), 71, 72, 87, 110–113, 123, 190
Gruening, Ernest, 311, 313
G-7 (financial powers), 372
GTE, 134
Guam, 305, 306–307, 315, 316, 404
Guantanamo Bay, 286
Guatemala, 218, 355, 395
Gutierrez, Luis, 233–234, 250, 254, 263

H

Haiti, 168, 330, 339, 378, 392
Hamilton, Lee, 232
Harrison, William Henry, 267
Harvard University, 267
Hatch, Orrin, 211
Hato Rey, 356
Hawaii, 125–126, 253, 299, 312, 314, 316, 403
Health Insurance Administration (ASES), 69–70, 132
Hearst, William Randolph, 221
Heirship laws, 288–289
Hemingway, Ernest, 333–334
Hemmings, Sally, 389
Hepatitis, 343
Hernandez, Andy, 273
Hernandez, Livan, 430
Hernandez Colon, Rafael, 147–148, 194, 195, 281, 288, 424
Hernandez Mayoral, Jose, 281, 282, 284, 285
Heroin, 329
Hexner, J. Tomas, 87, 88, 124, 126, 131, 132, 136–138, 141
High-Intensity Drug Trafficking Areas (HIDTA), 331, 335, 346, 366
High Intensity Financial Crime Areas (HIFCA), 366
Hispanic Americans, 273–274, 281, 288
"Hispanicizing," 47
Hispaniola, 386, 427
Hitler, Adolf, 439
HIV/AIDS, 86, 343
Hoffman, Fritz, 183
Hoffman-La Roche, 183
Holmes, Peter, 168
Holt, Thomas, 134
Holt Group, Inc., 133–134
Honolulu, Hawaii, 154
Hoover, Herbert, 185
Horn, Steve, 250–252
Hospital de San Alfonso (San Juan), 418
Hospitales de la Concepcion (San German), 418
House Appropriations Defense Subcommittee, 410
House Armed Services Committee, 408, 410
House Human Resources Committee, 220, 236, 241, 246
House Interior Committee, 220
House Rules Committee, 236, 246, 248, 262, 313, 314
House Ways and Means Committee, 176, 177, 194, 199, 200, 203, 204, 206, 209, 211
Housing and Urban Renewal Corporation of Puerto Rico, 86
Housing assistance, 90
H.R. 856 (1998), 239, 241–243, 245–250, 252, 255, 259, 261–264, 266, 268, 270, 291, 312, 383
H.R. 3024. *See* Young bill
H.R. 7674 (1950), 224
"Human capital," 71, 72
Hunter, Lawrence A., 136, 208–209
Hunter report, 138, 139, 141, 153, 155
Hurricane Georges, 68, 268
Hurricane Hugo, 86
Hurricane San Ciprian, 185
Hurricane San Ciriaco, 185
Hurricane San Felipe, 184–185

I

IberoAmerican Summit, 279–280, 280
Idaho, 423
Iglesias (labor leader), 387
Immigration, 44, 107
Imperialism, 260
Import duties, 151
Income taxes, 144–145
Independence, 15, 20, 29, 43, 46, 93, 127, 130, 139, 154, 156, 164, 165, 173, 184, 186, 187, 196, 220, 222, 223, 227, 230, 231, 234, 240–242, 248, 250, 251, 254, 263–264, 269, 270, 275, 277–279, 281–285, 293, 296, 298–300, 305, 306, 308, 314, 315, 348, 354, 371–372, 377, 393, 396, 397, 403, 404, 407, 412, 414, 416, 417, 420, 421, 426, 429, 441. *See also* Sovereignty
Independence Party (PIP), 230, 277, 280, 299, 397

Index

Independentistas, 186, 227, 234, 420
India, 166
Industrial Exemption Tax Act (1948), 175, 176, 188, 189, 192
Industrialization, 108
Infrastructure development, 132, 136
Inquisition, 385–387
Institute for Policy Innovation, 136, 138, 155
Insurance industry, 55–57, 97, 100, 102, 160, 161
Intercompany transfers, 191
Internal Revenue Code, 61, 109–110, 127. *See also under individual section number*
Internal Revenue Service (IRS), 116–117, 175, 176, 191–192, 335, 357, 359–363, 369, 370, 375, 376
International Labor Organization, 280
International Telephone and Telegraph Company, 382
Investment, 116–117, 168, 192–193, 202
"Investment strike," 194, 195, 197, 202, 210, 211
Iowa, 313
Iraq, 304, 307, 372, 399, 400
Irrizarri, Louis, 281, 282
IRS. *See* Internal Revenue Service
Israel, 259
Italy, 428
Izzo, Tom, 421

J

Jackson, Jesse, 301, 383, 407
Jamaica, 330, 342
Japan, 310
Japan, Inc., 153
Jefferson, Thomas, 253, 389
Jehovah's Witnesses, 390, 422
Jenkins, Glenn, 87, 88, 124, 126, 131, 132, 136–138, 141
Jews, 386–387, 422
Jobs, 10, 11, 47, 80, 89, 108, 114–115, 117–121, 138–139, 168, 189–192, 194, 202, 205, 207, 209–210, 245, 394, 412, 414, 431, 440. *See also* Employment; Unemployment
Johnson, Jay, 416

Johnson, Lyndon Baines, 227, 263, 424
Johnston, J. Bennett, 199
Joint Committee on Taxation, 201, 205, 210, 211
Joint Interagency Task Force, 300, 336, 413
Jones, William H., 222, 223
Jones Act (1917), 222, 265, 297, 306
Jones Act (1920), 153
Jones Bill, 405
Junta de Planificacion, 114

K

Kahn, Roger, 429
Kansas, 313
Kemp, Jack, 155
Kemp-Roth income tax cuts, 177
Kennedy, Edward, 267
Kennedy, Joe, 383
Kennedy, John F., 144, 283, 381, 420
Kennedy, Patrick, 267–268, 441
Kennedy Administration, 283
Kenya, 372
Keynesian economics, 142, 146, 148
King, Martin Luther, Jr., 303, 392
Klondike Gold Rush, 308
K-Mart, 411
Kosciusko, Thaddeus, 402
Kosovo, 385, 400

L

Labor, 121, 135, 137–138, 176, 188, 194
Laden, Osama bin, 276
Lafayette, Marquis de, 402
Laffer, Arthur, 147
Laffer Associates, 21, 142, 143, 149, 151
Laffer Curve, 147, 150
La Follette, Robert, 182
Lance, Bert, 367
Land ownership/reform, 184, 187
Landrieu, Mary, 270
Language, 42–43, 78–80. *See also* English language/"English First"; Spanish language
La Roche, Adele, 183
Latin America, 363, 366, 371, 374, 394
"Latinos," 395–397
Lau, Alvarez, 358

Lausel, Jose, 400
Leading Cultural and Economic indicators, 64, 75
League of United Latin American Citizens (LULAC), 265
Leahy, William D., 186
LeBron, Lolita, 276
Liberal Party, 187
Liberia, 416
Lincoln, Abraham, 381, 387
Lippmann, Walter, 313
Literacy, 71, 252
Lodge, Henry Cabot, 221
London, England, 366, 371
Longworth, Nicholas, 182
Lopez, Jennifer, 382
Los Angeles, California, 262, 384
Lott, Trent, 211, 263–266
Louisiana, 253, 289, 423
Louisiana Territory, 308, 332
Luis Lugo, Ramon, 237
LULAC (League of United Latin American Citizens), 265
Lutherans, 422
Luxembourg, 368

M
Madrid, Spain, 419, 427
Maine (battleship), 304–305
Maldonado, Alejo, 334
Mambo, 52–53
Manifest Destiny, 381
Manso, Alonso, 418–419
Manufacturing, 108, 112, 114–121, 123, 127, 168, 174–176, 181, 189–191, 193, 202, 207, 219, 243, 245, 403, 411
Marichal, Juan, 430, 431
Marijuana, 336, 342, 348–349
Marine Corps, 410, 416
Marino, John, 410, 416
Marriage, 76, 77, 144, 145, 151
Marshall Islands, 231, 315–317
Martin, Ricky, 301, 382
Martinez, Jose, 134
Massacre de Ponce, 297
Mater et Magistra (papal encyclical), 420
Mays, Willie, 431
McCaffrey, Barry, 335

McDonald, Mike, 360, 361, 363
McGrady, Tracy, 40
McKinley, William, 305, 308
McManus, James, 420, 421
Mechanical products industry, 189
Medalla, 140
Medal of Freedom, 433
Medellin cartel, 368
Medicaid, 70, 87
Medicare, 66, 74, 90
Mercado, Ferdinand, 279
Mercantilism, 332
MERCOSUR, 153, 156
Metropolitan Bus Authority, 69
Metropolitan Life, 55–56
Mexico, 154, 179, 218, 273, 336, 355, 360, 395, 429
Miami, Florida, 360–361, 364
Miami Herald, 378
Michigan, 310, 313
Micronesia, 232, 315, 316
Middle East, 377
Migration (from Puerto Rico), 106–108, 145, 195
Miles, Marc, 71, 89–91, 111, 122, 130, 137, 141
Miles, Nelson A., 216, 217, 221, 405
Military bases, 226. *See also* Vieques bombing range
Military service, 252
Miller Brewing Company, 140
Mills, Wilbur, 194–195
Milosevic, Slobodan, 383–384
Minimum wage laws, 89, 91, 103, 139, 151, 192, 206
Minnesota, 310, 422
Minnie Mouse (cartoon character), 371
MIRA (pro-independence group), 299
Mississippi, 124–125, 261, 263, 331, 422
Miss Universe contest, 382
Mona Passage, 378, 386
"Moncho's Other Family Business" (fictional story), 321–327
Money Mastery newsletter, 162
Monroe Doctrine, 185
Montreal Expos, 429–432
MONY (Mutual of New York), 56
Morales Carrion, Arturo, 405

Index

Morgan, Harry, 333
Morgan, J.P., 309
Mormons, 422
Mortality rate, 76
Moscoso, Guillermo, 413, 414
Moscoso, Teodoro, 194, 384–385
Moynihan, Pat, 43–44, 199, 317
Mueller, John, 71, 89–91, 111, 121–122, 130, 137, 141
Muñoz Marin, Luis, 79, 80, 108, 144, 174, 175, 186–188, 207, 223, 225, 227, 281–284, 420, 424
Muñoz Rivera, Luis, 223, 419
Murder, 84, 85
Murkowski, Frank, 215–216, 263, 265, 266, 291, 292
Mutual of New York (MONY), 56

N

NAEP. *See* National Assessment of Educational Progress
NAFTA. *See* North American Free Trade Agreement
Naguabo, 411
NAP. *See* Nutritional Assistance Program
Naples, Italy, 417
NASD (National Association of Securities Dealers), 160
National Assessment Governing Board, 78–79
National Assessment of Educational Progress (NAEP), 78–79, 137
National Association of Securities Dealers (NASD), 160
National enterprise zones, 155
National Federation of Republican Women (NFRW), 262–263
National Geographic, 45
Nationalist Party, 186
National Review Online Special, 261
National Science Foundation, 80, 82
Native Americans, 440
NATO, 406
Natter, Robert, 410
Navieras, 133–134
Neoricans, 394
Netherlands, 385, 418
Neuberger, Richard L., 311

New Deal, 174, 185, 284, 310
New Drug Applications (NDAs), 112
"A New Friend of Commonwealth" (fictional story), 351–354
New Frontier, 381
New Jersey, 378
New Mexico, 253
New Patriot Act, 373
New People's Party, 229
Newport, Rhode Island, 414
Newport News, Virginia, 414
New Progressive Party (PNP), 86, 133, 148, 229, 230, 237, 265, 277, 280, 299, 410, 423, 424
New Republican Party, 291–292
New York, New York, 358, 363–366, 371, 378, 382, 384, 385, 392, 393, 394, 396, 407, 410
New York Giants, 388
New York Mets, 430
The New York Times, 257, 404
New York Yankees, 431
New Zealand, 136
NFRW. *See* National Federation of Republican Women
Nickles, Don, 211, 263
Nixon, Richard, 146
No Child Left Behind, 73, 78, 155, 274–275
Non-Qualified Deferred Compensation, 160
Noriega, Manuel, 362, 368
North American Free Trade Agreement (NAFTA), 153, 154, 156
North Carolina, 409
Northern Ireland, 372
Northern Marianas, 282
Novello, Antonia, 293
NPP. *See* New Progressive Party
Nutritional Assistance Program (PAN), 74–75, 88, 90

O

OAS (Organization of American States), 287
Ochoa family, 368
Odishelidze, Alexander, 19
Office of National Drug Control Policy, 62

Office of the Commission for Financial Institutions (OCIF), 374
Official languages, 79
Oklahoma, 253, 308
Old San Juan, 376, 387, 405
Olympic games, 262
Omnibus Budget Reconciliation Act of 1993 (OBRA), 205
ONDCP. *See* U.S. Office of National Drug Control Policy
100 Years of Solitude (Gabriel Garcia Marquez), 95
Operation Bootstrap, 78, 105, 108, 112, 123, 142–144, 175
Operation Casablanca, 368
Operation Conquistador, 336
Operation Greenback, 299, 361, 362, 364, 366, 369
Operation Greenquest, 372
Operation HALCON, 336
Operation High Wire, 375
Operation Journey, 300, 336
Operation Lost Honor, 334
Opportunity cost, 122–123
Oregon, 313
O'Reilly, Alejandro, 239–240, 289, 297, 332, 427–428
Orellana, Manuel. *See* Rodriguez Orellana, Manuel
Orengo, Richard P., 399–400
Organic Act, Second (1912), 309
Organic Acts, First (1884), 308
Organization of American States (OAS), 287
Orlando, Florida, 218
The Orlando Sentinel, 47, 376, 411, 424
Oscar Berrios, Luis, 374–375
"Outsiders," 101–102

P
PACs. *See* Political action committees
Padilla, Francisco, 419
Padilla, Maria, 411
Palau, 315
Palladium, 54
Palmeiro, Rafael, 430
PAN. *See* Nutritional Assistance Program
Panama, 279, 357, 358, 362, 367, 368, 405, 429
Panama Canal, 406
Pan American Games, 421
"Panas," 98–100, 160
Pantojas-Garcia, Emilio, 86, 105, 115
Partido Autonomista (autonomist party), 419
Partido Popular Democratico. See Popular Democratic Party
Pasquera, 278, 286
PDP. *See* Popular Democratic Party
Pell grants, 66, 275
Pelzman, Joseph, 110–111, 127, 128, 129
Pennsylvania Avenue, 403
Pentecostals, 390, 422
People (magazine), 382
PER. *See* Republican Statehood Party
Per capita income, 125, 187, 190
Perez, Tony, 430, 431
Perot, Ross, 229
Personal income, 150
Petro-chemicals industry, 189, 190
Pharmaceutical industry, 11, 12, 61, 105, 111, 112, 114, 118–121, 165–169, 172, 176, 178–179, 181, 183, 189–194, 198, 202–207, 210, 212, 233–238, 247, 260, 268, 289, 309, 439, 441
Philadelphia Athletics, 431
Philippines, 181, 182, 185, 221, 242, 250, 285, 304–306
Pieras, Jaime, Jr., 401
Pinero, Jesus T., 223, 297
PIP. *See* Independence Party
Pittsburgh Pirates, 433
Platt Amendment (1902), 222, 305, 306
Plebiscites, 226–227, 231, 232, 239, 242, 271, 298–299
PNP. *See* New Progressive Party
Police force, 84–86, 345, 347, 375
Political action committees (PACs), 199–200
Ponce de Leon, Juan, 297, 418
Ponsa-Flores, Edda, 404
"The Poorhouse of the Caribbean," 392, 427
Pope Alexander VI, 418

Index

Pope John XXIII, 420, 421
Pope Leo XIII, 419
Popular Democratic Party (PDP), 21, 130, 132, 135, 144, 145, 147–149, 174, 187, 188, 194, 208, 210, 223, 224, 227, 229–231, 237, 243, 249, 264, 265, 268–271, 276, 277, 279–285, 299, 396, 420, 423–424
Populares. See Popular Democratic Party
Population density, 81
Portugal, 386
Possessions Corporation System of Taxation, 138, 174, 176, 182, 196
Poverty, 105–106, 108, 121, 124
Powell, Colin, 154, 280, 287
PPD. *See* Popular Democratic Party
Prepa (Puerto Electric Power Authority), 135
Prescription drugs, 74, 94, 212. *See also* Pharmaceutical industry
Price Waterhouse Coopers, 210
PRIDCO (Puerto Rico Industrial Development Co.), 121
"Prietusco" (mulatto artisan class), 389, 391
Prisons, 135
Privatization, 132–136, 141, 151
Prohibition, 333–334
Protestants, 390, 421
PRT. *See* Puerto Rico Telephone
PRUSA. *See* Puerto-Rico-USA Foundation
Public Broadcasting Service, 84
Public Law 81-600 (1950), 225, 282–283, 299
Public Law 447 (1952), 225
Puerto Rican Nationalist Party, 299
Puerto Rican Police, 375
Puerto Rican Regiment, 405
Puerto Ricans in Civic Action, 244
Puerto Rico Cement, 288
Puerto Rico Electric Power Authority (Prepa), 135
Puerto Rico First, Inc., 243–245
Puerto Rico Herald, 270–271, 280
Puerto Rico Industrial Development Co. (PRIDCO), 121
Puerto Rico Self-Determination Act. *See* Young bill

Puerto Rico Telephone (PRT), 134–135
Puerto-Rico-USA Foundation (PRUSA), 178, 202–204
Pujols, Albert, 430

Q
"Quebec argument," 250–252
Quinones, Denise, 382

R
Race, 42
Ramirez de Ferrer, Miriam, 244
Rangel, Charles, 199–202, 204, 205, 211
Rayburn, Sam, 313
Reagan, Ronald, 149, 150, 162, 168, 178, 196–197, 229, 261–262, 273, 423, 424
Reagan Administration, 177, 197, 198, 200, 202, 205, 315
Reagan Library, 263
Referendum (1993), 293
Reform Party (United States), 229
Reforms, 132–142
Regan, Don, 199
Reporters, 257–258
Republican Party ("GOP"), 71, 147, 162, 165, 198, 204, 206, 218, 230, 232, 234, 236, 237, 239, 243–245, 248, 251, 255–256, 258–263, 266, 271–275, 286, 287, 291, 294–296, 298, 309, 312, 313, 391, 412, 423–425, 441
Republican Statehood Party (PER), 227, 229, 423
Rerum Novarum (Papal encyclical), 419
Research and development, 81–82, 112
Resident Commissioner of Puerto Rico, 82, 92, 210
Revenue Tax Act (1921), 175
Rhode Island, 403
Richardson, Bill, 261, 441
Rijock, Kenneth, 371
Rivera, Geraldo, 382
Rivera, Victor, 84, 85
Rivero, Horacio, 293
Robinson, Frank, 432
Robinson, Jackie, 431
Rockefeller, Nelson, 304
Rodriguez, Charlie, 383

Rodriguez Orellana, Manuel, 164, 165, 234, 281
Rodriquez, Alex, 430
Rodriquez, Chi-Chi, 388
Rohrabacher, Dana, 255, 256
Roman, Ivan, 376
Rome, Italy, 419
Romero-Barcelo, Carlos, 21, 141, 148, 149, 150, 152
Roosevelt, Franklin D., 70, 284, 310, 311, 312, 406
Roosevelt, Theodore, 185, 221, 222
Roosevelt, Theodore, Jr., 185–186
Roosevelt Administration (1933-1945), 174, 185
Roosevelt Roads Naval Station, 94, 345, 406–407, 409, 410–412, 416, 417
Roseland, 54
Rossello, Pedro, 47, 79, 86, 133, 138, 170–171, 237, 239, 265, 270, 277–278, 285, 292, 300, 407, 424
Rota, Spain, 417
ROTHR (Relocatable Over-The-Horizon Radar), 412, 413
Rubin, Robert, 369
Rubio, Euripides, 437–438
Ruiz, Rivera, 169, 207
Rumsfeld, Donald, 147
Rum tax rebate, 140–141

S
S. 472 (1988), 265–266
S. 2019 (1996), 235, 236
Sales taxes, 141
Salsa music, 53
Sanchez-Vilella, Roberto, 227, 229, 283
Sandburg, Carl, 221
Sanes Rodriguez, David, 300
San Francisco Chronicle, 409
San Francisco Giants, 431
San Juan, Manuel, 356, 357
San Juan Batiste, 427
San Juan Rotary Club, 384
The San Juan Star, 169, 170, 211, 252, 410, 413, 416
Santiago, Benito, 430
Santorum, Rick, 211
Schlesinger, Arthur, 312

Scripps-Howard, 162
Sears, 411
SECO (Securities and Exchange Commission), 160
Secretary of the Treasury, 373
Section 246 (of Internal Revenue Code), 182
Section 262 (of Internal Revenue Code), 174, 199
Section 482 (of Internal Revenue Code), 175, 176
Section 931 (of Internal Revenue Code), 173–180, 190, 192–195
Section 936 (of Internal Revenue Code), 15, 47, 64, 66, 88, 105, 109–120, 122–123, 127, 130, 138, 142, 167–172, 177, 179–180, 193, 195–201, 208–209, 232–233, 238–239, 245, 289
Section 956 (of Internal Revenue Code), 206, 208, 209, 211, 289
Securities, 160, 161
Securities and Exchange Commission (SECO), 160
Self-rule, 185
Semi-conductor industry, 189
Senate Armed Services Committee, 410
Senate Committee on Energy and Natural Resources, 263
Senate Energy and Natural Resources Committee, 291
Senate Energy Committee, 270
Senate Finance Committee, 180
Senate Foreign Affairs Committee, 367, 368
Senate Judiciary Committee, 235
September 11, 2001 terrorist attacks, 276, 338, 372, 373, 375
Serrano, Jose, 233–234, 254, 410
Service-oriented jobs, 114
Seventh-Day Adventists, 390
Seward, Secretary of State, 308
Shapiro, Robert J., 63
Sharpton, Al, 407, 408
Shipping, 133–134, 153–154
Siberia, 413
Slate magazine, 103
Slater, Jon, 134–135

Index

Slavery, 297, 386, 387
Small businesses, 138, 141
Small Business Job Protection Act (1996), 206
Smith, Gordon, 180, 211
Smith, Howard, 313
SmithKline, 193
Smuggling, 330–334. *See also* Drugs and drug trade
"Smurfing," 366
Social reform, 187
Social Security, 62, 87, 90
Social services, 69
Social welfare agencies, 85–86
Solomon, Gerald, 246, 248, 250, 251, 253, 254, 258, 262–263, 273
Somocurcio, Monica, 412
Sosthenes, Hernand, 382
South Korea, 123, 124, 166
Sovereignty, 16, 41, 164, 225, 228, 231, 240–242, 269, 281–284, 296, 305, 315, 409, 417, 434, 456. *See also* Independence
Soviet Union, 260
Sowell, Thomas, 103, 115, 138
Spain, 221, 295, 297–298, 304, 305, 308, 332–333, 337, 386, 387, 389, 418, 419, 427, 428
"Spanglish," 98
Spanish-American War, 297, 405, 419, 420
Spanish language, 237, 250, 251, 252, 343
Spencer, Jack, 416
St. Martin (St. Maarten), 340
Statehood, 15, 22, 43, 86–91, 102, 125–127, 130–133, 139, 148, 154, 165, 186, 220, 223, 225, 227–232, 237, 240–245, 248–251, 254, 255, 261–265, 269, 270, 274, 275, 281–282, 284, 285, 288–289, 291–296, 299, 300, 309–315, 347–348, 354, 355, 391, 396, 397, 403, 404, 420–421, 423, 424, 426, 434
Statistical Abstract of the United States, 70
Status (of Puerto Rico), 15
Stone, W. Clement, 98–99
Suarez-Lasa, Sandra, 190
Supreme Court (Puerto Rico), 401–402. *See also* U.S. Supreme Court

Switzerland, 368
Swope, Guy, 186

T

Taft, Howard, 309
Taft Hotel, 54
Taino Indians, 297
Taiwan, 123, 124, 259
Tampa, Florida, 367, 368
TANF program. *See* Temporary Assistance to Needy Families program
Tapia Theater, 356
Tariffs, 20, 139, 183–184
Tauzin, Billy, 270, 300
Tax Equity and Fiscal Responsibility Tax Act (TEFRA), 178, 198, 200, 201
Taxes/taxation, 15, 20–22, 43–44, 61, 65, 66, 87, 88, 108–112, 115, 116, 118, 119, 127–130, 132, 138–142, 144–153, 177, 181–182, 232–234, 236, 239–240, 276, 288–289
Tax Reform Act (1976), 176–177, 195
Tax Reform Act (1986), 203, 204
TEFRA. *See* Tax Equity and Fiscal Responsibility Tax Act
Telephone industry, 134–135
Teller Amendment, 305
Temporary Assistance to Needy Families (TANF) program, 77, 89–90
Tennessee, 313, 382
Territorial Clause, 225, 231, 278, 283
Terrorism, 286, 299, 334, 343, 393
Texas, 218, 273, 356, 413
Textile industry, 120, 189
Thatcher, Margaret, 132
Thomas, Bill, 211
Thomas, Craig, 266, 270
Thomas, Dave, 433
Thornburgh, Richard, 282
Three Kings Day, 349
Tiant, Luis, 430
Title I funds, 73, 78
Tito, Josip Broz, 33–35, 51
Toa Alta, Puerto Rico, 400
Tobacco, 183
Tobin, James, 148
Toricelli, Robert, 266–267
Torruellas, Juan, 293

469

Tourism, 126, 132, 137
Trade, 134, 139, 183–184, 187, 194
Transfer payments, 121, 142–143, 192
"Transition tax," 89
Transportation, 69
Treaty of Paris (1898), 221, 223, 230, 305
Truman, Harry S., 224, *225*, 272, 283, 297, 299, 425
Trust Territory of the Pacific Islands, 315
Tugwell, Rexford, 174, 284, 420
Tydings Bill (1938), 296

U
Unemployment, 11, 43, 87–91, 103–104, 107–110, 121, 122, 138, 142, 145, 146, 149, 155, 159, 166, 197, 207, 392, 411
Unions. *See* Labor
United Kingdom, 117, 132, 185, 418
United Nations, 260, 280, 282, 307, 315, 317, 372, 426
United Stateholders. *See Estadistas Unidos*
University of Puerto Rico, 188
U.S. Armed Forces, 402, 406
U.S. Army, 54–55
U.S. Census Bureau, 138
U.S. Centers for Disease Control, 63
U.S. Chamber of Commerce, 234
U.S. Coast Guard, 330, 335–337
U.S. Constitution, 219, 225, 226, 229–231, 278, 283, 333, 401, 403, 404
U.S.-controlled areas, time until independence for, 302
U.S. Court of Appeals for the First Circuit (Boston), 401
U.S. Customs Service, 300, 335–337, 339, 343, 348, 361, 372, 375, 413
U.S. Department of Defense, 345, 410, 415, 441
U.S. Department of Education, 78
U.S. Department of Health and Human Services, 77
U.S. Department of Homeland Security, 83–84, 335, 343, 372
U.S. Department of Justice, 84, 343, 346, 401
U.S. Department of State, 154, 280, 317
U.S. Department of the Interior, 306

U.S. Department of the Treasury, 84, 88, 115, 120, 154, 177–179, 193, 195–205, 210, 211, 229, 236, 343, 359, 363, 368
U.S. Drug Enforcement Agency. *See* Drug Enforcement Agency
U.S. Hispanic Leadership Institute, 273
U.S. Navy, 285, 286, 300–301, 306, 308, 335, 343, 345, 406–411, 416, 417, 441
U.S. Office of National Drug Control Policy (ONDCP), 300, 331, 334, 335, 337, 342
U.S. Postal Service, 339
U.S. Presidential elections, 91, 92
U.S. Supreme Court, 278, 389, 423
U.S. Virgin Islands, 140, 161, 182, 330, 331, 355
USA PATRIOT Act, 373, 374
USA Team (basketball), 39–40

V
La Vamparita, 148–150
Variable annuities, 160
Velazquez, Nydia, 233–234, 254
Venezuela, 259, 331, 395, 429
Verona, Italy, 417
Victory Tax, 144, 145, 149, 150
Vieques bombing range, 46, 94, 131, 226, 276–277, 286, 300–301, 343, 345, 406–417, 424
Vietnam, 437, 438
Vigil, Michael S., 342
Virginia, 413
Virgin Islands. *See* U.S. Virgin Islands
Voting Rights Act, 423

W
Wages, 184, 192, 205. *See also* Minimum wage laws
The Wall Street Journal, 393
Wal-Mart, 411
Wanniski, Jude, 147
Washington, 404, 412, 414
The Washington Post, 257, 317, 399
The Washington Times, 243, 410
Welfare reform, 76–77, 245
Wendy's (restaurant chain), 433
West Side Story, 381–382, 395, 429

Index

West Virginia, 133
White House, 403, 425
Wickersham, James, 309, 310
Wilson, Woodrow, 405
Winship, Blanton, 186
Winship, Governor, 297
Wirthlin Worldwide, 422
Wisconsin, 310
Wolfowitz, Paul, 408
Wooden, John, 433
Woodward, Bob, 43, 44, 317
World Trade Organization (WTO), 153
World War I, 392, 402, 405
World War II, 186, 223, 310, 315, 392, 406
WTO (World Trade Organization), 153

Y

Young, Don, 216, 220, 234, 237, 239–241, 249, 254, 383, 441
Young bill (1996) (H.R. 3024) (Puerto Rico Self-Determination Act), 220, 233–237, 239–240, 243, 248, 249, 254, 257, 258, 260–262, 267, 270, 298
Yugoslavia, 30–35, 386